THE BOOK ®

D1244523

Suzuki GS500 Twin
Service and Repair Manual

Matthew Coombs and Phil Mather

(3238-248-8AB3)

Models covered

GS500EK	1989	GS500ET	1996
GS500EL	1990	GS500EV	1997
GS500EM	1991	GS500EW	1998
GS500EN	1992	GS500EX	1999
GS500EP	1993	GS500EY	2000
GS500ER	1994	GS500K1	2001
GS500ES	1995	GS500K2	2002

© Haynes Publishing 2002

A book in the **Haynes Service and Repair Manual Series**

ISBN **1 85960 985 6**

British Library Cataloguing in Publication Data
A catalogue record for this book is available from the British Library.

Library of Congress Control Number 2002111983

ABCDE
FGHIJ
KLMNO

Printed in the USA

Haynes Publishing
Sparkford, Yeovil, Somerset BA22 7JJ, England

Haynes North America, Inc
861 Lawrence Drive, Newbury Park, California 91320, USA

Editions Haynes
4, Rue de l'Abreuvoir
92415 COURBEVOIE CEDEX, France

Haynes Publishing Nordiska AB
Box 1504, 751 45 UPPSALA, Sweden

Contents

LIVING WITH YOUR SUZUKI GS

Introduction

Daily (pre-ride) checks

MAINTENANCE

Routine maintenance and servicing

Contents

REPAIRS AND OVERHAUL

Suzuki Every Which Way

by Julian Ryder

From Textile Machinery to Motorcycles

Suzuki were the second of Japan's Big Four motorcycle manufacturers to enter the business, and like Honda they started by bolting small two-stroke motors to bicycles. Unlike Honda, they had manufactured other products before turning to transportation in the aftermath of World War II. In fact Suzuki has been in business since the first decade of the 20th-Century when Michio Suzuki manufactured textile machinery.

The desperate need for transport in post-war Japan saw Suzuki make their first motorised bicycle in 1952, and the fact that by 1954 the company had changed its name to Suzuki Motor Company shows how quickly the sideline took over the whole company's activities. In their first full manufacturing year, Suzuki made nearly 4500 bikes and rapidly expanded into the world markets with a range of two-strokes.

Suzuki didn't make a four-stroke until 1977 when the GS750 double-overhead-cam across-the-frame four arrived. This was several years after Honda and Kawasaki had established the air-cooled four as the industry standard, but no motorcycle epitomises the era of what came to be known as the Universal Japanese motorcycle better than the GS. So well engineered were the original fours that you can clearly see their genes in the GS500 twins that are still going strong in the mid-1990s. Suzuki's ability to prolong the life of their products this way means that they are often thought of as a conservative company. This is hardly fair if you look at some of their landmark designs, most of which have been commercial as well as critical successes.

Two-stroke Success

Early racing efforts were bolstered by the arrival of Ernst Degner who defected from the East German MZ team at the Swedish GP of 1961, bringing with him the rotary-valve secrets of design genius Walter Kaaden. The new Suzuki 50 cc racer won its first GP on the Isle of Man the following year and winning the title easily. Only Honda and Ralph Bryans interrupted Suzuki's run of 50 cc titles from 1962 to 1968.

The T500 two-stroke twin

The arrival of the twin-cylinder 125 racer in 1963 enabled Hugh Anderson to win both 50 and 125 world titles. You may not think 50 cc racing would be exciting - until you learn that the final incarnation of the thing had 14 gears and could do well over 100 mph on fast circuits. Before pulling out of GPs in 1967 the 50 cc racer won six of the eight world titles chalked up by Suzuki during the 1960s as well as providing Mitsuo Itoh with the distinction of being the only Japanese rider to win an Isle of Man TT. Mr Itoh still works for Suzuki, he's in charge of their racing program.

Europe got the benefit of Suzuki's two-stroke expertise in a succession of air-cooled twins, the six-speed 250 cc Super Six being the most memorable, but the arrival in 1968 of the first of a series of 500 cc twins which were good looking, robust and versatile marked the start of mainstream success.

So confident were Suzuki of their two-stroke expertise that they even applied it to the burgeoning Superbike sector. The GT750 water-cooled triple arrived in 1972. It was big, fast and comfortable although the handling and stopping power did draw some comment. Whatever the drawbacks of the road bike, the engine was immensely successful in Superbike and Formula 750 racing. The roadster has its devotees, though, and is now a sought-after bike on the classic Japanese scene. Do not refer to it as the Water Buffalo in such company. Joking aside, the later disc-braked versions were quite civilised, but the audacious idea of using a big two-stroke motor in what was essentially a touring bike was a surprising success until the fuel crisis of the mid-'70s effectively killed off big strokers.

The same could be said of Suzuki's only real lemon, the RE5. This is still the only mass-produced bike to use the rotary (or Wankel) engine but never sold well. Fuel consumption in the mid-teens allled to frightening complexity and excess weight meant the RE5 was a non-starter in the sales race.

Development of the Four-stroke range

When Suzuki got round to building a four-stroke they did a very good job of it. The GS fours were built in 550, 650, 750, 850 1000 and 1100 cc sizes in sports, custom, roadster and even shaft-driven touring forms over many years. The GS1000 was in on the start of Superbike racing in the early 1970s and the GS850 shaft-driven tourer was around nearly 15 years later. The fours spawned a line of 400, 425, 450 and 500 cc GS twins that were essentially the middle half of the four with all their reliability. If there was ever a criticism of the GS models it was that with the exception of the GS1000S of 1980, colloquially known as the ice-cream van, the range was visually uninspiring.

They nearly made the same mistake when they launched the four-valve-head GSX750 in 1979. Fortunately, the original twin-shock

One of the later GT750 'kettle' models with front disc brakes

The GS400 was the first in a line of four-stroke twins

The GS750 led the way for a series of four cylinder models

version was soon replaced by the 'E'-model with Full-Floater rear suspension and a full set of all the gadgets the Japanese industry was then keen on and has since forgotten about, like 16-inch front wheels and anti-dive forks. The air-cooled GSX was like the GS built in 550, 750 and 1100 cc versions with a variety of half, full and touring fairings, but the GSX that is best remembered is the Katana that first appeared in 1981. The power was provided by an 1000 or 1100 cc GSX motor, but wrapped around it was the most outrageous styling package to come out of Japan. Designed by Hans Muth of Target Design, the Katana looked like nothing seen before or since. At the time there was as much anti feeling as praise, but now it is rightly regarded as a classic, a true milestone in motorcycle design. The factory have even started making 250 and 400 cc fours for the home market with the same styling as the 1981 bike.

Just to remind us that they'd still been building two-strokes for the likes of Barry Sheene, in 1986 Suzuki marketed a road-going version of their RG500 square-four racer which had put an end to the era of the four-stroke in 500 GPs when it appeared in 1974. In 1976 Suzuki not only won their first 500 title with Sheene, they sold RG500s over the counter and won every GP with them - with the exception of the Isle of Man TT which the works riders boycotted. Ten years on, the RG500 Gamma gave road riders the nearest experience they'd ever get to riding a GP bike. The fearsome beast could top 140 mph and only weighed 340 lb - the other alleged GP replicas were pussy cats compared to the Gamma's man-eating tiger.

The RG only lasted a few years and is already firmly in the category of collector's item; its four-stroke equivalent, the GSX-R, is still with us and looks like being so for many years. You have to look back to 1985 and its launch to realise just what a revolutionary step the GSX-R750 was: quite simply it was the first race replica. Not a bike dressed up to look like a race bike, but a genuine racer with lights on, a bike that could be taken straight to the track and win.

The first GSX-R, the 750, had a completely new motor cooled by oil rather than water and an aluminium cradle frame. It was sparse, a little twitchy and very, very fast. This time Suzuki got the looks right, blue and white bodywork based on the factory's racing colours and endurance-racer lookalike twin headlights. And then came the 1100 - the big GSX-R got progressively more brutal as it chased the Yamaha EXUP for the heavyweight championship.

And alongside all these mould-breaking designs, Suzuki were also making the best looking custom bikes to come out of Japan, the Intruders; the first race replica trail bike, the DR350; the sharpest 250 Supersports, the RGV250; and a bargain-basement 600, the Bandit. The Bandit proved so popular they went on to build 1200 and 750 cc versions of it. I suppose that's predictable, a range of four-stroke fours just like the GS and GSXs. It's just like the company really, sometimes predictable, admittedly - but never boring.

Suzuki's GSX-R range represented their cutting edge sports bikes

The GS500 Twin

If ever there was a bike bred to be a workhorse it's the GS500E. Its ancestry can be traced right back to the first generation of air-cooled GS motors, Suzuki's first four strokes incidentally. Those 550, 750 and 1000 cc fours gave rise to a 400 cc twin which grew over the years to 425 cc. Just like the fours, this twin used a roller-bearing bottom end and was considered unburstable. In 1985 the motor was bored out again, this time to 450 cc, but more significantly it got a plain bearing bottom end, bringing it into line with industry practice. This is the motor that in 1989 was bored out by another 3 mm to 74 mm and used to power the first GS500EK.

The motor may have been around for a good while in one form or another, but Suzuki did an excellent job with the totally new chassis and running gear to produce a motorcycle with looks sharp enough to belie its utilitarian specification. Here was a bike that was aimed at the rider on a budget, the rider who had just passed his or her test, and the big-city despatch riding market, yet it didn't look like a workhorse. Suzuki had got their planning right, the bike sold well and was well reviewed on both sides of the Atlantic.

There were very few signs of the GS500E being built down to a price, with the possible exception of the front fork. The front fork was very soft and did a good impression of a high-speed lift under even gentle braking. This complaint was addressed on the UK 1992 model, the GS500EN, by fitting higher-rate fork springs and the incorporation of preload adjusters in the fork top bolts.

The only mechanical modification to the GS related to the cylinder head. Like all air-cooled motors, the GS produced a good deal of noise when cold and a lot of it came from camshaft endfloat. From engine number 114497 onwards the clearance was opened

The GS500E

up to a theoretical 1 mm by taking 0.5 mm off the head casting and the same amount off the end of the camshaft. This clearance was shimmed up with a 1 mm shim to give 'almost no clearance when cold' - the theory being that differential rates of expansion between the cylinder head and the camshaft would produce working clearance once the motor was warm. Like the fork modification, it worked well enough to stop roadtesters mentioning the problem again.

Apart from a redesigned front brake caliper introduced on the 1996 GS500ET, the only other alterations made to the model up until 2001 were cosmetic. This was in keeping with the machine's 'budget bike' image, the established successful GS500E formula

requiring the factory to do no more than change the paint scheme once a year.

Several modifications were incorporated on the 2001 GS500K1. The two-piece handlebars were replaced with a one-piece bar clamped to the fork top yoke. The front fork preload adjusters (previously fitted to certain models) were discontinued, the length of the fork springs was increased and the fork oil capacity was reduced. Fork protectors were fitted to the tops of the fork sliders.

Carburettor size was increased and accelerator/decelerator cables replaced the single throttle cable of earlier models. New style side panels, rear light unit and turn indicators were fitted, and the fuel tank capacity was increased.

Acknowledgements

Our thanks are due to Bridge Motorcycles of Exeter and GT Motorcycles of Yeovil who supplied the machines featured in the photographs throughout this manual, to Mel Rawlings A.I.R.T.E. of MHR Engineering who carried out the mechanical work, and to Fowlers Motorcycles of Bristol who supplied a GS500E for the front cover photography. We would also like to thank the Avon Rubber Company, who kindly supplied information and technical assistance on tyre fitting, and NGK Spark Plugs (UK) Ltd for information on spark plug maintenance and electrode conditions.

Thanks are also due to Redcat Marketing and Kel Edge for supplying transparencies, and to Phil Flowers who carried out the front cover photography. The introduction, "Suzuki - Every Which Way" was written by Julian Ryder.

About this Manual

The aim of this manual is to help you get the best value from your motorcycle. It can do so in several ways. It can help you decide what work must be done, even if you choose to have it done by a dealer; it provides information and procedures for routine maintenance and servicing; and it offers diagnostic and repair procedures to follow when trouble occurs.

We hope you use the manual to tackle the work yourself. For many simpler jobs, doing it yourself may be quicker than arranging an appointment to get the motorcycle into a dealer and making the trips to leave it and pick it up. More importantly, a lot of money can be saved by avoiding the expense the shop must pass on to you to cover its labour and overhead costs. An added benefit is the sense of satisfaction and accomplishment that you feel after doing the job yourself.

References to the left or right side of the motorcycle assume you are sitting on the seat, facing forward.

We take great pride in the accuracy of information given in this manual, but motorcycle manufacturers make alterations and design changes during the production run of a particular motorcycle of which they do not inform us. No liability can be accepted by the authors or publishers for loss, damage or injury caused by any errors in, or omissions from, the information given.

GS500EK (1989), EL (1990) and EM (1991)

The GS500E was introduced in 1989. The motor, an air-cooled parallel twin with chain driven overhead camshafts, was based on Suzuki's earlier 450 cc unit, while the frame was of an all-new, steel twin spar cradle design. Front suspension was by conventional oil-damped telescopic forks and rear suspension was by a steel box-section swingarm controlled by monoshock and rising rate linkage. The bike was unfaired, but a fairing and belly pan were available as options.

Colours available: Pearl white, Italian red and Pearl black. The Pearl white option was discontinued in 1990 (GS500EL). The 1991 GS500EM was available in Jade green, Pegasus blue, Italian red and Pearl black.

GS500EN (1992) and EP (1993)

Higher rate springs and suspension preload adjusters were fitted to the front forks of UK models to reduce fork dive under braking.

Colours available: Italian red, Pearl black and Deep purple metallic. Colours remained the same for 1993 (GS500EP).

GS500ER (1994) and ES (1995)

Colours available: Light purple metallic, Candy red and Pearl black. The candy red option was replaced by Teal green in 1995 (GS500ES).

GS500ET (1996)

The design of the front brake caliper was changed. Colours available: candy red, teal green and pearl black.

GS500EV (1997) and EW (1998)

A clutch switch was incorporated into the safety circuit. Colours available: Candy red, Marine green, Deep blue and Pearl black. The green and black options were replaced by Aztec orange in 1998 (GS500EW).

GS500EX (1999)

Colours available: Forest green, Candy orange and Phlolina yellow.

GS500EY (2000)

Colours available: Pearl black, Candy orange and Jay blue.

GS500K1 (2001)

Longer front fork springs were fitted and the preload adjusters, where fitted, were discontinued. Fork protectors were fitted to the tops of the fork sliders. A one-piece handlebar was clamped to the fork top yoke. Carburettor size was increased and accelerator/decelerator cables and a new throttle twistgrip were fitted. The design of the side panels, rear light unit and turn indicators was changed. The seat and fuel tank were re-modelled and the tank capacity was increased.

Colours available: Grand blue, Abyss blue metallic and Pearl yellow.

GS500K2 (2002)

Colours available: Saturn black and Grand blue.

Dimensions and weights

Wheelbase (W)
- EK to EY models .... 1410 mm (55.51 in)
- K1 models onward .... 1405 mm (55.31 in)

Overall length (L)
- EK to EY models .... 2075 mm (81.69 in)
- K1 models onward .... 2080 mm (81.89 in)

Overall height (H)
- EK to EY models .... 1045 mm (41.14 in)
- K1 models onward .... 1080mm (42.52 in)

Overall width
- EK model .... 725 mm (28.54 in)
- EL to ER models .... 755 mm (29.72 in)
- ES to EY models .... 745 mm (29.33 in)
- K1 models onward .... 820 mm (32.28 in)

Seat height (S) .... 790 mm (31.10 in)

Ground clearance
- EK to EY models .... 155 mm (6.10 in)
- K1 models onward .... 150 mm (5.91 in)

Dry weight
- EK to EY models .... 169 kg (373 lb)
- K1 models onward .... 173 kg (381 lb)

Engine

Type .... Air-cooled, parallel twin cylinder four-stroke
Capacity .... 487 cc
Bore .... 74 mm
Stroke .... 56.6 mm
Compression ratio 9.0:1
Camshafts .... DOHC, chain driven
Valves .... 2 valves per cylinder
Fuel system
- EK to EY models .... 2 x 33 mm Mikuni BST33SS carburettors
- K1 models onward ..... 2 x 34 mm Mikuni BSR34SS carburettors
Ignition system .... Transistorised
Clutch .... Wet multi-plate
Transmission .... 6 speed constant mesh
Final drive
- Chain .... DID 520 VM (110 links)
- Sprockets .... 16 tooth front, 39 tooth rear

Chassis

Type .... Twin spar steel cradle
Rake
- EK to EY models .... 25° 30'
- K1 models onward .... 25°
Trail
- EK to EY models .... 95 mm
- K1 models onward .... 97 mm
Front suspension
- Type .... 37 mm oil damped telescopic forks, pre-load adjustment on certain models
- Travel .... 120 mm
Rear suspension
- Type .... Steel box section swingarm with monoshock
- Travel .... 115 mm
- Adjustments .... 7 position pre-load
Tyre sizes
- Front 110/70 17 54H
- Rear 130/70 17 62H
Brakes
- Front .... 1 x 310 mm disc with two-piston sliding caliper
- Rear .... 1 x 250 mm disc with two-piston opposed caliper

Performance data

Maximum power .... 52 bhp (38.8 kW) @ 9200 rpm
Maximum torque .... 30.4 lbf ft (41.2 Nm) @ 7500 rpm
Power-to-weight ratio (approximate) .... 0.30 bhp per kg (0.22 kW per kg)
Top speed .... 112 mph (180 km/h)

Acceleration
- Time taken to cover a 1/4 mile from a standing start ..... 14.2 seconds
- Terminal speed after 1/4 mile .... 92.5 mph (149 km/h)

Average fuel consumption
- Miles per Imp gal, miles per litre, litres per 100 km ..... 54 mpg, 12 mpl, 5.2 l/100 km

Fuel tank capacity*
- EK to EY models .... 17 litres (3.7 Imp gal, 4.5 US gal)
- K1 models onward .... 20 litres (4.4 Imp gal, 5.3 US gal)
- *reduced capacity for California models

Fuel tank range
- EK to EY models .... 204 miles (328 km)
- K1 models onward .... 240 miles (386 km)

Performance data sourced from Motor Cycle News road test features. See the MCN website for up-to-date biking news.

MCN www.motorcyclenews.com

Professional mechanics are trained in safe working procedures. However enthusiastic you may be about getting on with the job at hand, take the time to ensure that your safety is not put at risk. A moment's lack of attention can result in an accident, as can failure to observe simple precautions.

There will always be new ways of having accidents, and the following is not a comprehensive list of all dangers; it is intended rather to make you aware of the risks and to encourage a safe approach to all work you carry out on your bike.

Asbestos

● Certain friction, insulating, sealing and other products - such as brake pads, clutch linings, gaskets, etc. - contain asbestos. Extreme care must be taken to avoid inhalation of dust from such products since it is hazardous to health. If in doubt, assume that they do contain asbestos.

Fire

● Remember at all times that petrol is highly flammable. Never smoke or have any kind of naked flame around, when working on the vehicle. But the risk does not end there - a spark caused by an electrical short-circuit, by two metal surfaces contacting each other, by careless use of tools, or even by static electricity built up in your body under certain conditions, can ignite petrol vapour, which in a confined space is highly explosive. Never use petrol as a cleaning solvent. Use an approved safety solvent.

● Always disconnect the battery earth terminal before working on any part of the fuel or electrical system, and never risk spilling fuel on to a hot engine or exhaust.

● It is recommended that a fire extinguisher of a type suitable for fuel and electrical fires is kept handy in the garage or workplace at all times. Never try to extinguish a fuel or electrical fire with water.

Fumes

● Certain fumes are highly toxic and can quickly cause unconsciousness and even death if inhaled to any extent. Petrol vapour comes into this category, as do the vapours from certain solvents such as trichloro-ethylene. Any draining or pouring of such volatile fluids should be done in a well ventilated area.

● When using cleaning fluids and solvents, read the instructions carefully. Never use materials from unmarked containers - they may give off poisonous vapours.

● Never run the engine of a motor vehicle in an enclosed space such as a garage. Exhaust fumes contain carbon monoxide which is extremely poisonous; if you need to run the engine, always do so in the open air or at least have the rear of the vehicle outside the workplace.

The battery

● Never cause a spark, or allow a naked light near the vehicle's battery. It will normally be giving off a certain amount of hydrogen gas, which is highly explosive.

● Always disconnect the battery ground (earth) terminal before working on the fuel or electrical systems (except where noted).

● If possible, loosen the filler plugs or cover when charging the battery from an external source. Do not charge at an excessive rate or the battery may burst.

● Take care when topping up, cleaning or carrying the battery. The acid electrolyte, evenwhen diluted, is very corrosive and should not be allowed to contact the eyes or skin. Always wear rubber gloves and goggles or a face shield. If you ever need to prepare electrolyte yourself, always add the acid slowly to the water; never add the water to the acid.

Electricity

● When using an electric power tool, inspection light etc., always ensure that the appliance is correctly connected to its plug and that, where necessary, it is properly grounded (earthed). Do not use such appliances in damp conditions and, again, beware of creating a spark or applying excessive heat in the vicinity of fuel or fuel vapour. Also ensure that the appliances meet national safety standards.

● A severe electric shock can result from touching certain parts of the electrical system, such as the spark plug wires (HT leads), when the engine is running or being cranked, particularly if components are damp or the insulation is defective. Where an electronic ignition system is used, the secondary (HT) voltage is much higher and could prove fatal.

Remember...

✗ **Don't** start the engine without first ascertaining that the transmission is in neutral.

✗ **Don't** suddenly remove the pressure cap from a hot cooling system - cover it with a cloth and release the pressure gradually first, or you may get scalded by escaping coolant.

✗ **Don't** attempt to drain oil until you are sure it has cooled sufficiently to avoid scalding you.

✗ **Don't** grasp any part of the engine or exhaust system without first ascertaining that it is cool enough not to burn you.

✗ **Don't** allow brake fluid or antifreeze to contact the machine's paintwork or plastic components.

✗ **Don't** siphon toxic liquids such as fuel, hydraulic fluid or antifreeze by mouth, or allow them to remain on your skin.

✗ **Don't** inhale dust - it may be injurious to health (see Asbestos heading).

✗ **Don't** allow any spilled oil or grease to remain on the floor - wipe it up right away, before someone slips on it.

✗ **Don't** use ill-fitting spanners or other tools which may slip and cause injury.

✗ **Don't** lift a heavy component which may be beyond your capability - get assistance.

✗ **Don't** rush to finish a job or take unverified short cuts.

✗ **Don't** allow children or animals in or around an unattended vehicle.

✗ **Don't** inflate a tyre above the recommended pressure. Apart from overstressing the carcass, in extreme cases the tyre may blow off forcibly.

✔ **Do** ensure that the machine is supported securely at all times. This is especially important when the machine is blocked up to aid wheel or fork removal.

✔ **Do** take care when attempting to loosen a stubborn nut or bolt. It is generally better to pull on a spanner, rather than push, so that if you slip, you fall away from the machine rather than onto it.

✔ **Do** wear eye protection when using power tools such as drill, sander, bench grinder etc.

✔ **Do** use a barrier cream on your hands prior to undertaking dirty jobs - it will protect your skin from infection as well as making the dirt easier to remove afterwards; but make sure your hands aren't left slippery. Note that long-term contact with used engine oil can be a health hazard.

✔ **Do** keep loose clothing (cuffs, ties etc. and long hair) well out of the way of moving mechanical parts.

✔ **Do** remove rings, wristwatch etc., before working on the vehicle - especially the electrical system.

✔ **Do** keep your work area tidy - it is only too easy to fall over articles left lying around.

✔ **Do** exercise caution when compressing springs for removal or installation. Ensure that the tension is applied and released in a controlled manner, using suitable tools which preclude the possibility of the spring escaping violently.

✔ **Do** ensure that any lifting tackle used has a safe working load rating adequate for the job.

✔ **Do** get someone to check periodically that all is well, when working alone on the vehicle.

✔ **Do** carry out work in a logical sequence and check that everything is correctly assembled and tightened afterwards.

✔ **Do** remember that your vehicle's safety affects that of yourself and others. If in doubt on any point, get professional advice.

● If in spite of following these precautions, you are unfortunate enough to injure yourself, seek medical attention as soon as possible.

Frame and engine numbers

General

The frame number is stamped into the right-hand side of the steering head and is repeated on the identification plate. The engine number is stamped into the top of the crankcase, on the right-hand side, behind the cylinder block. Both of these numbers should be recorded and kept in a safe place so they can be furnished to law enforcement officials in the event of a theft. There is also a carburettor identification number on the side of each carburettor body.

The frame and engine numbers and carburettor identification number should also be kept in a handy place (such as with your driver's licence) so they are always available when purchasing or ordering parts for your machine.

UK models

Models are identified by their suffix letter (eg GS500E**K**). To determine the suffix letter, refer to the frame numbers in the following table. The first part of the frame number is the model code (eg GM51A), followed by the actual serial number. Note that the production year is not necessarily the same as the year of registration.

US models

The procedures in this manual identify the models by their suffix letter (eg GS500E**K**). On US models the suffix letter is included in the frame number. The first part of the frame number is the model code (JS1GM51A for 1989 to 1996 models and JS1VP52A for 1997-on), followed by a letter (see tables), then the actual frame number.

UK models		
Year	Suffix letter	Initial frame no.
1989	EK	GM51A-100001 on
1990	EL	GM51A-103616 on
1991	EM	GM51A-109642 on
1992	EN	GM51A-116511 on
1993	EP	GM51A-122409 on
1994	ER	GM51A-130124 on
1995	ES	GM51A-133783 on
1996	ET	GM51A-137535 on
1997	EV	GM51A-139551 on
1998	EW	GM51A-141323 on
1999	EX	GM51A-143268 on
2000	EY	JS1GM51A000504497 on
2001	K1	JS1BK111200100001 on
2002	K2	JS1BK111200100453 on

US models	
Year	Suffix letter
1989	EK
1990	EL
1991	EM
1992	EN
1993	EP
1994	ER
1995	ES
1996	ET
1997	EV
1998	EW
1999	EX
2000	EY
2001	K1
2002	K2

The identification plate is mounted on the right-hand side frame spar.

The frame number is stamped into the steering head right-hand side.

The engine number is stamped into the top of crankcase behind the cylinder block.

Buying spare parts

Once you have found all the identification numbers, record them for reference when buying parts. Since the manufacturers change specifications, parts and vendors (companies that manufacture various components on the machine), providing the ID numbers is the only way to be reasonably sure that you are buying the correct parts.

Whenever possible, take the worn part to the dealer so direct comparison with the new component can be made. Along the trail from the manufacturer to the parts shelf, there are numerous places that the part can end up with the wrong number or be listed incorrectly.

The two places to purchase new parts for your motorcycle - the accessory store and the franchised dealer - differ in the type of parts they carry. While dealers can obtain virtually every part for your motorcycle, the accessory dealer is usually limited to normal high wear items such as shock absorbers, tune-up parts, various engine gaskets, cables, chains, brake pads, etc. Rarely will an accessory outlet have major suspension components, cylinders, transmission gears, or cases.

Used parts can be obtained for roughly half the price of new ones, but you can't always be sure of what you're getting. Once again, take your worn part to the breaker (wrecking yard) for direct comparison.

Whether buying new, used or rebuilt parts, the best course is to deal directly with someone who specialises in parts for your particular make.

Engine/transmission oil level

Before you start
✔ Take the motorcycle on a short run to allow it to reach normal operating temperature.

Caution: Do not run the engine in an enclosed space such as a garage or workshop.

✔ Stop the engine and place the motorcycle on its centre stand. Allow it to stand undisturbed for a few minutes to allow the oil level to stabilise. Make sure the motorcycle is on level ground.

Bike care:
● If you have to add oil frequently, you should check whether you have any oil leaks. If there is no sign of oil leakage from the joints and gaskets the engine could be burning oil (see *Fault Finding*).

The correct oil
● Modern, high-revving engines place great demands on their oil. It is very important that the correct oil for your bike is used.
● Always top up with a good quality oil of the specified type and viscosity and do not overfill the engine.

Oil type	API grade SE or SF (minimum)
Oil viscosity	SAE 10W/40

1 Unscrew the oil filler cap from the right-hand side crankcase cover. The dipstick is integral with the oil filler cap, and is used to check the engine oil level.

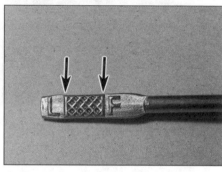

3 Remove the dipstick and observe the level of the oil, which should be somewhere in between the upper 'F' and lower 'L' level lines (arrows).

2 Using a clean rag or paper towel, wipe off all the oil from the dipstick, then insert the clean dipstick back into the engine, but do not screw it in.

4 If the level is below the 'L' line, top the engine up with the recommended grade and type of oil, to bring the level up to the 'F' line on the dipstick.

Battery electrolyte level

⚠ *Warning: Be extremely careful when handling or working around the battery - the electrolyte is very caustic.*

Before you start:
✔ Position the motorcycle on its centre stand on level ground. Remove the seat (see Chapter 7) for access to the battery.
✔ Use distilled water to top up the battery. Do not use tap water (except in an emergency).

Bike care:
● If the battery electrolyte level needs topping up frequently, it is likely that there is a problem either with the battery or with the charging system. Refer to Chapter 8 and investigate the problem.

1 The electrolyte level is visible through the translucent battery case - it should be between the upper MAX and lower level lines (arrows).

2 If the electrolyte is low the battery must be topped up with distilled water. Remove the cell caps . . .

3 . . . and fill each cell to the MAX level line with distilled water - do not overfill. On completion, mop up any spills and install the cell caps.

Brake fluid levels

⚠ *Warning: Brake hydraulic fluid can harm your eyes and damage painted surfaces, so use extreme caution when handling and pouring it and cover surrounding surfaces with rag. Do not use fluid that has been standing open for some time, as it absorbs moisture from the air which can cause a dangerous loss of braking effectiveness.*

Before you start:

✔ Position the motorcycle on its centre stand, and turn the handlebars until the top of the master cylinder is as level as possible. If necessary, tilt the motorcycle to make it level. Remove the seat (see Chapter 7) for access to the rear brake fluid reservoir.

✔ Make sure you have the correct hydraulic fluid - DOT 4 is recommended. Wrap a rag around the reservoir being worked on to ensure that any spillage does not come into contact with painted surfaces.

Bike care:

● The fluid in the front and rear brake master cylinder reservoirs will drop slightly as the brake pads wear down.
● If any fluid reservoir requires repeated topping-up this is an indication of a leak somewhere in the system, which should be investigated immediately.
● Check for signs of fluid leakage from the hydraulic hoses and components - if found, rectify immediately.
● Check the operation of both brakes before taking the machine on the road; if there is evidence of air in the system (spongy feel to lever or pedal), it must be bled (see Chapter 6).

1 The front brake fluid level is checked via the sightglass in the reservoir - it must be above the LOWER level mark (arrow).

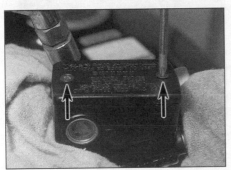

2 If the level is below the LOWER level mark, remove the two screws (arrows) to free the front brake fluid reservoir cover, plate and diaphragm.

3 Top up with new clean DOT 4 hydraulic fluid, until the level is above the LOWER mark. Take care to avoid spills (see **Warning** above).

4 Ensure that the diaphragm is correctly seated before installing the plate and cover.

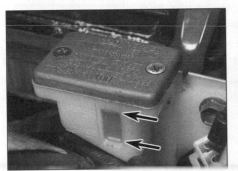

5 The rear brake fluid level can be seen through the translucent body of the reservoir. The fluid must lie between the LOWER and UPPER level marks (arrows).

6 Remove the two screws and lift off the cover and diaphragm. Top up with new clean DOT 4 brake fluid until the level is between the two level marks.

7 Check that the diaphragm is correctly folded before installing the cover.

Suspension, steering and drive chain

Suspension and steering:

● Check that the front and rear suspension operates smoothly without binding.
● Check that the suspension is adjusted as required.

● Check that the steering moves smoothly from lock-to-lock.

Drive chain:

● Check that the drive chain slack isn't excessive. If it requires adjustment, refer to Chapter 1.
● If the chain looks dry, lubricate it (see Chapter 1).

Tyres

The correct pressures:
● The tyre pressures must be checked when **cold**, not immediately after riding. If the motorcycle has just been ridden the tyres will be warm and their pressures will have increased. Note that extremely low tyre pressures may cause the tyre to slip on the rim or come off. High tyre pressures will cause abnormal tread wear and unsafe handling.

● Use an accurate pressure gauge.

● Proper air pressure will increase tyre life and provide maximum stability and ride comfort.

Tyre care:
● Check the tyres carefully for cuts, tears, embedded nails or other sharp objects and excessive wear. Operation of the motorcycle with excessively worn tyres is extremely hazardous, as traction and handling are directly affected.
● Check the condition of the tyre valve and ensure the dust cap is in place.
● Pick out any stones or nails which may have become embedded in the tyre tread.
● If tyre damage is apparent, or unexplained loss of pressure is experienced, seek the advice of a tyre fitting specialist without delay.

Tyre tread depth:
● At the time of writing UK law requires that tread depth must be at least 1 mm over 3/4 of the tread breadth all the way around the tyre, with no bald patches. Many riders, however, consider 2 mm tread depth minimum to be a safer limit. Suzuki recommend a minimum of 1.6 mm on the front and 2 mm on the rear.

● Many tyres now incorporate wear indicators in the tread. Identify the triangular pointer or TWI mark on the tyre sidewall to locate the indicator bars and replace the tyre if the tread has worn down to the bar.

1 Check the tyre pressures when the tyres are **cold** and keep them properly inflated.

2 Measure tread depth at the centre of the tyre using a tread depth gauge.

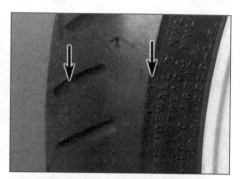

3 Tyre tread wear indicator bar and its location marking (usually an arrow, on this tyre TWI) on the sidewall (arrows).

Loading/speed	Front	Rear
Rider only	33 psi (2.25 bar)	36 psi (2.50 bar)
Rider and passenger	33 psi (2.25 bar)	41 psi (2.80 bar)

Legal and safety checks

Lighting and signalling:
● Take a minute to check that the headlight, taillight, brake light, instrument lights and turn signals all work correctly.
● Check that the horn sounds when the switch is operated.
● A working speedometer is a statutory requirement in the UK.

Safety:
● Check that the throttle grip rotates smoothly and snaps shut when released, in all steering positions.
● Check that the clutch lever operates smoothly and with the correct amount of freeplay (see Chapter 1).
● Check that the engine shuts off when the kill switch is operated.
● Check that sidestand return spring holds the stand securely up when retracted. The same applies to the centre stand.
● Check the operation of the sidestand switch as described in your owners manual.

Fuel:
● This may seem obvious, but check that you have enough fuel to complete your journey. If you notice signs of fuel leakage - rectify the cause immediately.
● Ensure you use the correct grade unleaded fuel - see Chapter 3 Specifications.

Chapter 1
Routine maintenance and servicing

Contents

Degrees of difficulty

Easy, suitable for novice with little experience		**Fairly easy,** suitable for beginner with some experience		**Fairly difficult,** suitable for competent DIY mechanic		**Difficult,** suitable for experienced DIY mechanic		**Very difficult,** suitable for expert DIY or professional	

1

Specifications

Engine

Valve clearances (COLD engine) - intake and exhaust	0.03 to 0.08 mm
Spark plugs	
Type	
Standard	NGK DPR8EA-9 or Nippondenso X24EPR-U9
For cold climate (below 5°C)	NGK DPR7EA-9 or Nippondenso X22EPR-U9
For extended high speed riding	NGK DPR9EA-9 or Nippondenso X27EPR-U9
Electrode gap	0.8 to 0.9 mm
Engine idle speed	1200 ± 100 rpm
Cylinder compression	
Standard	142 to 199 psi (10 to 14 bar)
Minimum (both cylinders)	142 psi (10 bar)*
Minimum (one cylinder)	114 psi (8 bar)*
Maximum difference between cylinders	28 psi (2 bar)
Oil pressure (with engine warm)	28 to 71 psi (2.0 to 5.0 bar) at 3000 rpm

*Note: If both cylinders record less than 142 psi (10 bar), overhaul is required (see text). If only one cylinder records less than 142 psi (10 bar) then the engine is good, as long as that cylinder is not below 114 psi (8 bar) and the difference between the two cylinders is less than 28 psi (2 bar).

Miscellaneous

Battery specific gravity		
Standard	1.28 at 20°C	
Minimum	1.22 at 20°C	
Clutch lever freeplay	10 to 15 mm	
Throttle cable freeplay	3 to 6 mm	
Drive chain		
Freeplay	20 to 30 mm	
Stretch limit (21 pin length - see text)	319.4 mm	
Brake pedal height		
EK to ER models	47 mm	
ES to EY models and K1 models onwards	55 mm	
Tyre pressures (cold)	**Front**	**Rear**
Rider	33 psi (2.25 bar)	36 psi (2.50 bar)
Rider and pillion	33 psi (2.25 bar)	41 psi (2.80 bar)
Tyre tread depth		
Front	1.6 mm minimum	
Rear	2 mm minimum	

Torque settings

Cylinder head 10 mm domed nuts	35 to 40 Nm
Cylinder head 6 mm plain nut	7 to 11 Nm
Exhaust downpipe clamp bolts	9 to 12 Nm
Silencer mounting bolt	18 to 28 Nm
Oil drain plug	20 to 25 Nm
Rear axle nut	
Nut with split-pin (US models)	50 to 80 Nm
Self-locking nut (UK models)	60 to 96 Nm
Steering stem bolt	35 to 55 Nm
Fork clamp bolts (top yoke)	18 to 28 Nm
Suspension linkage rod bolts	70 to 100 Nm
Suspension linkage arm bolt	70 to 100 Nm
Shock absorber mounting bolts	40 to 60 Nm
Swingarm pivot nut	55 to 88 Nm

Recommended lubricants and fluids

Drive chain lubricant	Engine oil or lubricant suitable for O-ring chains
Engine/transmission oil viscosity	SAE 10W/40
Engine/transmission oil type	API grade SE, SF or SG (minimum) motor oil
Engine/transmission oil capacity	
Oil change	2.6 litres
Oil and filter change	2.9 litres
Following engine overhaul - dry engine, new filter	3.2 litres
Brake fluid	DOT 4
Fork oil type	SAE 10W fork oil
Fork oil capacity	
UK EK to EM models and all US models	382 cc
UK EN to EY models	377 cc
UK K1 models onward	389 cc
Fork oil level*	
UK EK to EM models and all US models	99 mm
UK EN to EY models	105 mm
UK K1 models onward	91 mm

*Oil level is measured from the top of the tube with the fork spring removed and the leg fully compressed.

Miscellaneous	
Wheel bearings	Multi-purpose grease
Rear suspension bearings	Lithium-based grease
Steering head bearings	Multi-purpose grease
Cables, lever and stand pivot points	Motor oil
Throttle grip	Multi-purpose grease or dry film lubricant

Note: *The daily (pre-ride) checks outlined in the owner's manual covers those items which should be inspected on a daily basis. Always perform the pre-ride inspection at every maintenance interval (in addition to the procedures listed). The intervals listed below are the intervals recommended by the manufacturer for each particular operation during the model years covered in this manual. Your owner's manual may have different intervals for your model.*

Daily (pre-ride)

☐ See *'Daily (pre-ride) checks'* at the beginning of this manual.

After the initial 600 miles (1000 km)

Note: *This check is usually performed by a Suzuki dealer after the first 600 miles (1000 km) from new. Thereafter, maintenance is carried out according to the following intervals of the schedule.*

Every 600 miles (1000 km)

☐ Clean and lubricate the drive chain (Section 1).

Every 2000 miles (3000 km)

☐ Clean the air filter element (Section 2).

Every 4000 miles (6000 km) or 12 months

Carry out all the items under the Daily (pre-ride) checks and the 2000 mile (3000 km) check, plus the following

☐ Check the specific gravity of the battery electrolyte (Section 3).
☐ Tighten the cylinder head nuts and exhaust pipe bolts (Section 4).
☐ Check the valve clearances (Section 5).
☐ Check the spark plug gaps (Section 6).
☐ Check the fuel hoses and system components (Section 7).
☐ Change the engine oil and replace the oil filter (Section 8).
☐ Check and adjust the engine idle speed (Section 9).
☐ Check the operation of the clutch (Section 10).
☐ Check and adjust drive chain freeplay (Section 11).
☐ Check for drive chain wear and stretch (Section 12).
☐ Check the brake pads for wear (Section 13).
☐ Check the brakes for correct operation, and for fluid leakage (Section 14).
☐ Check the tyre and wheel condition, and the tyre tread depth (Section 15).

Every 4000 miles (6000 km) or 12 months (continued)

☐ Check the steering head bearing freeplay (Section 16).
☐ Check the tightness of all nuts and bolts (Section 17).

Every 7500 miles (12 000 km) or 2 years

Carry out all the items under the 4000 mile (6000 km) check, plus the following:

☐ Replace the air filter (Section 18).
☐ Replace the spark plugs (Section 19).
☐ Check the front and rear suspension (Section 20).

Every two years

☐ Change the brake fluid (Section 21).

Every four years

☐ Replace the brake hoses (Section 22).
☐ Replace the fuel hoses (Section 23).

Non-scheduled maintenance

☐ Check throttle/choke cable operation and freeplay (Section 24).
☐ Check carburettor synchronisation (Section 25).
☐ Check the headlight aim (Section 26).
☐ Check the wheel bearings (Section 27).
☐ Check and lubricate the stands, lever pivots and cables (Section 28).
☐ Change the front fork oil (Section 29).
☐ Check the cylinder compression (Section 30).
☐ Check the engine oil pressure (Section 31).
☐ Re-grease the steering head bearings (Section 32).
☐ Re-grease the swingarm and suspension linkage bearings (Section 33).
☐ Replace the brake master cylinder and caliper seals (Section 34).

1

Component locations on right-hand side

1 Rear brake fluid reservoir	4 Spark plug and valves	7 Brake pads	10 Oil drain plug
2 Carburettors	5 Front brake fluid reservoir	8 Oil filter	11 Oil filler plug
3 Idle speed screw	6 Throttle cable upper adjuster	9 Oil pressure switch	12 Brake pedal height adjuster

Component locations on left-hand side

1 Fork seals	4 Steering head bearings	7 Air filter	10 Drive chain
2 Clutch cable upper adjuster	5 Spark plug and valves	8 Remote fuel tap	11 Clutch cable lower adjuster
3 Choke cable adjuster	6 Fuel filter (main fuel cock)	9 Battery	12 Clutch release mechanism

Introduction

1 This Chapter is designed to help the home mechanic maintain his/her motorcycle for safety, economy, long life and peak performance.

2 Deciding where to start or plug into the routine maintenance schedule depends on several factors. If the warranty period on your motorcycle has just expired, and if it has been maintained according to the warranty standards, you may want to pick up routine maintenance as it coincides with the next mileage or calendar interval. If you have owned the machine for some time but have never performed any maintenance on it, then you may want to start at the nearest interval and include some additional procedures to ensure that nothing important is overlooked. If you have just had a major engine overhaul, then you may want to start the maintenance schedule from the beginning. If you have a used machine and have no knowledge of its history or maintenance record, you may desire to combine all the checks into one large service initially and then settle into the maintenance schedule prescribed.

3 Before beginning any maintenance or repair, the machine should be cleaned thoroughly, especially around the oil filter, spark plugs, valve cover, side panels, carburettors, etc. Cleaning will help ensure that dirt does not contaminate the engine and will allow you to detect wear and damage that could otherwise easily go unnoticed.

4 Certain maintenance information is sometimes printed on decals attached to the motorcycle. If the information on the decals differs from that included here, use the information on the decal.

Every 600 miles (1000 km)

1 Drive chain - cleaning and lubrication

Cleaning and lubrication

1 Place the machine on its centre stand. Rotate the back wheel whilst cleaning and lubricating the chain to better access all the links.

2 Wash the chain in paraffin (kerosene), then wipe it off and allow it to dry, using compressed air if available. If the chain is excessively dirty it should be removed from the machine and allowed to soak in the paraffin (see Chapter 5).

Caution: Don't use petrol (gasoline), solvent or other cleaning fluids which might damage its internal sealing properties. Don't use high-pressure water. The entire process shouldn't take longer than ten minutes - if it does, the O-rings in the chain rollers could be damaged.

3 The best time to lubricate the chain is after riding; when the chain is warm, the lubricant penetrates the joints between the side plates better than when cold.

4 Apply the specified lubricant (see Specifications at the beginning of the Chapter) to the area where the side plates overlap - not to the middle of the rollers. After applying the lubricant, let it soak in for a few minutes before wiping off any excess.

Caution: If using an aerosol drive chain oil make sure it is marked as being suitable for O-ring chains. The chain O-rings can be damaged by the solvents and additives contained in certain products.

HAYNES HiNT *Apply lubricant to the top of the lower chain run - the centrifugal force will work it into the chain when the bike is moving.*

Freeplay check and adjustment

5 After chain lubrication check the amount of freeplay as described in Section 11 and adjust if necessary.

Every 2000 miles (3000 km)

2 Air filter - cleaning

1 Remove the fuel tank (see Chapter 3).

2 Unscrew the four screws securing the air filter to the filter housing, noting the positions of the wiring loom and breather hose clamps and the arrow on the top of the filter which must point forward. Withdraw the filter from the housing **(see illustration)**.

3 Tap the filter on a hard surface to dislodge any dirt. If compressed air is available, use it to clean the element, directing the air from the outside of the element **(see illustration)**. If the element is torn or extremely dirty, replace it with a new one.

4 Install the filter by reversing the removal procedure, making sure that the arrow on the top of the filter is facing forward **(see illustration)**. Make sure that the filter is properly seated in the housing before fitting the screws.

Caution: If the machine is continually ridden in dusty conditions, the filter should be cleaned more frequently.

1

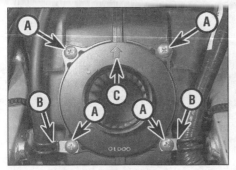

2.2 Air filter screws (A), wiring and breather hose clamps (B), directional arrow (C)

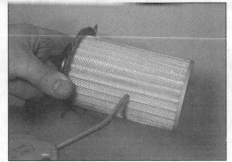

2.3 Clean the element using compressed air directed from the outside in

2.4 Install the filter with the arrow facing forward

Every 4000 miles (6000 km) or 12 months

3 Battery - electrolyte specific gravity check

1 Before checking the specific gravity of the battery electrolyte, make sure that the electrolyte level is correct (see *"Daily (pre-ride) checks).*
2 Using an hydrometer, check the specific gravity of each of the cells in the battery. If the readings obtained are less than that specified at the beginning of the Chapter, the battery should be charged (see Chapter 8). If an hydrometer is not available, have the battery checked by a Suzuki dealer.

4 Cylinder head nuts and exhaust system bolts - tightness check

1 Suzuki recommend that the cylinder head nuts and exhaust pipe bolts are checked to ensure they are tightened to their correct torque settings. The engine must be completely cool for these maintenance procedures, so let the machine sit overnight before beginning.

Cylinder head nuts

2 Remove the valve cover (see Chapter 2).
3 The cylinder head is secured by eight 10 mm domed nuts and one 6 mm bolt. Slacken the bolt at the front of the cylinder head (see illustration). The eight domed nuts are numbered for identification (see illustration).

Slacken the nuts evenly and a little at a time in a reverse of their numerical sequence until they are all slack.
4 Using a torque wrench, tighten the domed nuts evenly and a little at a time in numerical sequence to the torque setting specified at the beginning of the Chapter (see illustration 4.3b).
5 When the nuts are correctly torqued, tighten the plain bolt at the front of the cylinder head to the specified torque setting (see illustration 4.3a).
6 Install the valve cover (see Chapter 2).

Exhaust pipe bolts

7 Using a torque wrench, check that the exhaust downpipe clamp bolts and the silencer mounting bolt are tightened to the torque settings specified at the beginning of the Chapter (see illustrations).

4.3a Cylinder head front bolt (arrow)

4.3b Cylinder head nut TIGHTENING sequence

4.7a Exhaust downpipe clamp bolts (arrows)

4.7b Silencer mounting bolt (arrow)

5.3 The pulse generator cover is secured by three bolts (arrows)

5.5a The R.T mark must align with the middle of the left-hand pulse generator coil . . .

5.5b . . . and the notch in the end of each camshaft must face inwards (arrows)

5.5c Using a feeler gauge to check the valve clearances

1

5 Valve clearances - check and adjustment

1 The engine must be completely cool for this maintenance procedure, so let the machine sit overnight before beginning.
2 Remove the valve cover (see Chapter 2). Unscrew the spark plugs to allow the engine to be turned over easier (see Section 6).
3 Unscrew the three bolts securing the pulse generator coil cover to the right-hand side crankcase cover (see illustration). The engine can be rotated by using a 19 mm spanner on the timing rotor hexagon and turning it in a clockwise direction only. Alternatively, place the motorcycle on its centre stand, select a high gear and rotate the rear wheel by hand in its normal direction of rotation.
4 Make a chart or sketch of all four valve positions so that a note of each clearance can be made against the relevant valve.
5 Rotate the engine until the R.T mark on the rotor aligns with the centre of the left-hand pulse generator coil, and so that the notches in the right-hand end of each camshaft face each other (see illustrations). At this point insert a feeler gauge of the same thickness as the correct valve clearance (see Specifications) between the cam lobe base and shim of the right-hand cylinder intake and exhaust valves, and of the left-hand cylinder intake valve, and check that it is a firm sliding fit (see illustration). If it is not, use the feeler gauges to obtain the exact clearance. Record the measured clearance on the chart.
6 Rotate the engine so that the timing rotor turns through 360°, at which point the notches in the end of each camshaft now face away from each other. Measure the valve clearance of the left-hand cylinder exhaust valve using the method described in Step 5.
7 When all clearances have been measured and charted, identify whether the clearance on any valve falls outside that specified. If it does, the shim between the follower and the camshaft must be replaced with one of a thickness which will restore the correct clearance.
8 Shim replacement requires the use of the Suzuki service tool (Pt. No. 09916-64510) or a home-made equivalent which can be made out of a piece of plate steel (see illustration).

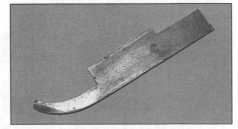

5.8 A home-made equivalent of the Suzuki tool

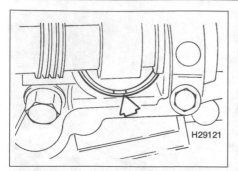

5.9 Turn the follower so that its notch (arrow) faces the middle of the engine

5.10 Using the tool to depress the cam follower

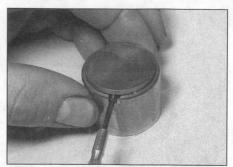

5.11a Prise the shim out of the follower (follower shown removed from engine) . . .

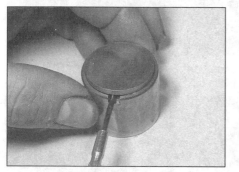

5.11b . . . and remove it using a pair of pliers

5.11c The shim size is marked on the underside of the shim

5.11d Measure the shim using a micrometer to confirm its size

9 Using your fingers, turn the cam follower of the valve in question so that its shim removing slot faces backwards (exhaust valve) or forwards (intake valve) (see illustration).

10 Fit the tool under the camshaft, making sure it contacts only the follower and not the shim, and press it down to depress the follower (see illustration).

11 Prise the shim out of the follower using a small screwdriver inserted in its slot and remove it using a pair of pliers (see illustrations). The shim size should be stamped on its face (see illustration). A shim size of 250 denotes a thickness of 2.5 mm, 245 is 2.45 mm. It is recommended that the shim is measured to check that it has not worn (see illustration). Shims are available in 0.05 mm increments from 2.15 to 3.10 mm.

12 Using the shim selection chart, find where the measured valve clearance and existing shim thickness values intersect and read off the shim size required (see illustration).

Obtain and install the replacement shim, noting that its size marking should be installed downwards and that the shim should be lubricated with engine oil.

13 Remove the tool from the follower. Rotate the crankshaft several turns to seat the new shim. Check the clearance again, then repeat the process for any other valves until the clearances are correct.

14 Install all disturbed components in a reverse of the removal sequence.

Valve Clearance (mm)	PRESENT SHIM SIZE - mm																			
	2.15	2.20	2.25	2.30	2.35	2.40	2.45	2.50	2.55	2.60	2.65	2.70	2.75	2.80	2.85	2.90	2.95	3.00	3.05	3.10
0.00~0.02		2.15	2.20	2.25	2.30	2.35	2.40	2.45	2.50	2.55	2.60	2.65	2.70	2.75	2.80	2.85	2.90	2.95	3.00	3.05
0.03~0.08	CORRECT CLEARANCE: NO ADJUSTMENT REQUIRED																			
0.09~0.13	2.20	2.25	2.30	2.35	2.40	2.45	2.50	2.55	2.60	2.65	2.70	2.75	2.80	2.85	2.90	2.95	3.00	3.05	3.10	
0.14~0.18	2.25	2.30	2.35	2.40	2.45	2.50	2.55	2.60	2.65	2.70	2.75	2.80	2.85	2.90	2.95	3.00	3.05	3.10		
0.19~0.23	2.30	2.35	2.40	2.45	2.50	2.55	2.60	2.65	2.70	2.75	2.80	2.85	2.90	2.95	3.00	3.05	3.10			
0.24~0.28	2.35	2.40	2.45	2.50	2.55	2.60	2.65	2.70	2.75	2.80	2.85	2.90	2.95	3.00	3.05	3.10				
0.29~0.33	2.40	2.45	2.50	2.55	2.60	2.65	2.70	2.75	2.80	2.85	2.90	2.95	3.00	3.05	3.10					
0.34~0.38	2.45	2.50	2.55	2.60	2.65	2.70	2.75	2.80	2.85	2.90	2.95	3.00	3.05	3.10						
0.39~0.43	2.50	2.55	2.60	2.65	2.70	2.75	2.80	2.85	2.90	2.95	3.00	3.05	3.10							
0.44~0.48	2.55	2.60	2.65	2.70	2.75	2.80	2.85	2.90	2.95	3.00	3.05	3.10								
0.49~0.53	2.60	2.65	2.70	2.75	2.80	2.85	2.90	2.95	3.00	3.05	3.10									
0.54~0.58	2.65	2.70	2.75	2.80	2.85	2.90	2.95	3.00	3.05	3.10										
0.59~0.63	2.70	2.75	2.80	2.85	2.90	2.95	3.00	3.05	3.10											
0.64~0.68	2.75	2.80	2.85	2.90	2.95	3.00	3.05	3.10												
0.69~0.73	2.80	2.85	2.90	2.95	3.00	3.05	3.10													
0.74~0.78	2.85	2.90	2.95	3.00	3.05	3.10														
0.79~0.83	2.90	2.95	3.00	3.05	3.10															
0.84~0.88	2.95	3.00	3.05	3.10																
0.89~0.93	3.00	3.05	3.10																	
0.94~0.98	3.05	3.10																		
0.99~1.03	3.10																			

EXAMPLE

Valve clearance	- 0.36 mm
Present shim size	- 2.45 mm
Shim size required	- 2.75 mm

5.12 Shim selection chart

H29122

6.4a Remove the spark plug cap . . .

6.4b . . . then unscrew the spark plug

6 Spark plugs - gap check and adjustment

1 Make sure your spark plug socket is the correct size before attempting to remove the plugs - a suitable one is supplied in the motorcycle's tool kit which is stored under the seat.

2 Remove the seat (see Chapter 7) and disconnect the battery negative (-ve) lead.

3 Clean the area around the plug caps to prevent any dirt falling into the spark plug channels.

4 Check that the cylinder location is marked on each plug lead, then pull the spark plug cap off each spark plug (see illustration). Using either the plug spanner supplied in the bike's toolkit or a deep plug socket, unscrew the plugs from the cylinder head (see illustration). Lay each plug out in relation to its cylinder; if either plug shows up a problem it will then be easy to identify the troublesome cylinder.

5 Inspect the electrodes for wear. Both the centre and side electrodes should have square edges and the side electrode should be of uniform thickness. Look for excessive deposits and evidence of a cracked or chipped insulator around the centre electrode. Compare your spark plugs to the colour spark plug reading chart at the end of this Manual. Check the threads, the washer and the ceramic insulator body for cracks and other damage.

6 If the electrodes are not excessively worn, and if the deposits can be easily removed with a wire brush, the plugs can be re-gapped and re-used (if no cracks or chips are visible in the insulator). If in doubt concerning the condition of the plugs, replace them with new ones, as the expense is minimal.

7 Cleaning spark plugs by sandblasting is permitted, provided you clean the plugs with a high flash-point solvent afterwards.

8 Before installing the plugs, make sure they are the correct type and heat range and check the gap between the electrodes (they are not pre-set on new plugs). For best results, use a wire-type gauge rather than a flat (feeler) gauge to check the gap (see illustrations). Compare the gap to that specified and adjust as necessary. If the gap must be adjusted, bend the side electrode only and be very careful not to chip or crack the insulator nose (see illustration). Make sure the washer is in place before installing each plug.

9 Since the cylinder head is made of aluminium, which is soft and easily damaged, thread the plugs into the head by hand (see illustration). Fit each plug finger-tight, then tighten by a further 1/4 turn with the tool supplied or a deep socket. Beware of over-tightening the plugs otherwise the threads in the head could be stripped.

10 Reconnect the spark plug caps, making sure they are securely connected to the correct cylinder.

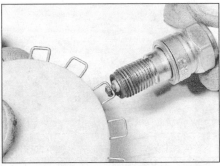

6.8a A wire type gauge is recommended to measure the spark plug electrode gap

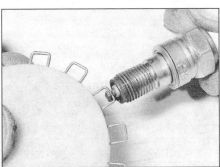

6.8b A blade type feeler gauge can also be used

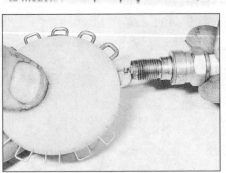

6.8c Adjust the electrode gap by bending the side electrode

6.9 Thread the plug in as far as possible by hand

1

7 Fuel system - check

Warning: Petrol (gasoline) is extremely flammable, so take extra precautions when you work on any part of the fuel system. Don't smoke or allow open flames or bare light bulbs near the work area, and don't work in a garage where a natural gas-type appliance is present. If you spill any fuel on your skin, rinse it off immediately with soap and water. When you perform any kind of work on the fuel system, wear safety glasses and have a fire extinguisher suitable for a Class B type fire (flammable liquids) on hand.

Check

1 Remove the fuel tank (see Chapter 3) and check the tank, the main fuel cock, the fuel tap, and the fuel hoses for signs of leakage, deterioration or damage; in particular check that there is no leakage from the fuel hoses. Replace any hoses which are cracked or deteriorated. On California models, also check the evaporative emission control system hoses between the fuel tank and charcoal canister and between the charcoal canister and carburettors.
2 If the fuel tap is leaking, remove the tap and tighten the four assembly screws on the back of the tap (see Chapter 3). If leakage persists remove the screws and disassemble the tap, noting how the components fit. Inspect all components for wear or damage. If any of the components are worn or damaged, a new tap must be fitted.
3 If the carburettor gaskets are leaking, the carburettors should be disassembled and rebuilt using new gaskets and seals (see Chapter 3).

Filter cleaning

4 Cleaning or replacement of the fuel filter is advised after a particularly high mileage has been covered. It is also necessary if fuel starvation is suspected.
5 The fuel filter is mounted in the tank and is integral with the main fuel cock. Remove the fuel tank and the main fuel cock (Chapter 3). Clean the gauze filter to remove all traces of dirt and fuel sediment. Check the gauze for holes. If any are found, a new filter should be fitted. Check the condition of the O-ring and replace it if it is in any way damaged or deteriorated.

8 Engine/transmission - oil and oil filter change

Warning: Be careful when draining the oil, as the exhaust pipes, the engine, and the oil itself can cause severe burns.

1 Consistent routine oil and filter changes are the single most important maintenance procedure you can perform on a motorcycle. The oil not only lubricates the internal parts of the engine, transmission and clutch, but it also acts as a coolant, a cleaner, a sealant, and a protectant. Because of these demands, the oil takes a terrific amount of abuse and should be replaced often with new oil of the recommended grade and type. Saving a little money on the difference in cost between a good oil and a cheap oil won't pay off if the engine is damaged.
2 Before changing the oil, warm up the engine so the oil will drain easily.
3 Put the motorcycle on its centre stand and position a clean drain tray below the engine. Unscrew the oil filler cap on the right-hand side crankcase cover to vent the crankcase and to act as a reminder that there is no oil in the engine (see illustration).
4 Next, unscrew the oil drain plug from the bottom of the engine and allow the oil to flow into the drain tray (see illustrations). Discard the sealing washer on the drain plug as it should be replaced whenever the plug is removed.
5 Position the oil drain tray so that it is below the oil filter. Unscrew the three nuts securing the oil filter cover to the front of the engine, then remove the cover along with its O-ring and spring (see illustration). Check the condition of the O-ring and replace it if it is damaged or deteriorated. Remove the old filter and wipe off any remaining oil from the filter cover sealing area (see illustration).
6 When the oil has completely drained, fit a new sealing washer over the drain plug. Fit the plug to the sump and tighten it to the torque setting specified at the beginning of the Chapter. Avoid overtightening, as damage to the sump will result.

8.3 Unscrew the oil filler cap

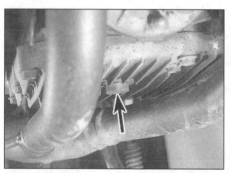

8.4a Unscrew the oil drain plug (arrow) . . .

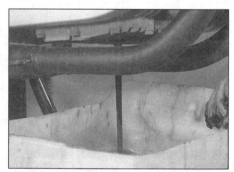

8.4b . . . and allow all the oil to drain

8.5a Unscrew the three nuts securing the oil filter cover . . .

8.5b . . . and remove the old filter

8.7a Install the new filter into the engine . . .

8.7b . . . then fit the O-ring onto the cover . . .

8.7c . . . followed by the spring . . .

8.7d . . . then fit the cover . . .

8.7e . . . and tighten its nuts securely

7 Install the new filter **(see illustration)**. Apply a smear of grease to the O-ring on the filter cover, then install the spring and the filter cover onto the engine and tighten the nuts securely **(see illustrations)**.

8 Refill the crankcase with oil to the proper level (see *Daily (pre-ride) checks*) with the recommended type and amount of oil, then install the filler cap. Start the engine and let it run for two or three minutes (make sure that the oil pressure light extinguishes after a few seconds). Shut it off, wait a few minutes, then check the oil level. If necessary, add more oil to bring the level up to the upper line on the dipstick. Check around the drain plug and filter cover for leaks.

9 The old oil drained from the engine cannot be re-used and should be disposed of properly. Check with your local refuse disposal company, disposal facility or environmental agency to see whether they will accept the used oil for recycling. Don't pour used oil into drains or onto the ground.

> **HAYNES HINT**
> *Check the old oil carefully - if it is very metallic coloured, then the engine is experiencing wear from break-in (new engine) or from insufficient lubrication. If there are flakes or chips of metal in the oil, then something is drastically wrong internally and the engine will have to be disassembled for inspection and repair. If there are pieces of fibre-like material in the oil, the clutch is experiencing excessive wear and should be checked.*

OIL CARE
FOLLOW THE CODE
OIL BANK LINE
0800 66 33 66
www.oilbankline.org.uk

Note: It is antisocial and illegal to dump oil down the drain. To find the location of your nearest oil recycling bank in the UK, call this number free. In the USA, note that any oil supplier must accept used oil for recycling.

9 Idle speed - check and adjustment

Idle speed check

1 Before adjusting the idle speed, make sure the valve clearances and spark plug gaps are correct. Also, turn the handlebars back-and-forth and see if the idle speed changes as this is done. If it does, the throttle cable may not be adjusted correctly, or may be worn out. This is a dangerous condition that can cause loss of control of the bike. Be sure to correct this problem before proceeding.

2 The engine should be at normal operating temperature, which is usually reached after 10 to 15 minutes of stop and go riding. Place the motorcycle on its centre stand and make sure the transmission is in neutral.

3 With the engine idling, adjust the idle speed by turning the throttle stop screw in or out until the idle speed listed in this Chapter's Specifications is obtained. The throttle stop screw is located under the right-hand carburettor **(see illustration)**.

4 Snap the throttle open and shut a few times, then recheck the idle speed. If necessary, repeat the adjustment procedure.

5 If a smooth, steady idle can't be achieved, the fuel/air mixture may be incorrect. Refer to Chapter 3 for additional information on adjusting the carburettors.

Throttle cable freeplay

6 At the same time as the idle speed is checked, measure the amount of freeplay is the throttle cable. This is measured in terms of twistgrip rotation, and is described in Section 24).

1

9.3 Throttle stop screw (arrow)

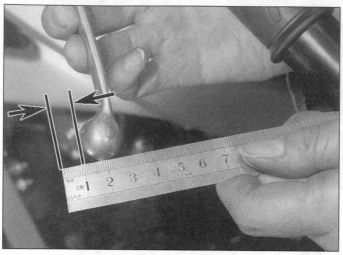

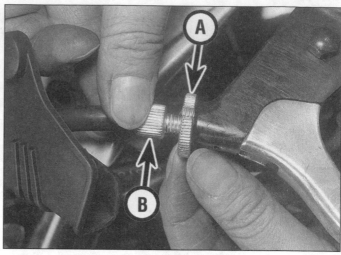

10.1 Measuring clutch lever freeplay

10.2 Lockring (A), adjuster (B) (lever end)

10 Clutch - check

1 Periodic adjustment of the clutch cable is necessary to compensate for cable stretch. Check that the amount of freeplay at the clutch lever end is within the specifications listed at the beginning of the Chapter **(see illustration)**. If adjustment is required, it can be made at either the lever end of the cable or at the clutch end.

2 To adjust cable freeplay at the lever, pull back the rubber cover, then loosen the locking ring and turn the adjuster in or out until the required amount of freeplay is obtained **(see illustration)**. To increase freeplay, turn the adjuster clockwise. To reduce freeplay, turn the adjuster anti-clockwise. Tighten the locking ring securely.

3 To adjust cable freeplay at the clutch, pull up the rubber cover on the top of the engine sprocket cover, then loosen the locknut and turn the adjuster until the required amount of freeplay is obtained **(see illustration)**. To increase freeplay, turn the adjuster clockwise. To reduce freeplay, turn the adjuster anti-clockwise. Tighten the locknut securely.

4 If all the adjustment has been taken up at the lever, reset the adjuster to give the maximum

amount of freeplay, then set the correct amount of freeplay using the adjuster at the clutch end of the cable. Subsequent adjustments can now be made using the lever adjuster only.

5 Clutch plate wear can be compensated for by adjustment of the clutch release mechanism set in the sprocket cover. If it is impossible to eliminate clutch drag or slip with cable adjustment, set the release mechanism freeplay as described in Chapter 2, Section 17. Always adjust the cable after release mechanism adjustment.

11 Drive chain - freeplay check and adjustment

Freeplay check

1 A neglected drive chain won't last long and can quickly damage the sprockets. Routine chain adjustment will ensure maximum chain and sprocket life.

2 To check the chain, shift the transmission into neutral and make sure the ignition switch is OFF. Place the machine on its centre stand.

3 Measure the amount of freeplay on the chain's bottom run, at a point midway between the two sprockets, then compare your measurement to the value listed in this

Chapter's Specifications **(see illustration)**. Since the chain will rarely wear evenly, rotate the rear wheel so that another section of chain can be checked; do this several times to check the entire length of chain. In some cases where lubrication has been neglected or the chain's O-rings have failed, corrosion and galling may cause the links to bind and kink, which effectively shortens the chain's length. If the chain is tight between the sprockets, rusty or kinked, or if any of the pins are loose or the rollers damaged, it's time to replace it with a new one. If you find a tight area, mark it with felt pen or paint, and repeat the measurement after the bike has been ridden. If the chain's still tight in the same area, it may be damaged or worn. Because a tight or kinked chain can damage the transmission output shaft bearing, it's a good idea to replace it.

Adjustment

4 Rotate the rear wheel until the chain is positioned with the tightest point at the centre of its bottom run, then place the machine on its sidestand.

5 On US models, remove the split pin from the rear axle nut, then on all models slacken the axle nut **(see illustration)**.

6 Adjust the chain adjusting nuts on the end of each side of the swingarm evenly until the amount of freeplay specified at the beginning

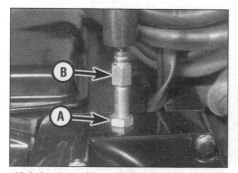

10.3 Locknut (A), adjuster (B) (clutch end)

11.3 Measuring drive chain freeplay

11.5 Slacken the axle nut . . .

11.6 . . . then adjust the chain by turning the adjuster nuts

11.7 The cut-out on each adjuster (arrow) must be in the same position relative to the notches in the swingarm

11.9 Tighten the axle nut to the specified torque setting

of the Chapter is obtained at the centre of the bottom run of the chain **(see illustration)**.

7 Following chain adjustment, check that the cut-out on the top of each chain adjuster is in the same position in relation to the notches on the swingarm **(see illustration)**. It is important that the mark on each adjuster aligns with the same notch; if not, the rear wheel will be out of alignment with the front.

8 If there is a discrepancy in the chain adjuster positions, adjust one of the chain adjusters so that its position is exactly the same as the other. Check the chain freeplay as described above and readjust if necessary.

9 Tighten the axle nut to the torque setting specified at the beginning of the Chapter, then tighten both chain adjuster nuts securely **(see illustration)**. On US models, fit a new split pin through the hole in the end of the axle and bend its ends securely around the axle nut.

12 Drive chain - wear and stretch check

1 Position the machine on its centre stand. Rotate the rear wheel slowly and check the entire length of the chain for damaged rollers, loose links and pins and replace if damage is found. If the chain has reached the end of its adjustment, it must be replaced.

2 The amount of chain stretch can be measured and compared to the stretch limit specified at the beginning of the Chapter. On US models, remove the split pin from the rear axle nut, then on all models slacken the axle nut **(see illustration 11.5)**. Tighten the chain

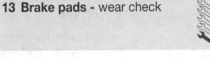

12.2 Measure distance between 1st and 21st pins to determine chain stretch

adjusting nuts on the end of each side of the swingarm evenly until the chain is tight **(see illustration 11.6)**. Measure along the bottom run the length of 21 pins (from the centre of the 1st pin to the centre of the 21st pin) and compare the result with the service limit specified at the beginning of the Chapter **(see illustration)**. Rotate the rear wheel so that several sections of the chain are measured, then calculate the average. If the chain exceeds the service limit it must be replaced (see Chapter 5). **Note:** *It is good practice to replace the chain and sprockets as a set.* Reset the chain freeplay as described in Section 11.

3 Check the teeth on the engine sprocket and the rear wheel sprocket for wear (Chapter 5).

4 Inspect the drive chain slider on the swingarm for excessive wear and replace it if necessary (see Chapter 5).

13 Brake pads - wear check

Front brake pads

1 The pads can be viewed from above or below the caliper mouth. The original equipment pads feature a wear indicator step (EK to ES models), a wear indicator cutout (ET to EY models) or a wear indicator groove (K1 models onward) in the friction material to denote the point at which the pads must be renewed **(see illustrations)**. If the pads are particularly dirty or you are in doubt about the amount of friction material remaining, remove the pads for inspection (see Chapter 6).

2 The pads must be renewed when they have worn down to the wear indicators to ensure braking efficiency and to avoid damage to the brake disc.

Rear brake pads

3 The pads can be viewed from the top of the caliper after removing the plastic cover. The original equipment pads feature a step or groove around the pad periphery to denote the point at which the pads must be replaced with new ones. If the pads are particularly dirty or you are in doubt about the amount of friction material remaining, remove the pads for inspection as described in Chapter 6.

1

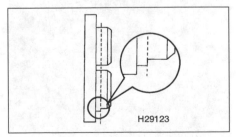

13.1a Front brake pad wear indicator step – EK to ES models

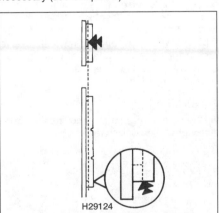

13.1b Front brake pad wear indicator cutout (arrow) – ET to EY models

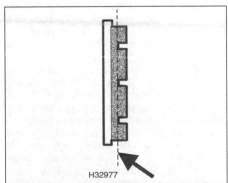

13.1c Front brake pad wear indicator groove (arrow) – K1 models onward

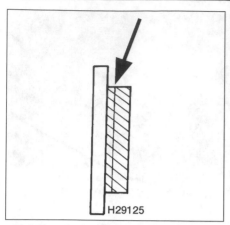

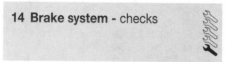

13.4 Rear brake pad wear indicator step or groove (arrow)

4 The pads must be replaced if the friction material has worn down level with the step or groove in the pad edge **(see illustration)**.

14 Brake system - checks

1 A routine general check of the brake system will ensure that any problems are discovered and remedied before the rider's safety is jeopardised.
2 Check the brake lever and pedal for loose connections, improper or rough action, excessive play, bends, and other damage. Replace any damaged parts with new ones (see Chapter 6).
3 Make sure all brake fasteners are tight. Check the brake pads for wear and make sure the fluid level in the reservoirs is correct (see *Daily (pre-ride) checks*). Look for leaks at the hose connections and check for cracks in the hoses. If the lever or pedal is spongy, bleed the brakes (see Chapter 6).
4 Make sure the brake light operates when the front brake lever is depressed. The front brake light switch is not adjustable. If it fails to operate properly, check it (see Chapter 8).
5 Make sure the brake light is activated just before the rear brake pedal takes effect. If adjustment is necessary, hold the switch and turn the adjusting nut on the switch body until the brake light is activated when required **(see illustration)**. If the switch doesn't operate the brake lights, check it (see Chapter 8).
6 Check the position of the brake pedal. The distance between the brake pedal pad and the top of the rider's footrest should be as specified at the beginning of the Chapter **(see illustration)**. If the pedal height is incorrect, slacken the locknut on the master cylinder pushrod, then turn the pushrod adjuster until the pedal is at the correct height **(see illustration)**. Tighten the locknut securely. Adjust the rear brake light switch after adjusting the pedal height (see Step 5).
7 The front brake lever has a span adjuster

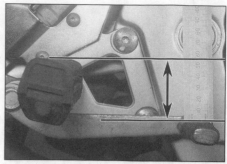

14.5 Rear brake light switch adjuster nut (arrow)

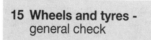
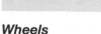

14.6b Master cylinder pushrod locknut (A) and adjuster (B)

which alters the distance of the lever from the handlebar **(see illustration)**. Pull the lever away from the handlebar and turn the adjuster knob until the setting which best suits the rider is obtained. Ensure the adjuster is never set between two positions.

15 Wheels and tyres - general check

Wheels

1 The cast wheels used are virtually maintenance free, but they should be kept clean and checked periodically for cracks and other damage. Also check the wheel runout and alignment (see Chapter 6). Never attempt to repair damaged cast wheels; they must be replaced with new ones. Check the valve rubber for signs of damage or deterioration and have it replaced if necessary. Also, make sure the valve stem cap is in place and tight.

Tyres

2 Check tyre condition and tread depth thoroughly - see Daily (pre-ride) checks.

16 Steering head bearing freeplay - check and adjustment

1 This motorcycle is equipped with tapered-roller type steering head bearings which can

14.6a Measuring rear brake pedal height

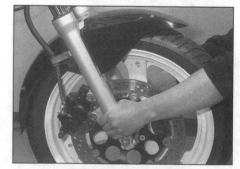

14.7 Adjusting the front brake lever span

become dented, rough or loose during normal use of the machine. In extreme cases, worn or loose steering head bearings can cause steering wobble - a condition that is potentially dangerous.

Check

2 Place the motorcycle on its centre stand. Raise the front wheel off the ground either by having an assistant push down on the rear or by placing a support under the engine.
3 Point the front wheel straight-ahead and slowly move the handlebars from side-to-side. Any dents or roughness in the bearing races will be felt and the bars will not move smoothly and freely.
4 Next, grasp the fork sliders and try to move them forward and backward **(see illustration)**. Any looseness in the steering head bearings will be felt as front-to-rear movement of the

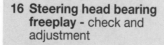

16.4 Checking for play in the steering head bearings

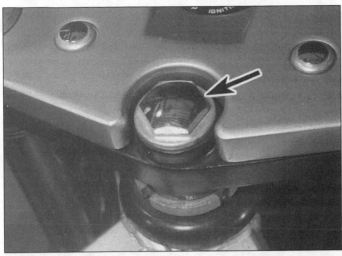

16.5a Slacken the steering stem bolt (arrow) . . .

16.5b . . . and each fork clamp bolt (arrow)

16.6 Adjust the bearings using a drift located into one of the notches in the adjuster ring

16.8 Tighten the steering stem bolt to the specified torque setting

forks. If play is felt in the bearings, adjust the steering head as follows.

 HAYNES HiNT *Freeplay in the fork due to worn fork bushes can be misinterpreted for steering head bearing play - do not confuse the two.*

Adjustment

5 Although not essential, it is wise to remove the fuel tank to avoid the possibility of damage should a tool slip while adjustment is being made (see Chapter 3). Slacken the steering stem bolt, then slacken the fork clamp bolts in the top yoke **(see illustrations)**.

6 Using a suitable drift located in one of the notches in the adjuster ring, slacken the adjuster ring slightly by tapping the drift with a hammer, until pressure is just released, then tighten it until all freeplay in the forks is removed, yet the steering is able to move freely from side to side **(see illustration)**. The

object is to set the adjuster ring so that the bearings are under a very light loading, just enough to remove any freeplay.

Caution: Take great care not to apply excessive pressure because this will cause premature failure of the bearings.

7 If the bearings cannot be set up properly, or if there is any binding, roughness or notchiness, they will have to be removed for inspection or replacement (see Chapter 5).

8 With the bearings correctly adjusted, tighten the steering stem bolt and the fork clamp bolts to the torque settings specified at the beginning of the Chapter **(see illustration)**.

9 Check the bearing adjustment as described above and re-adjust if necessary.

17 Nuts and bolts - tightness check

1 Since vibration of the machine tends to

loosen fasteners, all nuts, bolts, screws, etc. should be periodically checked for proper tightness.

2 Pay particular attention to the following:

> Spark plugs
> Engine oil drain plug
> Gearchange lever bolt
> Footrest and stand bolts
> Engine mounting bolts
> Shock absorber mounting bolts and suspension linkage bolts
> Handlebar bolts
> Front axle nut and clamp bolt
> Front fork clamp bolts (top & bottom yoke)
> Rear axle nut
> Swingarm pivot nut
> Brake caliper mounting bolts
> Brake hose banjo bolts and brake caliper bleed screws
> Brake disc bolts and rear sprocket nuts

3 If a torque wrench is available, use it along with the torque specifications at the beginning of this, or other, Chapters.

1

Every 7500 miles (12 000 km) or 2 years

18 Air filter - replacement

1 Remove the old air filter as described in Section 2 and install a new one.

19 Spark plugs - replacement

1 Remove the old spark plugs as described in Section 6 and install new ones.

20 Suspension - check

1 The suspension components must be maintained in top operating condition to ensure rider safety. Loose, worn or damaged suspension parts decrease the motorcycle's stability and control.

Front suspension

2 While standing alongside the motorcycle, apply the front brake and push on the handlebars to compress the forks several times. See if they move up-and-down smoothly without binding. If binding is felt, the forks should be disassembled and inspected (see Chapter 5).
3 Inspect the area above the dust seal for oil leakage, then carefully lever the dust seal upwards using a flat-bladed screwdriver and inspect the area around the fork seal **(see illustrations)**. If leakage is evident, the seals must be replaced (see Chapter 5).
4 Check the tightness of all suspension nuts and bolts to be sure none have worked loose.

Rear suspension

5 Inspect the rear shock for fluid leakage and tightness of its mountings. If leakage is found, the shock should be replaced (see Chapter 5).
6 With the aid of an assistant to support the bike, compress the rear suspension several times. It should move up and down freely without binding. If any binding is felt, the worn

20.3a Lever off the fork dust seal . . .

20.3b . . . and check for signs of oil leakage

20.7a Attempt to move the swingarm from side-to-side

20.7b Feel for up-and-down play in the rear suspension bearings

or faulty component must be identified and replaced. The problem could be due to either the shock absorber, the suspension linkage components or the swingarm components.
7 Position the motorcycle on its centre stand so that the rear wheel is off the ground. Grab the swingarm and rock it from side to side - there should be no discernible movement at the rear **(see illustration)**. If there's a little movement or a slight clicking can be heard, inspect the tightness of all the rear suspension mounting bolts and nuts, referring to the torque settings specified at the beginning of the Chapter, and re-check for movement. Next, grasp the top of the rear wheel and pull it upwards - there should be no discernible freeplay before the shock absorber begins to compress **(see illustration)**. Any freeplay felt in either check indicates worn bearings in the suspension linkage or swingarm, or worn shock absorber mountings. The worn

components must be replaced (see Chapter 5).
8 To make an accurate assessment of the swingarm bearings, remove the rear wheel (see Chapter 6) and the bolt securing the suspension linkage rods to the linkage arm (see Chapter 5). Grasp the rear of the swingarm with one hand and place your other hand at the junction of the swingarm and the frame. Try to move the rear of the swingarm from side-to-side. Any wear (play) in the bearings should be felt as movement between the swingarm and the frame at the front. If there is any play the swingarm will be felt to move forward and backward at the front (not from side-to-side). Next, move the swingarm up and down through its full travel. It should move freely, without any binding or rough spots. If any play in the swingarm is noted or if the swingarm does not move freely, the bearings must be removed for inspection or replacement (see Chapter 5).

Every 2 years

21 Brake fluid - change

1 The brake fluid should be replaced at the prescribed interval or whenever a master cylinder or caliper overhaul is carried out. Refer to the brake bleeding section in Chapter 6, noting that all old fluid must be pumped from the fluid reservoir and hydraulic line before filling with new DOT 4 fluid.

Every 4 years

22 Brake hoses - replacement

1 The hoses should be replaced regardless of their condition.
2 Refer to Chapter 6 and disconnect the brake hoses from the master cylinders and calipers. Always replace the banjo union sealing washers with new ones.

23 Fuel hoses - replacement

 Warning: *Petrol (gasoline) is extremely flammable, so take extra precautions when you* work on any part of the fuel system. Don't smoke or allow open flames or bare light bulbs near the work area, and don't work in a garage where a natural gas-type appliance is present. If you spill any fuel on your skin, rinse it off immediately with soap and water. When you perform any kind of work on the fuel system, wear safety glasses. It is also advisable to have a fire extinguisher suitable for a Class B type fire (flammable liquids) on hand - be sure you know how to use it.

All models

1 All fuel hoses should be replaced regardless of their condition.
2 Remove the fuel tank (see Chapter 3). Disconnect the fuel hoses from the fuel cock, fuel tap and from the carburettors, noting the routing of each hose and where it connects (see Chapter 3 if required). It is advisable to make a sketch of the various hoses before removing them to ensure they are correctly installed.
3 Secure each new hose to its unions using new clamps. Run the engine and check that there are no fuel leaks before taking the machine out on the road.

California models

4 The emission control system hoses should be replaced regardless of their condition. In addition to the fuel hoses mentioned above, replace the surge hose from the fuel tank to the charcoal canister, and the purge hose from the charcoal canister to the carburettors **(see illustration 14.1 in Chapter 3).**

Non-scheduled maintenance

24 Throttle and choke cable - check

Note: *The throttle cable and choke cable will stretch over a period of time necessitating adjustment.*

Throttle cable

1 Make sure the throttle grip rotates easily from fully closed to fully open with the front wheel turned at various angles. The grip should return automatically from fully open to fully closed when released.
2 If the throttle sticks, this is probably due to a cable fault. Remove the cable (see Chapter 3) and lubricate it (see Section 28). Install the cable, making sure it is correctly routed. If this fails to improve the operation of the throttle, the cable must be replaced. Note that in very rare cases the fault could lie in the carburettors rather than the cable, necessitating the removal of the carburettors and inspection of the throttle linkage (see Chapter 3).
3 With the throttle operating smoothly, check for a small amount of freeplay in the throttle twistgrip **(see illustration)**. The amount of freeplay in the cable, measured in terms of twistgrip rotation, should be as specified at the beginning of the Chapter. If adjustment is necessary, adjust the idle speed first (see Section 9).
4 The cable is adjustable at either the twistgrip end or the carburettor end. Minor adjustments should be made at the twistgrip end. To adjust the cable freeplay on EK to EY models, slacken the locknut on the cable adjuster and rotate the adjuster until the correct amount of freeplay is obtained, then tighten the locknut against the adjuster **(see illustration)**.
5 To adjust the cable freeplay on K1 models onward, slacken the locknut on the decelerator cable adjuster and set the adjuster to give maximum freeplay, then slacken the locknut on the accelerator cable adjuster and rotate the adjuster until the correct amount of freeplay is obtained **(see illustration)**. Tighten the locknut against the adjuster. Hold the twistgrip in the closed position and rotate the decelerator cable adjuster until resistance is felt in the cable, then tighten the locknut against the adjuster.
6 If all the adjustment has been taken up at

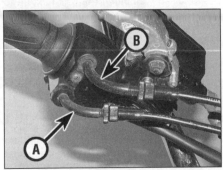
24.3 Throttle cable freeplay is measured in terms of twistgrip rotation

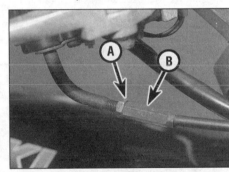
24.4 Throttle cable adjuster locknut (A) and adjuster (B) – twistgrip end, EK to EY models

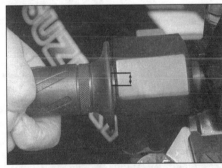
24.5 Decelerator cable (A) and accelerator cable (B) – twistgrip end, K1 models onwards

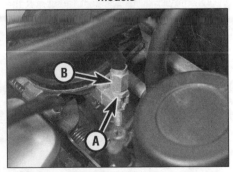
24.6 Throttle cable adjuster locknut (A) and adjuster (B) – carburettor end, EK to EY models

1

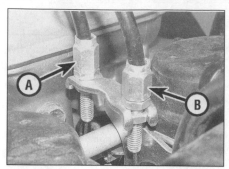

24.7 Decelerator cable (A) and accelerator cable (B) – carburettor end, K1 models onwards

25.5a Remove the vacuum take-off caps . . .

25.5b . . . and the vacuum hose (K1 models onward)

the twistgrip on EK to EY models, re-set the adjuster to give maximum freeplay, then set the correct amount of freeplay at the carburettors by slackening the locknut and turning the adjuster as required **(see illustration)**. Tighten the locknut on completion, and make sure the lower nut is still captive in the bottom of the adjuster. Subsequent adjustments can now be made at the twistgrip end.

7 If all the adjustment has been taken up at the twistgrip on K1 models onward, reset the accelerator and decelerator cable adjusters to give maximum freeplay, then set the correct amount of freeplay at the carburettors. Slacken the accelerator cable locknut and turn the adjuster as required **(see illustration)**. Tighten the locknut on completion and make sure the lower nut is still captive in the bottom of the adjuster. Hold the twistgrip in the closed position and rotate the decelerator cable adjuster until resistance is felt in the cable, then tighten the locknut and make sure the lower nut is still captive in the bottom of the adjuster.

8 Check that the throttle twistgrip operates smoothly and snaps shut quickly when released.

9 With the engine idling, turn the handlebars through the full extent of their travel. The idle speed should not change. If it does, the cable may be incorrectly routed - correct this condition before riding the bike (see Chapter 3).

Choke cable

10 If the choke does not operate smoothly this is probably due to a cable fault. Remove the cable (see Chapter 3) and lubricate it (see Section 28). Install the cable, routing it so it takes the smoothest route possible.

11 Check for a small amount of freeplay in the cable and adjust it if necessary using the adjuster at the lever end of the cable, using the method described in Step 4 above for the throttle cable (throttle end). If this fails to improve the operation of the choke, the cable must be replaced. Note that in very rare cases the fault could lie in the carburettors rather than the cable, necessitating the removal of the carburettors and inspection of the choke valves (see Chapter 3).

25 Carburettors - synchronisation

Note: *The carburettors will go out of synchronisation over a period of time, resulting in decreased fuel mileage, increased engine temperature, less than ideal throttle response and higher vibration levels.*

⚠️ **Warning: Petrol (gasoline) is extremely flammable, so take extra precautions when you work on any part of the fuel system. Don't smoke or allow open flames or bare light bulbs near the work area, and don't work in a garage where a natural gas-type appliance is present. If you spill any fuel on your skin, rinse it off immediately with soap and water. When you perform any kind of work on the fuel system, wear safety glasses and have a fire extinguisher suitable for a Class B type fire (flammable liquids) on hand.**

⚠️ **Warning: Take great care not to burn your hand on the hot engine unit when accessing the gauge take-off points on the intake manifolds. Do not allow exhaust gases to build up in the work area; either perform the check outside or use an exhaust gas extraction system.**

1 Carburettor synchronisation is simply the process of adjusting the carburettors so they pass the same amount of fuel/air mixture to each cylinder. This is done by measuring the vacuum produced in each cylinder. Before synchronising the carburettors, make sure the valve clearances are properly set.

2 To properly synchronise the carburettors, you will need some sort of vacuum gauge set-up with a gauge for each cylinder, or a manometer, which is a calibrated tube arrangement that utilises columns of mercury or steel rods to indicate engine vacuum. If using a mercury manometer, extra precautions must be taken during use and storage of the instrument as mercury is a liquid, and extremely toxic. Because of the nature of the synchronisation procedure and the need for special instruments, most owners leave the task to a Suzuki dealer.

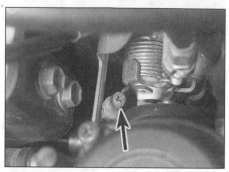

25.8 Carburettor synchronisation screw (arrow)

3 Start the engine and let it run until it reaches normal operating temperature, then shut it off.

4 Remove the fuel tank (see Chapter 3).

5 On EK to EY models, remove the vacuum take-off cap from the top of each carburettor **(see illustration)**. On K1 models onward, remove the take-off cap from the left-hand carburettor and the vacuum hose from the right-hand carburettor **(see illustration)**. Connect the gauge hoses to the take-off adapters. Make sure that are no air leaks as false readings will result.

6 Arrange a temporary fuel supply, either by using a small temporary tank or by using extra long fuel pipes to the now remote fuel tank. Alternatively, position the tank on a suitable base on the motorcycle, taking care not to scratch any paintwork, and making sure that the tank is safely and securely supported.

7 Start the engine and increase the idle speed to 1750 rpm using the throttle stop screw under the right-hand carburettor **(see illustration 9.3)**. If the gauges are fitted with damping adjustment, set this so that the needle flutter is just eliminated but so that they can still respond to small changes in pressure. The vacuum readings for both of the cylinders should be the same. If the vacuum readings vary, proceed as follows.

Caution: Do not allow the engine to overheat. If necessary, stop the engine and allow it to cool before starting again.

8 The carburettors are adjusted by turning the synchronising screw situated in-between the carburettors, in the throttle linkage **(see illustration)**. The screw is accessed using a

long screwdriver. Turn the screw until the reading on each gauge is the same. **Note:** *Do not press down on the screw whilst adjusting it, otherwise a false reading will be obtained.* When the carburettors are synchronised, open and close the throttle quickly to settle the linkage, and recheck the gauge readings, readjusting if necessary.

9 When the adjustment is complete, recheck the vacuum readings, then adjust the idle speed by turning the throttle stop screw until the idle speed listed in this Chapter's Specifications is obtained.

10 Stop the engine. Remove the gauge hoses and replace the take-off caps. Detach the temporary fuel supply and install the fuel tank (see Chapter 3).

26 Headlight - aim check and adjustment

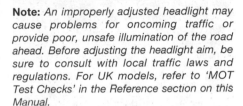

Note: *An improperly adjusted headlight may cause problems for oncoming traffic or provide poor, unsafe illumination of the road ahead. Before adjusting the headlight aim, be sure to consult with local traffic laws and regulations. For UK models, refer to 'MOT Test Checks' in the Reference section on this Manual.*

1 The headlight beam can be adjusted both horizontally and vertically. Check first that the tyre pressures are correct and the suspension is adjusted as required. The machine must be off its stand and on level ground, with the fuel tank half full and with an assistant sitting on the seat. If the bike is usually ridden with a passenger on the back, have a second assistant to do this.

2 Horizontal adjustment is made by turning the adjuster screw in the headlight rim **(see illustration)**. Turn it clockwise to move the beam to the right, and anti-clockwise to move it to the left.

3 Vertical adjustment is made by slackening the headlight mounting bolts and the bolt in

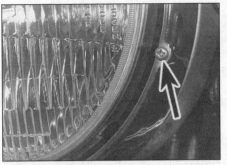

26.2 Headlight beam horizontal adjuster (arrow)

the guide on the lower right-hand side of the headlight shell and tilting the light up or down as required **(see illustration)**. Tighten the bolts securely after the adjustment has been made.

27 Wheel bearings - check

Note: *Wheel bearings should be checked periodically for wear. Worn bearings will cause handling and stability problems.*

1 Place the motorcycle on its centre stand. With the wheel raised off the ground slightly, check for any play in the bearings by pushing and pulling the wheel against the hub **(see illustration)**. Also rotate the wheel and check that it spins smoothly.

2 If any play is detected in the hub, or if the wheel does not rotate smoothly (and this is not due to brake drag), the wheel bearings must be removed and inspected for wear or damage (see Chapter 6).

28 Stands, lever pivots and cables - lubrication

Note: *Since the controls, cables and various*

26.3 Headlight mounting bolt (arrow)

other components of a motorcycle are exposed to the elements, they should be lubricated periodically to ensure safe and trouble-free operation.

Pivot points

1 The footrest pivots, clutch and brake lever pivots, brake pedal pivot and stand pivots should be lubricated frequently. In order for the lubricant to be applied where it will do the most good, the component should be disassembled. However, if chain and cable lubricant is being used, it can be applied to the pivot joint gaps and will usually work its way into the areas where friction occurs.

2 If motor oil or light grease is being used, apply it sparingly as it may attract dirt (which could cause the controls to bind or wear at an accelerated rate). **Note:** *One of the best lubricants for the control lever pivots is a dry-film lubricant (available from many sources by different names).*

Cables

3 To lubricate the cables, disconnect the relevant cable at its upper end, then lubricate the cable with a pressure adapter **(see illustration)**. See Chapter 2 for clutch cable removal and Chapter 3 for the choke and throttle cable removal.

1

27.1 Checking for play in the wheel bearings

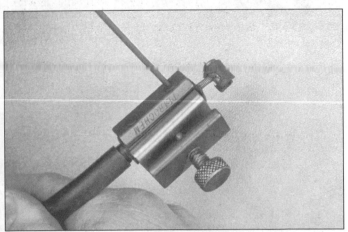

28.3 Lubricating a cable with a pressure lubricator. Make sure the tool seals around the inner cable

4 The speedometer and tachometer cables should be removed (see Chapter 8) and the inner cable withdrawn from the outer cable and lubricated with motor oil or cable lubricant. Do not lubricate the upper few inches of the cable as the lubricant may travel up into the instrument head.

29 Front forks - oil change

Note: *The fork oil will deteriorate over a period of time with a loss of its damping properties.*
1 Remove the front forks (see Chapter 5).
2 Carefully unscrew the fork top bolt **(see illustration)**.

 Warning: The fork spring is pressing on the fork top bolt with considerable pressure. Unscrew

29.2 Unscrew the fork top bolt

29.5a Pour the oil into the top of the tube

29.6b ... followed by the spacer ...

the bolt very carefully, keeping a downward pressure on it and release it slowly as it is likely to spring clear. It is advisable to wear some form of eye and face protection when carrying out this operation.

3 Slide the fork tube down into the slider and withdraw the disc washer (where fitted), spacer, spring seat and spring from the tube, noting which way up they fit.
4 Invert the fork leg over a suitable container and pump the fork vigorously to expel as much fork oil as possible. Allow the fork oil to drain for a few minutes.
5 Fully compress the fork, and pour in the oil using the amount and type specified at the beginning of the Chapter **(see illustration)**. Slowly pump the forks up and down a few times to fully distribute the oil. The oil level should also be measured and adjustment made by adding or subtracting oil. Fully compress the fork tube into the slider and measure the fork oil level from the top of the tube **(see illustration)**. Add or subtract fork oil until the oil is at the level specified in the Specifications Section of this Chapter.
6 Install the spring seat with its shouldered side down into the spring, then install the spring into the fork tube, followed by the spacer, and where fitted, the disc washer **(see illustrations)**.
7 Inspect the O-ring on the fork top bolt and replace it if it shows any signs of damage or deterioration **(see illustration)**. Install the top bolt carefully into the fork tube, keeping the

29.5b Measure the oil level with the fork held vertical

29.6c ... and the disc washer (where fitted)

fork tube fully extended whilst pressing on the spring and making sure the top bolt is not cross-threaded. **Note:** *The top bolt can be tightened at this stage if the tube is held between the padded jaws of a vice, but do not risk distorting the tube by doing so. A better method is to tighten the top bolt when the fork has been installed in the bike and is securely held in the yokes.*

 Warning: It will be necessary to compress the spring by pressing it down using the top bolt to engage the threads of the top bolt with the fork tube. This is a potentially dangerous operation and should be performed with care, using an assistant if necessary. Wipe off any excess oil before starting to prevent the possibility of slipping.

TOOL TIP *Use a ratchet-type tool when installing the fork top bolt. This makes it unnecessary to remove the tool from the bolt whilst threading it in making it easier to maintain a downward pressure on the spring.*

8 Install the front forks (see Chapter 5).

30 Engine - cylinder compression check

1 Among other things, poor engine performance may be caused by leaking

29.6a Fit the spring seat, shouldered side down, into the top of the spring, then install the spring into the fork tube ...

29.7 Replace the O-ring (arrow) if it is worn or damaged

valves, incorrect valve clearances, a leaking head gasket, or worn pistons, rings and/or cylinder walls. A cylinder compression check will help pinpoint these conditions and can also indicate the presence of excessive carbon deposits in the cylinder heads.

2 Make sure the valve clearances are correctly set (see Section 5) and that the cylinder head nuts are tightened to the correct torque setting (see Section 4).

3 Refer to *Fault Finding Equipment* in the Reference section for details of the compression test.

31 Engine - oil pressure check

Note: *An oil pressure check is essential if the oil pressure warning light indicates a problem, but can be carried out as a routine check of the lubrication system.*

1 To check the oil pressure, a suitable gauge and adapter piece (which screws into the crankcase) will be needed. Suzuki provide a kit (Pt. Nos. 09915-74510 and 09915-77330) for this purpose.

2 Warm the engine up to normal operating temperature then stop it.

3 Unscrew the plug from the bottom of the right-hand crankcase cover and swiftly screw the adapter into the crankcase threads **(see illustration)**. Connect the gauge to the adapter.

4 Start the engine and increase the engine speed to 3000 rpm whilst watching the gauge

31.3 Oil pressure gauge adapter plug (arrow)

reading. The oil pressure should be similar to that given in the Specifications at the start of this Chapter.

5 If the pressure is significantly lower than the standard, either the pressure regulator is stuck open, the oil pump is faulty, the oil strainer is blocked, or there is other engine damage. Begin diagnosis by checking the oil strainer and regulator, then the oil pump (see Chapter 2). If those items check out okay, chances are the bearing oil clearances are excessive and the engine needs to be overhauled.

6 If the pressure is too high, the regulator is stuck closed and must be checked (see Chapter 2).

7 Stop the engine and unscrew the gauge and adapter from the crankcase.

8 Install the crankcase plug using a new sealing washer, and tighten it securely. Check the oil level (see Daily (pre-ride) checks).

32 Steering head - bearing lubrication

Note: *Grease will harden over time, or may be washed out by high-pressure washers, necessitating repacking with fresh grease.*

1 Disassemble the steering head for re-greasing of the bearings. Refer to Chapter 5 for details.

33 Rear suspension - bearing lubrication

Note: *Grease will harden over time, or may be \washed out by high-pressure washers, necessitating repacking with fresh grease.*

1 The suspension components are not equipped with grease nipples. Remove the swingarm and the suspension linkage as described in Chapter 5 for greasing of the bearings.

34 Brake calipers and master cylinders - seal replacement

Note: *Brake seals will deteriorate over a period of time, leading to sticking operation or leakage.*

1 Refer to Chapter 6 and dismantle the components for seal replacement.

1

Notes

Chapter 2
Engine, clutch and transmission

Contents

2

Degrees of difficulty

Easy, suitable for novice with little experience

Fairly easy, suitable for beginner with some experience

Fairly difficult, suitable for competent DIY mechanic

Difficult, suitable for experienced DIY mechanic

Very difficult, suitable for expert DIY or professional

Specifications

General
Engine
 Type . . . . Four-stroke parallel twin
 Capacity . . . . 487 cc
 Bore . . . . 74.0 mm
 Stroke . . . . 56.6 mm
 Compression ratio . . . . 9.0 to 1
Clutch . . . . Wet multi-plate
Transmission . . . . Six-speed constant mesh
Final drive . . . . Chain and sprockets

Camshafts and camchain
Camshaft
  Intake lobe height
    UK ER to EY models and K1 models onward
      Standard .... 36.090 to 36.130 mm
      Service limit (min) .... 35.80 mm
    All other models
      Standard .... 36.789 to 36.819 mm
      Service limit (min) .... 36.49 mm
  Exhaust lobe height
    UK ER to EY models and K1 models onward
      Standard .... 36.090 to 36.130 mm
      Service limit (min) .... 35.80 mm
    All other models
      Standard .... 36.291 to 36.321 mm
      Service limit (min) .... 36.00 mm
  Journal diameter .... 21.959 to 21.980 mm
  Journal holder diameter .... 22.012 to 22.025 mm
  Journal oil clearance
    Standard .... 0.032 to 0.066 mm
    Service limit (max) .... 0.15 mm
  Runout (max) .... 0.10 mm
Camchain
  21 pin length (max) .... 158.0 mm

Cylinder head
Warpage (max) .... 0.10 mm

Valves, guides and springs
Valve clearances .... see Chapter 1
Intake valve
  Head diameter .... 39 mm
  Stem diameter .... 6.960 to 6.975 mm
  Guide bore diameter .... 7.000 to 7.015 mm
  Stem to guide clearance .... 0.025 to 0.055 mm
  Valve stem deflection (max) .... 0.35 mm
  Valve margin thickness (min) .... 0.50 mm
  Seat width .... 1.0 to 1.2 mm
  Valve lift .... 8.5 mm
  Head runout (max) .... 0.03 mm
  Stem runout (max) .... 0.05 mm
Exhaust valve
  Head diameter .... 32 mm
  Stem diameter .... 6.945 to 6.960 mm
  Guide bore diameter .... 7.000 to 7.015 mm
  Stem to guide clearance .... 0.040 to 0.070 mm
  Valve stem deflection (max) .... 0.35 mm
  Valve margin thickness (min) .... 0.50 mm
  Seat width .... 1.0 to 1.2 mm
  Valve lift .... 8.0 mm
  Head runout (max) .... 0.03 mm
  Stem runout (max) .... 0.05 mm
Valve spring free length (min) - intake and exhaust
  Inner spring .... 35.6 mm
  Outer spring .... 40.6 mm

Cylinder block
Bore
  Standard .... 74.000 to 74.015 mm
  Service limit (max) .... 74.08 mm
Warpage (max) .... 0.10 mm
Cylinder compression .... see Chapter 1

Pistons

Piston diameter (measured 15.0 mm up from skirt, at 90° to piston pin axis)
Standard .... 73.945 to 73.960 mm
Service limit (min) .... 73.880 mm
1st oversize .... + 0.5 mm
2nd oversize .... + 1.0 mm
Piston-to-bore clearance
Standard .... 0.050 to 0.060 mm
Service limit (max) .... 0.12 mm
Piston pin diameter
Standard .... 17.995 to 18.000 mm
Service limit (min) .... 17.98 mm
Piston pin bore
Standard .... 18.002 to 18.008 mm
Service limit (max) .... 18.03 mm

Piston rings

End gap (free)
Top ring
Standard .... 7.0 mm (approx)
Service limit (min) .... 5.6 mm
2nd ring
Standard .... 11.0 mm (approx)
Service limit (min) .... 8.8 mm
End gap (installed) - top and 2nd rings
Standard .... 0.10 to 0.25 mm
Service limit (max) .... 0.70 mm
Piston ring thickness (top and 2nd rings) .... 1.17 to 1.19 mm
Piston ring groove width
Top and 2nd rings .... 1.21 to 1.23 mm
Oil ring .... 2.51 to 2.53 mm
Ring-to-groove clearance
Top ring (max) .... 0.18 mm
2nd ring (max) .... 0.15 mm
Oversize ring identification
Top and 2nd rings
1st oversize 50
2nd oversize 100
Oil ring (standard Red)
1st oversize .... Blue
2nd oversize .... Yellow

Crankshaft and bearings

Journal diameter .... 31.976 to 32.000 mm
Main bearing oil clearance
Standard .... 0.020 to 0.044 mm
Service limit (max) .... 0.08 mm
Runout (max) .... 0.05 mm
Thrust bearing thickness
Standard .... 2.950 to 2.975 mm
Service limit (min) .... 2.850 mm

Balancer shaft

Journal diameter
EK to EM models .... 31.976 to 32.000 mm
EN to EY models and K1 models onward .... 31.984 to 32.000 mm
Bearing oil clearance
Standard .... 0.020 to 0.044 mm
Service limit (max) .... 0.08 mm
Spring free length (min) .... 14.9 mm

Connecting rods

Small-end internal diameter
Standard .... 18.006 to 18.014 mm
Service limit (max) .... 18.04 mm
Big-end side clearance
Standard .... 0.1 to 0.2 mm
Service limit (max) .... 0.3 mm

2

Connecting rods (continued)

Big-end width	22.95 to 23.00 mm
Crankpin width	23.10 to 23.15 mm
Crankpin diameter	33.976 to 34.000 mm
Big-end oil clearance	
Standard	0.024 to 0.048 mm
Service limit (max)	0.08 mm

Lubrication system

Oil pressure	see Chapter 1

Clutch

Friction plate	
Quantity	7
Thickness	
Standard	2.92 to 3.08 mm
Service limit (min)	2.62 mm
Tab width	
Standard	15.8 to 16.0 mm
Service limit (min)	15.0 mm
Plain plate	
Quantity	6
Warpage (max)	0.1 mm
Spring free length (min)	60.8 mm

Transmission

Gear ratios (No. of teeth)	
Primary reduction	2.714 to 1 (76/28T)
1st gear	2.461 to 1 (32/13T)
2nd gear	1.777 to 1 (32/18T)
3rd gear	1.380 to 1 (29/21T)
4th gear	1.125 to 1 (27/24T)
5th gear	0.961 to 1 (25/26T)
6th gear	0.851 to 1 (23/27T)
Final reduction	2.437 to 1 (39/16T)
Input shaft length (see text)	114.7 to 114.8 mm

Selector drum and forks

Selector fork-to-groove clearance	
Standard	0.1 to 0.3 mm
Service limit (max)	0.5 mm
Selector fork end thickness	5.3 to 5.4 mm
Selector fork groove width in gears	5.5 to 5.6 mm

Torque settings

Engine mounting bolt nuts	60 to 72 Nm
Right-hand side frame downtube bolt nuts	25 to 38 Nm
Valve cover bolts	13 to 15 Nm
Camchain tensioner bolts	6 to 8 Nm
Rear camchain guide bolts	4 to 7 Nm
Camshaft sprocket bolts	17 to 19 Nm
Camshaft journal cap bolts	8 to 12 Nm
Cylinder head 10 mm domed nuts	35 to 40 Nm
Cylinder head 6 mm bolt	8 to 12 Nm
Clutch nut	40 to 60 Nm
Clutch pressure plate bolts	4 to 6 Nm
Oil pump screws	8 to 12 Nm
Starter clutch Allen bolts	15 to 20 Nm
Sump (oil pan) bolts	12 to 16 Nm
Oil pressure regulator	17 to 20 Nm
Crankcase bolts	
8 mm bolts	20 to 24 Nm
6 mm bolts	9 to 13 Nm
Primary drive gear nut	90 to 110 Nm
Balancer shaft end bolt	35 to 45 Nm
Connecting rod nuts	
Initial setting (see text)	22 to 28 Nm
Final setting	30 to 34 Nm

1 General information

The engine/transmission unit is an air-cooled parallel twin, fitted across the frame. The engine has two valves per cylinder, operated by double overhead camshafts. The camshafts are chain driven off the crankshaft and run in plain bearings.

The engine/transmission unit is constructed in aluminium alloy with the crankcase being divided horizontally. The crankcase incorporates a wet sump (oil pan), pressure fed lubrication system, and houses a gear driven oil pump. The one-piece forged crankshaft runs in four main bearings. The left-hand end of the crankshaft carries the alternator rotor, whilst the right-hand end carries the ignition rotor and pulse generator coils.

The clutch is of the wet multi-plate type and is gear driven off the crankshaft. The transmission is of the six-speed constant mesh type. Drive is taken to the rear wheel by chain.

2 Operations possible with the engine in the frame

The components and assemblies listed below can be removed without having to remove the engine/transmission assembly from the frame. If however, a number of areas require attention at the same time, removal of the engine is recommended.

Valve cover
Camchain tensioner
Camshafts
Cylinder head
Cylinder block, pistons and piston rings
Ignition rotor and pulse generator coil
Clutch
Oil pump
Gearchange mechanism
*   (external components)*
Alternator
Starter clutch and idle gear
Sump (oil pan), oil strainer and oil
*   pressure relief valve*
Starter motor

3 Operations requiring engine removal

It is necessary to remove the engine/transmission assembly from the frame and separate the crankcase halves to gain access to the following components.

Transmission shafts
Selector drum and forks
Crankshaft and bearings
Balancer shaft and bearings
Connecting rod big-ends and bearings

4 Major engine repair - general note

1 It is not always easy to determine when or if an engine should be completely overhauled, as a number of factors must be considered.

2 High mileage is not necessarily an indication that an overhaul is needed, while low mileage, on the other hand, does not preclude the need for an overhaul. Frequency of servicing is probably the single most important consideration. An engine that has regular and frequent oil and filter changes, as well as other required maintenance, will most likely give many miles of reliable service. Conversely, a neglected engine, or one which has not been run in properly, may require an overhaul very early in its life.

3 Exhaust smoke and excessive oil consumption are both indications that piston rings and/or valve guides are in need of attention, although make sure that the fault is not due to oil leakage.

4 If the engine is making obvious knocking or rumbling noises, the connecting rod and/or main bearings are probably at fault.

5 Loss of power, rough running, valve train noise and high fuel consumption rates may also point to the need for an overhaul, especially if all are present at the same time. If a complete tune-up does not help, major mechanical work is the only solution.

6 An engine overhaul generally involves restoring the internal parts to the specifications of a new engine. The piston rings and main and connecting rod bearings are usually replaced and the cylinder walls honed or, if necessary, re-bored during a major overhaul. Generally the valve seats are re-ground, since they are usually in less than perfect condition at this point. The end result should be a like new engine that will give as many trouble-free miles as the original.

7 Before beginning the overhaul, read through the related procedures to familiarise yourself with the scope and requirements of the job. Overhauling an engine is not all that difficult, but it is time consuming. Plan on the bike being tied up for a minimum of two weeks. Check on the availability of parts and make sure any necessary special tools, equipment and supplies are obtained in advance.

8 Most work can be done with typical workshop hand tools, although a number of precision measuring tools are required for inspecting parts to determine if they must be replaced. Often a dealer will handle the inspection of parts and offer advice concerning reconditioning and replacement. As a general rule, time is the primary cost of an overhaul so it does not pay to install worn or substandard parts.

9 As a final note, to ensure maximum life and minimum trouble from a rebuilt engine, everything must be assembled with care in a spotlessly clean environment.

5 Engine - removal and installation

Note: *The engine is very heavy. Engine removal and installation should be carried out with the aid of at least one assistant; personal injury or damage could occur if the engine falls or is dropped. A hydraulic or mechanical floor jack should be used to support and lower or raise the engine if possible.*

Removal

1 Position the bike on its centre stand. Work can be made easier by raising the machine to a suitable working height on a hydraulic ramp or a suitable platform.

2 If the engine is dirty, particularly around its mountings, wash it thoroughly before starting any major dismantling work. This will make work much easier and rule out the possibility of caked on lumps of dirt falling into some vital component.

3 Drain the engine oil and remove the oil filter (see Chapter 1).

4 Remove the seat and the side panels (see Chapter 7) and disconnect the battery negative (-ve) lead (see Chapter 8). Trace the negative lead to its connector and disconnect it. Feed the lead through to the engine and coil it on the crankcase, noting its routing.

5 Remove the fuel tank (see Chapter 3).

6 Slacken the screws securing the ignition control unit to the left-hand side of the frame to allow the connectors of the wiring routed behind the unit to pass through. The ignition control unit can be removed if preferred (see Chapter 4).

7 Remove the carburettors (see Chapter 3). Plug the engine intake manifolds with clean rag.

8 Unscrew the knurled ring securing the lower end of the tachometer cable to its drive unit on the front of the cylinder head and withdraw the cable inner end from the drive unit **(see illustration)**.

9 Disconnect the spark plug leads from the plugs and secure them clear of the engine.

10 Trace the starter motor cable back from the starter motor (located under a cover behind the cylinder block) to the starter relay,

2

5.8 Unscrew the knurled ring (arrow) to release the tachometer cable

5.10 Pull back the rubber cover (arrow) and disconnect the starter motor lead from its terminal on the relay

5.11 Unscrew the gearchange lever pinch bolt (arrow)

releasing it from its clamp on the frame tube. Peel back the rubber cover from the relay, then unscrew the nut securing the cable to its terminal and disconnect the cable **(see illustration)**. Pull the cable back to the starter motor, noting its routing, and coil it on top of the crankcase so that it does not impede engine removal.

11 Unscrew the gearchange lever pinch bolt and remove the lever from the shaft, noting any alignment marks on the lever and the shaft **(see illustration)**. If no marks are visible, make your own before removing the lever so that it can be correctly aligned with the shaft on installation.

12 Remove the front sprocket (Chapter 5).

13 Remove the exhaust system (Chapter 3).

14 Trace the ignition pulse generator and oil pressure switch wiring back from the base of the right-hand side crankcase cover and disconnect it at its connector. Release the wiring from any clips or ties, noting its routing, and coil it on top of the crankcase so that it does not impede engine removal.

15 Trace the alternator wiring back from the top of the sprocket cover on the left-hand side of the engine and disconnect it at its bullet connectors. Release the wiring from any clips

or ties, noting its routing, and coil it on top of the crankcase so that it does not impede engine removal.

16 Trace the neutral switch wiring back from the top of the sprocket cover and disconnect it at its connector. Release the wiring from any clips or ties, noting its routing, and coil it on top of the crankcase so that it does not impede engine removal.

17 At this point, position an hydraulic or mechanical jack under the engine with a block of wood between the jack head and sump (oil

pan) **(see illustration)**. Make sure the jack is centrally positioned so the engine will not topple when the last mounting bolt is removed. Take the weight of the engine on the jack.

18 Unscrew the nuts on the six bolts which secure the right-hand side frame downtube to the rest of the frame, then withdraw the bolts **(see illustrations)**.

19 Unscrew the nuts on both the upper and lower front engine mounting bolts, then remove the right-hand side frame downtube **(see illustrations)**. Remove the spacers from

5.17 Support the engine using a jack and a block of wood

5.18a Right-hand side frame downtube is secured by two bolts at the rear (arrows) . . .

5.18b . . . and four at the front (arrows)

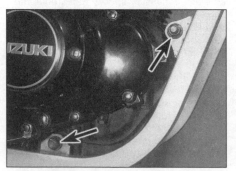

5.19a Unscrew the front engine bolt nuts (arrows) . . .

5.19b . . . and remove the frame downtube

the end of each front mounting bolt, noting that the longer spacer fits on the upper mounting bolt.
20 Make sure the engine is properly supported on the jack, and have an assistant support it as well. Unscrew the nuts on both the upper and lower rear engine mounting bolts, then withdraw all four engine bolts from the left-hand side of the machine **(see illustration)**. Note which bolt fits where as they are all of different length. Recover the spacers from the front engine bolts, noting that the longer spacer fits on the upper mounting bolt.
21 The engine can now be removed from the frame. Check that all wiring, cables and hoses are well clear, then lower the jack and manoeuvre the engine out of the right-hand side of the frame.
22 The engine mounting bolt nuts are self-locking, and as such can be only used once. Discard all the nuts and replace them with new ones on installation.

Installation

23 Installation is the reverse of removal, noting the following points:
a) Make sure no wires, cables or hoses become trapped between the engine and the frame when installing the engine.
b) The engine mounting bolts are all of different length. Make sure the correct bolt is installed in its correct location. The longest bolt (255 mm) is the front upper mounting bolt. The second longest bolt (240 mm) is the front lower mounting bolt. The third longest bolt (170 mm) is the rear upper mounting bolt. The shortest bolt (160 mm) is the rear lower mounting bolt. Install the bolts from the left-hand side.
c) When installing the front engine mounting bolts, make sure the long spacers are installed on each end of the upper bolt and the short spacers are installed on each end of the lower bolt **(see illustrations)**.
d) Use new self-locking nuts on the engine

mounting bolts. Do not fully tighten any of the bolts until they have all been installed. Make sure the spacers are correctly positioned.
e) Tighten the engine mounting bolt nuts, the right-hand side frame downtube bolt nuts and any other bolts and nuts to the torque settings specified at the beginning of the Chapter.
f) Use new gaskets on the exhaust pipe connections.
g) Align the marks made on the gearchange lever and shaft when installing the lever onto the shaft, and tighten the pinch bolt securely **(see illustration)**.
h) Make sure all wires, cables and hoses are correctly routed and connected, and secured by any clips or ties.
i) Refill the engine with oil and install a new filter (see Chapter 1).
j) Adjust the drive chain freeplay (Chapter 1).
k) Adjust the throttle and clutch freeplay (see Chapter 1).

5.20 Unscrew the rear engine bolt nuts (arrows)

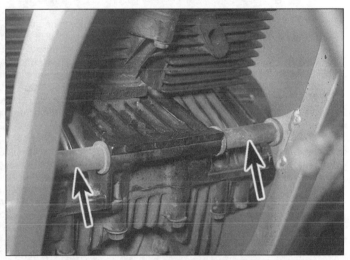
5.23a Front upper mounting bolt spacers (arrows)

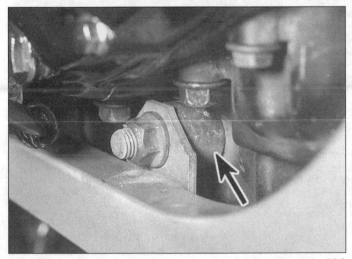
5.23b Front lower mounting bolt spacer (arrow) (one on each side)

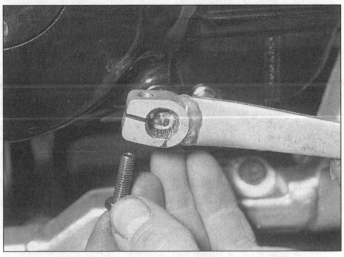
5.23c Align the previously made marks when installing the gearchange lever

2

6.4 An engine support made from pieces of 2 x 4 inch wood

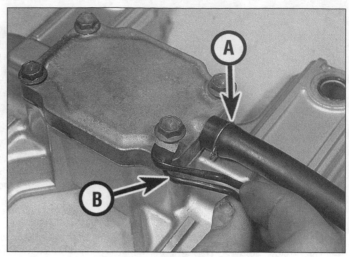

7.3 Detach the breather hose (A)
and release the choke cable from its clamp (B)

6 Engine disassembly and reassembly - general information

Disassembly

1 Before disassembling the engine, the external surfaces of the unit should be thoroughly cleaned and degreased. This will prevent contamination of the engine internals, and will also make working a lot easier and cleaner. A high flash-point solvent, such as paraffin (kerosene) can be used, or better still, a proprietary engine degreaser. Use old paintbrushes and toothbrushes to work the solvent into the various recesses of the engine casings. Take care to exclude solvent or water from the electrical components and intake and exhaust ports.

 Warning: The use of petrol (gasoline) as a cleaning agent should be avoided because of the risk of fire.

2 When clean and dry, arrange the unit on the workbench, leaving suitable clear area for working. Gather a selection of small containers and plastic bags so that parts can be grouped together in an easily identifiable manner. Some paper and a pen should be on hand to permit notes to be made and labels attached where necessary. A supply of clean rag is also required.

3 Before commencing work, read through the appropriate section so that some idea of the necessary procedure can be gained. When removing various engine components it should be noted that great force is seldom required, unless specified. In many cases, a component's reluctance to be removed is indicative of an incorrect approach or removal method. If in any doubt, re-check with the text.

4 An engine support stand made from short lengths of 2 x 4 inch wood bolted together into a rectangle will help support the engine **(see illustration)**. The perimeter of the mount should be just big enough to accommodate the sump (oil pan) within it so that the engine rests on its crankcase.

5 When disassembling the engine, keep 'mated' parts together (including gears, cylinders, pistons, connecting rods, valves, etc. that have been in contact with each other during engine operation). These 'mated' parts must be reused or replaced as an assembly.

6 Engine/transmission disassembly should be done in the following general order with reference to the appropriate Sections.

> *Remove the valve covers*
> *Remove the camchain tensioner and camchain guide blades*
> *Remove the camshafts*
> *Remove the cylinder head*
> *Remove the cylinder block*
> *Remove the pistons*
> *Remove the ignition rotor and pulse generator coil assembly (see Chapter 4)*
> *Remove the clutch*
> *Remove the oil pump*
> *Remove the gearchange mechanism external components*
> *Remove the alternator (see Chapter 8)*
> *Remove the starter clutch and idle gear*
> *Remove the sump (oil pan)*
> *Remove the starter motor (see Chapter 8)*
> *Separate the crankcase halves*
> *Remove the transmission shafts/gears*
> *Remove the shift drum and forks*
> *Remove the crankshaft and connecting rods*
> *Remove the balancer shaft*

Reassembly

7 Reassembly is accomplished by reversing the general disassembly sequence.

7 Valve cover - removal and installation

Note: *The valve cover can be removed with the engine in the frame. If the engine has been removed, ignore the steps which do not apply.*

Removal

1 Remove the seat and the side panels (see Chapter 7) and disconnect the battery negative (-ve) lead.

2 Remove the fuel tank (see Chapter 3).

3 Release the clamp securing the breather hose to the breather cover on the top of the valve cover, and detach the hose **(see illustration)**. Also release the choke cable from its clamp on the breather cover.

4 Disconnect the spark plug leads from the plugs and secure them clear of the engine.

5 Remove the cap (early models) from each of the six valve cover bolts, then unscrew the bolts and remove them along with their rubber O-rings **(see illustration)**. Discard the O-rings as new ones must be used on installation.

7.5 The valve cover is secured by six bolts (arrows)

7.9 Make sure the gasket fits correctly into is groove

7.10a Install the valve cover . . .

7.10b . . . then fit new O-rings . . .

7.10c . . . and secure the cover with its bolts . . .

7.10d . . . tightening them to the specified torque setting

6 Lift the valve cover off the cylinder head. If it is stuck, do not try to lever it off with a screwdriver. Tap it gently around the sides with a rubber hammer to dislodge it.

Installation

7 Examine the valve cover gasket for signs of damage or deterioration and replace it if necessary.
8 Clean the mating surfaces of the cylinder head and the valve cover with lacquer thinner, acetone or brake system cleaner.
9 If a new gasket is being used, apply a smear of a suitable adhesive (such as Suzuki Bond No. 1207B) into the groove in the valve cover. Install the gasket into the valve cover, making sure it fits correctly into the groove **(see illustration)**. Also apply the adhesive to the half-circles on the gasket where they fit into the cutouts in the cylinder head.
10 Position the cover on the cylinder head, making sure the gasket stays in place **(see illustration)**. Install the cover bolts, using new O-rings, and tighten them to the torque setting specified at the beginning of the Chapter **(see illustrations)**. On early models, insert the caps into the heads of the valve cover bolts.
11 Install the remaining components in the reverse order of removal.

8 Camchain tensioner and camchain guide blades - removal, inspection & installation

Note: *The camchain tensioner and guide blades can be removed with the engine in the frame.*

Camchain tensioner

Removal

1 Unscrew the two camchain tensioner mounting bolts and withdraw the tensioner from the back of the cylinder block **(see illustration)**.
2 Remove the gasket from the base of the tensioner or from the cylinder block and discard it as a new one must be used on installation.

Inspection

3 Examine the tensioner components for signs of wear or damage.
4 Remove the plug from the middle of the tensioner cap. Using a flat-bladed screwdriver, turn the slotted end of the tensioner clockwise to release the tension. Remove the screwdriver and check that the tensioner plunger springs back out of the tensioner body.
5 If the tensioner is worn or damaged, or if the plunger is seized in the body or the spring mechanism broken, the tensioner must be replaced. The internal components of the tensioner are not available individually.

Installation

6 Fit a new gasket, using a smear of sealant to keep it in place **(see illustration)**.

8.1 Camchain tensioner mounting bolts (arrows)

8.6 Fit a new gasket . . .

8.8a . . . then install the tensioner . . .

8.8b . . . and secure it with its bolts, keeping the screwdriver located in the slot

8.10 Fit the plug into the end of the tensioner

7 If not already done, remove the plug from the middle of the tensioner cap, and using a flat-bladed screwdriver, turn the slotted end of the tensioner clockwise until the plunger is fully retracted into the tensioner body. Keep the screwdriver located in the slotted end of the tensioner to prevent it from unwinding itself and allowing the plunger to spring out.

8 Keeping the screwdriver located, fit the tensioner into the cylinder block and install the tensioner mounting bolts **(see illustrations)**. Tighten the bolts to the torque setting specified at the beginning of the Chapter.

9 Remove the screwdriver from the end of the tensioner. As the slotted end turns itself back, the tensioner automatically sets itself to the correct tension against the camchain. It is advisable to remove the valve cover (see Section 7) and check that the camchain is tensioned.

10 Fit the plug into the tensioner cap **(see illustration)**.

Camchain guide blades

Removal

11 Remove the valve cover (see Section 7).

12 Lift the front camchain guide blade out of the front of the camchain tunnel, noting which way round it fits and how it locates in the cutouts in the cylinder head **(see illustration)**.

13 The top camchain guide, located in the valve cover, should be inspected in situ prior to removal, and removed only if necessary. To remove the guide, unscrew the four bolts securing the breather cover to the top of the valve cover and remove the breather cover and its gasket **(see illustration)**. Take care not to lose the wire mesh filter inside the cover. Unscrew the two screws securing the top camchain guide to the valve cover and

remove the guide, noting which way round it fits **(see illustration)**.

14 To inspect or remove the rear camchain guide it is first necessary to displace the rear camshaft (see Section 10). Having done that, the guide can be inspected in situ **(see illustration)**. Support the guide with your finger or grasp it with a pair of pliers, using an assistant if required, then unscrew the two bolts securing the guide to the cylinder head, taking great care not to allow the guide to fall down the camchain tunnel and into the crankcase **(see illustration)**.

Inspection

15 Examine the sliding surface of the guides for signs of wear or damage, and replace them if necessary.

Installation

16 Apply a suitable non-permanent thread

8.12 Lift the front camchain guide blade out of the engine

8.13a The breather cover is secured by four bolts (arrows)

8.13b The camchain guide is secured to the valve cover by two screws (arrows)

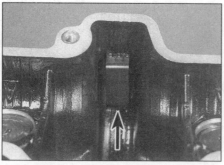

8.14a Rear camchain guide (arrow)

8.14b The rear camchain guide is secured to the cylinder head by two bolts (arrows)

8.17 Make sure the mesh filter is in place in the breather cover

8.18a The bottom of the front blade must locate in its seat (arrow) . . .

8.18b . . . and the lugs in their cutouts (arrows)

locking compound to the threads of the rear camchain guide bolts. Install the rear guide onto the cylinder head, taking great care not to drop it down the camchain tunnel and into the crankcase, and tighten the bolts to the torque setting specified at the beginning of the Chapter. Install the rear camshaft (see Section 10).

17 If removed, install the top camchain guide onto the valve cover and tighten its screws securely. Install the breather cover with its mesh filter and tighten its bolts securely **(see illustration)**.

18 Install the front guide blade into the front of the camchain tunnel, making sure it locates correctly in its seat and its lugs locate in their cutouts in the cylinder head **(see illustrations)**.

19 Install the valve cover (see Section 7).

---

9 Camchain and camchain tensioner blade - removal, inspection and installation

Note: *To remove the camchain and the camchain tensioner blade the engine must be removed from the frame and the crankcases separated.*

Camchain

Removal

1 Remove the crankshaft (see Section 29).
2 Slip the camchain off the crankshaft **(see illustration)**.

Inspection

3 Pull the chain tight to remove any slack, then measure the length of 21 pins (from the centre of the 1st pin to the centre of the 21st pin - see illustration 12.2 in Chapter 1) and compare the result with the service limit specified at the beginning of the Chapter. If the chain has stretched beyond the service limit, it must be replaced.

Installation

4 Slip the camchain onto its sprocket on the crankshaft, making sure it is properly engaged.
5 Install the crankshaft (see Section 29).

Camchain tensioner blade

Removal

6 Separate the crankcase halves (Section 23).
7 Remove the two rubber cushions from the upper crankcase half, noting which way up they fit, then lift the camchain tensioner blade

out of its cutouts in the crankcase, noting which way round it fits **(see illustration)**. Don't lose the pin which fits into the end of the blade.

Inspection

8 Examine the sliding surface of the tensioner blade for signs of wear or damage, and replace it if necessary. Check the condition of the rubber cushions and replace them if they are damaged or deteriorated.

Installation

9 If removed, install the pin into the end of the blade **(see illustration)**. Install the tensioner blade into the upper crankcase half, making sure it is the correct way round and its pin locates correctly in the cutouts **(see illustration)**. Fit the rubber cushions into the cutouts with the rounded ends facing away from the tensioner blade pin **(see illustration)**.
10 Reassemble the crankcase halves (see Section 23).

9.2 Slip the camchain off the crankshaft sprocket

9.7 Remove the two rubber cushions (arrows)

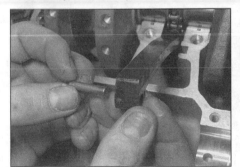

9.9a Install the pin into the blade . . .

9.9b . . . then install the blade, locating the pin in the cutouts (arrows)

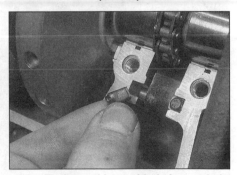

9.9c Fit the cushions with their rounded ends facing out

2

10.2a The pulse generator cover is secured by three screws (arrows)

10.2b The R.T mark must align with the middle of the left-hand pulse generator coil . . .

10.2c . . . and the notch in the end of each camshaft must face inwards (arrows)

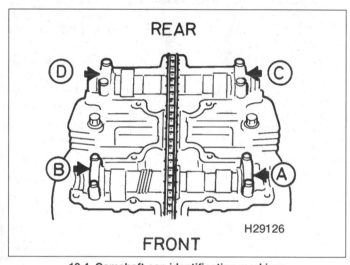

10.4 Camshaft cap identification markings

10 Camshafts and followers - removal, inspection and installation

Note: *The camshafts and followers can be removed with the engine in the frame.*

Removal

1 Remove the valve cover (see Section 7).
2 Unscrew the three screws securing the pulse generator coil cover to the right-hand side crankcase cover **(see illustration)**. The engine can be rotated by using a 19 mm spanner on the timing rotor and turning it in a clockwise direction only. Alternatively, place the motorcycle on its centre stand, select a high gear and rotate the rear wheel by hand in its normal direction of rotation. Rotate the engine until the R.T mark on the rotor aligns with the centre of the left-hand pulse

generator coil, and so that the notches in the right-hand end of each camshaft face each other **(see illustrations)**. To ease reassembly, make alignment marks on the sprockets, chain and camshafts with a felt pen.
3 Remove the camchain tensioner and the front camchain guide blade (see Section 8).
4 Before disturbing the camshaft journal caps, check for the identification markings, which should be the letters A, B, C and D, one for each cap, cast into their top surfaces and facing out **(see illustration)**. These markings ensure that the caps can be matched up to their original journals on installation. If no markings are visible, mark your own using a felt pen. If necessary, make a sketch of the layout as an aid for installation.
5 Working on one camshaft at a time, slacken all cap bolts evenly and a little at a time in a criss-cross sequence, then remove the caps **(see illustration)**. Retrieve the dowels from

either the cap or the cylinder head if they are loose.
6 Slip the camchain off the sprocket and withdraw the camshaft and sprocket. On P, R, S, T and V models, note the shim fitted to the

10.5 Unscrew the camshaft cap bolts and remove the caps

10.6 Slip the chain off the sprocket and remove the shim (arrow)

10.8 Remove each follower with its shim

left-hand end of the camshaft and remove it for safe-keeping **(see illustration)**.

7 Repeat the procedure for the other camshaft. Tie the camchain up to prevent it from dropping down into the crankcase, and do not allow it to go slack as it could bind between the crankshaft sprocket and the crankcase. Cover the top of the cylinder head with a rag to prevent anything falling into the engine.

8 Obtain a container which is divided into four compartments, and label each compartment with the location of its corresponding valve in the cylinder head and whether it belongs with an intake or an exhaust valve. Pick each shim and follower out of the cylinder head and store them in the corresponding compartment in the container **(see illustration)**.

9 If necessary, bend back the locking tabs on the plate fitted under the camshaft sprocket mounting bolts, then unscrew the two bolts securing each sprocket to its camshaft and remove the plate, noting how it fits, and the sprocket. Note that the intake camshaft sprocket is marked with IN and exhaust camshaft sprocket with EX, and that these markings face the right-hand side of the engine. If the locking tabs on the sprocket bolt plates are damaged or worn, discard the plates and replace them with new ones.

Inspection

10 Inspect the cam bearing surfaces of the head and the caps. Look for score marks, deep scratches and evidence of spalling (a pitted appearance). Check the camshaft lobes for heat discoloration (blue appearance), score marks, chipped areas, flat spots and spalling **(see illustrations)**. Measure the height of each lobe with a micrometer and compare the reading with the specifications at the beginning of the Chapter **(see illustration)**. If wear is excessive the amount of valve lift is reduced which results in poor engine performance. The camshaft must be replaced (see **Haynes Hint**).

11 Check the amount of camshaft runout by supporting each end of the camshaft on V-blocks, and measuring any runout using a dial gauge. If the runout exceeds the specified limit the camshaft must be replaced.

12 The camshaft bearing oil clearance should then be checked using a product known as Plastigauge.

13 Clean the camshafts, the bearing surfaces in the cylinder head and the caps with a clean, lint-free cloth, then lay the camshafts in place in the cylinder head.

14 Cut strips of Plastigauge and lay one piece on each bearing journal, parallel with the camshaft centreline **(see illustration)**. Make sure the camshaft cap dowels are installed and fit the caps in their proper positions as noted on removal **(see illustration 10.4)**. Ensuring the camshafts are not rotated at all, tighten all cap bolts evenly and a little at a time in a criss-cross sequence, until the torque setting specified at the beginning of the Chapter is reached. Repeat for the other camshaft.

15 Now unscrew the bolts evenly and a little at a time in a criss-cross sequence, then

2

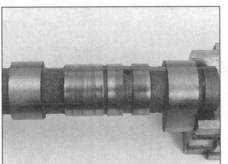

10.10a Check the journal surfaces of the camshaft for scratches or wear

10.10b Check the lobes of the camshaft for wear - here's an example of damage requiring camshaft replacement (or repair)

10.10c Measure the height of the camshaft lobes with a micrometer

10.14 Place a strip of Plastigauge on each bearing journal

10.16 Measure the crushed Plastigauge using the scale on the pack to obtain the oil clearance

carefully lift off the caps, again making sure the camshaft is not rotated. Repeat on the other camshaft.

16 To determine the oil clearance, compare the crushed Plastigauge (at its widest point) on each journal to the scale printed on the Plastigauge container **(see illustration)**.

17 Compare the results to this Chapter's Specifications. If the oil clearance is greater than specified, measure the diameter of the camshaft bearing journal with a micrometer. If it is within specifications, replace the cylinder head and bearing caps. If the journal diameter is less than the specified limit, replace the camshaft with a new one and recheck the clearance. If the clearance is still too great, also replace the cylinder head and bearing caps.

 HAYNES HiNT *Before replacing the camshafts or the cylinder head and camshaft caps because of damage, check with local machine shops specialising in motorcycle engineering work. In the case of the camshafts, it may be possible for cam lobes to be welded, reground and hardened, at a cost far lower than that of a new camshaft. If the bearing surfaces in the cylinder head are damaged, it may be possible for them to be bored out to accept bearing inserts. Due to the cost of a new cylinder head, it is recommended that all options be explored.*

18 Except in cases of oil starvation, the camchain wears very little. If the chain has stretched excessively (see Section 9 for inspection procedure), which makes it difficult to maintain proper tension, it must be replaced.
19 Check the sprockets for chipped teeth and other damage, replacing them if necessary. Note that if new sprockets are installed, a new camchain must also be installed. If the sprockets are worn, the camchain is also worn, and also the sprocket on the crankshaft (which can only be remedied by replacing the crankshaft). If wear this severe is apparent, the entire engine should be disassembled for inspection.
20 Check the front chain guide blade and the top and rear chain guides for wear or damage

(see Section 8). If they are worn or damaged, the chain may be worn out or improperly tensioned. Check the operation of the camchain tensioner (see Section 8).
21 Inspect the outer surfaces of the cam followers for evidence of scoring or other damage. If a follower is in poor condition, it is probable that the bore in which it works is also damaged. Check for clearance between the followers and their bores. Whilst no specifications are given, if slack is excessive, replace the followers. If the bores are seriously out-of-round or tapered, the cylinder head and the followers must be replaced.

Installation

22 Lubricate each follower and its shim with engine oil and install them in the cylinder head **(see illustration 10.8)**. **Note:** *It is most important that the followers and shims are returned to their original valves otherwise the valve clearances will be inaccurate.*
23 If removed, install each sprocket onto its camshaft, making sure the sprocket marked with IN is fitted on the intake camshaft (also marked IN), and the sprocket marked EX is fitted to the exhaust camshaft (also marked EX), and that these markings face the right-hand end of the camshaft, which is identified by a notch in its end. Apply a smear of a suitable non-permanent thread locking compound to the sprocket bolts, then install them with their locking plate, using a new one if necessary, and tighten them to the torque setting specified at the beginning of the Chapter. Bend up the tabs on the locking plate to secure the bolts **(see illustration)**. On

10.23a Bend up each tab on the lockplate (arrow) to secure the bolts

10.26 Install the exhaust camshaft

P, R, S, T and V models, also make sure that the shim fitted to the left-hand end of each camshaft is installed before installation of the camshaft **(see illustration)**.
24 Position the crankshaft as described in Step 2.
25 Apply a smear of clean engine oil to the cylinder head camshaft bearing surfaces. Apply a coating of molybdenum paste (such as Suzuki Moly paste) to the camshaft journals, making sure they are completely covered.
26 Check that the camchain is engaged around the lower sprocket teeth on the crankshaft and that the crankshaft is positioned as described in Step 2. Install the exhaust camshaft (identified by EX) through the camchain **(see illustration)** and position it so that the notch in its right-hand end faces the right-hand side of the engine and points backwards, and so that the arrow marked "1" on the sprocket points forwards and is flush with the top of the cylinder head mating surface, and the arrow marked "2" points vertically upwards **(see illustration 10.27)**. Keeping the front run of the chain taut engage the chain on the sprocket teeth.
27 Starting with the camchain pin that is directly above the arrow marked "2" on the exhaust camshaft sprocket, count eighteen pins along the chain towards the intake side. Install the intake camshaft (identified by IN) through the camchain so that the notch in its right-hand end faces the right-hand side of the engine and points forwards, and engage the sprocket with the chain so that the arrow marked "3" on the sprocket aligns with the eighteenth pin **(see illustration)**.

10.23b Fit the shim onto the left-hand end of the camshaft

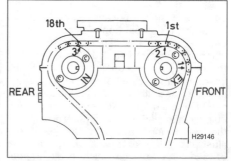

10.27 The cam chain and sprockets must be set up as shown

10.29a Install the journal cap dowels if removed . . .

10.29b . . . followed by the journal caps

10.29c Tighten the cap bolts to the specified torque setting

10.33 Install the pulse generator coil assembly cover

28 Before proceeding further, check that everything aligns as described in Steps 2, 26 and 27. If it doesn't, the valve timing will be inaccurate and the valves will contact the pistons when the engine is turned over.

29 Oil the camshaft journal caps. Ensure the camshaft cap dowels are installed then fit the caps **(see illustrations)**, making sure they are in their proper positions as noted on removal **(see illustration 10.4)**. Tighten the cap bolts on one camshaft evenly and a little at a time in a criss-cross sequence, until the specified torque setting is reached **(see illustration)**. Repeat for the other camshaft.

30 With all caps tightened down, check that the valve timing marks still align (see Steps 2, 26 and 27). Check that each camshaft is not pinched by turning the crankshaft a few degrees in each direction with a 19 mm spanner on the timing rotor.

31 Install the front camchain guide and the camchain tensioner (see Section 8).

32 If any of the valve components have been

replaced, check the valve clearances (see Chapter 1).

33 Install the pulse generator coil cover onto the right-hand crankcase cover and tighten its screws securely **(see illustration)**.

34 Install the valve cover (see Section 7).

35 Check the engine oil level and top up if necessary (see Chapter 1).

11 Cylinder head - removal and installation

Caution: *The engine must be completely cool before beginning this procedure or the cylinder head may become warped.*

Note: *The cylinder head can be removed with the engine in the frame. If the engine has already been removed, ignore the steps which don't apply.*

Removal

1 Remove the exhaust system (Chapter 3).

2 Remove the carburettors (see Chapter 3).

3 Remove the spark plugs (see Chapter 1).

4 Remove the camshafts (see Section 10).

5 The cylinder head has eight 10 mm domed nuts and one 6 mm bolt. Unscrew the bolt on the front of the cylinder head **(see illustration)**. The eight domed nuts are numbered for identification **(see illustration 11.16a)**. Slacken

11.5 Unscrew the cylinder head front bolt (arrow)

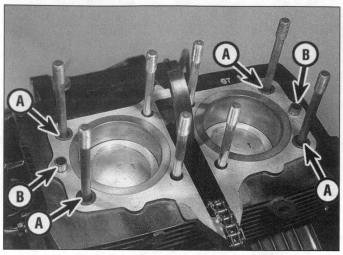

11.7 Remove the stud O-rings (A) and the dowels (B),
if they are loose

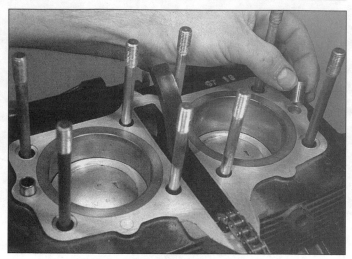

11.11 Install the two dowels, if removed

the nuts evenly and a little at a time in a **reverse** of their numerical sequence until they are all slack. Remove all the nuts and their washers, taking great care not to drop any of them into the crankcase. Discard the washers as new ones must be used.

6 Pull the cylinder head up off the studs. If it is stuck, tap around the joint faces of the cylinder head with a soft-faced mallet to free the head. Do not attempt to free the head by inserting a screwdriver between the head and cylinder block - you'll damage the sealing surfaces.

7 Lift the head off the block, and remove it from the engine. Remove the old cylinder head gasket and the O-rings which fit around the cylinder head studs **(see illustration)**. Stuff a clean rag into the camchain tunnel to prevent any debris falling into the engine. Discard the gasket and O-rings as new ones must be used.

8 If they are loose, remove the two dowels from the cylinder block studs **(see illustration 11.7)**. If either appears to be missing it is probably stuck in the underside of the cylinder head.

9 Check the cylinder head gasket and the mating surfaces on the cylinder head and block for signs of leakage, which could indicate warpage. Refer to Section 13 and check the flatness of the cylinder head.

10 Clean all traces of old gasket material from the cylinder head and block. If a scraper is used, take care not to scratch or gouge the soft aluminium. Be careful not to let any of the gasket material fall into the crankcase, the cylinder bores or the oil passages.

Installation

11 If removed, install the two dowels onto the cylinder block studs **(see illustration)**. Lubricate the cylinder bores with engine oil.

12 Fit a new O-ring onto each cylinder head stud and press it into its recess in the top of the cylinder block **(see illustration)**. Check that they are properly seated.

13 Ensure the cylinder head and block mating surfaces are clean, then lay the new head gasket in place on the cylinder block, making sure all the holes are correctly aligned and that the UP letters stamped out of the gasket read the correct way round **(see illustrations)**. Never re-use the old gasket.

11.12 Fit a new O-ring around each stud

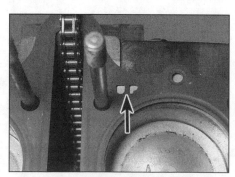

11.13b . . . making sure the UP mark
(arrow) reads correctly

14 Carefully lower the cylinder head over the studs and onto the block **(see illustration)**. It is helpful to have an assistant to pass the camchain up through the tunnel and slip a piece of wire through it to prevent it falling back into the engine. Keep the chain taut to prevent it becoming disengaged from the crankshaft sprocket.

15 Install the eight domed nuts using new washers and tighten them finger-tight **(see illustrations)**.

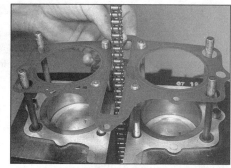

11.13a Fit the new cylinder head
gasket . . .

11.14 Lower the cylinder head
onto the block

11.15a Fit new washers onto the studs . . .

11.15b . . . then install the domed cylinder head nuts

11.16a Cylinder head nut TIGHTENING sequence

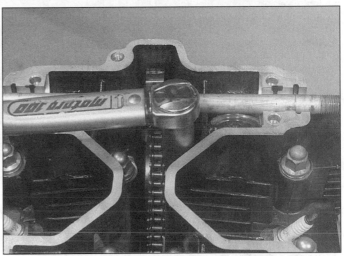

11.16b Tighten the cylinder head nuts to the specified torque • . .

16 The nuts are numbered for identification **(see illustration)**. Tighten the nuts evenly and a little at a time in their numerical sequence to the torque setting specified at the beginning of the Chapter **(see illustration)**.
17 When the nuts are correctly torqued, install the bolt in the front of the cylinder head and tighten it to the specified torque setting **(see illustration)**.

11.17 . . . then install the front cylinder head bolt

18 Install the camshafts (see Section 10).
19 Install the spark plugs (see Chapter 1).
20 Install the carburettors (see Chapter 3).
21 Install the exhaust system (see Chapter 3).

12 Valves/valve seats/valve guides - servicing

1 Because of the complex nature of this job and the special tools and equipment required, most owners leave servicing of the valves, valve seats and valve guides to a professional.
2 The home mechanic can, however, remove the valves from the cylinder head, clean and check the components for wear and grind in the valves (see Section 13).
3 After the valve service has been performed, the head will be in like-new condition. When the head is returned, be sure to clean it again very thoroughly before installation on the engine to remove any metal particles or abrasive grit that may still be present from the valve service operations. Use compressed air, if available, to blow out all the holes and passages.

13 Cylinder head and valves - disassembly, inspection and reassembly

1 As mentioned in the previous section, valve servicing, valve seat re-cutting and valve guide replacement should be left to a Suzuki dealer. However, disassembly, cleaning and inspection of the valves and related components can be done (if the necessary special tools are available) by the home mechanic. This way no expense is incurred if the inspection reveals that overhaul is not required at this time.
2 To disassemble the valve components without the risk of damaging them, a valve spring compressor is absolutely necessary.

2

13.5a Collets can be freed once valve has been compressed

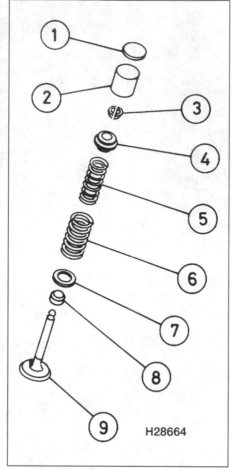

H28664

13.5b Valve components

1	Shim	6 Outer spring
2	Follower	7 Spring seat
3	Collets	8 Stem seal
4	Spring retainer	9 Valve
5	Inner spring	

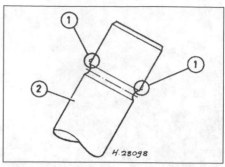

13.5c Remove any burrs (1) if the valve stem (2) won't pull through the guide

Disassembly

3 Before proceeding, arrange to label and store the valves along with their related components in such a way that they can be returned to their original locations without getting mixed up. A good way to do this is to obtain a container which is divided into four compartments, and to label each compartment with the identity of the valve which will be stored in it (ie left- or right-hand cylinder, intake or exhaust valve).

4 If not already done, clean all traces of old gasket material from the cylinder head. If a scraper is used, take care not to scratch or gouge the soft aluminium. Carefully scrape all carbon deposits out of the combustion chamber area. A hand held wire brush or a piece of fine emery cloth can be used once the majority of deposits have been scraped away. Do not use a wire brush mounted in a drill motor, or one with extremely stiff bristles, as the head material is soft and may be eroded away or scratched by the wire brush.

5 Compress the valve spring on the first valve with a spring compressor, then remove the collets (see illustration) and the retainer, noting which way up it fits, from the valve assembly (see illustration). Do not compress the springs any more than is absolutely necessary. Carefully release the valve spring compressor and remove the springs and the valve from the head. If the valve binds in the guide (won't pull through), push it back into the head and deburr the area around the collet groove with a very fine file or whetstone (see illustration).

6 Repeat the procedure for the remaining valves. Remember to keep the parts for each valve together and in order so they can be reinstalled in the same location.

7 Once the valves have been removed and labelled, pull the valve stem seals off the top of the valve guides with pliers and discard them (the old seals should never be reused), then remove the spring seats, noting which way up they fit.

8 Next, clean the cylinder head with solvent and dry it thoroughly. Compressed air will speed the drying process and ensure that all holes and recessed areas are clean.

9 Clean all of the valve springs, collets, retainers and spring seats with solvent and dry them thoroughly. Do the parts from one valve at a time so that no mixing of parts between valves occurs.

10 Scrape off any deposits that may have formed on the valve, then use a motorised wire brush to remove deposits from the valve heads and stems. Again, make sure the valves do not get mixed up.

Inspection

11 Inspect the head very carefully for cracks and other damage. If cracks are found, a new head will be required. Check the cam bearing surfaces for wear and evidence of seizure. Check the camshafts and followers for wear as well (see Section 10).

12 Using a precision straightedge and a feeler gauge which corresponds to the warpage limit listed in the specifications at the beginning of the Chapter, check the head gasket mating surface for warpage. Lay the straightedge lengthways, across the head and diagonally, intersecting the stud holes, and try

to slip the feeler gauge under it on either side of the combustion chamber (see illustration). If the feeler gauge can be inserted between the straightedge and the cylinder head, the head is warped and must be either machined or, if warpage is excessive, replaced with a new one.

13 Examine the valve seats in the combustion chamber. If they are pitted, cracked or burned, the head will require work beyond the scope of the home mechanic. Measure the valve seat width and compare it to this Chapter's Specifications (see illustration). If it exceeds the service limit, or if it varies around its circumference, valve overhaul is required.

14 Clean the valve guides to remove any carbon build-up, then install the valve in its guide so that its face is 10 mm above the

13.12 Lay a precision straightedge across the cylinder head and try to slide a feeler gauge of the specified thickness (equal to the maximum allowable warpage) under it

13.13 Measure the valve seat width with a ruler (or for greater precision, use a vernier caliper)

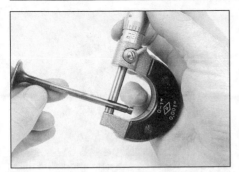

13.14a Measure the valve stem diameter with a micrometer

13.14b Insert a small hole gauge into the valve guide and expand it so there's a slight drag when it's pulled out

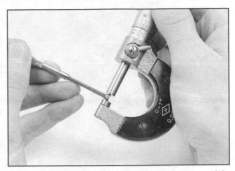

13.14c Measure the small hole gauge with a micrometer

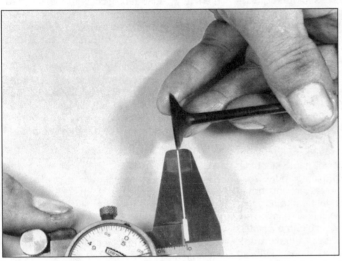

13.15 Measure the valve margin thickness as shown

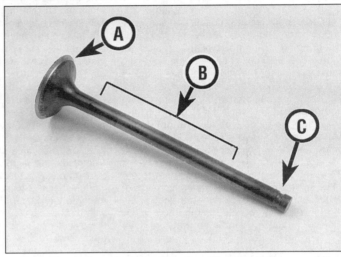

13.16 Check the valve face (A), stem (B) and collet groove (C) for signs of wear and damage

seat. Mount a dial gauge against the side of the valve face and measure the amount of side clearance (deflection) between the valve stem and its guide in two perpendicular directions. If the clearance exceeds the limit specified, remove the valve and measure the valve stem diameter **(see illustration)**. Also measure the inside diameters of the guides (at both ends and the centre of the guide) with a small hole gauge and micrometer **(see illustrations)**. The guides are measured at the ends and at the centre to determine if they are worn in a bell-mouth pattern (more wear at the ends). If the valve stem or guide is worn beyond its limit, it must be renewed.

15 Carefully inspect each valve face for cracks, pits and burned spots. Measure the valve margin thickness and compare it to the Specifications **(see illustration)**. If it is thinner than specified, renew the valve.

16 Check the valve stem and the collet groove area for cracks **(see illustration)**. Rotate the valve and check for any obvious indication that it is bent. Check the end of the stem for pitting and excessive wear. The presence of any of the above conditions indicates the need for valve servicing.

17 Using V-blocks and a dial gauge, measure the valve stem runout and the valve head runout and compare the results to the specifications. If either measurement exceeds the service limit, the valve must be replaced.

18 Check the end of each valve spring for wear and pitting. Measure the spring free length and compare it to that listed in the specifications **(see illustration)**. If any spring is shorter than specified it has sagged and must be replaced. Also place the spring upright on a flat surface and check it for bend by placing a ruler or set-square against it **(see**

illustration). If the bend in any spring is excessive, it must be replaced.

19 Check the spring retainers and collets for obvious wear and cracks. Any questionable parts should not be reused, as extensive damage will occur in the event of failure during engine operation.

20 If the inspection indicates that no overhaul work is required, the valve components can be reinstalled in the head.

Reassembly

21 Before installing the valves in the head,

2

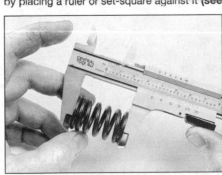

13.18a Measure the free length of the valve springs

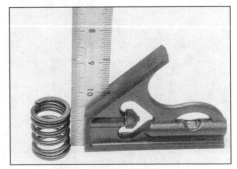

13.18b Check the valve springs for squareness

13.22 Apply grinding compound sparingly, in small dabs, to the valve face only

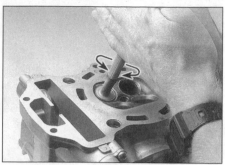

13.23a Rotate the valve grinding tool back and forth between the palms of your hands

13.23b The face and seat should be the specified width and with a smooth, unbroken appearance (arrow)

they should be ground in (lapped) to ensure a positive seal between the valves and seats. This procedure requires coarse and fine valve grinding compound and a valve grinding tool. If a grinding tool is not available, a piece of rubber or plastic hose can be slipped over the valve stem (after the valve has been installed in the guide) and used to turn the valve.

22 Apply a small amount of coarse grinding compound to the valve face, then slip the valve into the guide **(see illustration)**. **Note:** Make sure each valve is installed in its correct guide and be careful not to get any grinding compound on the valve stem.

23 Attach the grinding tool (or hose) to the valve and rotate the tool between the palms of your hands. Use a back-and-forth motion (as though rubbing your hands together) rather than a circular motion (ie so that the valve rotates alternately clockwise and anti-clockwise rather than in one direction only) **(see illustration)**. Lift the valve off the seat and turn it at regular intervals to distribute the grinding compound properly. Continue the grinding procedure until the valve face and seat contact area is of uniform width and unbroken around the entire circumference of the valve face and seat **(see illustration)**.

24 Carefully remove the valve from the guide and wipe off all traces of grinding compound. Use solvent to clean the valve and wipe the seat area thoroughly with a solvent soaked cloth.

25 Repeat the procedure with fine valve grinding compound, then repeat the entire procedure for the remaining valves.

26 Lay the spring seats in place in the

cylinder head with their shouldered side facing up so that they fit into the base of the springs (the spring seat can be identified from the spring retainer by its larger internal diameter - be sure not to mix up the two), then install new valve stem seals on each of the guides. Use an appropriate size deep socket to push the seals over the end of the valve guide until they are felt to clip into place. Don't twist or cock them, or they will not seal properly against the valve stems. Also, don't remove them again or they will be damaged.

27 Coat the valve stem with molybdenum disulphide grease, then install it into its guide, rotating it slowly to avoid damaging the seal. Check that the valve moves up and down freely in the guide. Next, install the springs, with their closer wound coils facing down into the cylinder head (and, if visible, the painted pink end facing up) **(see illustration)**, followed by the spring retainer, with its shouldered side facing down so that it fits into the top of the spring.

28 Compress the springs with the valve spring compressor and install the collets. When compressing the springs, depress them only as far as is absolutely necessary to slip the collets into place. Apply a small amount of grease to the collets to help hold them in place as the pressure is released from the springs **(see illustration)**. Make certain that the collets are securely locked in their retaining grooves.

29 Assemble the other valve assemblies as described in Steps 27 and 28.

30 Support the cylinder head on blocks so the valves can't contact the workbench top,

then very gently tap each of the valve stems with a soft-faced hammer. This will help seat the collets in their grooves.

 HAYNES HINT *Check for proper sealing of the valves by pouring a small amount of solvent into each of the valve ports. If the solvent leaks past any valve into the combustion chamber area the valve grinding operation on that valve should be repeated.*

14 Cylinder block - removal, inspection and installation

Note: The cylinder block can be removed with the engine in the frame.

Removal

1 Remove the cylinder head (see Section 11).
2 Lift the cylinder block up to remove it from the studs. If it is stuck, tap around the joint faces of the block with a soft-faced mallet to free it from the crankcase. Don't attempt to free the block by inserting a screwdriver between it and the crankcase - you'll damage the sealing surfaces. When the block is removed, stuff clean rags around the pistons to prevent anything falling into the crankcase.
3 Note the location of the two dowels which will be either on the bottom of the block or in the crankcase **(see illustration)**; remove them if they are loose.

13.27 Install the springs with their closely spaced coils down (against the cylinder head)

13.28 A small dab of grease will help to keep the collets in place on the valve while the spring is released

14.3 Remove the dowels (arrows) if they are loose

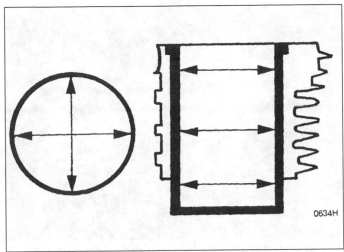

14.7 Cylinder bore wear measurement points

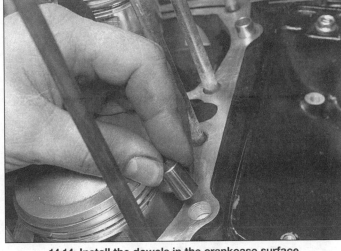

14.14 Install the dowels in the crankcase surface

4 Remove the gasket and clean all traces of old gasket material from the cylinder block and crankcase mating surfaces. If a scraper is used, take care not to scratch or gouge the soft aluminium. Be careful not to let any of the gasket material fall into the crankcase or the oil passages.

Inspection

5 Do not attempt to separate the cylinder liners from the cylinder block.

6 Check the cylinder walls carefully for scratches and score marks. A rebore will be necessary to remove any deep scores.

7 Using telescoping gauges (see *Mechanics Tools and Tips* in the Reference section), check the dimensions of each cylinder to assess the amount of wear, taper and ovality. Measure near the top (but below the level of the top piston ring at TDC), centre and bottom (but above the level of the oil ring at BDC) of the bore, both parallel to and across the crankshaft axis **(see illustration)**. Calculate any differences between the measurements taken to determine any taper and ovality in the bore. Compare the results to the specifications at the beginning of the Chapter. If the cylinders are tapered, oval, or worn beyond the service limits, or badly scratched, scuffed or scored, have them rebored and honed by a Suzuki dealer or specialist motorcycle repair shop. If the cylinders are rebored, they will require oversize pistons and rings.

8 If the precision measuring tools are not available, take the block to a Suzuki dealer or specialist motorcycle repair shop for assessment and advice.

9 If the cylinders are in good condition and the piston-to-bore clearance is within specifications (see Section 15), the cylinders should be honed (de-glazed). To carry out this task, you will need the proper size flexible hone with fine stones (see *Tools* in the Reference section), or a bottle-brush type hone, plenty of light oil or honing oil, some clean rags and an electric drill motor.

10 Hold the block sideways (so that the bores are horizontal rather than vertical) in a vice with soft jaws or cushioned with wooden blocks. Mount the hone in the drill motor, compress the stones and insert the hone into the cylinder. Thoroughly lubricate the cylinder, then turn on the drill and move the hone up and down in the cylinder at a pace which produces a fine cross-hatch pattern on the cylinder wall with the lines intersecting at an angle of approximately 60°. Be sure to use plenty of lubricant and do not take off any more material than is necessary to produce the desired effect. Do not withdraw the hone from the cylinder while it is still turning. Switch off the drill and continue to move it up and down in the cylinder until it has stopped turning, then compress the stones and withdraw the hone. Wipe the oil from the cylinder and repeat the procedure on the other cylinder. Remember, do not take too much material from the cylinder wall.

11 Wash the cylinders thoroughly with warm soapy water to remove all traces of the abrasive grit produced during the honing operation. Be sure to run a brush through the bolt holes and flush them with running water. After rinsing, dry the cylinders thoroughly and apply a thin coat of light, rust-preventative oil to all machined surfaces.

12 If you do not have the equipment or desire to perform the honing operation, take the block to a Suzuki dealer or specialist motorcycle repair shop.

Installation

13 Check that the mating surfaces of the cylinder block and crankcase are free from oil or pieces of old gasket.

14 If removed, install the dowels into their correct locations in the crankcase, and push them firmly home **(see illustration)**.

15 Remove the rags from around the pistons, and lay the new base gasket in place on the crankcase, making sure all the holes are correctly aligned and that the UP letters stamped out of the gasket read the correct way round **(see illustrations)**. Never re-use the old gasket.

16 Check that the piston ring end gaps are correctly positioned **(see illustration 16.14)**. If required, install piston ring clamps onto the pistons to ease their entry into the bores as the block is lowered. This is not essential as each cylinder has a good lead-in enabling the piston rings to be hand-fed into the bores. If possible, have an assistant to support the block while this is done.

17 Lubricate the cylinder bores, pistons and piston rings with clean engine oil, then install

2

14.15a Fit the new base gasket . . .

14.15b . . . making sure the UP mark reads correctly

14.17 Carefully lower the block onto the pistons

15.2 Note the arrowhead stamped into each piston crown (arrow) which must face forward

the block down over the studs until the piston crowns fit into the bores (see illustration). At this stage feed the camchain up through the block and secure it in place with a piece of wire to prevent it from falling back down.

18 Gently push down on the cylinder block, making sure the pistons enter the bores squarely and do not get cocked sideways. If piston ring clamps are not being used, carefully compress and feed each ring into the bore as the block is lowered. If necessary, use a soft-faced mallet to gently tap the block down, but do not use force if the block appears to be stuck as the pistons and/or rings will be damaged. If clamps are used, remove them once the pistons are in the bore.

19 When the pistons are correctly installed in the cylinders, press the block down onto the base gasket.

20 Install the cylinder head (see Section 11).

15 Pistons - removal, inspection and installation

Note: The pistons can be removed with the engine in the frame.

Removal

1 Remove the cylinder block (see Section 14).
2 Before removing the piston from the connecting rod, stuff a clean rag into the hole around the rod to prevent the circlips or anything else from falling into the crankcase. Use a felt marker pen to write the cylinder identity on the crown of each piston (or on the skirt if the piston is dirty and going to be cleaned). Each piston should also have an arrowhead marked on its crown which should face forwards (see illustration). If this is not visible, mark the piston accordingly so that it can be installed the correct way round.
3 Prise out the circlip on one side of the piston using needle-nose pliers or a small flat-bladed screwdriver inserted into the notch (see illustration). Push the piston pin out

from the other side to free the piston from the connecting rod (see illustration). Remove the other circlip and discard them as new ones must be used. When the piston has been removed, install its pin back into its bore so that related parts do not get mixed up. Rotate the crankshaft so that the best access is obtained for each piston.

> **HAYNES HINT** *If a piston pin is a tight fit in the piston bosses, soak a rag in boiling water then wring it out and wrap it around the piston - this will expand the alloy piston enough to release its grip on the pin.*

Inspection

4 Before the inspection process can be carried out, the pistons must be cleaned and the old piston rings removed. Note that if the cylinders are being rebored, piston inspection can be overlooked as new ones will be fitted.
5 Using your thumbs or a piston ring removal and installation tool, carefully remove the rings from the pistons (see illustration). Do not nick or gouge the pistons in the process. Carefully note which way up each ring fits in its groove as they must be installed in their original positions if being re-used. The upper surface of each ring is marked with the letter N at one end (see illustration).

15.3a Use the notch (arrow) to aid removal of the circlip . . .

15.3b . . . then push the pin out from the other side and withdraw it from the piston

15.5a Removing the piston rings using a ring removal and installation tool

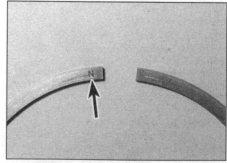

15.5b Note the letter N (arrow) which must face up

15.11 Measure the piston ring-to-groove clearance with a feeler gauge

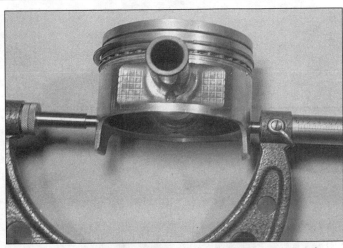

15.12 Measure the piston diameter with a micrometer at the specified distance from the bottom of the skirt

6 Scrape all traces of carbon from the tops of the plstons. A hand-held wire brush or a piece of fine emery cloth can be used once most of the deposits have been scraped away. Do not, under any circumstances, use a wire brush mounted in a drill motor to remove deposits from the pistons; the piston material is soft and will be eroded away by the wire brush.

7 Use a piston ring groove cleaning tool to remove any carbon deposits from the ring grooves. If a tool is not available, a piece broken off an old ring will do the job. Be very careful to remove only the carbon deposits. Do not remove any metal and do not nick or gouge the sides of the ring grooves.

8 Once the deposits have been removed, clean each of the pistons with solvent and dry thoroughly. If the identification previously marked on the piston is cleaned off, re-mark it with the correct identity. Make sure the oil return holes below the oil ring groove are clear.

9 Carefully inspect each piston for cracks around the skirt, at the pin bosses and at the ring lands. Normal piston wear appears as even, vertical wear on the thrust surfaces of the piston and slight looseness of the top ring in its groove. If the skirt is scored or scuffed, the engine may have been suffering from overheating and/or abnormal combustion, which caused excessively high operating temperatures. The oil pump should be checked thoroughly. Also check that the circlip grooves are not damaged.

10 A hole in the piston crown is an indication that abnormal combustion (pre-ignition) was occurring. Burned areas at the edge of the piston crown are usually evidence of spark knock (detonation). If any of the above problems exist, the causes must be corrected or the damage will occur again.

11 Measure the piston ring-to-groove clearance by laying each piston ring in its groove and slipping a feeler gauge in beside it **(see illustration)**. Check the clearance at three or four locations around the groove. If the clearance is greater than specified, replace both the piston and rings as a set. If

new rings are being used, measure the clearance using the new rings. If the clearance is greater than that specified, the piston is worn and must be replaced. **Note:** *Make sure you have the correct ring for the groove - the two compression rings can be identified by their profile* **(see illustration 16.12)**.

12 Check the piston-to-bore clearance by measuring the bore (see Section 14) and the piston diameter. Make sure each piston is matched to its correct cylinder. Measure the piston 15.0 mm up from the bottom of the skirt and at 90° to the piston pin axis **(see illustration)**. Subtract the piston diameter from the bore diameter to obtain the

clearance. If it is greater than the specified figure, the piston must be replaced (assuming the bore itself is within limits, otherwise a rebore is necessary).

13 Apply clean engine oil to the piston pin, insert it into the piston and check for any freeplay between the two **(see illustration)**. Measure the pin external diameter and the pin bore in the piston and compare the measurements to the specifications at the beginning of the Chapter **(see illustrations)**. Repeat the measurements between the pin and the connecting rod small-end **(see illustration)**. Replace components that are worn beyond the specified limits.

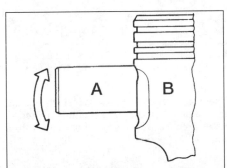

15.13a Slip the pin (A) into the piston (B). If it's loose, replace the piston and pin

15.13b Measure the external diameter of the pin . . .

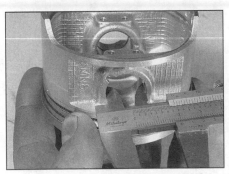

15.13c . . . the internal diameter of the bore in the piston . . .

15.13d . . . and the internal diameter of the connecting rod small-end

2

15.17 Always use new circlips to secure the piston pin

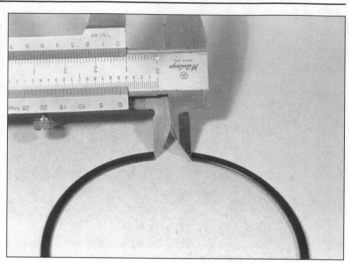

16.3 Measuring piston ring free end gap

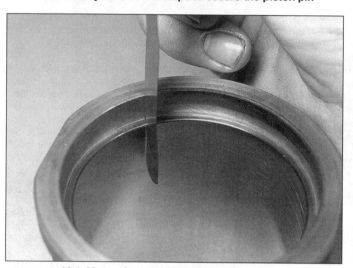

16.4 Measuring piston ring installed end gap

16.6 Ring end gap can be enlarged by clamping a file in a vice and filing the ring ends

14 If the pistons are to be replaced, ensure the correct size of piston is ordered. Suzuki produce two oversize pistons as well as the standard piston. The oversize pistons available are: +0.5 mm and +1.00 mm. **Note:** *Oversize pistons usually have their relevant size stamped on top of the piston crown, eg a 0.50 mm oversize piston will be marked 0.50. Be sure to obtain the correct oversize rings for the pistons.*

Installation

15 Inspect and install the piston rings (see Section 16).
16 Lubricate the piston pin, the piston pin bore and the connecting rod small-end bore with clean engine oil.
17 Install a new circlip in one side of the piston (do not re-use old circlips) **(see illustration)**. Line up the piston on its correct connecting rod, making sure the arrow on the piston crown points forwards, and insert the piston pin from the other side **(see illustration 15.3b)**. Secure the pin with the other new circlip. When installing the circlips, compress

them only just enough to fit them in the piston, and make sure they are properly seated in their grooves with the open end away from the removal notch.

16 Piston rings -
inspection and installation

1 It is good practice to replace the piston rings when an engine is being overhauled. Before installing the new piston rings, the ring end gaps must be checked, both free and installed.
2 Lay out the pistons and the new ring sets so the rings will be matched with the same piston and cylinder during the end gap measurement procedure and engine assembly.
3 To measure the free end gap of each ring, lay each ring on a flat surface and measure the gap between the ends of the ring using a vernier caliper **(see illustration)**. Compare the

results to the specifications at the beginning of the Chapter and replace any ring that is below its service limit.
4 To measure the installed end gap, insert the top ring into the top of the cylinder and square it up with the cylinder walls by pushing it in with the top of the piston. The ring should be about 20 mm below the top edge of the cylinder. To measure the end gap, slip a feeler gauge between the ends of the ring and compare the measurement to the specifications at the beginning of the Chapter **(see illustration)**.
5 If the gap is larger or smaller than specified, double check to make sure that you have the correct rings before proceeding.
6 If the gap is too small, it must be enlarged or the ring ends may come in contact with each other during engine operation, which can cause serious damage. The end gap can be increased by filing the ring ends very carefully with a fine file. When performing this operation, file only from the outside in **(see illustration)**.
7 Excess end gap is not critical unless it is

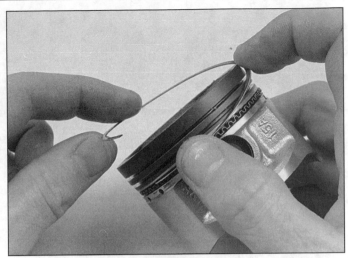

16.10a Install the oil ring expander in its groove . . .

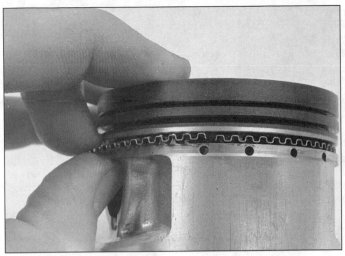

16.10b . . . and fit the side rails each side of it. The oil ring must be installed by hand

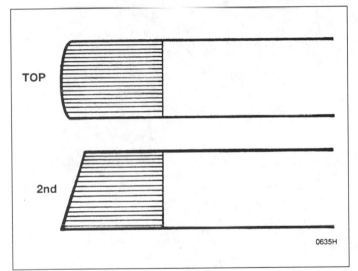

16.12 Don't confuse the top ring with the second ring

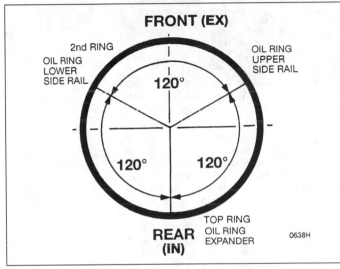

16.14 Arrange the ring end gaps like this

greater than 0.7 mm. Again, double check to make sure you have the correct rings for your engine and check that the bore is not worn.

8 Repeat the procedure for each ring that will be installed in the cylinders. Remember to keep the rings, pistons and cylinders matched up.

9 Once the ring end gaps have been checked/corrected, the rings can be installed on the pistons.

10 The oil control ring (lowest on the piston) is installed first. It is composed of three separate components, namely the expander and the upper and lower side rails. Slip the expander into the groove, then install the upper side rail. Do not use a piston ring installation tool on the oil ring side rails as they may be damaged. Instead, place one end of the side rail into the groove between the expander and the ring land. Hold it firmly in place and slide a finger around the piston while pushing the rail into the groove. Next,

install the lower side rail in the same manner **(see illustrations)**. Make sure the ends of the expander do not overlap.

11 After the three oil ring components have been installed, check to make sure that both the upper and lower side rails can be turned smoothly in the ring groove.

12 Install the second (middle) ring next. It can be readily distinguished from the top ring by its cross-section shape **(see illustration)**. To avoid breaking the ring, use a piston ring installation tool and make sure that the identification letter N near the end gap is facing up **(see illustration 15.5b)**. Fit the ring into the middle groove on the piston. Do not expand the ring any more than is necessary to slide it into place.

13 Finally, install the top ring in the same manner. The top ring can be distinguished from the second ring by its cross-section shape **(see illustration 16.12)**. Also, its face is

chrome-plated. Make sure the identification letter N near the end gap is facing up **(see illustration 15.5b)**.

14 Once the rings are correctly installed, check they move freely without snagging and stagger their end gaps as shown **(see illustration)**.

---

17 Clutch - removal, inspection and installation

Note: *The clutch can be removed with the engine in the frame.*

Removal

1 Drain the engine oil (refer to Chapter 1).

2 Unscrew the three bolts securing the circular pulse generator assembly cover to the right-

17.2a The pulse generator assembly cover is secured by three bolts (arrows)

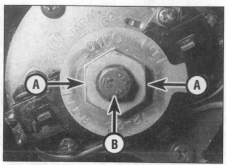

17.2b Counter-hold the rotor using a 19 mm spanner on the flats (A) and unscrew the rotor bolt (B)

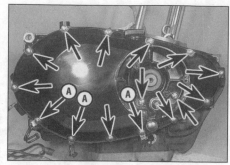

17.3 The crankcase cover is secured by fifteen bolts (arrows). Note the positions of the wiring clips on three of the bolts (A)

17.4 Note the positions of the two dowels (arrows) and remove them if they are loose

hand side crankcase cover **(see illustration)**. Remove the cover. Using a 19 mm spanner to counter-hold the timing rotor, unscrew the bolt in the centre of the rotor which secures it to the end of the crankshaft **(see illustration)**. Remove the rotor, noting how the pin in the end of the crankshaft locates in the slot in the rotor. The oil pressure switch can remain in the crankcase cover, but its wire must be disconnected. Remove the pulse generator coil assembly by removing its two screws (see illustration 4.10 in Chapter 4).

3 Working in a criss-cross pattern, evenly slacken the fifteen right-hand side crankcase cover retaining bolts, noting the position of the cable clips **(see illustration)**. Lift the cover away from the engine, being prepared to catch any residual oil which may be released as the cover is removed.

4 Remove the gasket and discard it. Note the positions of the two locating dowels fitted to the crankcase and remove them for safe-keeping if they are loose **(see illustration)**.

5 Working in a criss-cross pattern, gradually and evenly slacken the clutch pressure plate retaining bolts until spring pressure is released **(see illustrations)**. To stop the clutch from turning while initially loosening the bolts, either put the engine into gear and have an assistant apply the rear brake (if the engine is in the frame), or jam the primary drive and driven gears together using the blade of a large screwdriver (if the engine has been removed). Remove the bolts, spacers and

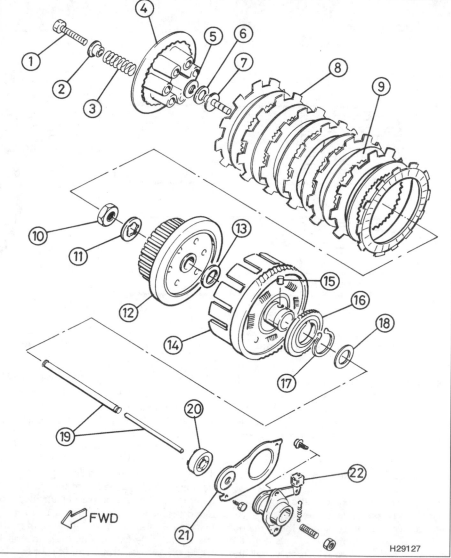

17.5a Clutch components

1 Pressure plate bolt	7 Pushrod end piece	13 Outer thrustwasher	18 Inner thrust washer
2 Spacer	8 Friction plates	14 Clutch housing	19 Pushrods
3 Spring	9 Plain plates	15 Pin	20 Pushrod oil seal
4 Pressure plate	10 Clutch nut	16 Oil pump drivegear	21 Retainer plate
5 Thrust washer	11 Lockwasher	17 Circlip	22 Release mechanism
6 Release bearing	12 Clutch centre		

17.5b Clutch pressure plate bolts (arrows)

17.5c Remove the pressure plate . . .

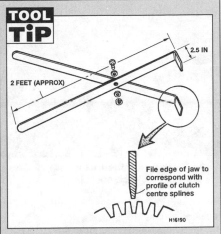

A clutch centre holding tool can easily be made using two strips of steel bent over at the ends and bolted together in the middle

17.5d . . . followed by the thrust washer, release bearing and pushrod end piece

17.7 Bend back the tabs on the lockwasher to release the clutch nut

springs, then withdraw the pressure plate (see illustration). Remove the thrust washer, release bearing and pushrod end piece from either the back of the pressure plate or the end of the input shaft (see illustration). If required, withdraw the clutch pushrod right-hand half from the crankshaft - it will either have to be poked through from the other side using the left-hand half of the pushrod (requiring removal of the front sprocket cover), or the engine will have to be tipped on its side.

6 Grasp the complete set of clutch plates and remove them as a pack. Unless new plates are being fitted, keep them in their original order.

7 Bend back the tabs on the clutch nut lockwasher (see illustration). To remove the clutch nut the input shaft must be locked. This can be done in two ways. If the engine is in the frame, engage 1st gear and have an assistant hold the rear brake on hard with the rear tyre in firm contact with the ground. Alternatively, the Suzuki service tool (Pt. No. 09920-53710), or a similar home-made tool made from two strips of steel bent at the ends and bolted together in the middle (see Tool tip), can be used to stop the clutch centre from turning whilst the nut is slackened (see illustration 17.20e). Unscrew the nut and remove the lockwasher from the input shaft, noting how it fits. Discard the lockwasher as a new one must be used on installation.

8 Remove the clutch centre from the shaft, followed by the outer thrust washer.

9 Remove the clutch housing from the shaft, followed by the inner thrust washer.

10 The oil pump drive gear is secured to the back of the clutch housing by a circlip (see illustration). If necessary, remove the circlip,

then remove the gear, noting which way round it fits and how it locates onto the pin in the housing. If the pin is loose, remove it for safekeeping.

Inspection

11 After an extended period of service the clutch friction plates will wear and promote

17.10 The oil pump drive gear is secured to the housing by a circlip (arrow)

17.11b . . . and the width of their tabs

clutch slip. Measure the thickness of each friction plate and the width of their tabs using a vernier caliper (see illustrations). If any plate has worn to or beyond the service limits given in the Specifications at the beginning of the Chapter, the friction plates must be replaced as a set. Also, if any of the plates smell burnt or are glazed, they must be replaced as a set.

12 The plain plates should not show any signs of excess heating (bluing). Check for warpage using a flat surface and feeler gauges (see illustration). If any plate exceeds the maximum permissible amount of warpage, or

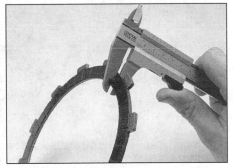

17.11a Measure the thickness of the friction plates . . .

17.12 Check the plain plates for warpage

2

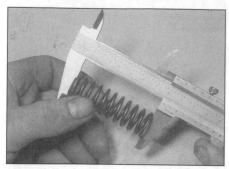

17.13 Measure the free length of the clutch springs

shows signs of bluing, all plain plates must be replaced as a set.

13 Measure the free length of each clutch spring using a vernier caliper **(see illustration)**. If any spring is below the service limit specified, replace all the springs as a set.

14 Inspect the clutch assembly for burrs and indentations on the edges of the protruding tabs of the friction plates and/or slots in the edge of the housing with which they engage. Similarly check for wear between the inner tongues of the plain plates and the slots in the clutch centre. Wear of this nature will cause clutch drag and slow disengagement during

gear changes, since the plates will snag when the pressure plate is lifted. With care a small amount of wear can be corrected by dressing with a fine file, but if this is excessive the worn components should be replaced.

15 Check the pressure plate, release bearing, pushrod end piece and thrust washer for signs of roughness, wear or damage, and replace any parts as necessary. Check that the right-hand pushrod is straight by rolling it on a flat surface.

16 Unscrew the gearchange lever pinch bolt and remove the lever from the shaft, noting any alignment marks on the lever and the shaft **(see illustration 18.1a)**. If no marks are visible, make your own before removing the lever so that it can be correctly aligned with the shaft on installation. Unscrew the bolts securing the engine sprocket cover to the crankcase and draw the cover away from the engine **(see illustration 18.1b)**. Note the position of the dowel and remove it if it is loose. Check the clutch release actuating mechanism for smooth operation and any signs of wear or damage **(see illustration)**. Unscrew the two screws securing the mechanism to the cover and remove the mechanism if required. Withdraw the clutch pushrod left-hand half and check it for straightness by rolling it on a flat surface **(see illustration)**. Check the

pushrod oil seal for signs of leakage and replace it if necessary, noting that it is secured by a retainer plate. Remove the engine sprocket (see Chapter 5) and bend back the tabs on the retainer plate, then unscrew the bolts and remove the plate. Lever out the old oil seal, then drive a new one squarely into place and secure it with the retainer plate. Bend up the tabs on the plate to secure the bolts.

Installation

17 Remove all traces of old gasket from the crankcase and crankcase cover surfaces.

18 If removed, install the pin into the hole in the back of the clutch housing, then install the oil pump drive gear onto the back of the housing, making sure that its raised inner edge faces the clutch and that the slot in the inner edge locates over the pin **(see illustrations)**. Secure the gear in place with its circlip, making sure it is properly seated in its groove **(see illustration)**.

19 Slide the inner thrust washer onto the end of the input shaft, then lubricate the clutch housing bush with clean engine oil and slide the housing onto the shaft, making sure it engages correctly with the teeth on the primary drive gear **(see illustrations)**.

20 Slide the outer thrust washer onto the

17.16a Check the release mechanism for smooth action

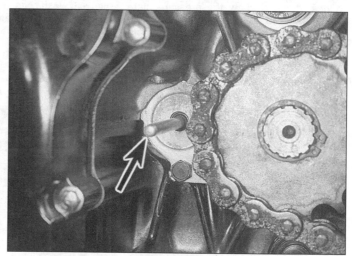

17.16b Withdraw the left-hand pushrod (arrow) and check it for straightness

17.18a Fit the pin into its hole . . .

17.18b . . . then install the oil pump drive gear, locating its slot (A) over the pin (B) . . .

17.18c . . . and secure it with the circlip

17.19a Slide the inner thrust washer onto the shaft . . .

17.19b . . . followed by the clutch housing

shaft, then install the clutch centre onto the shaft splines **(see illustrations)**. Fit a new lockwasher onto the shaft splines, then install the clutch nut. Using the method employed on dismantling to lock the input shaft, tighten the nut to the specified torque **(see illustrations)**. **Note:** *Check that the clutch centre rotates freely after tightening.* Bend up the tabs of the lockwasher to secure the nut **(see illustration)**.

21 Build up the clutch plates in the clutch housing, starting with a friction plate, then a plain plate and alternating friction and plain plates until all are installed **(see illustrations)**. Coat each plate with clean engine oil prior to installation.

17.20a Slide the outer thrust washer onto the shaft . . .

17.20b . . . followed by the clutch centre

17.20c Slide lockwasher onto the shaft . . .

17.20d . . . then install the clutch nut . . .

17.20e . . . tighten to the specified torque

2

17.20f Bend up the lockwasher tabs

17.21a Install a friction plate first . . .

17.21b . . . followed by a plain plate

17.22a Install the right-hand pushrod . . .

17.22b . . . followed by the pushrod end piece . . .

17.22c . . . the release bearing . . .

17.22d . . . and the thrust washer

22 Install the pushrod right-hand half (if removed) into the end of the input shaft, followed by the pushrod end piece (see illustrations). Lubricate both sides of the release bearing and thrust washer with clean engine oil, then install them onto the push-rod end piece (see illustrations).

23 Install the pressure plate onto the clutch (see illustration). Install the springs and the spacers, making sure that the shouldered side of the spacer fits into the spring, then install the pressure plate bolts. Tighten the bolts evenly in a criss-cross sequence to the torque setting specified at the beginning of this Chapter, using the method employed on removal (see Step 5) to stop the clutch from turning (see illustrations).

24 If removed, insert the right-hand side crankcase cover dowels into the crankcase (see illustration 17.4), then place a new gasket onto the crankcase, making sure that it locates correctly over the dowels (see illustration).

25 Check the condition of the crankshaft right-hand end oil seal in the crankcase cover. If it is worn or damaged, or shows signs of leakage, lever out the old seal using a flat-bladed screwdriver, and drive a new seal into place using a seal driver or suitably sized

17.23a Install the pressure plate . . .

17.23b . . . followed by the springs . . .

17.23c . . . their spacers . . .

17.23d . . . and the bolts

17.24 Fit a new gasket onto the crankcase

17.25a Lever out the old seal . . .

17.25b . . . then install a new seal . . .

17.25c . . . and drive it squarely into place

17.25d Install the crankcase cover

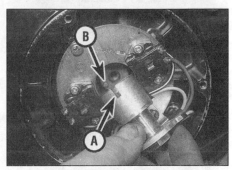

17.26a Locate the rotor slot (A) over the pin (B)

17.26b Install the rotor bolt . . .

17.26c . . . and tighten it to the specified torque whilst counter-holding the rotor

17.27 Install the pulse generator assembly cover

socket (see illustrations). Apply a smear of grease to the lips of the oil seal and install the crankcase cover (see illustration), and tighten its bolts evenly in a criss-cross sequence, making sure that all the wiring clamps are in their correct positions (see illustration 17.3).

26 Install the pulse generator coil assembly and tighten its two screws securely, noting that the lower screw also secures a wire clamp. Apply a smear of sealant to the edges of the wiring grommet and seat it in the casing. Reconnect the oil pressure switch wire. Install the timing rotor onto the end of the crankshaft, making sure the slot in the rotor locates correctly over the pin in the end of the crankshaft (see illustration). Using a 19 mm spanner to counter-hold the rotor, install the rotor bolt and tighten it to the torque setting specified at the beginning of the Chapter (see illustrations).

27 Install the pulse generator assembly cover and tighten its bolts securely (see

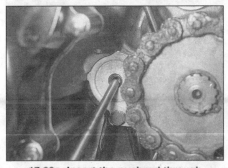

17.28a Insert the pushrod through the oil seal

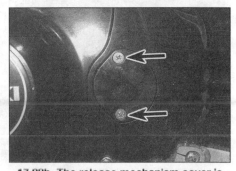

17.28b The release mechanism cover is secured by two screws (arrows)

illustration). Connect the pulse generator wiring at its connector behind the left-hand side panel.

28 If disassembled, install the clutch release mechanism in the engine sprocket cover and tighten its screws securely. Insert the pushrod left-hand half through the oil seal and into the input shaft, then install the sprocket cover and

tighten its bolts securely (see illustration). Unscrew the two screws securing the release mechanism cover to the sprocket cover, then loosen the locknut on the release mechanism adjuster screw (see illustration). Unscrew the adjuster screw a few turns, then screw it in until resistance is met as it contacts the end of the pushrod. From this position, unscrew the

2

17.28c Slacken the locknut and adjust the screw as described

adjuster 1/4 to 1/2 a turn, then tighten the locknut securely **(see illustration)**. Install the release mechanism cover. Install the gearchange lever onto its shaft, align the punch marks, and tighten the pinch bolt securely.

29 Check and adjust the amount of clutch lever freeplay (see Chapter 1).
30 Refill the engine with oil (see Chapter 1).

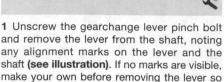

18 Clutch cable – removal and installation

1 Unscrew the gearchange lever pinch bolt and remove the lever from the shaft, noting any alignment marks on the lever and the shaft **(see illustration)**. If no marks are visible, make your own before removing the lever so that it can be correctly aligned with the shaft on installation. Unscrew the bolts securing the engine sprocket cover to the crankcase and remove the cover **(see illustration)**.
2 Bend out the tab in the cable retainer on the end of the release mechanism arm **(see**

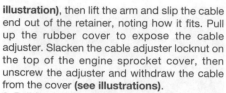

illustration), then lift the arm and slip the cable end out of the retainer, noting how it fits. Pull up the rubber cover to expose the cable adjuster. Slacken the cable adjuster locknut on the top of the engine sprocket cover, then unscrew the adjuster and withdraw the cable from the cover **(see illustrations)**.
3 Pull back the rubber cover from the clutch adjuster at the handlebar end of the cable **(see illustration)**. Fully slacken the lockwheel then screw the adjuster fully in **(see illustration 18.4)**. This resets it to the beginning of its adjustment span.
4 Align the slots in the adjuster and lockwheel with that in the lever bracket, then pull the outer cable end from the socket in the adjuster and release the inner cable from the lever **(see illustrations)**. Remove the cable from the machine, noting its routing.
5 Installation is the reverse of removal, making

18.1a Unscrew the pinch bolt (arrow) and remove the lever

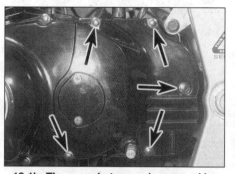

18.1b The sprocket cover is secured by five bolts (arrows)

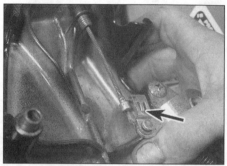

18.2a Bend out the retainer tab (arrow), then slip the cable end out of its retainer

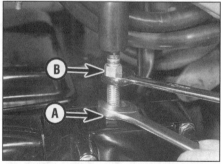

18.2b Slacken the locknut (A) and unscrew the adjuster (B) . . .

18.2c . . . then withdraw the cable from the cover

18.3 Pull back the rubber cover . . .

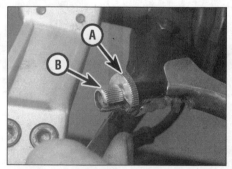

18.4a . . . then slacken lockwheel (A) and screw in adjuster (B) so the slots align, then remove the cable from the adjuster . . .

18.4b . . . and the lever

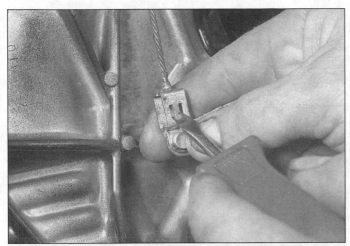

18.5 Bend in the retainer tab to secure the cable end

19.2a Remove circlip (arrow) and slide the gear off the shaft . . .

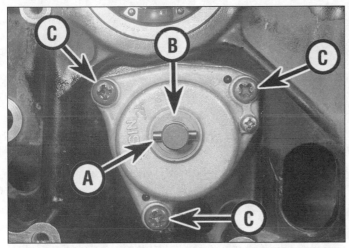

19.2b . . . then slide out drive pin (A) and remove washer (B). The pump is secured to the crankcase by three screws (C)

19.3 Remove the two O-rings (arrows)

sure the cable is correctly routed. Bend in the retainer to secure the cable end **(see illustration)**. Check the clutch release actuating mechanism for smooth operation and any signs of wear or damage. Adjust the amount of clutch lever freeplay (see Chapter 1).

19 Oil pump - removal, inspection and installation

Note: *The oil pump can be removed with the engine in the frame.*

Removal

1 Remove the clutch (see Section 17).
2 Remove the circlip securing the oil pump driven gear to the pump, then remove the gear, noting how and which way round it fits **(see illustration)**. Remove the drive pin and washer from the pump shaft **(see illustration)**.
3 Remove the three screws securing the pump to the crankcase **(see illustration 19.2b)**, then withdraw the pump and remove

the two O-rings **(see illustration)**. Discard the O-rings as new ones must be used.

Inspection

4 Inspect the pump body for any obvious damage such as cracks or distortion, and check that the shaft rotates freely and without any side-to-side play or excessive endfloat.
5 The oil pump fitted to this machine is not serviceable and Suzuki provide no inspection

procedure or specifications for it. If the pump is suspected of being faulty, it must be replaced as a unit.

Installation

6 Install the new O-rings onto the ends of the oilways, then install the pump **(see illustration)**. Apply a suitable non-permanent thread locking compound to the threads of the pump screws **(see illustration)** and tighten

19.6a Fit new O-rings to the oilways, then install the pump

19.6b Apply a thread locking compound to the pump screws

2

19.7a Slide the washer onto the shaft . . .

19.7b . . . then install the drive pin into its hole

19.7c Fit the gear over the drive pin . . .

19.7d . . . and secure it with the circlip

them to the torque setting specified at the beginning of the Chapter.

7 Fit the washer and drive pin onto the pump shaft, making sure that the drive pin is central **(see illustrations)**. Install the driven gear with its marked side facing out, making sure the drive pin locates correctly into the slot in the gear **(see illustration)**. Secure the driven gear with its circlip, making sure it fits correctly in its groove **(see illustration)**.

8 Install the clutch (see Section 17).

20 Gearchange mechanism - removal, inspection and installation

Note: *The gearchange mechanism can be removed with the engine in the frame.*

Removal

1 Remove the clutch (see Section 17).

2 Unscrew the gearchange lever pinch bolt and remove the lever from the shaft. Note any punch marks on the arm and the shaft which

must be aligned on installation **(see illustration 18.1a)**. If no marks are visible, make some of your own as an aid to installation.

3 Unscrew the bolt securing the selector drum stopper arm to the crankcase. Unhook the return spring from the input shaft bearing retainer plate and remove the stopper arm **(see illustration)**. Note how the stopper arm roller locates on the change pins in the selector drum.

4 Note how the gearchange selector arm claw fits onto the change pins in the selector drum, and how the gearchange shaft centralising spring ends fit on each side of the locating pin, then move the selector arm claw down off the change pins and withdraw the gearchange shaft from the engine **(see illustration)**.

5 If necessary, unscrew the screw securing the change pin holder plate to the selector

20.3 Unscrew the stopper arm bolt (A) and release the spring from the retainer plate (B)

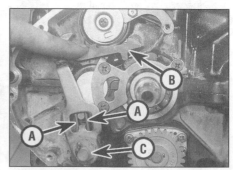

20.4 Note how the centralising spring ends locate (A), then move selector arm (B) off the drum and withdraw shaft (C)

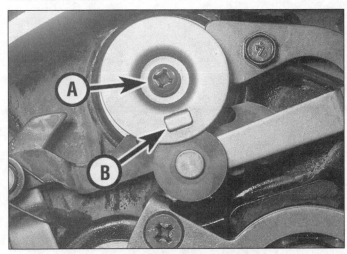

20.5 Remove the screw (A) to release the plate, noting how it locates over the neutral pin (B)

20.6 Remove the E-clip (A) to release the spring. Note how the spring ends locate (B)

drum, then remove the plate, noting how the recess in the plate locates over the neutral change pin **(see illustration)**. Remove the change pins, noting the position of the differently shaped neutral pin and taking care not to lose any of them.

Inspection

6 Inspect the selector arm and the stopper arm return springs and the shaft centralising spring. If they are fatigued, worn or damaged they must be replaced. To replace the selector arm spring, remove the E-clip and slide the spring off, noting how its ends locate **(see illustration)**. Check the gearchange shaft for straightness and damage to the splines. If the shaft is bent you can attempt to straighten it, but if the splines are damaged the shaft must be replaced.

7 Unscrew the bolts securing the engine sprocket cover to the crankcase and draw the cover away from the engine **(see illustration 18.1b)**. Note the position of the dowel and remove it if it is loose. Check the condition of the gearchange shaft oil seal set in the left-hand side of the crankcase. If it is damaged or deteriorated it must be replaced with a new one. Lever out the old seal and drive the new one squarely into place using a seal driver or suitable socket.

8 Inspect the selector arm claw, the stopper arm roller and the change pins. If they are worn or damaged they must be replaced.

Installation

9 If removed, install the change pins into the end of the selector drum, making sure the neutral pin is correctly located, then install the holder plate, making sure it locates correctly on the change pins and the neutral pin locates in the recess in the plate **(see illustration 20.5)**. Apply a non-permanent thread locking compound to the threads of the holder plate screw, then install the screw and tighten it securely.

20.10a Slide the centralising spring and spacer onto the shaft . . .

10 If removed, slide the centralising spring and spacer onto the gearchange shaft and locate the spring ends either side of the pin **(see illustrations)**. Smear clean engine oil over the gearchange shaft then install the assembly into its hole in the engine, placing the selector arm in position on the selector drum change pins, and making sure the centralising spring ends are correctly located on each side of the pins on the shaft arm and the crankcase **(see illustrations)**.

11 Apply a suitable non-permanent thread locking compound to the threads of the stopper arm bolt, then install the bolt through the stopper arm **(see illustration)**. Install the

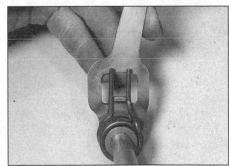

20.10b . . . and locate the spring ends as shown

20.10c Install the shaft . . .

20.10d . . . and locate the spring ends as shown

20.11a Apply a thread locking compound to the stopper arm bolt

2

20.11b Hook the return spring into its hole in the retainer plate (arrow)

20.11c The installed assembly should be as shown

assembly onto the crankcase, positioning the stopper arm roller onto the neutral change pin and hooking the return spring into the hole in the input shaft bearing retainer plate **(see illustrations)**. Tighten the bolt securely. Make sure the stopper arm is free to move and is returned by the pressure of the spring.

12 Install the engine sprocket cover and tighten its screws securely. Install the gearchange lever onto the end of the shaft on the left-hand side of the engine, aligning the punch marks on the arm and shaft, and check that the mechanism works correctly. Tighten the pinch bolt securely.

13 Install the clutch (see Section 17).

21 Starter clutch and gear assembly - removal, inspection and installation

Note: *The starter clutch and idle gear assembly can be removed with the engine in the frame.*

Removal

1 Remove the left-hand side panel (see Chapter 7). Trace the alternator wiring back

from the top of the engine sprocket cover and disconnect it at the connectors. Release the wiring from any clips or ties.

2 Unscrew the gearchange lever pinch bolt and remove the lever from the shaft, noting any alignment marks on the lever and the shaft **(see illustration 18.1a)**. If no marks are visible, make your own before removing the lever so that it can be correctly aligned with the shaft on installation. Unscrew the bolts securing the engine sprocket cover to the crankcase and move the cover aside **(see illustration 18.1b)**. There is no need to detach the clutch cable from the cover. Release the alternator wiring from the clamp next to the neutral switch.

3 Working in a criss-cross pattern, evenly slacken the left-hand side crankcase cover retaining bolts **(see illustration)**. Lift the cover away from the engine, being prepared to catch any residual oil which may be released as the cover is removed. Remove the gasket and discard it. Note the position of the locating dowel fitted to the crankcase and remove it for safe-keeping if it is loose. Note how the idle/reduction gear shaft end locates in the socket in the crankcase cover, acting as a second dowel.

4 Withdraw the starter idle/reduction gear shaft then remove the gear, noting which way round it fits **(see illustration)**. Remove the alternator rotor (see Chapter 8). The starter driven gear should come away with the rotor. If it doesn't, remove it from the crankshaft. The starter clutch is secured to the back of the rotor by three Allen bolts **(see illustration)**.

Inspection

5 Install the starter driven gear into the starter clutch (if removed) and, with the rotor face down on a workbench, check that the gear rotates freely in an anti-clockwise direction and locks against the rotor in a clockwise direction. If it doesn't, replace the starter clutch.

6 Withdraw the starter driven gear from the starter clutch. If it appears stuck, rotate it anti-clockwise as you withdraw it to free it from the starter clutch. Check the bearing surface of the starter driven gear hub and the condition of the rollers inside the clutch body **(see illustrations)**. If the bearing surface shows signs of excessive wear or the rollers are damaged, marked or flattened at any point, they should be replaced.

7 Remove the rollers and check the plungers

21.3 The left-hand side crankcase cover is secured by ten bolts (arrows)

21.4a Withdraw the shaft (A) and remove the idle/reduction gear (B)

21.4b The starter clutch is secured to the back of the rotor by three bolts (arrows)

21.6a Check the condition of the starter driven gear hub . . .

21.6b . . . and the rollers in the clutch

21.7 Remove the rollers and check the plungers and springs

and springs for signs of deformation or damage **(see illustration)**. Make sure the plungers move freely in their sockets.

8 Check that the three Allen bolts securing the starter clutch to the rotor are tight **(see illustration 21.4b)**. If any are loose, unscrew all the bolts, then apply a suitable non-permanent thread locking compound to their threads and tighten them to the specified torque setting. Lubricate the starter clutch rollers with new engine oil.

9 Examine the teeth of the starter idle/ reduction gear and the corresponding teeth of the starter driven gear and starter motor drive shaft. Replace the gears and/or starter motor if worn or chipped teeth are discovered on related gears.

Installation

10 Lubricate the hub of the starter driven gear with clean engine oil, then install the

starter driven gear into the starter clutch, rotating it anti-clockwise as you do so to spread the rollers and allow the hub of the gear to enter.

11 Install the alternator rotor (see Chapter 8).

12 Lubricate the idle/reduction gear shaft with clean engine oil, then install the idle/reduction gear followed by its shaft, making sure the smaller pinion on the idle/reduction gear faces outwards and meshes correctly with the teeth of the starter driven gear, and the teeth of the larger pinion mesh correctly with the teeth of the starter motor shaft **(see illustrations)**.

13 If removed, insert the dowel in the crankcase, then install the crankcase cover using a new gasket, making sure it locates correctly onto the dowel and the idle/ reduction gear shaft **(see illustrations)**. Tighten the cover bolts evenly in a criss-cross sequence.

22 Sump (oil pan), oil strainer and oil pressure regulator - removal and installation

Note: *The sump (oil pan) and strainer can be removed with the engine in the frame. If work is being carried out with the engine removed ignore the preliminary steps. To remove the oil pressure regulator the engine must be removed from the frame and the crankcases separated.*

Sump (oil pan) and oil strainer

Removal

1 Remove the exhaust system (Chapter 3).

2 Drain the engine oil (see Chapter 1).

3 Unscrew the sump (oil pan) bolts, slackening them evenly in a criss-cross sequence to prevent distortion **(see illustration)**. Remove

21.12a Install the idle/reduction gear . . .

21.12b . . . followed by its shaft . . .

21.12c . . . making sure all pinions mesh as shown

21.13a Make sure the dowel (arrow) is installed, then fit a new gasket . . .

21.13b . . . and install the cover

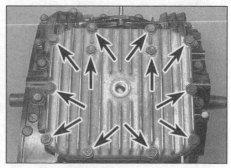

22.3 The sump (oil pan) is secured by twelve bolts (arrows)

2

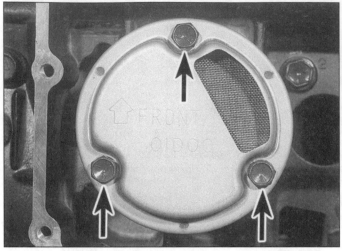

22.4 The oil strainer is secured by three bolts (arrows)

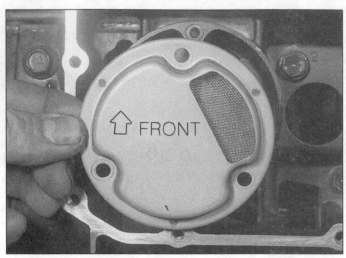

22.6 Make sure the arrow on the strainer points to the front of the engine

22.7 Lay the gasket in place . . .

22.8 . . . then install the sump (oil pan)

the sump (oil pan) and its gasket. Discard the gasket as a new one must be used.
4 Unscrew the three bolts securing the oil strainer to the underside of the crankcase, noting the arrow on the strainer which must point forwards **(see illustration)**.

Inspection

5 Make sure the oil strainer is clean and remove any debris caught in the mesh. Inspect the strainer for any signs of wear or damage and replace it if necessary.

Installation

6 Install the oil strainer onto the underside of the crankcase, making sure the arrow points to the front of the engine, and tighten its bolts securely **(see illustration)**.
7 Remove all traces of gasket from the sump (oil pan) and crankcase mating surfaces, then lay a new gasket onto the sump (oil pan) (if the engine is in the frame) or onto the crankcase (if the engine has been removed and is positioned upside down on the work surface)

(see illustration). Make sure the holes in the gasket align correctly with the oil passages.
8 Position the sump (oil pan) onto the crankcase and install the bolts, and tighten them evenly in a criss-cross pattern to the torque setting specified at the beginning of the Chapter **(see illustration)**.
9 Install the exhaust system (see Chapter 3).
10 Fill the engine with the correct type and quantity of oil as described in Chapter 1. Start the engine and check for leaks around the sump (oil pan).

Oil pressure regulator

Removal

11 Separate the crankcase halves (see Section 23).
12 Unscrew the oil pressure regulator from the lower crankcase half and remove it with its washer **(see illustration)**.

Inspection

13 Check that the pressure regulator plunger

moves freely in the plunger body, and inspect it for signs of wear or damage. Replace the regulator and its washer if necessary.

Installation

14 Install the oil pressure regulator and its washer onto the lower crankcase half and tighten it to the torque setting specified at the beginning of the Chapter.

22.12 Oil pressure regulator location

23 Crankcase -
separation and reassembly

Note: *References to the right- and left-hand ends of the transmission shafts are made as though the engine is the correct way up, even though throughout this procedure it is upside down. Therefore the right-hand end of a shaft will actually be on your left as you look down onto the underside of the upper crankcase assembly.*

Separation

1 To access the crankshaft and connecting rods, balancer shaft, bearings and transmission components, the crankcase must be split into two parts.

2 To enable the crankcases to be separated, the engine must be removed from the frame (see Section 5). Before the crankcases can be separated, the camchain tensioner, camshafts, cylinder head, cylinder block, ignition pulse generator coil assembly, clutch, oil pump, gearchange mechanism, alternator, starter clutch and starter idle/reduction gear, sump (oil pan), oil strainer, oil filter and starter motor must be removed. See the relevant Sections or

Chapters for details. **Note:** *If the crankcases are being separated to inspect or access the transmission components, or to inspect the crankshaft or balancer shaft, the engine top-end components (camchain tensioner, camshafts, cylinder head, cylinder block, pistons) can remain in situ. However, if removal of the crankshaft and connecting rod assemblies is intended, full disassembly of the top-end is necessary.*

3 Remove the three screws securing the transmission input shaft bearing retainer plate to the right-hand side of the crankcase and remove the plate, noting how it fits **(see illustration)**.

4 Bend back the tabs on the retainer plate for the transmission output shaft bearing and the clutch pushrod oil seal, located on the left - hand side of the crankcase **(see illustration)**. Unscrew the two bolts and remove the plate.

5 Unscrew the single crankcase bolt located next to the starter motor housing in the upper crankcase half **(see illustration)**.

6 Turn the engine upside down so that it rests on the cylinder head studs and the back of the upper crankcase half.

7 Working in a **reverse** of the tightening sequence **(see illustration 23.19)**, and noting that two of the bolts (Nos. 1 and 3) are located

inside the oil filter housing and are accessed by the holes in the crankcase using a socket extension, slacken each crankcase bolt a little a time until they are all finger-tight, then remove the bolts. **Note:** *As each bolt is removed, store it in its relative position in a cardboard template of the crankcase halves. This will ensure all bolts are installed in the correct location on reassembly. Store the engine earth (ground) cable with its bolt (No. 24).*

8 Carefully lift the lower crankcase half off the upper half, using a large screwdriver in the leverage points and a soft-faced hammer to tap around the joint to initially separate the halves if necessary **(see illustrations)**. **Note:** *If the halves do not separate easily, make sure all fasteners have been removed. Do not try and separate the halves by levering against the crankcase mating surfaces as they are easily scored and will leak oil. Use only the special leverage points.* The lower crankcase half will come away by itself, leaving the crankshaft, balancer shaft, camchain tensioner blade, transmission shafts, selector drum and selector forks in the upper crankcase half. Note that the transmission shaft oil seals should be replaced whenever the crankcase halves are separated, irrespective of whether the shafts are to be removed or disassembled. There is no need to

23.3 The input shaft bearing retainer plate is secured by three screws

23.4 Bend back the tabs (arrows), then unscrew the bolts and remove the plate

23.5 Unscrew the single crankcase bolt in the upper crankcase half (arrow)

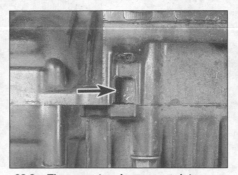

23.8a There are two leverage points, one at the front of the engine (arrow) . . .

23.8b . . . and one at the back (arrow)

2

23.8c Output shaft oil seals (A), and input shaft oil seal (B)

23.8d The input shaft seal simply lifts away

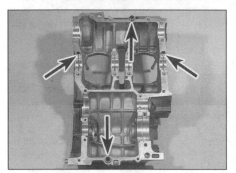

23.9 Remove the four dowels (arrows) if they are loose

23.15 Apply a suitable sealant to the crankcase mating surface . . .

remove the shafts from the crankcase, though it may be necessary to lift the end of the output shaft slightly so that the seals slide off the end of the shaft easily **(see illustration)**. The input shaft oil seal butts against the end of the shaft and can simply be lifted away **(see illustration)**.

9 Remove the four locating dowels from the crankcase if they are loose (they could be in either crankcase half), noting their locations **(see illustration)**.

Reassembly

10 Remove all traces of sealant from the crankcase mating surfaces.

11 If the transmission shafts have not been removed from the crankcase, slide new output shaft oil seals onto the left-hand end of the shaft, lifting it slightly if necessary **(see illustration 25.6 and 23.8c)**. Make sure the selector forks return into their grooves if the shaft is lifted. Position the input shaft oil seal against the left-hand end of the shaft **(see illustrations 23.8d and c)**.

12 Ensure that all components and their bearings are in place in the upper and lower crankcase halves. Check that the crankshaft thrust bearings and the transmission bearing locating pins and half-ring retainers are all correctly located, and that the camchain

tensioner blade, its cushions, and all oil jets have been installed, if removed.

13 Generously lubricate the transmission shafts, selector drum and forks, and the crankshaft and balancer shaft, particularly around the bearings, with clean engine oil, then use a rag soaked in high flash-point solvent to wipe over the gasket surfaces of both halves to remove all traces of oil.

14 Install the four locating dowels in the upper crankcase half **(see illustration 21.9)**. Make sure that the gear selector drum is in the neutral position.

15 Apply a small amount of suitable sealant to the mating surface of the lower crankcase half **(see illustration)**. **Caution:** *Do not apply an excessive amount of sealant, as it will ooze out when the case halves are assembled and may obstruct oil passages.*

16 Check again that all components are in position, particularly that the bearing shells are still correctly located in the lower crankcase half, then carefully install the lower crankcase half down onto the upper crankcase half **(see illustration)**. Make sure the dowels all locate correctly into the lower crankcase half.

17 Check that the lower crankcase half is correctly seated. **Note:** *The crankcase halves should fit together without being forced. If the casings are not correctly seated, remove the lower crankcase half and investigate the problem. Do not attempt to pull them together using the crankcase bolts as the casing will crack and be ruined.*

18 Check that the transmission shafts rotate freely and independently in neutral, then rotate the selector drum by hand and select each gear in turn whilst rotating the input shaft. Check that all gears can be selected and that the shafts rotate freely in every gear.

19 Clean the threads of the crankcase bolts and insert them in their original locations, not forgetting the engine earth (ground) cable secured by bolt No. 24 **(see illustration)**. Secure all bolts finger-tight at first, then

23.16 . . . then assemble the crankcase halves

23.19 Crankcase bolt TIGHTENING sequence

23.21 Do not forget the single upper crankcase bolt

23.22a Install the output shaft retainer plate . . .

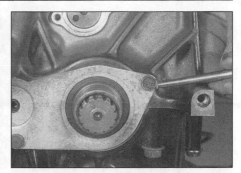

23.22b . . . and bend up the tabs to lock the bolts

23.23a Install the input shaft retainer plate . . .

23.23b . . . applying a thread locking compound to its screws

tighten the bolts a little at a time and in the numerical sequence shown to the torque settings specified at the beginning of the Chapter. When torquing the bolts, be sure to distinguish correctly between the 8 mm bolts and the 6 mm bolts.

20 With all crankcase fasteners tightened, check that the crankshaft and transmission shafts rotate smoothly and easily. Check the operation of the transmission in each gear (see Step 18). If there are any signs of undue stiffness, tight or rough spots, or of any other problem, the fault must be rectified before proceeding further.

21 Turn the engine over. Install the single upper crankcase half bolt and tighten it to the specified torque setting **(see illustration)**.

22 Install the retainer plate for the transmission output shaft bearing and the clutch pushrod oil seal onto the left-hand side of the crankcase **(see illustration)**. Tighten the bolts securely, then bend up the tabs on the plate to lock them in place **(see illustration)**.

23 Install the transmission input shaft bearing retainer plate onto the right-hand side of the crankcase **(see illustration)**. Apply a suitable non-permanent thread locking compound to the threads of the screws and tighten them securely **(see illustration)**.

24 Install all other removed assemblies in the reverse of the sequence given in Step 2.

24 Crankcase - inspection and servicing

1 After the crankcases have been separated, remove the crankshaft, balancer shaft, camchain tensioner blade, oil pressure regulator, neutral switch and transmission components, referring to the relevant Sections of this Chapter and to Chapter 8 for the neutral switch. Remove the cylinder oil jet from the side of each cylinder hole in the top of the upper crankcase half, and check the condition of their O-rings, replacing them if necessary **(see illustration)**. Also remove the balancer shaft oil jets and the transmission input shaft oil jet from the bearing cutouts in the lower crankcase half **(see illustrations)**. Remove the screws securing each oil

deflector plate to the lower crankcase half and remove the plates, noting how they fit.

2 The crankcases should be cleaned thoroughly with new solvent and dried with compressed air. All oil passages and oil jets should be blown out with compressed air.

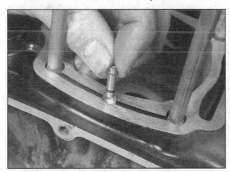

24.1a Cylinder oil jet location

24.1c Input shaft oil jet location (arrow)

3 All traces of old gasket sealant should be removed from the mating surfaces. Minor damage to the surfaces can be cleaned up with a fine sharpening stone or grindstone. *Caution: Be very careful not to nick or gouge the crankcase mating surfaces or oil*

24.1b Balancer shaft oil jet locations (arrows)

24.1d Each oil deflector plate is secured by two screws (arrows)

2

leaks will result. Check both crankcase halves very carefully for cracks and other damage.

4 Small cracks or holes in aluminium castings may be repaired with an epoxy resin adhesive as a temporary measure. Permanent repairs can only be effected by argon-arc welding, and only a specialist in this process is in a position to advise on the economy or practical aspect of such a repair. If any damage is found that can't be repaired, replace the crankcase halves as a set.

5 Damaged threads can be economically reclaimed by using a diamond section wire insert, of the Helicoil type, which is easily fitted after drilling and re-tapping the affected thread (see *Tools and Mechanics Tips* in the Reference section of this Manual).

6 Sheared studs or screws can usually be removed with screw extractors, which consist of a tapered, left thread screw of very hard steel. These are inserted into a pre-drilled hole in the stud, and usually succeed in dislodging the most stubborn stud or screw (see *Tools and Mechanics Tips* in the Reference section of this Manual).

7 Check that all the cylinder head studs are tight in the crankcase halves. If any are loose, remove them using a stud extractor tool, then clean their threads and apply a suitable non-permanent thread locking compound and tighten them securely.

8 Install the removed oil jets and oil deflector plates into their correct locations **(see**

illustrations 24.1a, b, c and d). Apply clean engine oil to the cylinder oil jet O-rings, and apply a suitable non-permanent thread locking compound to the threads of the oil deflector plate screws and tighten them securely. Install all other components and assemblies, referring to the relevant Sections of this Chapter and to Chapter 8, before reassembling the crankcase halves.

25 Transmission shafts - removal and installation

Note: *To remove the transmission shafts the engine must be removed from the frame and the crankcases separated.*

Note: *References to the right- and left-hand ends of the transmission shafts are made as though the engine is the correct way up, even though throughout this procedure it is upside down. Therefore the right-hand end of a shaft will actually be on your left as you look down onto the underside of the upper crankcase assembly.*

Removal

1 Separate the crankcase halves (Section 23). Note the positions of the bearing locating pins on the right-hand end of the input shaft and on each end of the output shaft.

2 Lift the input shaft and output shaft out of the crankcase, noting their relative positions in the crankcase and how they fit, and noting

how the selector forks engage in the grooves on the gear pinions.

3 Remove the bearing half-ring retainers and the input shaft left-hand bearing dowel from the upper crankcase half, noting how they fit **(see illustrations 25.5a, b and c)**. If they are not in their slots or hole in the crankcase, remove them from the bearings themselves on the shafts.

4 Remove the oil seals from the left-hand end of the output shaft, noting how they fit, and discard them as new ones must be used **(see illustration)**. Also remove the input shaft oil seal, which will probably have remained in the crankcase **(see illustration 23.8d)**. If necessary, the input shaft and output shaft can be disassembled and inspected for wear or damage (see Section 26).

Installation

5 Install the input shaft and output shaft bearing half-ring retainers into their slots in the upper crankcase half, and install the input shaft left-hand end bearing dowel into its hole **(see illustrations)**.

6 Slide new oil seals onto the left-hand end of the output shaft, having first coated the seal lips with grease **(see illustration)**.

7 Lower the input shaft into position in the upper crankcase, making sure the hole in the left-hand bearing engages correctly with the dowel, the middle selector fork engages correctly in its groove in the 3rd/4th gear pinion, and the bearing pin and groove on the right-hand bearing engage correctly with the

25.4 Slide the two oil seals (arrows) off the end of the output shaft and discard them

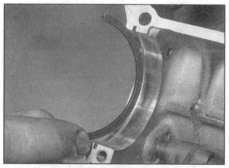

25.5a Fit the input shaft bearing retainer . . .

25.5b . . . and the output shaft bearing retainer into their slots . . .

25.5c . . . and the input shaft bearing dowel into its hole

25.6 Make sure the oil seals are installed the correct way round

25.7a Make sure the dowel (A) locates in the hole (B), and the fork (C) fits into its groove (D)

25.7b Position the bearing pin (A) against the crankcase, and make sure the half-ring retainer (B) is engaged in its slots

recess in the crankcase and bearing half-ring retainer **(see illustrations)**. Install the oil seal against the left-hand end of the shaft **(see illustration 23.8d and c)**.

8 Lower the output shaft into position in the crankcase half, making sure the outer selector forks engage correctly in their grooves in the 5th and 6th gear pinions. Make sure the bearing pins engage correctly with the recesses in the crankcase, and the groove in the left-hand bearing engages correctly with the bearing half-ring retainer **(see illustrations)**.

9 Make sure both transmission shafts are correctly seated and their related pinions are correctly engaged **(see illustration)**.

Caution: If the input shaft bearing locating pin and/or output shaft half-ring or dowel pin are not correctly engaged, the crankcase halves will not seat correctly.

10 Position the gears in the neutral position and check the shafts are free to rotate easily and independently (ie the input shaft can turn whilst the output shaft is held stationary) before proceeding further. Also check that the selector drum and forks rotate or move freely.

11 Reassembly the crankcase halves as described in Section 24.

---

26 Transmission shafts -
disassembly, inspection and reassembly

Note: *References to the right- and left-hand ends of the transmission shafts are made as though they are installed in the engine and the engine is the correct way up.*

1 Remove the transmission shafts from the upper crankcase half (see Section 25). Always disassemble the transmission shafts separately to avoid mixing up the components.

Input shaft

Disassembly

HAYNES HiNT *When disassembling the transmission shafts, place the parts on a long rod or thread a wire through them to keep them in order and facing the proper direction.*

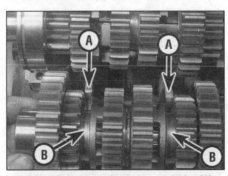

25.8a Make sure the selector forks (A) fit into their grooves (B)

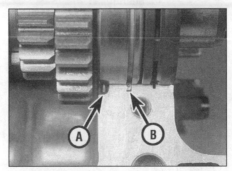

25.8c . . . against the crankcase, and make sure the half-ring retainer (B) is engaged in its slot

2 Remove the bearing from the left-hand end of the shaft **(see illustration)**.

3 The 2nd gear pinion is a press fit on the shaft, and must be removed using a puller **(see illustration)**. **Note:** *Suzuki advise that the 2nd gear pinion can only be removed and installed twice before replacement of the input shaft is necessary.*

4 Slide the 6th gear pinion and combined 3rd/4th gear pinion off the shaft.

5 Remove the circlip securing the 5th gear

25.8b Position the bearing pins (A) . . .

25.9 The installed transmission assembly should be as shown

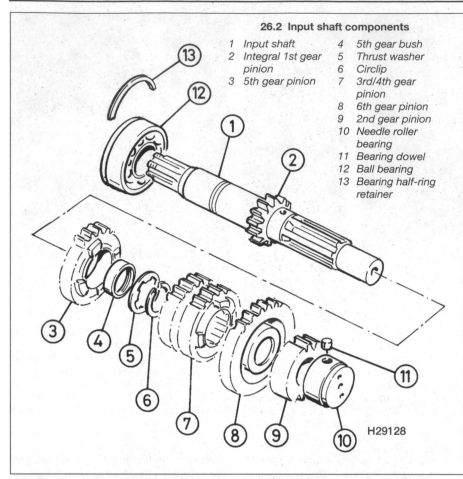

26.2 Input shaft components

1	Input shaft	4	5th gear bush
2	Integral 1st gear pinion	5	Thrust washer
3	5th gear pinion	6	Circlip
		7	3rd/4th gear pinion
		8	6th gear pinion
		9	2nd gear pinion
		10	Needle roller bearing
		11	Bearing dowel
		12	Ball bearing
		13	Bearing half-ring retainer

H29128

pinion, then slide the thrust washer and the pinion off the shaft, followed by the 5th gear bush.

6 The 1st gear pinion is integral with the shaft.

Inspection

7 Wash all of the components in clean solvent and dry them off.

8 Check the gear teeth for cracking chipping, pitting and other obvious wear or damage. Any pinion that is damaged as such must be replaced.

9 Inspect the dogs and the dog holes in the gears for cracks, chips, and excessive wear especially in the form of rounded edges. Make sure mating gears engage properly. Replace the paired gears as a set if necessary.

10 Check for signs of scoring or bluing on the pinions, bush and shaft. This could be caused by overheating due to inadequate lubrication. Check that all the oil holes and passages are clear. Replace any damaged components.

11 Check that each pinion moves freely on the shaft or bush (5th gear pinion) but without undue freeplay. Check that the 5th gear bush moves freely on the shaft but without undue freeplay.

12 The shaft is unlikely to sustain damage unless the engine has seized, placing an unusually high loading on the transmission, or the machine has covered a very high mileage. Check the surface of the shaft, especially where a pinion turns on it, and replace the shaft if it has scored or picked up, or if there are any cracks.

13 Check the ball bearing for play or roughness, and that it is a tight fit on the shaft. Replace the bearing if it is worn, loose or damaged, using a bearing puller to remove it (see illustration). If one is not available, carefully lever it off using a pair of tyre levers (see illustration). Install the bearing using a press. Install the needle roller bearing onto the shaft, and check it for play or roughness. Replace the bearing if it is worn or damaged.

14 Check the washers and replace any that are bent or appear weakened or worn. Discard all the circlips as new ones must be used.

Reassembly

15 During reassembly, apply molybdenum paste or engine oil to the mating surfaces of the shaft, pinions and bush. When installing the circlips, do not expand their ends any further than is necessary, and install them so that the chamfered side faces the pinion it secures (see illustration).

16 Slide the 5th gear bush and 5th gear pinion, with its dogs facing away from the integral 1st gear, onto the left-hand end of the shaft (see illustrations). Install the thrust washer and circlip, making sure that the circlip locates correctly in the groove in the shaft (see illustrations).

17 Slide the combined 3rd/4th gear pinion

26.3 Using a puller to remove the 2nd gear pinion

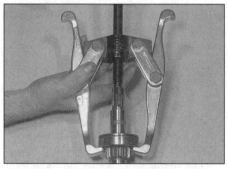

26.13a Use a puller to remove the bearing . . .

26.13b . . . or lever it off with a pair of tyre levers

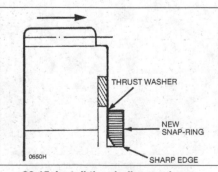

THRUST WASHER

NEW SNAP-RING

SHARP EDGE

0650H

26.15 Install the circlips as shown

26.16a Install the bush . . .

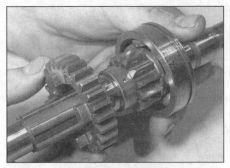

26.16b . . . followed by 5th gear pinion . . .

26.16c . . . the thrust washer . . .

26.16d . . . and the circlip . . .

26.16e . . . making sure it locates correctly in its groove

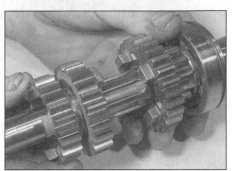

26.17 Install the combined 3rd/4th gear pinion . . .

onto the shaft, so that the larger (4th gear) pinion faces the 5th gear pinion dogs (see illustration).

18 Slide the 6th gear pinion onto the shaft so that its dog holes face the dogs on the 3rd gear pinion (see illustration).

19 The 2nd gear pinion is a press fit onto the shaft and must be installed using a press (see illustration). Note: Suzuki advise that the 2nd gear pinion can only be removed and installed twice before replacement of the input shaft is necessary. Apply a suitable non-permanent thread locking compound to the internal surface of the pinion, and press the pinion onto the shaft so that the distance between its outer edge and the outer edge of the integral

1st gear pinion is as specified at the beginning of the Chapter (see illustration). After installing the 2nd gear pinion, check that the 6th gear pinion rotates freely on the shaft.

20 Slide the needle roller bearing onto the shaft end (see illustration). Check that all components have been correctly installed (see illustration).

26.18 . . . followed by the 6th gear pinion

26.19a Install 2nd gear using a press . . .

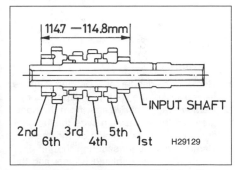

26.19b . . . to the specified depth

1147 —114.8mm

INPUT SHAFT

2nd 6th 3rd 4th 5th 1st H29129

2

26.20a Install the needle bearing onto the end of the shaft

26.20b The assembled shaft should be as shown

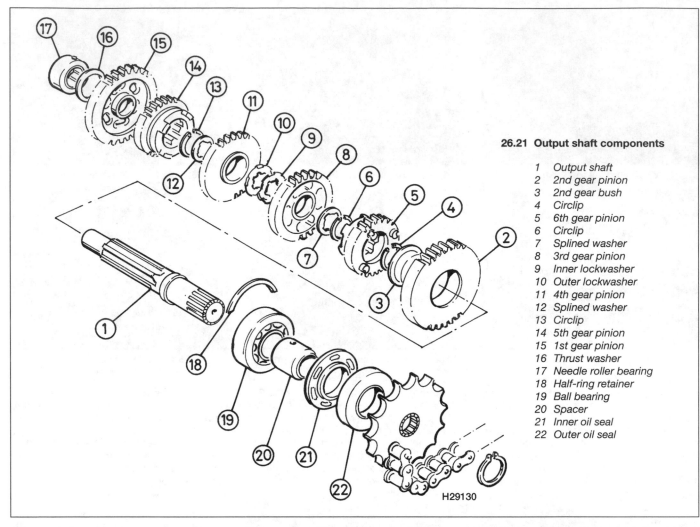

26.21 Output shaft components

1   Output shaft
2   2nd gear pinion
3   2nd gear bush
4   Circlip
5   6th gear pinion
6   Circlip
7   Splined washer
8   3rd gear pinion
9   Inner lockwasher
10 Outer lockwasher
11 4th gear pinion
12 Splined washer
13 Circlip
14 5th gear pinion
15 1st gear pinion
16 Thrust washer
17 Needle roller bearing
18 Half-ring retainer
19 Ball bearing
20 Spacer
21 Inner oil seal
22 Outer oil seal

H29130

Output shaft

Disassembly

21 Remove the needle roller bearing from the right-hand end of the shaft (see illustration).
22 Remove the thrust washer from the right-hand end of the shaft, then slide the 1st gear pinion and the 5th gear pinion off the shaft.
23 Remove the circlip securing the 4th gear pinion, then slide the splined washer and the pinion off the shaft.
24 Slide the two lockwashers off the shaft, noting how they fit, followed by the 3rd gear pinion and the splined washer.
25 Remove the circlip securing the 6th gear pinion, then slide the pinion off the shaft.
26 Remove the circlip securing the 2nd gear pinion, then slide the 2nd gear bush and the pinion off the shaft.

Inspection

27 Wash all of the components in clean solvent and dry them off.
28 Check the gear teeth for cracking, chipping, pitting and other obvious wear or damage. Any pinion that is damaged as such must be replaced.

29 Inspect the dogs and the dog holes in the gears for cracks, chips, and excessive wear especially in the form of rounded edges. Make sure mating gears engage properly. Replace the paired gears as a set if necessary.
30 Check for signs of scoring or bluing on the pinions, bush and shaft. This could be caused by overheating due to inadequate lubrication. Check that all the oil holes and passages are clear.
31 Check that each pinion moves freely on the shaft or bush (2nd gear pinion) but without undue freeplay. Check that the 2nd gear bush moves freely on the shaft but without undue freeplay.
32 The shaft is unlikely to sustain damage unless the engine has seized, placing an unusually high loading on the transmission, or the machine has covered a very high mileage. Check the surface of the shaft, especially where a pinion turns on it, and replace the shaft if it has scored or picked up, or if there are any cracks.
33 Check the ball bearing for play or roughness, and that it is a tight fit on the shaft. Replace the bearing if it is worn, loose or damaged, using a bearing puller to remove it

and the spacer (see illustration). If one is not available, carefully lever them off using a pair of tyre levers (see illustration 26.13b). Install the bearing using a press. Install the needle roller bearing onto the shaft, and check it for play or roughness. Replace the bearing if it is worn or damaged.
34 Check the washers and replace any that are bent or appear weakened or worn. Discard all the circlips as new ones must be used.

26.33 Use a puller and draw the spacer off with the bearing

26.36a Install the 2nd gear pinion . . .

26.36b . . . and its bush . . .

26.36c . . . and secure them with the circlip

Reassembly

35 During reassembly, apply molybdenum paste or engine oil to the mating surfaces of the shaft, pinions and bush. When installing the circlips, do not expand their ends any furthor than is necessary, and install them so that the chamfered side faces the pinion it secures (see illustration 26.15).

36 Slide the 2nd gear pinion and its bush onto the shaft, so that the collared side of the bush faces away from the bearing, and secure them in place with the circlip, making sure that it is properly seated in its groove (see illustrations).

37 Slide the 6th gear pinion onto the shaft with its selector fork groove facing away from the 2nd gear pinion, and secure it in place with the circlip, making sure it is properly seated in its groove (see illustrations).

38 Slide the splined washer, followed by the

26.37a Install the 6th gear pinion . . .

26.37b . . . and secure it with the circlip

3rd gear pinion onto the shaft (see illustrations). Slide the inner lockwasher onto the shaft until it aligns with its groove, then turn it in the groove so that its splines align with those on the shaft (see illustrations). Slide the outer lockwasher onto the shaft so

that its tabs fit into the slots in the inner lockwasher, thus locking it in place (see illustration).

39 Slide the 4th gear pinion onto the shaft, followed by the splined washer, and secure them in place with the circlip, making sure

26.38a Install the splined washer . . .

26.38b . . . followed by the 3rd gear pinion

26.38c Install the inner lockwasher . . .

2

26.38d . . . and align it as shown

26.38e Install outer lockwasher so its tabs engage in the slots in the inner lockwasher

26.39a Install the 4th gear pinion . . .

26.39b . . . and the splined washer . . .

26.39c . . . and secure them with the circlip

26.40a Install the 5th gear pinion . . .

26.40b . . . followed by 1st gear pinion . . .

26.40c . . . and the thrust washer

26.41a Install the bearing onto the end of the shaft

26.41b The assembled shaft should be as shown

that it is properly seated in its groove (see illustrations).

40 Slide the 6th gear pinion onto the shaft with its selector fork groove facing the 4th gear pinion, followed by the 1st gear pinion and the thrust washer (see illustrations).

41 Slide the needle roller bearing onto the shaft end (see illustration). Check that all components have been correctly installed (see illustration).

27 Selector drum and forks - removal, inspection and installation

Note: *Access can be gained to the stopper arm and selector arm with the engine in the frame and the clutch removed (Section 20). All other operations require the engine to be removed and the crankcases to be separated.*
Note: *References to the right- and left-hand*

sides or ends of the crankcases or other components are made as though the engine is the correct way up, even though throughout this procedure it is upside down. Therefore the right-hand end of a component will actually be on your left as you look down onto the underside of the upper crankcase assembly.

Removal

1 Separate the crankcase halves and remove the transmission shafts (Sections 23 and 25).
2 Unscrew the selector fork shaft retaining screw from the right-hand side of the upper crankcase half (see illustration). Supporting the selector forks, withdraw the shaft and then remove the forks, noting the correct location and which way round each fork fits. Once removed from the crankcase, it is a good idea to slide the forks back onto the shaft, in their correct order, as an aid to installation.
3 Unscrew the bolt securing the neutral detent plunger in the top of the upper crankcase half, noting that it is under spring pressure (see illustration). Remove the bolt slowly so that the spring does not expel itself, and remove the sealing washer. Withdraw the spring and the plunger, noting which way up it fits.
4 Remove the neutral switch (see Chapter 8).
5 Unscrew the bolt securing the selector drum retainer plate to the right-hand side of

27.2 This screw (arrow) retains the selector fork shaft

27.3 Unscrew the bolt and withdraw the spring and plunger

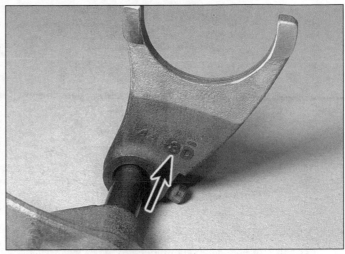

27.5 Unscrew the retainer plate bolt (arrow), then remove the plate and withdraw the selector drum

27.6 Note the identification number on each selector fork (arrow)

the upper crankcase half, then remove the plate and withdraw the selector drum from the crankcase, noting how they fit **(see illustration)**. Note the washer that fits onto the left-hand end of the selector drum, and that it may remain stuck against the drum bearing in the crankcase.

6 Note that each selector fork is numbered for identification. The left-hand fork is number 3, the middle fork is number 2, and the right-hand fork is number 1 **(see illustration)**. The numbers must face the right-hand side of the engine.

Inspection

7 Inspect the selector forks for any signs of wear or damage, especially around the fork ends where they engage with the groove in the pinion. Check that each fork fits correctly in its pinion groove. Check closely to see if the forks are bent. If the forks are in any way damaged they must be replaced.

8 With the fork engaged with its pinion groove, measure the fork-to-groove clearance using a feeler gauge, and compare the result to the specifications at the beginning of the Chapter **(see illustration)**. If the clearance exceeds the service limit specified, measure the thickness of the fork ends and the width of the gear grooves and compare the readings to the specifications **(see illustrations)**. Replace whichever components are worn beyond their specifications.

9 Check that the forks fit correctly on their shaft. They should move freely with a light fit but no appreciable free play. Check that the fork shaft holes in the crankcases are not worn or damaged.

10 The selector fork shaft can be checked for trueness by rolling it along a flat surface. A bent rod will cause difficulty in selecting gears and make the gearshift action heavy. Replace the shaft if it is bent.

11 Inspect the selector drum grooves and selector fork guide pins for signs of wear or damage. If either component shows signs of wear or damage the selector(s) and drum must be replaced.

12 Check that the selector drum bearing rotates freely and has no sign of freeplay between it and the crankcase. Replace the bearing if necessary. Drift the bearing out of the crankcase, noting that once it has been removed it cannot be re-used. Draw or drive the new bearing onto place, making sure it

enters squarely. Also check the drum journal hole in the crankcase for wear or damage.

Installation

13 Fit the washer onto the left-hand end of the selector drum, then install the drum into the crankcase, positioning it so that the neutral position plunger detent aligns with the hole in the top of the crankcase **(see illustration)**. Apply a suitable non-permanent thread locking compound to the threads of the selector drum retainer plate bolt, then

2

27.8a Measure the fork-to-groove clearance using a feeler gauge

27.8b Measure the thickness of the fork end . . .

27.8c . . . and the width of the groove

27.13a Install the selector drum into the crankcase

27.13b Apply a thread locking compound to the retainer plate bolt

27.13c Install a suitable bolt to locate the other end of the plate (arrow), then tighten the retainer plate bolt securely

27.14a Install the plunger . . .

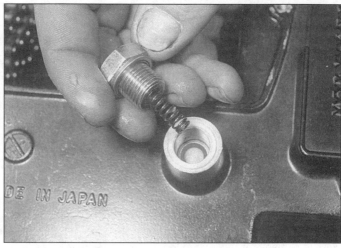

27.14b . . . followed by the spring and bolt

install the plate against the end of the selector drum **(see illustration)**. Temporarily install a suitable bolt to locate the other end of the plate and stop it from becoming misaligned, then tighten the retainer plate bolt securely **(see illustration)**.

14 Install the neutral position plunger into the hole in the top of the crankcase, making sure it is the correct way up and locates into the detent in the selector drum **(see illustration)**. Check the condition of the sealing washer on the bolt, using a new one if necessary, then install the spring into the end of the bolt. Install the bolt, making sure the spring end locates correctly in the top of the plunger and tighten it securely **(see illustration)**.

15 Lubricate the selector fork shaft with clean engine oil and slide it into its bore in the

crankcase **(see illustration)**. As the shaft is installed, fit each selector fork in turn, making sure it is in its correct location and the right way round (see Step 6), and that its guide pin locates in its track in the selector drum **(see illustration)**. Apply a suitable non-permanent thread locking compound to the threads of the selector fork shaft retaining screw and install it into the crankcase **(see illustration)**.

27.15a Slide the shaft into the crankcase . . .

27.15b . . . fitting numbered selector forks in their correct positions and making sure their guide pins fit into the tracks (arrow)

27.15c Apply a thread locking compound to the screw and tighten it securely

16 Install the neutral switch (see Chapter 8).
17 Install the transmission shafts (see Section 25).

28 Main and connecting rod bearings - general information

1 Even though main and connecting rod bearings are generally replaced with new ones during the engine overhaul, the old bearings should be retained for close examination as they may reveal valuable information about the condition of the engine.
2 Bearing failure occurs mainly because of lack of lubrication, the presence of dirt or other foreign particles, overloading the engine and/or corrosion. Regardless of the cause of bearing failure, it must be corrected before the engine is reassembled to prevent it from happening again.
3 When examining the connecting rod bearings, remove them from the connecting rods and caps and lay them out on a clean surface in the same general position as their location on the crankshaft journals. This will enable you to match any noted bearing problems with the corresponding crankshaft journal.
4 Dirt and other foreign particles get into the engine in a variety of ways. It may be left in the engine during assembly or it may pass through filters or breathers. It may get into the oil and from there into the bearings. Metal chips from machining operations and normal engine wear are often present. Abrasives are sometimes left in engine components after reconditioning operations, especially when parts are not thoroughly cleaned using the proper cleaning methods. Whatever the source, these foreign objects often end up imbedded in the soft bearing material and are easily recognised. Large particles will not

imbed in the bearing and will score or gouge the bearing and journal. The best prevention for this cause of bearing failure is to clean all parts thoroughly and keep everything spotlessly clean during engine reassembly. Frequent and regular oil and filter changes are also recommended.
5 Lack of lubrication or lubrication breakdown has a number of interrelated causes. Excessive heat (which thins the oil), overloading (which squeezes the oil from the bearing face) and oil leakage or throw off (from excessive bearing clearances, worn oil pump or high engine speeds) all contribute to lubrication breakdown. Blocked oil passages will also starve a bearing and destroy it. When lack of lubrication is the cause of bearing failure, the bearing material is wiped or extruded from the steel backing of the bearing. Temperatures may increase to the point where the steel backing and the journal turn blue from overheating.
6 Riding habits can have a definite effect on bearing life. Full throttle low speed operation, or labouring (lugging) the engine, puts very high loads on bearings, which tend to squeeze out the oil film. These loads cause the bearings to flex, which produces fine cracks in the bearing face (fatigue failure). Eventually the bearing material will loosen in pieces and tear away from the steel backing. Short trip riding leads to corrosion of bearings, as insufficient engine heat is produced to drive off the condensed water and corrosive gases produced. These products collect in the engine oil, forming acid and sludge. As the oil is carried to the engine bearings, the acid attacks and corrodes the bearing material.
7 Incorrect bearing installation during engine assembly will lead to bearing failure as well. Tight fitting bearings which leave insufficient bearing oil clearances result in oil starvation. Dirt or foreign particles trapped behind a bearing insert result in high spots on the bearing which lead to failure.

8 To avoid bearing problems, clean all parts thoroughly before reassembly, double check all bearing clearance measurements and lubricate the new bearings with clean engine oil during installation.

29 Crankshaft and main bearings - removal, inspection and installation

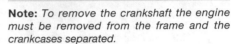

Note: *To remove the crankshaft the engine must be removed from the frame and the crankcases separated.*

Removal

1 Separate the crankcase halves (Section 23).
2 Lift the crankshaft out of the upper crankcase half, noting the position of the thrust bearings between each inner crank web and the main bearing housing **(see illustration)**. If the crankshaft appears stuck, tap it gently using a soft-faced mallet. Remove the thrust bearings, noting how they fit.
3 If required, remove the connecting rods from the crankshaft (see Section 31), and disengage the camchain from its sprocket.
4 If required, remove the nut securing the primary drive gear to the right-hand end of the crankshaft **(see illustration)**. Remove the nut and its washer, noting which way round it fits, then slide the gear off the end of the shaft, noting how it locates over the Woodruff key. If the key is loose, remove it for safekeeping.

Inspection

5 Clean the crankshaft with solvent, using a rifle-cleaning brush to scrub out the oil passages. If available, blow the crank dry with compressed air, and also blow through the oil passages. Check the camchain sprocket and the balancer shaft drive gear for wear or damage. If any of the sprocket or gear teeth are excessively worn, chipped or broken, the crankshaft must be replaced. Similarly check

2

29.2 Note the thrust bearings between the crank web and the bearing housing (arrows)

29.4 Unscrew the nut (arrow) to release the primary drive gear

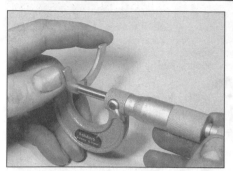

29.9 Measure the thickness of each thrust bearing

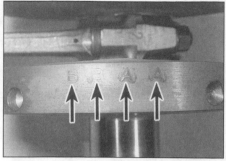

29.10a Crankshaft main bearing journal size codes (arrows)

29.10b Crankshaft main bearing housing size codes (arrows)

29.14 Make sure the tab on the shell locates in the slot in the housing (arrow)

29.16 Place a strip of Plastigauge on each bearing journal

the primary drive gear, which, if damaged or worn, is available as an individual component.

6 Refer to Section 28 and examine the main bearings. If they are scored, badly scuffed or appear to have been seized, new bearings must be installed. Always replace the main bearings as a set. If they are badly damaged, check the corresponding crankshaft journal. Evidence of extreme heat, such as discoloration, indicates that lubrication failure has occurred. Be sure to thoroughly check the oil pump and pressure regulator as well as all oil holes and passages before reassembling the engine.

7 The crankshaft journals should be given a close visual examination, paying particular attention where damaged bearings have been discovered. If the journals are scored or pitted in any way a new crankshaft will be required. Undersizes are not available, precluding the option of re-grinding the crankshaft.

8 Place the crankshaft on V-blocks and check the runout at the main bearing journals using a dial gauge. Compare the reading to the maximum specified at the beginning of the Chapter. If the runout exceeds the limit, the crankshaft must be replaced.

9 Measure the thickness of each thrust bearing using a micrometer, and compare the result to the specifications at the beginning of the Chapter (see illustration). If the thickness measured is below the service limit specified, the thrust bearings must be replaced.

Bearing shell selection

10 Replacement bearing shells for the main bearings are supplied on a selected fit basis. Codes stamped in the crankshaft and crankcase are used to identify the correct replacement bearings. The crankshaft main bearing journal size letters, one letter for each journal (either an A, a B or a C), are stamped on the outside of the crankshaft left-hand web (see illustration). The corresponding main bearing housing size letters (either an A or a B), are stamped into the rear of the upper crankcase half (see illustration). The first letter of each set of four is for the outer left-hand journal, the second for the inner left, the third for the inner right and the fourth for the outer right.

11 A range of bearing shells is available. To

select the correct bearing for a particular journal, using the table below cross-refer the main bearing journal size letter (stamped on the crank web) with the main bearing housing size letter (stamped on the crankcase) to determine the colour code of the bearing required. For example, if the journal size is C, and the housing size is B, then the bearing required is Yellow.

	Crankshaft journal code		
	A	B	C
Crankcase housing code			
A	Green	Black	Brown
B	Black	Brown	Yellow

Oil clearance check

Note: *The balancer shaft bearing oil clearance should be checked simultaneously with the crankshaft main bearing oil clearance (see Section 30).*

12 Whether new bearing shells are being fitted or the original ones are being re-used, the main bearing oil clearance should be checked before the engine is reassembled.

13 Clean the backs of the bearing shells and the bearing housings in both crankcase halves.

14 Press the bearing shells into their locations, ensuring that the tab on each shell

engages in the notch in the crankcase (see illustration). Make sure the bearings are fitted in the correct locations and take care not to touch any shell's bearing surface with your fingers.

15 Ensure the shells and crankshaft are clean and dry. Lay the crankshaft in position in the upper crankcase.

16 Cut several lengths of the appropriate size Plastigauge (they should be slightly shorter than the width of the crankshaft journal). Place a strand of Plastigauge on each (cleaned) journal (see illustration). Make sure the crankshaft is not rotated.

17 Carefully install the lower crankcase half on to the upper half. Make sure that the selector forks (if fitted) engage with their respective slots in the transmission gears as the halves are joined. Check that the lower crankcase half is correctly seated. **Note:** *Do not tighten the crankcase bolts if the casing is not correctly seated.* Install the lower crankcase bolts numbers 1 to 12 (see illustration 23.19) in their original locations and tighten them a little at a time in sequence to the torque setting specified at the beginning of the Chapter. When torquing the bolts, be sure to distinguish correctly between the 8 mm bolts and the 6 mm bolts. Make sure that the crankshaft is not rotated as the bolts are tightened.

18 Slacken each bolt in reverse sequence starting at number 12 and working backwards to number 1. Slacken each bolt a little at a time until they are all finger-tight, then remove the bolts. Carefully lift off the lower crankcase half, making sure the Plastigauge is not disturbed.

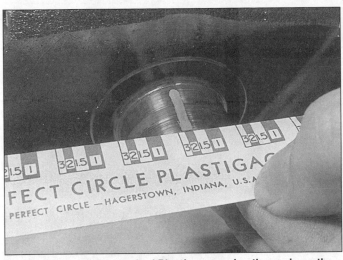

29.19 Measure the crushed Plastigauge using the scale on the pack to obtain the clearance

29.25 Lubricate the shells generously

19 Compare the width of the crushed Plastigauge on each crankshaft journal to the scale printed on the Plastigauge envelope to obtain the main bearing oil clearance **(see illustration)**. Compare the reading to the specifications at the beginning of the Chapter.
20 If the clearance is not within the specified limits, the bearing shells may be the wrong grade (or excessively worn if the original inserts are being reused). Before deciding that different grade shells are needed, make sure that no dirt or oil was trapped between the bearing shells and the crankcase halves when the clearance was measured. If the clearance is excessive, even with new shells (of the correct size), the crankshaft journal is worn and the crankshaft should be replaced.
21 On completion carefully scrape away all traces of the Plastigauge material from the crankshaft journal and bearing shells; use a fingernail or other object which is unlikely to score them.

Installation

22 If removed, install the Woodruff key into its slot in the right-hand end of the crankshaft, then slide the primary drive gear onto the shaft, making sure the slot in the gear locates over the key. Fit the washer with its concave (dished) side facing the gear, then tighten the primary drive gear nut to the torque setting specified at the beginning of the Chapter.
23 If removed, install the connecting rods onto the crankshaft (see Section 31), and engage the camchain onto its sprocket.
24 Clean the backs of the bearing shells and the bearing recesses in both crankcase halves. If new shells are being fitted, ensure that all traces of the protective grease are cleaned off using paraffin (kerosene). Wipe dry the shells and crankcase halves with a lint-free cloth. Make sure all the oil passages and holes are clear, and blow them through with compressed air if it is available.
25 Lubricate each shell, preferable with

molybdenum paste, or if not available then with clean engine oil **(see illustration)**. Press the bearing shells into their locations. Make sure the tab on each shell engages in the notch in the casing **(see illustration 29.14)**. Make sure the bearings are fitted in the correct locations and take care not to touch any shell's bearing surface with your fingers.
26 Rotate the balancer shaft until the dot on its driven gear faces backwards. Lower the crankshaft into position in the upper crankcase, feeding the camchain down

through its tunnel, and engage the crankshaft with the balancer shaft so that the dot on the drive gear on the crankshaft aligns with the dot on the driven gear on the balancer shaft **(see illustrations)**.
27 Install the thrust bearings into their locations on the outside of each inner main bearing housing in the upper crankcase half, making sure that the oil groove faces outside towards the crankshaft web **(see illustrations)**.
28 Reassemble the crankcase halves (see Section 23).

29.26a Install the crankshaft . . .

29.26b . . . making sure the dot on its drive gear aligns with that on the balancer driven gear (arrows)

29.27a Make sure the oil groove (arrow) faces the crank web . . .

29.27b . . . then slide the thrust bearings into position

2

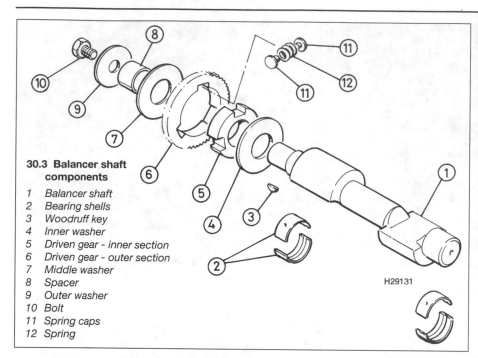

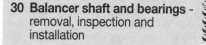

30.3 Balancer shaft components

1 Balancer shaft
2 Bearing shells
3 Woodruff key
4 Inner washer
5 Driven gear - inner section
6 Driven gear - outer section
7 Middle washer
8 Spacer
9 Outer washer
10 Bolt
11 Spring caps
12 Spring

H29131

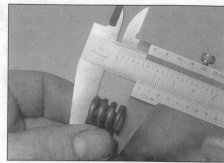

30.8 Measure the free length of each damper spring

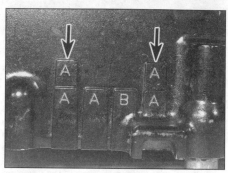

30.9 Balancer shaft bearing housing size letters (arrows)

30 Balancer shaft and bearings - removal, inspection and installation

Note: To remove the balancer shaft the engine must be removed from the frame and the crankcases separated.

Removal

1 Separate the crankcase halves (Section 23).
2 Lift the balancer shaft out of the upper crankcase half, noting how it fits. If it appears stuck, tap it gently using a soft-faced mallet.
3 If required, unscrew the bolt in the right-hand end of the balancer shaft, then remove the outer washer, the spacer and the middle washer **(see illustration)**. Using a flat-bladed screwdriver, carefully lever each damper spring out of its slot in the driven gear, taking care not to lose their end caps. Slide the driven gear outer section off the shaft, noting how it fits. If the driven gear inner section needs to be removed, use a puller. If a puller is not available, carefully lever it off using a pair of tyre levers. Note how it locates over the Woodruff key. If it is loose, remove the Woodruff key from its slot in the shaft, then remove the inner washer.

Inspection

4 Clean the balancer shaft with solvent, using a rifle-cleaning brush to scrub out the oil passages. If available, blow the shaft dry with compressed air, and also blow through the oil passages.
5 Refer to Section 28 and examine the bearings. If they are scored, badly scuffed or appear to have been seized, new bearings must be installed. Always replace the bearings as a set. If they are badly damaged, check the

corresponding balancer shaft journal. Evidence of extreme heat, such as discoloration, indicates that lubrication failure has occurred. Be sure to thoroughly check the oil pump and pressure regulator as well as all oil holes and passages before reassembling the engine.
6 The balancer shaft journals should be given a close visual examination, paying particular attention where damaged bearings have been discovered. If the journals are scored or pitted in any way a new balancer shaft will be required. Undersizes are not available, precluding the option of re-grinding the shaft.
7 Check the balancer shaft driven gear sections for wear or damage. If any of the teeth on the outer section are excessively worn, chipped or broken, the gear must be replaced. Note that the inner section of the gear is not available as an individual component, but comes as part of the balancer shaft assembly.
8 Measure the free length of each damper spring (with the spring caps removed), and compare the result to the specifications at the beginning of the chapter **(see illustration)**. If the free length of any spring is below the service limit specified, replace all three springs.

Bearing shell selection

9 Replacement bearing shells for the balancer shaft bearings are supplied on a selected fit basis. Code numbers stamped on the balancer and crankcase are used to identify the correct replacement bearings. The balancer shaft bearing journal size letters, one letter for each journal (either an A, a B or a C), are stamped on the outside of each web on the balancer shaft; the letter on the left-hand web is for the left-hand journal, the letter on the right-hand web is for the right-hand journal. The corresponding bearing housing

size letters (either an A or a B) are stamped into the rear of the upper crankcase half **(see illustration)**. The left-hand letter is for the left journal, the right-hand letter for the right-hand journal.
10 A range of bearing shells is available. To select the correct bearing for a particular journal, using the table below cross-refer the bearing journal size letter (stamped on the web) with the bearing housing size letter (stamped on the crankcase) to determine the colour code of the bearing required. For example, if the journal size is C, and the housing size is B, then the bearing required is Yellow.

	Balancer shaft journal code		
	A	B	C
Crankcase housing code			
A	Green	Black	Brown
B	Black	Brown	Yellow

Oil clearance check

Note: The crankshaft main bearing oil clearance should be checked simultaneously with the balancer shaft bearing oil clearance (see Section 29).
11 Whether new bearing shells are being fitted or the original ones are being re-used, the bearing oil clearance should be checked before the engine is reassembled. Note that

the shaft must be fully assembled for this procedure as the spacer acts as the bearing journal (see Step 21).

12 Clean the backs of the bearing shells and the bearing housings in both crankcase halves.
13 Press the bearing shells into their locations, ensuring that the tab on each shell engages in the notch in the crankcase **(see illustration 29.14)**. Make sure the bearings are fitted in the correct locations and take care not to touch any shell's bearing surface with your fingers.
14 Ensure the shells and balancer shaft are clean and dry. Lay the shaft in position in the upper crankcase.
15 Cut several lengths of the appropriate size Plastigauge (they should be slightly shorter than the width of the journal). Place a strand of Plastigauge on each (cleaned) journal **(see illustration 29.16)**. Make sure the balancer shaft is not rotated.
16 Carefully install the lower crankcase half on to the upper half. Make sure that the selector forks (if fitted) engage with their respective slots in the transmission gears as the halves are joined. Check that the lower crankcase half is correctly seated. **Note:** *Do not tighten the crankcase bolts if the casing is not correctly seated.* Install the lower crankcase bolts numbers 1 to 12 **(see illustration 23.19)** in their original locations and tighten them a little at a time in sequence to the torque setting specified at the beginning of the Chapter. When torquing the bolts, be sure to distinguish correctly between the 8 mm bolts and the 6 mm bolts. Make sure that the balancer shaft is not rotated as the bolts are tightened.
17 Slacken each bolt in reverse sequence starting at number 12 and working backwards

to number 1. Slacken each bolt a little at a time until they are all finger-tight, then remove the bolts. Carefully lift off the lower crankcase half, making sure the Plastigauge is not disturbed.
18 Compare the width of the crushed Plastigauge on each journal to the scale printed on the Plastigauge envelope to obtain the bearing oil clearance **(see illustration 29.19)**. Compare the reading to the specifications at the beginning of the Chapter.
19 If the clearance is not within the specified limits, the bearing shells may be the wrong grade (or excessively worn if the original inserts are being reused). Before deciding that different grade shells are needed, make sure that no dirt or oil was trapped between the bearing shells and the crankcase halves when the clearance was measured. If the clearance is excessive, even with new shells (of the correct size), the journal is worn and the balancer shaft should be replaced.
20 On completion carefully scrape away all traces of the Plastigauge material from the

shaft journal and bearing shells; use a fingernail or other object which is unlikely to score them.

Installation

21 If removed, slide the inner washer on to the right-hand end of the balancer shaft, then locate the Woodruff key into its slot in the shaft. Drive or press the inner section of the driven gear onto the shaft, making sure that the punch mark faces outwards and that the slot locates correctly over the Woodruff key **(see illustration)**. Slide the outer section of the driven gear over the inner section, making sure that the punch mark on the outer section aligns with that of the inner **(see illustration)**. Fit the caps into the ends of each spring, then compress the springs with pliers and install them into their slots in the driven gear assembly, making sure they are properly seated **(see illustrations)**. Slide the middle washer, the spacer and the outer washer onto the shaft, then install the end bolt and tighten it to the specified torque **(see illustrations)**.

30.21a Make sure the punch mark (A) faces out and the key locates in its slot (B)

30.21b Make sure the punch marks on each section are aligned (arrows)

30.21c Fit the caps into the spring ends . . .

30.21d . . . and fit the springs into their slots

30.21e Install the middle washer . . .

30.21f . . . the spacer . . .

30.21g . . . and the outer washer . . .

30.21h . . . and secure them with the bolt

30.23a Install the shells . . .

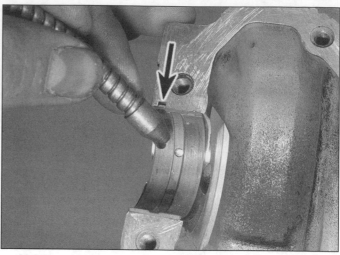

30.23b . . . making sure the tab locates in the notch (arrow), and lubricate them generously

22 Clean the backs of the bearing shells and the bearing recesses in both crankcase halves. If new shells are being fitted, ensure that all traces of the protective grease are cleaned off using paraffin (kerosene). Wipe dry the shells and crankcase halves with a lint-free cloth. Make sure all the oil passages and holes are clear, and blow them through with compressed air if it is available.

23 Press the bearing shells into their locations (see illustration). Make sure the tab on each shell engages in the notch in the casing. Lubricate each shell, preferably with molybdenum paste, or if not available with clean engine oil (see illustration). Make sure the bearings are fitted in the correct locations and take care not to touch any shell's bearing surface with your fingers.

24 Rotate the crankshaft until the dot on its drive gear faces forwards. Lower the balancer shaft into position in the upper crankcase, and engage the balancer shaft with the crankshaft so the dot on the drive gear on the crankshaft aligns with the dot on the driven gear on the balancer shaft (see illustration 29.26b).

25 Reassemble the crankcase halves (see Section 23).

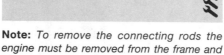

31 Connecting rods - removal, inspection and installation

Note: To remove the connecting rods the engine must be removed from the frame and the crankcases separated.

Removal

1 Remove the crankshaft (see Section 29).
2 Before removing the rods from the crankshaft, measure the side clearance on each rod with a feeler gauge (see illustration). If the clearance on any rod is greater than the service limit listed in this Chapter's Specifications, measure the big-end and crankpin widths as described in Step 7.
3 Using paint or a felt marker pen, mark the relevant cylinder identity on each connecting rod and bearing. Mark across the cap-to-connecting rod join to ensure that the cap is fitted the correct way around on reassembly.
4 Unscrew the big-end cap nuts and separate the connecting rod, cap and both bearing shells from the crankpin (see illustration). Do

not remove the bolts from the connecting rods. Keep the rod, cap, nuts and (if they are to be reused) the bearing shells together in their correct positions to ensure correct installation.

Inspection

5 Check the connecting rods for cracks and other obvious damage.
6 If not already done (see Section 15), apply clean engine oil to the piston pin, insert it into the connecting rod small-end and check for any freeplay between the two (see illustration). Measure the pin external diameter and the small-end bore diameter and compare the measurements to the specifications at the beginning of the Chapter (see illustrations 15.13b and 15.13d). Replace components that are worn beyond the specified limits.
7 If the side clearance measured in Step 2 exceeds the service limit specified, measure the width of the connecting rod big-end and the width of the crankpin (see illustrations). Compare the results to the specifications at the beginning of the Chapter, and replace whichever component exceeds those specifications.

31.2 Measure the connecting rod side clearance using a feeler gauge

31.4 Unscrew the cap nuts and separate the connecting rods from the crankpins

31.6 Slip the piston pin into the rod's small-end and rock it back and forth to check for looseness

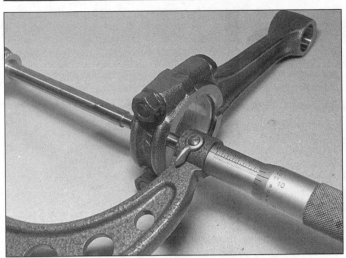

31.7a Measure the width of the connecting rod . . .

31.7b . . . and of the corresponding crankpin

8 Refer to Section 28 and examine the connecting rod bearing shells. If they are scored, badly scuffed or appear to have seized, new shells must be installed. Always replace the shells in the connecting rods as a set. If they are badly damaged, check the corresponding crankpin. Evidence of extreme heat, such as discoloration, indicates that lubrication failure has occurred. Be sure to thoroughly check the oil pump and pressure relief valve as well as all oil holes and passages before reassembling the engine.

9 Have the rods checked for twist and bend by a Suzuki dealer if you are in doubt about their straightness.

Bearing shell selection

10 Replacement bearing shells for the big-end bearings are supplied on a selected fit basis. Codes stamped on the crankshaft and connecting rod are used to identify the correct replacement bearings. The crankpin journal size numbers are stamped on the crankshaft inner left-hand web and will be either a 1, a 2 or a 3 (see illustration). The number coming after the L is for the left-hand big-end, and the number coming before the R is for the right-hand big-end. The connecting rod size code

is marked on the flat face of the connecting rod and cap and will be either a 1 or a 2 (see illustration).

11 A range of bearing shells is available. To select the correct bearing for a particular big-end, using the table below cross-refer the crankpin journal size number (stamped on the web) with the connecting rod size letter (stamped on the rod) to determine the colour code of the bearing required. For example, if the connecting rod size is 2, and the crankpin size is 3, then the bearing required is Yellow.

	Crankpin code		
	1	2	3
Rod code			
1	Green	Black	Brown
2	Black	Brown	Yellow

Oil clearance check

12 Whether new bearing shells are being fitted or the original ones are being re-used,

the connecting rod bearing oil clearance should be checked prior to reassembly.

13 Clean the backs of the bearing shells and the bearing locations in both the connecting rod and cap.

14 Press the bearing shells into their locations, ensuring that the tab on each shell engages the notch in the connecting rod/cap (see illustration). Make sure the bearings are fitted in the correct locations and take care not to touch any shell's bearing surface with your fingers.

15 Cut two lengths of the appropriate size Plastigauge (they should be slightly shorter than the width of the crankpin). Place a strand of Plastigauge on each (cleaned) crankpin journal and fit the (clean) connecting rod assemblies, shells and caps (see illustration 29.16). Make sure the cap is fitted the correct way around so the previously made markings align and tighten the bearing cap nuts in two stages, first to the initial torque setting specified at the beginning of the Chapter, and then to the final torque setting specified, whilst ensuring that the connecting rod does not rotate. Slacken the cap nuts and remove the connecting rod assemblies, again taking great care not to rotate the crankshaft.

2

31.10a Crankpin journal size numbers (arrows)

31.10b Connecting rod size code

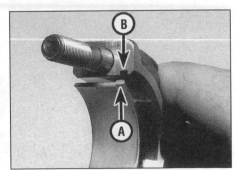

31.14 Make sure the tab (A) locates in the notch (B)

31.20 Tighten the connecting rod cap nuts to the specified torque setting in two stages

16 Compare the width of the crushed Plastigauge on each crankpin to the scale printed on the Plastigauge envelope to obtain the connecting rod bearing oil clearance **(see illustration 29.19)**.

17 If the clearance is not within the limits specified, the bearing shells may be the wrong grade (or excessively worn if the original shells are being reused). Before deciding that different grade shells are needed, make sure that no dirt or oil was trapped between the bearing shells and the connecting rod or cap when the clearance was measured. If the clearance is excessive, even with new shells (of the correct size), the crankpin is worn and the crankshaft should be replaced.

18 On completion carefully scrape away all traces of the Plastigauge material from the crankpin and bearing shells using a fingernail or other object which is unlikely to score the shells.

Installation

19 Install the bearing shells in the connecting rods and caps, aligning the notch in the bearing with the groove in the rod or cap **(see illustration 31.14)**. Lubricate the shells, preferably with molybdenum paste, or if not available with clean engine oil, and assemble the components on the crankpin so that the connecting rod size letter is facing backwards. Tighten the nuts finger-tight at this stage. Check to make sure that all components have been returned to their original locations using the marks made on disassembly.

20 Tighten the bearing cap nuts in two stages, first to the initial torque setting specified at the beginning of the Chapter, and then to the final torque setting specified **(see illustration)**.

21 Check that the rods rotate smoothly and freely on the crankpin. If there are any signs of roughness or tightness, remove the rods and re-check the bearing clearance.

22 Install the crankshaft (see Section 29).

32 Initial start-up after overhaul

1 Make sure the engine oil level is correct (see *Daily (pre-ride) checks*).

2 Pull the plug caps off the spark plugs and insert a spare spark plug into each cap. Position the spare plugs so that their bodies are earthed (grounded) against the engine. Turn on the ignition switch and crank the engine over with the starter until the oil pressure indicator light goes off (which indicates that oil pressure exists). Turn off the ignition. Remove the spare spark plugs and reconnect the plug caps.

3 Make sure there is fuel in the tank, then turn the remote fuel tap to the ON position and operate the choke.

4 Start the engine and allow it to run at a moderately fast idle until it reaches operating temperature.

Caution: If the oil pressure indicator light doesn't go off, or it comes on while the engine is running, stop the engine immediately.

5 Check carefully for oil leaks and make sure the transmission and controls, especially the brakes, function properly before road testing the machine. Refer to Section 33 for the recommended running-in procedure.

6 Upon completion of the road test, and after the engine has cooled down completely, recheck the valve clearances (see Chapter 1) and check the engine oil level (see *Daily (pre-ride) checks*).

33 Recommended running-in procedure

1 Treat the machine gently for the first few miles to make sure oil has circulated throughout the engine and any new parts installed have started to seat.

2 Even greater care is necessary if the engine has been rebored or a new crankshaft has been installed. In the case of a rebore, the bike will have to be run in as when new. This means greater use of the transmission and a restraining hand on the throttle until at least 500 miles (800 km) have been covered. There's no point in keeping to any set speed limit - the main idea is to keep from labouring the engine and to gradually increase performance up to the 500 mile (800 km) mark. These recommendations can be lessened to an extent when only a new crankshaft is installed. Experience is the best guide, since it's easy to tell when an engine is running freely. The table below shows maximum engine speed limitations, which Suzuki provide for new motorcycles, can be used as a guide.

3 If a lubrication failure is suspected, stop the engine immediately and try to find the cause. If an engine is run without oil, even for a short period of time, severe damage will occur.

Up to 500 miles (800 km)	5000 rpm max	Vary throttle position/speed
500 to 1000 miles (800 to 1600 km)	8000 rpm max	Vary throttle position/speed. Use full throttle for short bursts
Over 1000 miles (1600 km)	10 000 rpm max	Do not exceed tachometer red line

Chapter 3
Fuel and exhaust systems

Contents

Degrees of difficulty

Easy, suitable for novice with little experience	Fairly easy, suitable for beginner with some experience	Fairly difficult, suitable for competent DIY mechanic	Difficult, suitable for experienced DIY mechanic	Very difficult, suitable for expert DIY or professional

Specifications

Fuel

Grade	Unleaded, minimum 91 RON (Research Octane Number)
Fuel tank capacity	
EK to EY models (California)	15 litres
EK to EY models (all others)	17 litres
K1 models onward (California)	19 litres
K1 models onward (all others)	20 litres
Reserve capacity	
EK to EY models	3.5 litres
K1 models onward	4.3 litres

Carburettors

Type	
EK to EY models	Mikuni BST33SS
K1 models onward	Mikuni BSR34SS

Carburettor adjustments

Pilot screw setting	
UK EK to EP models	$1 \frac{1}{4}$ turns out
UK ER and ES models	$1 \frac{7}{8}$ turns out
UK ET to EY models	2 turns out
UK K1 models onward	$2 \frac{3}{4}$ turns out
all US models	pre-set
Float height	
EK to EY models	14.6 ± 1.0 mm
K1 models onward	13.0 ± 1.0 mm
Idle speed	see Chapter 1

3

Jet sizes

Pilot jet
    UK EK to EY models 40
    US EK to EY models 37.7
    K1 models onward 17.5
Pilot air jet
    UK EK to EP models, and US 49-state models .... 1.3 mm
    UK ER to EY models .... 1.2 mm
    California models .... 1.35 mm
    K1 models onward 165
Needle jet
    UK EK to EY models 0-2
    US EK to EY models 0-3
    K1 models onward P-5M
Jet needle
    UK EK to EY models .... 5DH9 (clip position – 3rd groove from top)
    US EK to EY models 5DH8
    UK K1 models onward .... 5DH41 (clip position – 2nd groove from top)
    US K1 models onward 5DH42
Main jet
    UK EK to EP models 120
    UK ER and ES models
        Left-hand carburettor 125
        Right-hand carburettor 122.5
    UK ET to EY models and K1 models onward 115
    US models EK to EY 122.5
    US K1 models onward 127.5
Main air jet .... 0.5 mm
Starter jet 42.5

Torque settings

Exhaust system
    Downpipe bolts .... 9 to 12 Nm
    Silencer bolt .... 18 to 28 Nm

---

1 General information and precautions

General information

The fuel system consists of the fuel tank, the main fuel cock and filter, the remote fuel tap, the carburettors, fuel hoses and control cables.

The main fuel cock mounted on the underside of the fuel tank incorporates a filter which sits inside the tank. The remote fuel tap is of the vacuum type.

The carburettors used on all models are Mikuni CV types. For cold starting, a choke lever mounted on the left-handlebar and connected by a cable, controls an enrichment circuit in the carburettor.

Air is drawn into the carburettors via an air filter which is housed under the fuel tank.

The exhaust system is a one-piece two-into-one design.

Many of the fuel system service procedures are considered routine maintenance items and for that reason are included in Chapter 1.

Precautions

 Warning: Petrol (gasoline) is extremely flammable, so take extra precautions when you work on any part of the fuel system. Don't smoke or allow open flames or bare light bulbs near the work area, and don't work in a garage where a natural gas-type appliance is present. If you spill any fuel on your skin, rinse it off immediately with soap and water. When you perform any kind of work on the fuel system, wear safety glasses and have a fire extinguisher suitable for a class B type fire (flammable liquids) on hand.

Always perform service procedures in a well-ventilated area to prevent a build-up of fumes.

Never work in a building containing a gas appliance with a pilot light, or any other form of naked flame. Ensure that there are no naked light bulbs or any sources of flame or sparks nearby.

Do not smoke (or allow anyone else to smoke) while in the vicinity of petrol (gasoline) or of components containing it. Remember the possible presence of vapour from these sources and move well clear before smoking.

Check all electrical equipment belonging to the house, garage or workshop where work is being undertaken (see the Safety first! section of this manual). Remember that certain electrical appliances such as drills, cutters etc. create sparks in the normal course of operation and must not be used near petrol (gasoline) or any component containing it.

Again, remember the possible presence of fumes before using electrical equipment.

Always mop up any spilt fuel and safely dispose of the rag used.

Any stored fuel that is drained off during servicing work must be kept in sealed containers that are suitable for holding petrol (gasoline), and clearly marked as such; the containers themselves should be kept in a safe place. Note that this last point applies equally to the fuel tank if it is removed from the machine; also remember to keep its cap closed at all times.

Read the Safety first! section of this manual carefully before starting work.

Owners of machines used in the US, particularly California, should note that their machines must comply at all times with Federal or State legislation governing the permissible levels of noise and of pollutants such as unburnt hydrocarbons, carbon monoxide etc. that can be emitted by those machines. All vehicles offered for sale must comply with legislation in force at the date of manufacture and must not subsequently be altered in any way which will affect their emission of noise or of pollutants.

In practice, this means that adjustments may not be made to any part of the fuel, ignition or exhaust systems by anyone who is not authorised or mechanically qualified to do so, or who does not have the tools, equipment and data necessary to properly carry out the task. Also if any part of these systems is to be replaced it must be replaced with only genuine Suzuki components or by components which are approved under the relevant legislation. The machine must never be used with any part of these systems removed, modified or damaged.

2 Fuel tank, main fuel cock and remote fuel tap - removal and installation

 Warning: Refer to the precautions given in Section 1 before starting work.

Fuel tank

Removal

1 Make sure the fuel tap is turned to the ON position and the fuel cap is secure.
2 Remove the seat and the side panels (see Chapter 7), then disconnect the battery, negative (-ve) terminal first.
3 Unscrew the bolt securing each side of the tank to the frame (see illustration).
4 Raise the tank at the rear and, using a flat-bladed screwdriver inserted from the right-hand side, turn the tap on the back of the main fuel cock to the OFF position (see illustration). Release the clamps securing the fuel hoses to

2.3 A single bolt (arrow) secures each side of the tank to the frame

their unions on the main fuel cock and detach the hoses, noting their location (see illustration). Also detach the water drain hose from its union on the underside of the tank.
5 Remove the tank by carefully drawing it back and away from the bike. Take care not to lose the mounting rubbers from the front of the tank and from between the sides of the tank and the frame, noting how they fit.
6 Inspect the tank mounting rubbers for signs of damage or deterioration and replace them if necessary. Also inspect the rubbers on the fuel tank mounting bracket. If necessary, unscrew the two bolts securing the bracket to the tank and remove the bracket, noting how the rubbers and the spacer fit (see illustration). Replace the rubbers if necessary.

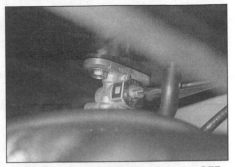

2.4a Turn the main fuel cock to the OFF position using a flat-bladed screwdriver

Installation

7 If removed, install the tank mounting bracket, making sure the rubbers and spacers are correctly positioned, and tighten the bracket bolts securely. Check that the front and side tank rubbers are fitted, then carefully lower the fuel tank into position, making sure the rubbers remain in place and that the bracket at the front locates correctly around the front rubber (see illustration).
8 With the tank raised at the rear, attach the water drain hose and the fuel hoses to their unions (see illustrations). Make sure that the fuel hose that is attached to the front (left-hand) union on the remote fuel tap is attached to the upper (rear) union on the main

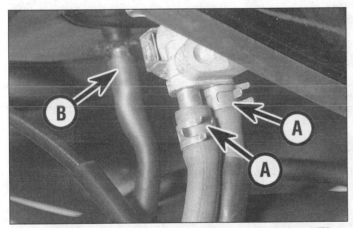

2.4b Detach the fuel hoses (A) and the water drain hose (B)

2.6 The tank bracket is secured to the tank by two bolts (arrows)

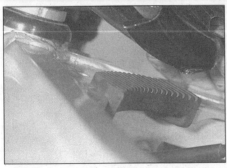

2.7 Make sure the tank locates correctly at the front

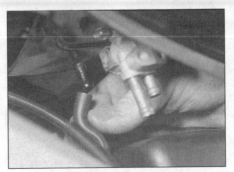

2.8a Attach the water drain hose . . .

2.8b . . . and the fuel hoses

3

2.9 Secure the tank with its bolts

2.13a The fuel cock is secured to the tank by two screws (arrows)

2.13b Clean the filter and check it for holes

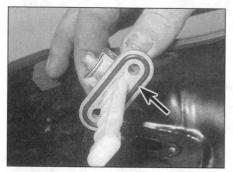

2.13c Check the condition of the O-ring (arrow) and replace it if necessary

2.14 Install the fuel cock with its tap (arrow) facing in

fuel cock. Secure the fuel hoses with their clamps. Check that the fuel hoses are secure on their unions on the remote fuel tap and turn the main fuel cock to the ON position. Lower the tank and check that it is properly seated and is not pinching any control cables or wires. Check that there is no sign of fuel leakage.

9 Install the tank mounting bolts and tighten them securely **(see illustration)**.

10 Connect the battery, fitting the negative (-ve) terminal last. With the remote fuel tap in the ON or RES position start the engine and check that there is no sign of fuel leakage, then shut if off.

11 Install the seat and the side panels (see Chapter 7).

Main fuel cock

Removal

12 Remove the fuel tank (see above).

13 The main fuel cock should not be removed unnecessarily from the tank to prevent the possibility of damaging the O-ring or the filter, and should not be dismantled. If the main fuel cock is being removed, connect drain hoses to the fuel cock unions and insert their ends in a container suitable and large enough for storing the petrol (gasoline). Turn the fuel cock tap to the ON position **(see illustration 2.4a)**, and allow the tank to fully drain. Unscrew the two screws securing the main fuel cock to the underside of the tank and withdraw it from the tank **(see illustration)**. Clean the gauze filter to remove all traces of dirt and fuel sediment **(see illustration)**. Check the gauze for holes. If any are found, a new filter should be fitted. Check the condition of the O-ring and replace it if it is in any way damaged or deteriorated **(see illustration)**.

Installation

14 If removed, install the main fuel cock into

the tank so that the tap faces in, using a new O-ring if necessary, and tighten its bolts securely **(see illustration)**. Check that the fuel cock is in the OFF position.

15 Install the fuel tank (see above).

Remote fuel tap

Removal

16 Make sure the fuel tap is turned to the ON position.

17 Remove the seat and the side panels (see Chapter 7), then disconnect the battery, negative (-ve) terminal first.

18 Unscrew the bolt securing each side of the rear of the tank to the frame **(see illustration 2.3)**.

19 Raise the tank at the rear and, using a flat-bladed screwdriver inserted from the right-hand side, turn the tap on the back of the main fuel cock mounted on the underside of the left-hand side of the tank to the OFF position **(see illustration 2.4a)**.

20 Unscrew the bolt or bolts (K1 models onward) securing the tap to the frame and displace the tap **(see illustrations)**.

21 Bearing in mind that a small amount of residual fuel will flow from the fuel hoses, release the clamps securing the hoses to the unions on the tap and detach the hoses, noting their location **(see illustrations 2.20a and b)**. Detach the carburettor vacuum hose from the union on the back of the tap.

22 Replacement parts are not available for the fuel tap; if the tap leaks fuel, it must be renewed. Access can be gained to the diaphragm by removing the cover on the back

2.20a Fuel tap on EK to EY models . . .

2.20b . . . and K1 models onward

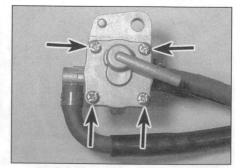

2.22a Tap diaphragm cover retaining screws – EK to EY models

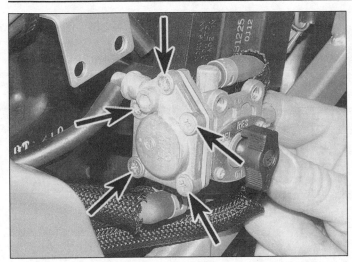

2.22b Tap diaphragm cover retaining screws – K1 models onward

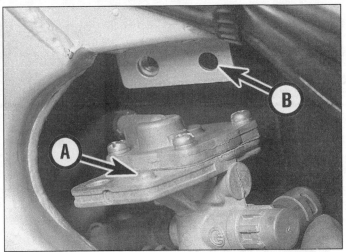

2.24 The lug (A) locates in the hole (B) – EK to EY models

or the side (K1 models onward) of the tap body (see illustrations). Although the diaphragm is not available separately from the tap, it can be examined for holes or splits to confirm faulty tap operation.

Installation

23 Attach the carburettor vacuum hose to the union on the back of the tap body. On EK to EY models, attach the carburettor supply hose to the inner union on the forward side of the tap and secure it with the clamp. On K1 models onward, attach the carburettor supply hose to the union on the bottom of the tap and secure it with its clamp. Attach the fuel hoses to their unions and secure them with the clamps. On EK to EY models, ensure the fuel hose attached to the rear union on the main fuel cock is attached to the outer union on the forwards side of the tap. On K1 models onward, ensure the fuel hose attached to the rear union on the main fuel cock is attached to the top (RES) union on the remote tap.
24 Install the tap onto the frame bracket. On EK to EY models, ensure the lug on the back of the tap locates in the hole in the bracket (see illustration). Tighten the mounting bolt(s) securely.
25 Check that the fuel hoses are secure on their unions on the fuel tap, and turn the main fuel cock to the ON position (see illustration 2.4a). Lower the tank and check that it is properly seated and is not pinching any control cables or wires. Turn the tap to the PRI position and check that there is no sign of fuel leakage.
26 Install the tank mounting bolts and tighten them securely (see illustration 2.9).
27 Connect the battery, fitting the negative (-ve) terminal last. Turn the tap to the ON or RES position. Start the engine and check that there is no sign of fuel leakage, then shut if off.
28 Install the seat and the side panels (see Chapter 8).

3 Fuel tank - cleaning and repair

1 All repairs to the fuel tank should be carried out by a professional who has experience in this critical and potentially dangerous work. Even after cleaning and flushing of the fuel system, explosive fumes can remain and ignite during repair of the tank.
2 If the fuel tank is removed from the bike, it should not be placed in an area where sparks or open flames could ignite the fumes coming out of the tank. Be especially careful inside garages where a natural gas-type appliance is located, because the pilot light could cause an explosion.

4 Idle fuel/air mixture adjustment - general information

1 Due to the increased emphasis on controlling motorcycle exhaust emissions, certain governmental regulations have been formulated which directly affect the carburation of this machine. In order to comply with the regulations, the carburettors on US models are sealed so they can't be tampered with. The pilot screws on other models are accessible, but the use of an exhaust gas analyser is the only accurate way to adjust the idle fuel/air mixture and be sure the machine doesn't exceed the emissions regulations.
2 The pilot screws are set to their correct position by the manufacturer and should not be adjusted unless it is necessary to do so for a carburettor overhaul. If the screws are adjusted they should be reset to the settings specified at the beginning of the Chapter.
3 If the engine runs extremely rough at idle or continually stalls, and if a carburettor overhaul does not cure the problem, take the motorcycle

to a Suzuki dealer equipped with an exhaust gas analyser. They will be able to properly adjust the idle fuel/air mixture to achieve a smooth idle and restore low speed performance.

5 Carburettor overhaul - general information

1 Poor engine performance, hesitation, hard starting, stalling, flooding and backfiring are all signs that major carburettor maintenance may be required.
2 Keep in mind that many so-called carburettor problems are really not carburettor problems at all, but mechanical problems within the engine or ignition system malfunctions. Try to establish for certain that the carburettors are in need of maintenance before beginning a major overhaul.
3 Check the fuel filter inside the tank, the fuel hoses, the intake adapter clamps, the air filter, the ignition system, the spark plugs and carburettor synchronisation before assuming that a carburettor overhaul is required.
4 Most carburettor problems are caused by dirt particles, varnish and other deposits which build up in and block the fuel and air passages. Also, in time, gaskets and O-rings shrink or deteriorate and cause fuel and air leaks which lead to poor performance.
5 When overhauling the carburettors, disassemble them completely and clean the parts thoroughly with a carburettor cleaning solvent and dry them with filtered, unlubricated compressed air. Blow through the fuel and air passages with compressed air to force out any dirt that may have been loosened but not removed by the solvent. Once the cleaning process is complete, reassemble the carburettor using new gaskets and O-rings.
6 Before disassembling the carburettors, make sure you have all the necessary O-rings and seals (either obtained individually or as a rebuild

3

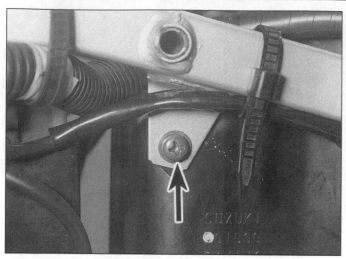

6.2a Remove the screw (arrow) on each side of the air filter housing . . .

6.2b . . . and detach the breather hose from its union

kit), some carburettor cleaner, a supply of clean rags, some means of blowing out the carburettor passages and a clean place to work. It is recommended that only one carburettor be overhauled at a time to avoid mixing up parts.

6 Carburettors - removal and installation

 Warning: Refer to the precautions given in Section 1 before starting work.

Removal

1 Remove the fuel tank (see Section 2).
2 Unscrew the two screws at the back of the air filter housing, one on each side, which secure the housing to the frame **(see illustration)**. Also release the clamp securing the breather hose to the front of the housing and detach the hose from its union **(see illustration)**.
3 Make sure the remote fuel tap is switched to the ON position, then release the clamp securing the carburettor supply hose to its union in between the carburettor float chambers and detach the hose **(see illustration)**. On K1 models onward, release the clamp securing the carburettor vacuum hose and detach the hose.
4 Detach the throttle cable(s) from the carburettors (see Section 10).
5 Detach the choke cable from the carburettors (see Section 11).
6 Slacken the clamps securing the air filter housing rubbers to the carburettor air intakes. Manoeuvre the air filter housing backwards so that the rubbers detach from the carburettor intakes and provide clearance for the carburettors to be removed.
7 Slacken the clamps securing the carburettors to the cylinder head intake adapters and ease the carburettors off the

adapters, noting how they fit **(see illustrations)**. Lift the carburettors up out of the top of the frame, noting the routing of the various hoses. **Note:** *Keep the carburettors upright to prevent fuel spillage from the float chambers and the possibility of the piston diaphragms being damaged.*
8 Place a suitable container below the float chambers then slacken the drain screws and drain all the fuel from the carburettors **(see illustration)**. Once all the fuel has been drained, tighten the drain screws securely.
9 If necessary, unscrew the bolts securing the intake adapters to the cylinder head and remove the adapters and O-rings, noting how

6.3 Detach fuel hose from union between carburettor float chambers (arrow)

6.7b . . . and remove the carburettors

they fit. Discard the O-rings as new ones must be used.

Installation

10 Installation is the reverse of removal, noting the following.

a) *Check for cracks or splits in the cylinder head intake adapters and the air filter housing rubbers, and replace them if necessary.*
b) *Make sure that the air filter housing and the cylinder head intake adapters are fully engaged with the carburettors and that their retaining clamps are securely tightened.*

6.7a Slacken the clamp screws . . .

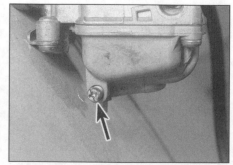

6.8 Carburettor drain screw (arrow)

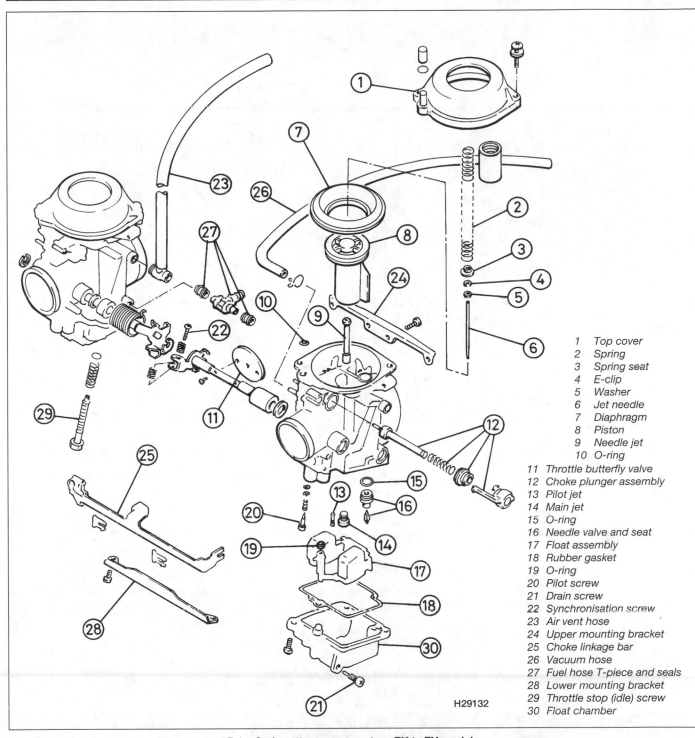

1   Top cover
2   Spring
3   Spring seat
4   E-clip
5   Washer
6   Jet needle
7   Diaphragm
8   Piston
9   Needle jet
10 O-ring
11 Throttle butterfly valve
12 Choke plunger assembly
13 Pilot jet
14 Main jet
15 O-ring
16 Needle valve and seat
17 Float assembly
18 Rubber gasket
19 O-ring
20 Pilot screw
21 Drain screw
22 Synchronisation screw
23 Air vent hose
24 Upper mounting bracket
25 Choke linkage bar
26 Vacuum hose
27 Fuel hose T-piece and seals
28 Lower mounting bracket
29 Throttle stop (idle) screw
30 Float chamber

H29132

7.1a Carburettor components – EK to EY models

3

c) Make sure all hoses are correctly routed and secured and not trapped or kinked.

d) Check the operation of the choke and throttle cables and adjust them as necessary (see Chapter 1).

e) Check idle speed and carburettor synchronisation and adjust as necessary (see Chapter 1).

7 Carburettors - disassembly, cleaning and inspection

⚠ **Warning: Refer to the precautions given in Section 1 before starting work.**

Disassembly

1 Remove the carburettors from the machine as described in the previous Section. **Note:** *Do not separate the carburettors unless absolutely necessary; each carburettor can be dismantled sufficiently for all normal cleaning and adjustments while in place on the mounting brackets. Dismantle the carburettors*

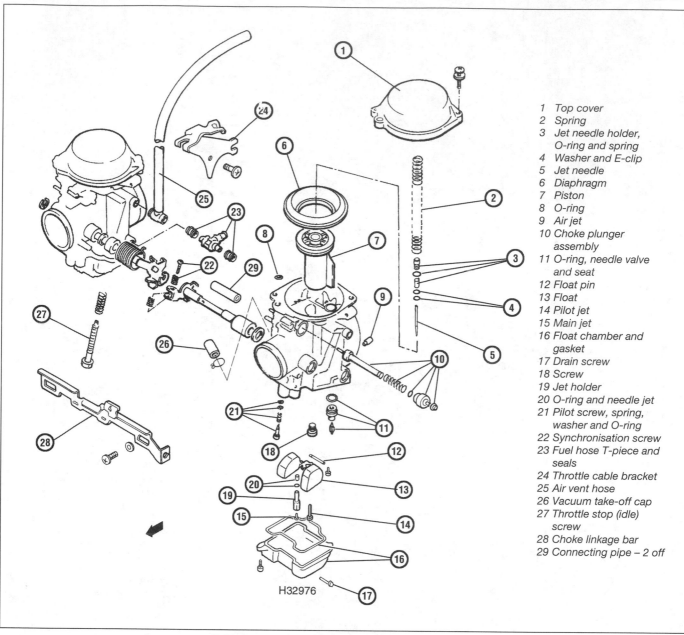

1 Top cover
2 Spring
3 Jet needle holder,
  O-ring and spring
4 Washer and E-clip
5 Jet needle
6 Diaphragm
7 Piston
8 O-ring
9 Air jet
10 Choke plunger
   assembly
11 O-ring, needle valve
   and seat
12 Float pin
13 Float
14 Pilot jet
15 Main jet
16 Float chamber and
   gasket
17 Drain screw
18 Screw
19 Jet holder
20 O-ring and needle jet
21 Pilot screw, spring,
   washer and O-ring
22 Synchronisation screw
23 Fuel hose T-piece and
   seals
24 Throttle cable bracket
25 Air vent hose
26 Vacuum take-off cap
27 Throttle stop (idle)
   screw
28 Choke linkage bar
29 Connecting pipe – 2 off

H32976

7.1b Carburettor components – K1 models onward

7.2 The carburettor top cover is secured by two screws (arrows)

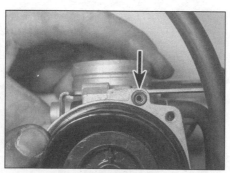

7.3 Remove the carburettor body O-ring

separately to avoid interchanging parts **(see illustration)**.

2 Unscrew and remove the top cover retaining screws **(see illustration)**. Lift off the cover and remove the spring from inside the piston.

3 Remove the O-ring from the top edge of the carburettor body and discard it as a new one must be fitted **(see illustration)**.

4 Carefully peel the diaphragm away from its sealing groove in the carburettor and withdraw the diaphragm and piston assembly **(see illustration)**.

Caution: Do not use a sharp instrument to displace the diaphragm as it is easily damaged.

7.4 Withdraw the diaphragm and piston assembly from the carburettor

7.5a Withdraw the jet needle assembly – EK to EY models

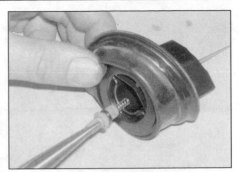

7.5b Withdraw the jet needle holder – K1 models onward

5 On EK to EY models, push the jet needle up from the bottom of the piston and withdraw it from the top (see illustration). Take care not to lose the spring seat, E-clip and washer. If they are removed from the needle, note which notch the E-clip is fitted in. On K1 models onward, withdraw the jet needle holder from inside the piston using a pair of thin-nosed pliers – it is a press fit, held by an O-ring (see illustration). Note the spring fitted into the bottom of the holder. Push the jet needle up from the bottom of the piston and withdraw it from the top, noting the washer on the top of the needle. Note which notch on the needle the E-clip is fitted in.
6 Unscrew the screws securing the float chamber to the base of the carburettor and

remove the float chamber, noting how it fits (see illustration). Remove the rubber gasket and discard it as a new one must be used.
7 On EK to EY models, carefully prise the float assembly out of the carburettor body, noting how it fits (see illustration). Remove the O-ring and discard it as a new one must be used. On K1 models onward, withdraw the float pin using a pair of thin-nosed pliers and lift out the float assembly. Unhook the needle valve from the tab on the float, noting how it fits (see illustration). Remove the float needle valve seat and its O-ring (see illustration). Discard the O-ring as a new one must be used.
8 Unscrew and remove the main jet (see illustration).

9 With the main jet removed the piston guide and needle jet can now be withdrawn through the top of the carburettor (see illustration). Note which way round the guide fits into the carburettor body. Discard the O-ring on the bottom of the guide as a new one must be used. Push the needle jet up from the bottom and remove it from the guide
10 Unscrew and remove the pilot jet (see illustration 7.8).
11 On UK models, the pilot screw can be removed from the carburettor, but note that its setting will be disturbed (see Haynes Hint). Unscrew and remove the pilot screw along with its spring, washer and O-ring (see illustration). Discard the O-ring as a new one must be used.

7.6 The float chamber is secured by two screws (arrows)

7.7a Lift the float assembly out of its socket (arrow) – EK to EY models . . .

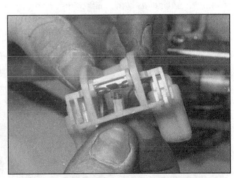

7.7b . . . and remove the needle valve from the float

7.7c Withdraw the needle valve seat (arrow)

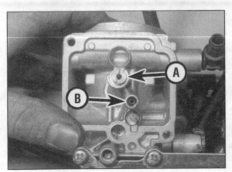

7.8 Main jet (A), pilot jet (B)

7.9 Withdraw the piston guide and needle jet

3

7.11 Note the setting of the pilot screw (arrow) before removing it

7.12a On EK to EY models, slide the clips (arrows) out to release the choke linkage bar . . .

7.12b . . . and compress the clip ends (arrows) to release the choke plunger assembly

HAYNES HiNT

To record the pilot screw's current setting, turn the screw in until it seats lightly, counting the number of turns necessary to achieve this, then fully unscrew it. On installation, the screw is simply backed out the number of turns you've recorded.

12 On EK to EY models, push out the clips securing the choke linkage bar to the carburettors, then remove the choke linkage bar from the plungers, noting how it fits **(see illustration)**. Compress the clip ends securing the choke plunger to the carburettor body and withdraw the plunger, noting how it fits **(see illustration)**. On K1 models onward, undo the two screws retaining the choke linkage bar and remove the screws and washers. Detach the linkage bar from the plungers, noting how it fits. Unscrew the choke plunger nut and withdraw the plunger assembly from the carburettor body. Take care not to lose the spring and O-ring when removing the nut.

Cleaning

Caution: Use only a petroleum-based solvent for carburettor cleaning. Don't use caustic cleaners.

13 Submerge the metal components in the solvent for approximately thirty minutes (or longer, if the directions recommend it).
14 After the carburettor has soaked long enough for the cleaner to loosen and dissolve most of the varnish and other deposits, use a nylon-bristled brush to remove the stubborn deposits. Rinse it again, then dry it with compressed air.
15 Use a jet of compressed air to blow out all of the fuel and air passages in the main and upper body **(see illustration)**.
Caution: Never clean the jets or passages with a piece of wire or a drill bit, as they will be enlarged, causing the fuel and air metering rates to be upset.

Inspection

16 Check the operation of the choke plunger. If it doesn't move smoothly, inspect the needle on the end of the choke plunger, the spring and the plunger linkage bar. Replace any component that is worn, damaged or bent **(see illustration)**.
17 If removed from the carburettor, check the tapered portion of the pilot screw, the spring and O-ring for wear or damage. Replace them if necessary.
18 Check the carburettor body, float chamber and top cover for cracks, distorted

sealing surfaces and other damage. If any defects are found, replace the faulty component, although replacement of the entire carburettor will probably be necessary (check with a Suzuki dealer on the availability of separate components).
19 Check the piston diaphragm for splits, holes and general deterioration.

HAYNES HiNT

Holding the diaphragm up to a light will help reveal holes.

20 Insert the piston guide and piston in the carburettor body and check that the piston moves up-and-down smoothly. Check the surface of the piston for wear. If it's worn excessively or doesn't move smoothly in the guide, replace the components as necessary.
21 Check the jet needle for straightness by rolling it on a flat surface such as a piece of glass (having first removed the spring seat, E-clip and washer, noting which notch the E-clip fits into). Replace it if it's bent or if the tip is worn.
22 Check the tip of the float needle valve and the valve seat. If either has grooves or scratches in it, or is in any way worn, they must be replaced as a set.

7.15 Do not forget the air passages in the inlets (arrows). The jet (A) can be removed if required

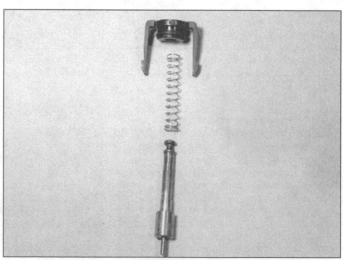

7.16 Choke plunger assembly – EK to EY models

23 Operate the throttle shaft to make sure the throttle butterfly valve opens and closes smoothly. If it doesn't, cleaning the throttle linkage may help. Dismantle the throttle shaft assembly for further inspection if necessary **(see illustration 7.1)**.

24 Check the floats for damage. This will usually be apparent by the presence of fuel inside one of the floats. If the floats are damaged, they must be replaced.

8 Carburettors - separation and joining

 Warning: Refer to the precautions given in Section 1 before proceeding.

Separation

1 The carburettors do not need to be separated for normal overhaul. If you need to separate them (to replace a carburettor body, for example), refer to the following procedure.

2 Remove the carburettors from the machine (see Section 6). Mark the body of each carburettor with its cylinder location to ensure that it is positioned correctly on reassembly.

3 Make a note of how the throttle return springs, linkage assembly and carburettor synchronisation springs are arranged to ensure that they are fitted correctly on reassembly **(see illustration)**. Also note the arrangement of the various hoses and their unions.

4 Remove the choke linkage bar as described in Section 7, Step 12. On EK to EY models, remove the screws securing the carburettors to the two mounting brackets and remove the brackets **(see illustrations)**.

5 Carefully separate the carburettors. Retrieve the synchronisation springs and note the fitting of the fuel hose T-piece and its seals, and the air vent hose T-piece as they are separated.

Joining

6 Assembly is the reverse of the disassembly procedure, noting the following.
  a) Make sure the fuel hose T-piece and seals and the air vent hose T-piece are correctly and securely inserted into the carburettors.
  b) Install the synchronisation spring after the carburettors are joined together. Make sure it is correctly and squarely seated **(see illustration 8.3)**.
  c) On EK to EY models, apply a suitable non-permanent thread locking compound to the carburettor bracket screws and tighten them securely.
  d) Check the operation of both the choke and throttle linkages ensuring that both operate smoothly and return quickly under spring pressure before installing the carburettors on the machine.
  e) Install the carburettors (see Section 6) and check carburettor synchronisation and idle speed (see Chapter 1).

9 Carburettors - reassembly and float height check

 Warning: Refer to the precautions given in Section 1 before proceeding

Note: *Before disassembling the carburettors, make sure you have all the necessary O-rings and seals (either obtained individually or as a rebuild kit), some carburettor cleaner, a supply of clean rags, some means of blowing out the carburettor passages and a clean place to work. It is recommended that only one carburettor be overhauled at a time to avoid mixing up parts. Take care not to overtighten the carburettor jets and screws, as they are easily damaged.*

1 Install the choke plunger assembly into the carburettor body. On EK to EY models, make sure the clips locate correctly in their holes **(see illustration 7.12b)**. Fit the choke linkage bar onto the plungers, making sure the slots in the arms locate correctly behind the nipple on the end of each choke plunger **(see illustration)**. On EK to EY models, secure the linkage bar in place with the clips, making sure their ends locate over the ends of the slide guide **(see illustration)**. On K1 models onward, secure the linkage bar with the washers and screws.

2 Install the pilot screw (if removed) along with its spring, washer and O-ring, turning it in until it seats lightly **(see illustration 7.11)**.

8.3 Note the arrangement of the throttle linkage assembly and various springs before disassembly

8.4a Unscrew the upper mounting bracket screws (arrows) . . .

8.4b . . . and the lower mounting bracket screws (arrows)

3

9.1a Make sure linkage bar slots locate correctly behind the choke plunger nipples

9.1b Secure the bar with the clips

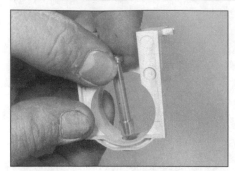

9.3a Install the needle jet into the guide

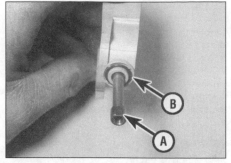

9.3b . . . noting the flat (A) which must align with the corresponding flat in the carburettor. Fit a new O-ring (B)

9.3c The main jet screws into the bottom of the needle jet

9.4 Install the pilot jet

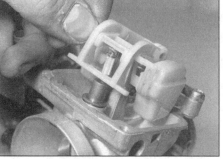

9.5 Install the needle valve seat using a new O-ring

Install the guide assembly into the carburettor body, making sure it is the right way round and properly seated (see illustration 7.9). Screw the main jet into the end of the needle jet (see illustration).

4 Install the pilot jet (see illustration).

5 Install a new O-ring around the float needle valve seat and install the seat into the carburettor body (see illustration).

6 Hook the float needle valve onto the tab on the float assembly (see illustration 7.7b). On EK to EY models, fit a new O-ring to the base of the float assembly, then carefully press the assembly into the carburettor body, making sure that the needle valve enters the seat and that the tab locates correctly in its cut-out (see illustrations). On K1 models onward, position the float assembly in the carburettor, making sure the needle valve locates in the seat, then install the pivot pin.

Now, turn the screw out the number of turns previously recorded, or as specified at the beginning of the Chapter.

3 Fit the jet needle into the piston guide,

noting the flat on the bottom of the jet which must align with the corresponding flat in the carburettor (see illustration). Fit a new O-ring onto the base of the guide (see illustration).

7 To check the float height, hold the carburettor so the float hangs down, then tilt it back until the needle valve is just seated, but not so far that the needle's spring-loaded tip is compressed. Measure the height of the bottom of the float above the gasket face (with the gasket removed) with an accurate ruler (see illustration). The correct setting should be as given in the Specifications at the beginning of the Chapter. If it is incorrect, adjust the float height by carefully bending the float tab a little at a time until the correct height is obtained. Repeat the procedure on the other carburettor.

8 With the float height checked, fit a new gasket to the float chamber, making sure it is

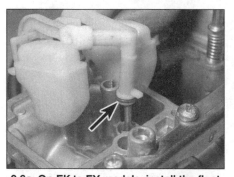

9.6a On EK to EY models, install the float assembly using a new O-ring (arrow) . . .

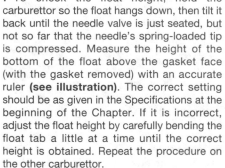

9.6b . . . making sure the needle valve enters its seat . . .

9.6c . . . and the tab (arrow) locates in its cutout

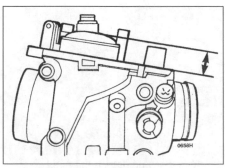

9.7 Measure the height of the float above the gasket surface

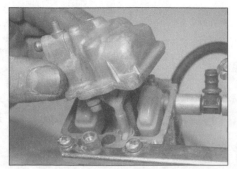

9.8 Install the float chamber using a new gasket

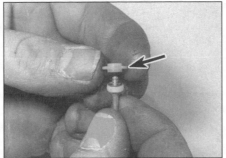

9.9a Make sure the E-clip (A) is in its correct groove, then fit the washer (B) . . .

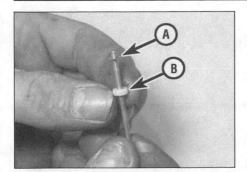

9.9b . . . and the spring seat (arrow)

9.11a Install the spring . . .

9.11b . . . and the top cover

seated properly in its groove, then install the chamber on the carburettor and tighten its screws securely (see illustration).

9 On EK to EY models, ensure the E-clip is secure in the specified notch in the jet needle,

then slide the washer underneath it and the spring seat on top of it (see illustrations). Install the jet needle into the diaphragm assembly (see illustration 7.5). On K1 models onward, ensure the E-clip is secure in the

specified notch in the jet needle, then fit the washer on top of the clip. Check that the spring and O-ring are fitted to the needle holder – use a new O-ring if necessary. Fit the jet needle into the piston, then install the needle holder and press it down until it is secure.

10 Insert the diaphragm assembly into the piston guide and lightly push the piston down, ensuring the needle is correctly aligned with the needle jet (see illustration 7.4). Press the diaphragm outer edge into its groove, making sure it is correctly seated. Check the diaphragm is not creased, and that the piston moves smoothly up and down in the guide.

11 Fit a new O-ring into the top edge of the carburettor body (see illustration 7.3). Install the spring into the diaphragm assembly, then fit the top cover to the carburettor, and tighten its screws securely (see illustrations).

12 Install the carburettors (see Section 6).

10 Throttle cable(s) - removal and installation

⚠️ Warning: Refer to the precautions given in Section 1 before proceeding.

Removal

Note: EK to EY models are fitted with a single throttle cable. K1 models onward are fitted with an accelerator and decelerator cable.

1 Remove the fuel tank (see Section 3).

2 Slacken the adjuster locknut and unscrew the adjuster until the captive nut becomes free and can be fully unscrewed from the adjuster (see illustrations). Lift the adjuster out of its bracket and detach the inner cable nipple from the throttle cam (see illustrations).

3 Unscrew the two right-hand side handlebar switch/throttle pulley housing screws and separate the switch halves. On EK to EY models, one of these screws secures the throttle cable elbow retainer plate (see illustration). On K1 models onward, the accelerator cable elbow retainer plate is secured by a separate screw and the decelerator cable elbow is secured by a

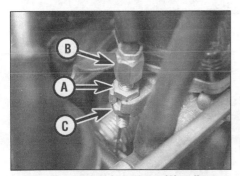

10.2a Throttle cable locknut (A), adjuster (B) and captive nut – EK to EY models

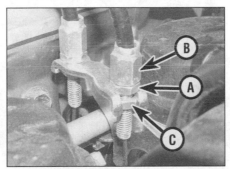

10.2b Throttle cable locknut (A), adjuster (B) and captive nut (C) – K1 models onward

10.2c Lift the adjuster out of the bracket . . .

10.2d . . . and detach the nipple (A) from the cam (B)

10.3a On EK to EY models the throttle cable retainer plate (arrow) is secured by the front housing screw

3

10.3b Accelerator cable retainer plate (A) and decelerator cable knurled ring (B) – K1 models onward

10.3c Detach the cable nipple (arrow) from the pulley – EK to EY models

10.3d Detach the cable nipples (arrows) from the pulley – K1 models onward

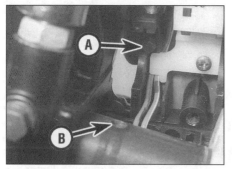

10.7a Make sure the pin (A) locates in the hole (B)

10.7b Make sure the cable retainer is secured by the screw

(see illustration 10.2b or a). Make sure the captive nut is held in the bracket.

9 Operate the throttle to check that it opens and closes freely.

10 Check and adjust the throttle cable freeplay (see Chapter 1). Turn the handlebars back and forth to make sure the cable doesn't cause the steering to bind.

11 Install the fuel tank (see Section 2).

12 Start the engine and check that the idle speed does not rise as the handlebars are turned. If it does, the throttle cable is routed incorrectly. Correct the problem before riding the motorcycle.

knurled ring (see illustration). Detach the cable nipple from the pulley, then remove the cable from the housing, noting how it fits (see illustrations).

4 Remove the cable noting its correct routing.

Installation

5 Install the cable making sure it is correctly routed. The cable must not interfere with any other component and should not be kinked or bent sharply.

6 Install the cable elbow into the lower half of the switch/throttle pulley housing. Lubricate the cable nipple with multi-purpose grease and install it into the throttle pulley (see illustration 10.3c or 3d).

7 Fit the two halves of the housing onto the handlebar so that the pin in the upper half of the housing locates in the hole in the top of the

handlebar (see illustration). Install the screws, making sure the elbow retainer is correctly positioned on EK to EY models, and tighten them securely (see illustration). On K1 models onward, install the screw for the accelerator cable elbow retainer plate and the knurled ring for the decelerator cable elbow finger-tight and align the cables, then tighten the screw and the knurled ring securely.

8 Lubricate the lower cable nipple with multi-purpose grease and attach it to the carburettor throttle cam (see illustration 10.2d). On K1 models onward, the accelerator cable should run around the back edge of the cam and the decelerator cable should run around the front edge of the cam. Install the cable adjuster into the mounting bracket, then thread the captive nut onto the lower end of the adjuster and tighten the locknut securely

11 Choke cable - removal and installation

Removal

1 Remove the fuel tank (see Section 2).

2 Free the choke outer cable from its bracket on the carburettor and detach the inner cable from the choke linkage bar (see illustration). Note how the spring ends locate on the bracket and the linkage bar.

3 Unscrew the two left-hand side handlebar switch/choke lever housing screws, one of which secures the choke cable elbow via a retainer plate. Separate the two switch halves, noting how the lever fits into the housing (see illustration). Detach the cable nipple from the choke lever (see illustration), then withdraw the cable and elbow from the housing.

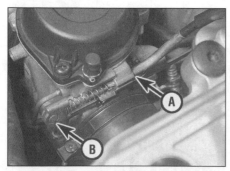

11.2 Pull the outer cable end out of its housing (A), then pull back the spring and detach the nipple (B) from the linkage bar

11.3a Note how the front screw secures the choke cable retainer plate

11.3b Detach the nipple from the lever

11.6a Make sure the lever fits correctly into the housing lower half

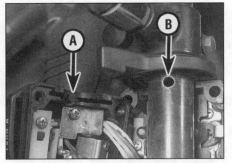
11.6b Make sure the pin (A) locates into the hole (B)

11.7 Fit the nipple into the linkage bar

4 Remove the cable from the machine noting its correct routing.

Installation

5 Install the cable making sure it is correctly routed. The cable must not interfere with any other component and should not be kinked or bent sharply.
6 Lubricate the upper cable nipple with multi-purpose grease. Install the cable in the switch/choke lever housing and attach the nipple to the choke lever **(see illustration 11.3b)**. Fit the two halves of the housing onto the handlebar, making sure the lever fits correctly into the lower half **(see illustration)**, and the pin in the upper half locates in the hole in the top of the handlebar **(see illustration)**. Install the screws, making sure the elbow retainer is correctly positioned, and tighten them securely **(see illustration 11.3a)**.

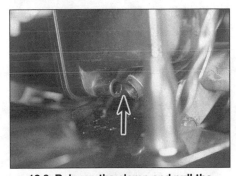
12.3 Release the clamp and pull the drain hose off its union (arrow)

7 Lubricate the cable lower nipple with multi-purpose grease and attach it to the choke linkage bar on the carburettor **(see illustration)**. Fit the outer cable into its bracket, making sure the spring ends locate correctly **(see illustration 11.2)**.
8 Check the choke cable operation and check for a small amount of freeplay (see Chapter 1).
9 Install the fuel tank (see Section 2).

12 Air filter housing - removal and installation

Removal

1 Remove the fuel tank (see Section 2). Unscrew the bolt securing the remote fuel tap to the frame and displace the tap **(see illustration 2.20)**. There is no need to detach the fuel hoses.
2 Slacken the clamps securing the air filter housing rubbers to the carburettor air intakes.
3 Release the clamp securing the air filter drain hose to the base of the air filter housing and detach the hose from its union **(see illustration)**.
4 Release the clamp securing the breather hose to the front of the housing and detach the hose from its union **(see illustration 6.2b)**.
5 Remove the two screws located at the back of the air filter housing, one on each side, which secure the housing to the frame **(see illustration 6.2a)**. Manoeuvre the air filter

housing backwards in order that the rubbers detach from the carburettor intakes, then carefully lift the housing out of the frame **(see illustration)**.

Installation

6 Installation is the reverse of removal. Make sure all the hoses are correctly installed and secured by their clamps. If the rubbers have been removed from the housing, make sure they are installed with the tab located at the top and between the two pins on the housing **(see illustration)**.

13 Exhaust system - removal and installation

> ⚠ **Warning: If the engine has been running the exhaust system will be very hot. Allow the system to cool before carrying out any work.**

Removal

1 The exhaust system is a one-piece design and must therefore be removed as a complete assembly. It is not possible to separate the silencer from the downpipes.
2 Unscrew the downpipe flange retaining bolts from the cylinder head **(see illustration)**.
3 Supporting the system, unscrew and remove the silencer mounting nut and bolt, then remove the system from the machine **(see**

3

12.5 Manoeuvre the housing out of the frame

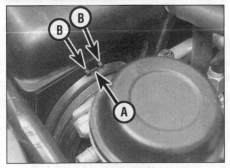
12.6 The tab (A) must fit between the two pins (B)

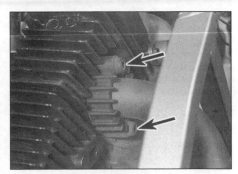
13.2 Each downpipe is secured by two bolts (arrows)

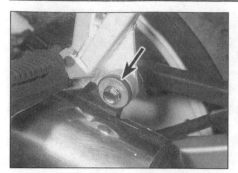

13.3 The silencer is secured by a single bolt (arrow)

13.4 Remove the old gasket from each port (arrows) . . .

13.5 . . . and install a new one

13.6a Manoeuvre the system into place . . .

13.6b . . . then install the downpipe bolts . . .

13.6c . . . and the silencer bolt

illustration). Check the condition of the rubber bush in the footrest bracket and replace it if necessary, noting the fitting of the spacer.

4 Remove the gasket from each port in the cylinder head and discard them as new ones must be fitted **(see illustration)**.

Installation

5 Fit a new gasket into each of the cylinder head ports **(see illustration)**. Apply a smear of grease to the gaskets to keep them in place whilst fitting the downpipe if necessary.

6 Manoeuvre the system into position so that the head of each downpipe is located in its port in the cylinder head and install the flange bolts finger-tight to hold the system in place **(see illustrations)**. Supporting the system, align the silencer mounting bracket with its mounting hole and install the bolt with its washer but do not yet tighten the nut **(see illustration)**. Now tighten the flange bolts to the specified torque setting, then fit the nut to the silencer mounting bolt and tighten the bolt to the specified torque setting.

7 Run the engine and check the system for leaks.

14 Evaporative emission control system (California models only) - general information

1 On all California models, an evaporative loss system is fitted **(see illustration)**. This system prevents the escape of fuel vapours into the atmosphere and functions as follows.

2 When the engine is stopped, fuel vapour from the tank is directed into a charcoal canister (located under the battery box) where it is absorbed and stored whilst the motorcycle is standing. When the engine is started, intake manifold depression draws the vapours which are stored in the canister into the carburettors to be burned during the normal combustion process.

3 The fuel tank incorporates a special vapour collection chamber which allows the vapours to pass into the canister. The tank vent pipe also incorporates a roll-over valve which closes and prevents any fuel from escaping through it in the event of the bike falling over. The tank filler cap has a one way valve which allows air into the tank as the volume of fuel decreases, but prevents any fuel vapour from escaping.

4 The system is not adjustable and can be tested only by a Suzuki dealer. Checks which can be performed by the owner are given in Chapter 1.

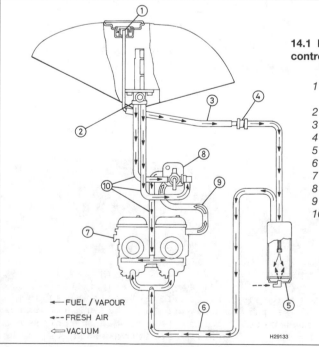

14.1 Evaporative emission control system - California models only

1 Fuel tank vapour separator
2 Main fuel cock
3 Surge hose
4 Roll-over valve
5 Charcoal canister
6 Purge hose
7 Carburettors
8 Remote fuel tap
9 Vacuum hose
10 Fuel hoses

FUEL / VAPOUR
FRESH AIR
VACUUM

H29133

Chapter 4
Ignition system

Contents

Degrees of difficulty

Easy, suitable for novice with little experience	**Fairly easy,** suitable for beginner with some experience	**Fairly difficult,** suitable for competent DIY mechanic	**Difficult,** suitable for experienced DIY mechanic	**Very difficult,** suitable for expert DIY or professional 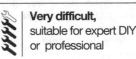

Specifications

General information
Cylinder identification . . . .   Left (alternator side), Right (clutch side)
Spark plugs . . . .   See Chapter 1

Ignition timing
At idle
 California models . . . .   5° BTDC
 All other models . . . .   12° BTDC
Full advance . . . .   40° BTDC @ 4000 rpm

Pulse generator coils
Resistance . . . .   250 to 420 ohms

Ignition HT coils
Primary winding resistance . . . .   3.0 to 6.0 ohms
Secondary winding resistance (with plug lead and cap) . . . .   18 to 30 K ohms

Torque setting
Timing rotor bolt . . . .   17 to 23 Nm

---

1 General information

All models are fitted with a fully transistorised electronic ignition system, which due to its lack of mechanical parts is totally maintenance free. The system comprises a rotor, pulse generator coils, ignition control unit and ignition HT coils (refer to the wiring diagrams at the end of Chapter 8 for details).

The trigger on the rotor, which is fitted to the right-hand end of the crankshaft, magnetically operates the pulse generator coils as the crankshaft rotates. The pulse generator coils send a signal to the ignition control unit which then supplies the ignition HT coils with the power necessary to produce a spark at the plugs.

The system uses two coils mounted on each side of the frame behind the steering head. The right-hand coil supplies the right cylinder spark plug and the left-hand coil supplies the left cylinder plug.

The ignition control unit incorporates an electronic advance system controlled by signals generated by the rotor and the pick-up coil.

The system incorporates a safety interlock circuit which will cut the ignition if the sidestand is put down whilst the engine is running and in gear, or if a gear is selected whilst the engine is running and the sidestand is down.

Because of their nature, the individual ignition system components can be checked but not repaired. If ignition system troubles occur, and the faulty component can be isolated, the only cure for the problem is to replace the part with a new one. Keep in mind

that most electrical parts, once purchased, cannot be returned. To avoid unnecessary expense, make very sure the faulty component has been positively identified before buying a replacement part.

2 Ignition system - check

 Warning: The energy levels in electronic systems can be very high. On no account should the ignition be switched on whilst the plugs or plug caps are being held. Shocks from the HT circuit can be most unpleasant. Secondly, it is vital that the engine is not turned over or run with either of the plug caps removed, and that the plugs are soundly earthed (grounded)

when the system is checked for sparking. The ignition system components can be seriously damaged if the HT circuit becomes isolated.

1 As no means of adjustment is available, any failure of the system can be traced to failure of a system component or a simple wiring fault. Of the two possibilities, the latter is far more likely. In the event of failure, check the system in a logical fashion, as described below.

2 Disconnect the HT lead from both cylinder spark plugs. Connect each lead to a spare spark plug and lay each plug on the engine with the threads contacting the engine. If necessary, hold each spark plug with an insulated tool.

 Warning: Do not remove the spark plugs from the engine to perform this check - atomised fuel pumped out of the open spark plug hole could ignite, causing severe injury!

3 Having observed the above precautions, check that the kill switch is in the RUN position, turn the ignition switch ON and turn the engine over on the starter motor. If the system is in good condition a regular, fat blue spark should be evident at each plug electrode. If the spark appears thin or yellowish, or is non-existent, further investigation will be necessary. Before proceeding further, turn the ignition off and remove the key as a safety measure.

4 The ignition system must be able to produce a spark which is capable of jumping a particular size gap. Suzuki specify that a healthy system should produce a spark capable of jumping 8 mm. A simple testing tool can be made to test the minimum gap across which the spark will jump (see **Tool Tip**).

5 Connect one of the spark plug HT leads from one coil to the protruding electrode on the test tool, and clip the tool to a good earth (ground) on the engine or frame. Check that the kill switch is in the RUN position, turn the ignition switch ON and turn the engine over on the starter motor. If the system is in good

TOOL TiP

A simple spark gap testing tool can be made from a block of wood, a large alligator clip and two nails, one of which is fashioned so that a spark plug cap or bare HT lead end can be connected to its end. Make sure the gap between the two nail ends is the same as specified.

condition a regular, fat blue spark should be seen to jump the gap between the nail ends. Repeat the test for the other coil. If the test results are good the entire ignition system can be considered good. If the spark appears thin or yellowish, or is non-existent, further investigation will be necessary.

6 Ignition faults can be divided into two categories, namely those where the ignition system has failed completely, and those which are due to a partial failure. The likely faults are listed below, starting with the most probable source of failure. Work through the list systematically, referring to the subsequent sections for full details of the necessary checks and tests. **Note:** *Before checking the following items ensure that the battery is fully charged and that all fuses are in good condition.*

a) *Loose, corroded or damaged wiring connections, broken or shorted wiring between any of the component parts of the ignition system (see Chapter 8).*

b) *Faulty HT lead or spark plug cap, faulty spark plug, dirty, worn or corroded plug electrodes, or incorrect electrode gap.*

c) *Faulty ignition switch or engine kill switch (see Chapter 8).*

d) *Faulty neutral or sidestand switch (see Chapter 8).*

e) *Faulty pulse generator coils or damaged rotor.*

f) *Faulty ignition HT coil(s).*

g) *Faulty ignition control unit.*

7 If the above checks don't reveal the cause of the problem, have the ignition system tested by a Suzuki dealer. Suzuki produce a tester which can perform a complete diagnostic analysis of the ignition system.

3 Ignition HT coils - check, removal and installation

Check

1 In order to determine conclusively that the ignition coils are defective, they should be tested by a Suzuki dealer equipped with the special diagnostic tester.

2 However, the coils can be checked visually (for cracks and other damage) and the primary and secondary coil resistances can be measured with a multimeter. If the coils are undamaged, and if the resistance readings are as specified at the beginning of the Chapter, they are probably capable of proper operation.

3 Remove the seat (see Chapter 7) and disconnect the battery negative (-ve) lead. To gain access to the coils, remove the fuel tank (see Chapter 3). The coils are mounted on each side of the frame behind the steering stem **(see illustration)**.

4 Disconnect the primary circuit electrical connectors from the coil being tested and the HT lead from the spark plug **(see illustration)**. Mark the locations of all wires and leads before disconnecting them.

3.3 The coils are mounted on each side of the frame behind the steering stem, and are secured by two bolts (arrows)

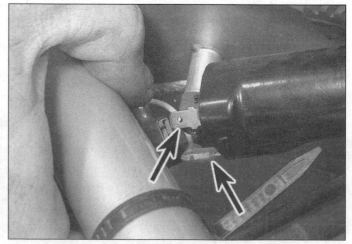

3.4 Disconnect the primary circuit connectors (arrows)

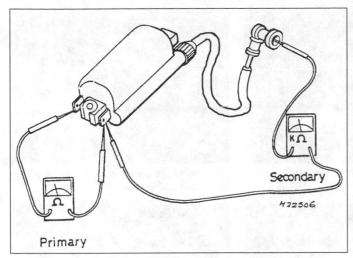

3.5 Ignition coil winding test connections

4.7 The pulse generator coil assembly cover
is secured by three bolts

5 Set the meter to the ohms x 1 scale and measure the resistance between the primary circuit terminals **(see illustration)**. This will give a resistance reading of the primary windings and should be consistent with the value given in the Specifications at the beginning of the Chapter.

6 To check the condition of the secondary windings, set the meter to the K ohm scale. Connect one meter probe to one of the primary circuit terminals and the other probe to the spark plug cap on the HT lead **(see illustration 3.5)**. If the reading obtained is not within the range shown in the Specifications, it is likely that the coil is defective.

7 Should any of the above checks not produce the expected result, have your findings confirmed on the diagnostic tester (see Step 1). If the coil is confirmed faulty, it must be replaced; the coil is a sealed unit and cannot therefore be repaired.

Removal

8 Remove the seat (see Chapter 7) and disconnect the battery negative (-ve) lead, then remove the fuel tank (see Chapter 3).

9 The coils are mounted on each side of the frame behind the steering stem. Disconnect the primary circuit electrical connectors from the coils **(see illustration 3.4)** and disconnect the HT leads from the spark plugs. Mark the locations of all wires and leads before disconnecting them.

10 Unscrew the two bolts securing each coil to the frame, noting the position of the spacers, and remove the coils **(see illustration 3.3)**. Note the routing of the HT leads.

Installation

11 Installation is the reverse of removal. Make sure the wiring connectors and HT leads are securely connected.

| 4 | **Pulse generator coils** - check, removal and installation |

Check

1 Remove the seat and the left-hand side panel (see Chapter 7) and disconnect the battery negative (-ve) lead.

2 Trace the pulse generator coil wiring back from the right-hand side crankcase cover and disconnect it at the 4-pin connector. Using a multimeter set to the ohms x 100 scale, measure the resistance first between the brown and black/blue wires, and then between the green/white and black/blue wires, on the pick-up coil side of the connector.

3 Compare the reading obtained with that given in the Specifications at the beginning of this Chapter. The pick-up coils must be replaced if the reading obtained differs greatly from that given, particularly if the meter indicates a short circuit (no measurable resistance) or an open circuit (infinite, or very high resistance).

4 If one or both pick-up coils are thought to be faulty, first check that this is not due to a

damaged or broken wire from the coil to the connector; pinched or broken wires can usually be repaired. Note that the pick-up coils are not available individually but come as a pair along with their mounting plate.

Removal

5 Remove the seat and the left-hand side panel (see Chapter 7) and disconnect the battery negative (-ve) lead.

6 Trace the pulse generator coil wiring back from the right-hand side crankcase cover and disconnect it at the 4-pin connector. Free the wiring from any clips or ties.

7 Unscrew the three bolts securing the circular pulse generator assembly cover to the right-hand side crankcase cover **(see illustration)**. Remove the cover.

8 Using a 19 mm spanner to counter-hold the timing rotor hex, unscrew the bolt in the centre of the rotor which secures it to the end of the crankshaft **(see illustration)**. Remove the rotor, noting how the pin in the end of the crankshaft locates in the slot in the rotor.

9 Slacken the screw securing the wire to the terminal on the oil pressure switch and detach the wire **(see illustration)**.

10 Unscrew the two screws securing the

4.8 Use a spanner on the hex (A) to counter-hold the rotor, then unscrew the rotor bolt (B)

4.9 Slacken the screw (arrow) and disconnect the oil pressure switch wire

4

4.10 The pulse generator coil assembly is secured by two screws (arrows)

4.13 Apply sealant to the grommet

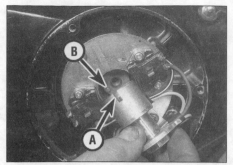

4.15a Make sure the slot in the timing rotor (A) locates over the pin (B)

4.15b Install the rotor bolt . . .

4.15c . . . and tighten it to the specified torque while counter-holding the rotor

4.16 Install the pulse generator assembly cover

pulse generator coil assembly mounting plate to the crankcase cover (see illustration). Remove the rubber wiring grommet from its recess in the crankcase cover and remove the coil assembly, noting how it fits.

11 Examine the rotor for signs of damage and replace it if necessary.

Installation

12 Install the pulse generator coil assembly onto the crankcase cover and tighten the assembly mounting screws securely (see illustration 4.10).

13 Apply a smear of sealant to the rubber wiring seal and fit the grommet in its recess in the crankcase (see illustration).

14 Connect the oil pressure switch wire to its terminal on the switch and tighten the screw securely (see illustration 4.9).

15 Install the timing rotor onto the end of the crankshaft, making sure the slot in the rotor locates correctly over the pin in the end of the crankshaft (see illustration). Using a 19 mm spanner to counter-hold the rotor, install the rotor bolt and tighten it to the torque setting specified at the beginning of the Chapter (see illustrations).

16 Install the pulse generator assembly cover and tighten its bolts securely (see illustration).

17 Route the wiring up to the connector and reconnect it. Secure the wiring in its clips or ties.

18 Reconnect the battery negative (-ve) lead and install the seat and side panel (see Chapter 7).

5 Ignition control unit - check, removal and installation

Check

1 If the tests shown in the preceding Sections have failed to isolate the cause of an ignition fault, it is likely that the ignition control unit itself is faulty. No test details are available with which the unit can be tested on home workshop equipment. Take the machine to a Suzuki dealer for testing on the diagnostic tester.

Removal

2 Remove the seat and the left-hand side panel (see Chapter 7) and disconnect the battery negative (-ve) lead.

5.3 Disconnect the two ignition control unit wiring connectors

3 Trace the wiring from the ignition control unit and disconnect it at the connectors (see illustration).

4 Unscrew the two screws securing the ignition control unit to the frame and remove the unit.

Installation

5 Installation is the reverse of removal. Make sure the wiring connectors are correctly and securely connected.

6 Ignition timing - general information and check

General information

1 Since no provision exists for adjusting the ignition timing and since no component is subject to mechanical wear, there is no need for regular checks; only if investigating a fault such as a loss of power or a misfire, should the ignition timing be checked.

2 The ignition timing is checked dynamically (engine running) using a stroboscopic light. The inexpensive neon lamps should be adequate in theory, but in practice may produce a pulse of such low intensity that the timing mark remains indistinct. If possible, one of the more precise xenon tube lamps should be used, powered by an external source of the appropriate voltage. **Note:** *Do not use the machine's own battery as an incorrect reading may result from stray impulses within the machine's electrical system.*

Check

3 Warm the engine up to normal operating temperature then stop it.

4 Unscrew the three bolts securing the circular pulse generator assembly cover to the right-hand side crankcase cover **(see illustration 4.7)**.

5 The timing mark on the rotor is an F which indicates the firing point at idle speed for the right-hand cylinder **(see illustration)**. The static timing mark with which this should align is the contact on the pulse generator coil.

The rotor timing mark can be highlighted with white paint (typist's correction fluid is ideal) to make it more visible under the stroboscopic light.

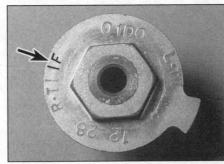

6.5 Ignition rotor timing mark

6 Connect the timing light to the right-hand cylinder HT lead as described in the manufacturer's instructions.

7 Start the engine and aim the light at the static timing mark.

8 With the machine idling at the specified speed, the timing mark should align with the static timing mark.

9 Slowly increase the engine speed whilst observing the timing mark. The timing mark should move anti-clockwise, increasing in relation to the engine speed until it reaches full advance (no identification mark).

10 As already stated, there is no means of adjustment of the ignition timing on these machines. If the ignition timing is incorrect, or suspected of being incorrect, one of the ignition system components is at fault, and the system must be tested as described in the preceding Sections of this Chapter.

11 When the check is complete, install the cover and tighten its bolts securely **(see illustration 4.16)**.

4

Chapter 5
Frame, suspension and final drive

Contents

Degrees of difficulty

Easy, suitable for novice with little experience	**Fairly easy,** suitable for beginner with some experience	**Fairly difficult,** suitable for competent DIY mechanic 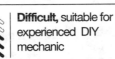	**Difficult,** suitable for experienced DIY mechanic	**Very difficult,** suitable for expert DIY or professional

Specifications

Front forks

Oil type . . . . SAE 10W fork oil
Oil capacity
  UK EK to EM models, all US models . . . . 382 cc
  UK EN to EY models . . . . 377 cc
  UK K1 models onward . . . . 389 cc
Oil level*
  UK EK to EM models, all US models . . . . 99 mm
  UK EN to EY models . . . . 105 mm
  UK K1 models onward . . . . 91 mm
Spring free length (service limit)
  UK EK to EM models . . . . 254 mm
  UK EN to EY models . . . . 303 mm
  UK K1 models onward . . . . 336 mm
  US EK to EY models . . . . 254 mm
  US K1 models onward . . . . 270 mm
Tube runout limit . . . . 0.2 mm
Oil level is measured from the top of the tube with the fork spring removed and the leg fully compressed

Rear suspension

Swingarm pivot pin runout (max) . . . . 0.3 mm

5

Torque settings

Handlebar clamp pinch bolts	8 to 12 Nm
Handlebar bracket nuts	27 to 42 Nm
Front brake master cylinder clamp bolts	8 to 12 Nm
Fork clamp bolts (top yoke)	18 to 28 Nm
Fork clamp bolts (bottom yoke)	25 to 40 Nm
Fork damper rod Allen bolt	15 to 25 Nm
Steering head bearing adjuster nut	40 to 50 Nm
Steering stem bolt	35 to 55 Nm
Shock absorber mounting bolts	40 to 60 Nm
Suspension linkage rod bolts	70 to 100 Nm
Suspension linkage arm bolt	70 to 100 Nm
Swingarm pivot nut	55 to 88 Nm
Brake torque arm nuts	22 to 35 Nm
Rear sprocket nuts	40 to 60 Nm

1 General information

All models use a full cradle twin spar steel frame.

Front suspension is by a pair of conventional oil-damped telescopic forks. On certain models the forks are adjustable for pre-load.

At the rear, a box-section steel swingarm acts on a single shock absorber via a linkage which provides a rising rate system. The shock absorber is adjustable for pre-load.

The drive to the rear wheel is by chain. A rubber damper system (often called a 'cush drive') is fitted between the rear wheel coupling and the wheel.

2 Frame - inspection and repair

1 The frame should not require attention unless accident damage has occurred. In most cases, frame replacement is the only satisfactory remedy for such damage. A few frame specialists have the jigs and other equipment necessary for straightening the frame to the required standard of accuracy, but even then there is no simple way of assessing to what extent the frame may have been over stressed.

2 After the machine has accumulated a lot of miles, the frame should be examined closely for signs of cracking or splitting at the welded joints. Loose engine mounting bolts can cause ovaling or fracturing of the mounting tabs. Minor damage can often be repaired by welding, depending on the extent and nature of the damage.

3 Remember that a frame which is out of alignment will cause handling problems. If misalignment is suspected as the result of an accident, it will be necessary to strip the machine completely so the frame can be thoroughly checked.

3 Footrests and brackets - removal and installation

Footrests

Removal

1 Remove the E-clip and washer from the bottom of the footrest pivot pin, then withdraw the pivot pin and remove the footrest (see illustration). Take care not to lose the rubber washer which fits on the inner end of the footrest.

2 If necessary, the footrest rubber can be separated from the footrest by removing the washer from the inner end of the footrest and sliding the rubber off the rest.

Installation

3 Installation is the reverse of removal.

Right-hand footrest bracket

Removal

4 Remove the rider's footrest (see Step 1).

5 Unhook the brake pedal return spring from the bracket and the brake light switch spring from the master cylinder pushrod actuating arm (see illustration). Depress the retaining tabs on the underside of the brake light switch adjuster nut and remove the switch from its bracket.

6 Slacken the pinch bolt securing the pushrod actuating arm to the brake pedal shaft, noting the alignment punch mark on the shaft which aligns with the gap in the arm (see illustration 3.5). If no mark is visible, make your own before removing the pedal so that it can be correctly aligned with the arm on installation. Withdraw the brake pedal from the arm and the footrest bracket.

3.1 Remove the E-clip (arrow) and withdraw the pin from the top to free the footrest

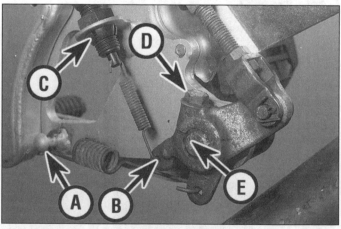

3.5 Brake pedal return spring (A), brake light switch spring (B), brake light switch retaining tabs (C), actuating arm pinch bolt (D). Note the punch mark (E)

7 Unscrew the two bolts securing the master cylinder to the bracket and remove the bracket **(see illustration)**. Support the master cylinder so that no strain is placed on its hoses.
8 Unscrew two bolts securing the bracket to the frame and remove the bracket **(see illustration)**. If required, unscrew the remaining bolt securing the foot guard to the bracket and separate the two.

Installation

9 Installation is the reverse of removal. Align the punch mark on the brake pedal shaft with the gap in the master cylinder pushrod actuating arm to ensure the brake pedal is installed at the correct height **(see illustration 3.5)**. Tighten the pinch bolt securely.

Left-hand footrest bracket

Removal

10 Remove the rider's footrest (see Step 1).
11 Unscrew the two bolts securing the bracket to the frame and remove the bracket **(see illustration)**. If required, unscrew the bolts securing the foot guard to the bracket and separate the two.

Installation

12 Installation is the reverse of removal.

---

4 Stands -
removal and installation

Centre stand

1 The centre stand is secured in the frame by two pivot bolts which fit inside spacers in the stand pivots. Support the bike on its sidestand and free one end of the centre stand springs. Where fitted, remove the split pin from the inner end of each bolt. Unscrew the bolts and remove the stand **(see illustration)**. Withdraw the spacer from each pivot. Discard the split pins (where fitted) as a new ones must be used.
2 Inspect the stand, spacers and bolts for signs of wear and replace them if necessary. Apply a smear of grease to the outside of the spacers and the bolts and fit the stand back

on the bike, tightening the bolts securely. Where fitted, use a new split pin on the pivot bolt ends. Reconnect the return springs.
3 Make sure the springs are in good condition and capable of holding the stand up when not in use. A broken or weak spring is an obvious safety hazard.

Sidestand

4 The sidestand is attached to a bracket on the frame. Springs anchored to the bracket ensure that the stand is held in the retracted or extended position.
5 Support the bike on its centre stand.
6 Free the stand springs and unscrew the nut from the pivot bolt **(see illustration)**. Withdraw the pivot bolt to free the stand from its bracket. On installation apply grease to the pivot bolt shank and tighten the nut securely. Reconnect the sidestand springs and check

that the return spring holds the stand securely up when not in use - an accident is almost certain to occur if the stand extends while the machine is in motion.
7 For check and replacement of the sidestand switch see Chapter 8.

---

5 Handlebars -
removal and installation

All models with two-piece handlebars

Note: *For access to the top yoke and steering head bearings, the handlebars can be removed as a complete assembly (see below) rather than individually.*

Right-hand handlebar removal

1 Unscrew the two screws on the underside of the switch housing, then separate the switch halves and remove them from the handlebar, noting how they fit.
2 Unscrew the two clamp bolts securing the front brake master cylinder assembly to the handlebar and lift the assembly away **(see illustration)**. Support the assembly in an upright position and so that no strain is placed on the hose. Disconnect the brake light switch wiring connectors.
3 Unscrew the handlebar clamp pinch bolts and withdraw the handlebar from the clamp, noting how the bolts fit into the

3.7 Master cylinder mounting bolts (arrows)

3.8 Footrest bracket mounting bolts (arrows)

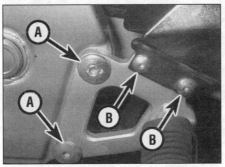
3.11 Footrest bracket mounting bolts (A), foot guard mounting bolts (B)

4.1 Centre stand mounting bolts (arrows)

4.6 Sidestand pivot bolt nut (arrow)

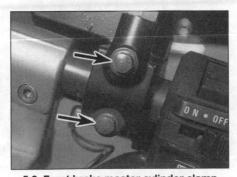
5.2 Front brake master cylinder clamp bolts (arrows)

5.3 Handlebar clamp pinch bolts (arrows)

5.4 Handlebar end weight retaining screw (arrow)

5.5 Handlebar clamp mounting bolts (arrows)

alignment cutouts in the handlebar **(see illustration)**.

4 If necessary, unscrew the handlebar end-weight retaining screw, then remove the cap, weight and spacer from the end of the handlebar and slide off the throttle twistgrip **(see illustration)**. If replacing the grip, it may be necessary to slit it using a sharp knife as it is adhered to the throttle twist.

5 If necessary, unscrew the bolts securing the handlebar clamp to the handlebar bracket and remove the clamp **(see illustration)**.

Right-hand handlebar installation

6 Installation is the reverse of removal, noting the following.

a) *Fit the handlebar so that the clamp bolts fit into the cutouts, thus aligning it correctly* **(see illustration)**.

b) *If removed, apply a smear of grease to the inside of the throttle twistgrip and a suitable non-permanent locking compound to the threads of the handlebar end-weight retaining screw.*

c) *If a new grip is being fitted, stick it to the throttle twist using a suitable adhesive.*

d) *Tighten the handlebar clamp pinch bolts to the torque setting specified at the beginning of the Chapter.*

e) *Make sure the front brake master cylinder assembly clamp is installed with the clamp mating surfaces aligned with the punch mark on the top of the handlebar* **(see illustration)**. *Tighten fully the upper bolt first, then the lower bolt, to the specified torque setting.*

f) *Make sure the pin in the upper switch housing locates in the hole in the handlebar.*

Left-hand handlebar removal

7 Unscrew the two screws on the underside of the switch housing, then separate the switch halves and remove them from the handlebar, noting how they fit.

8 Slacken the clutch lever assembly bracket pinch bolt **(see illustration)**.

9 Unscrew the handlebar clamp pinch bolts and withdraw the handlebar from the clamp, noting how the bolts fit into the alignment cutouts in the handlebar **(see illustration 5.3)**. Slide the clutch lever assembly off the handlebar as you withdraw it.

10 If necessary, unscrew the handlebar end-weight retaining screw, then remove the cap, weight and spacer from the end of the handlebar **(see illustration 5.4)**. If you are replacing the grip, it may be necessary to slit it using a sharp knife as it is adhered to the handlebar.

11 If necessary, unscrew the bolts securing the handlebar clamp to the handlebar bracket and remove the clamp **(see illustration 5.5)**.

Left-hand handlebar installation

12 Installation is the reverse of removal, noting the following.

a) *Fit the handlebar so that the clamp bolts fit into the cutouts, thus aligning it correctly* **(see illustration 5.6a)**.

b) *If removed, apply a suitable non-permanent locking compound to the threads of the handlebar end-weight retaining screw.*

5.6a Note the cutouts (arrows) for the clamp pinch bolts

5.8 Clutch lever assembly bracket pinch bolt (arrow)

c) *If a new grip is being fitted, stick it to the handlebar using a suitable adhesive.*

d) *Tighten the handlebar clamp pinch bolts to the torque setting specified at the beginning of the Chapter.*

e) *Make sure the clutch lever assembly clamp is installed with the clamp mating surfaces aligned with the punch mark on the underside of the handlebar* **(see illustration)**. *Tighten the clutch lever assembly pinch bolt securely.*

f) *Make sure the pin in the upper switch housing locates in the hole in the handlebar.*

Complete assembly removal

13 Unscrew the nuts on the bolts securing the instrument cluster and displace the cluster **(see illustration)**. There is no need to disconnect the instrument cluster wiring or speedometer cable.

14 Remove the switch housings, master

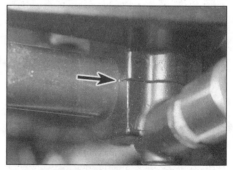

5.6b Punch mark (arrow) must align with master cylinder clamp mating surfaces

5.12 Punch mark (arrow) must align with the clutch lever clamp mating surfaces

5.13 Instrument cluster mounting bolt nut (arrow)

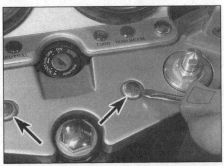

5.15a Remove the caps (arrows) . . .

in the adjuster and lockwheel with that in the lever bracket, then pull the outer cable end from the socket in the adjuster and release the inner cable from the lever. If it is to be removed, slacken the clutch lever assembly bracket pinch bolt. It can only be slid off the handlebar after removal of the grip.

20 Prise out the caps from the bolts securing the handlebar clamps, then unscrew the bolts and remove the clamps and the handlebars **(see illustrations)**. If necessary, unscrew the nuts and remove the bolts securing the handlebar bracket to the top yoke **(see illustration)**.

21 If necessary, unscrew the handlebar end-weight retaining screws, then remove the weights from the end of the handlebars. If replacing the grips, it may be necessary to slit them using a sharp knife as they are adhered to the throttle twist (right-hand) and the handlebar (left-hand).

Installation

22 Installation is the reverse of removal. Position the handlebars so that the ridges are central in the clamp mounts and the punch mark aligns with the split in the clamp **(see illustration)**. Fit the clamps so that their punch mark faces forwards and tighten the handlebar mounting bolts securely.

23 If removed, apply a suitable non-permanent locking compound to the handlebar end-weight retaining screws. If new grips are being fitted, secure them using a suitable adhesive. Make sure the front brake master cylinder assembly clamp is installed with the clamp mating surfaces aligned with the punch mark on the handlebar. Tighten fully the upper bolt first, then the lower bolt, to the specified torque setting.

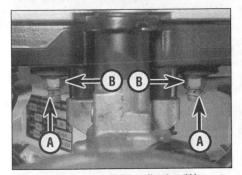

5.15b . . . and the split pins (A), then unscrew the nuts (B) . . .

5.15c . . . and remove the bolts (arrows)

cylinder assembly and clutch lever assembly from the handlebars, following the appropriate steps above. **Note:** *If required, the handlebars can be displaced for access to the top yoke and steering head bearings without removing the switch housings, the front brake master cylinder assembly and the clutch lever assembly.*

15 Prise out the cap from the top and remove the split pin from the bottom of each bolt securing the handlebar bracket to the top yoke **(see illustrations)**. Unscrew the nuts and withdraw the bolts, then lift the handlebar bracket assembly off the top yoke, noting how it fits **(see illustration)**.

Complete assembly installation

16 Installation is the reverse of removal. Tighten the handlebar bracket nuts to the torque setting specified at the beginning of the Chapter. Use new split pins if necessary.

All models with one-piece handlebars

Removal
Note: *If required, the handlebars can be displaced for access to the fork top bolts or the top yoke without removing the switch housings and the front brake master cylinder assembly and the clutch lever assembly.*

17 Remove the screws securing both the left- and right-hand switch housings to the handlebar, then separate teh switch halves and remove them from the handlebar, noting how they fit.

18 Unscrew the two clamp bolts securing the front brake master cylinder assembly to the handlebar and lift the assembly away. Support the assembly in an upright position and so that

no strain is placed on the hose. Disconnect the brake light switch wiring connectors.

19 Pull back the rubber cover from the clutch lever assembly. Fully slacken the lockwheel then screw the adjuster fully in. Align the slots

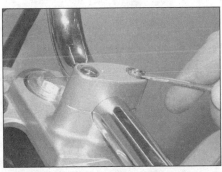

5.20a Remove the caps . . .

5.20b . . . then undo the handlebar clamp bolts

5.20c Handlebar bracket is retained by two nuts and bolts

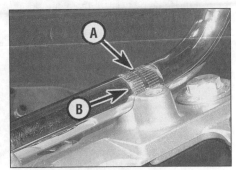

5.22 Handlebar positioning ridges (A) and punch mark (B)

5

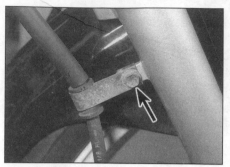

6.2 Brake hose clamp bolt (arrow)

6.3 Top yoke fork clamp bolt (arrow)

6.4a Note the alignment of the fork with the handlebar bracket as an aid to installation

6 Forks -
removal and installation

Removal

1 Remove the front wheel (see Chapter 6).
2 Remove the front mudguard and brace (see Chapter 7). Unscrew the bolt securing the brake hose clamp to the right-hand fork (see illustration).
3 Slacken, but do not remove, the fork clamp bolts in the top yoke (see illustration). If the forks are to be disassembled, or if the fork oil is being changed, it is advisable to slacken the fork top bolts at this stage. On UK K, L and M and US EK to EY models, first remove the top bolt cap. On models with pre-load adjusters in the fork top bolts, set the pre-load adjuster to its minimum setting (see Section 12). On models with one-piece handlebars, displace the handlebars if required for improved access to the top bolts (see Section 5).

 HAYNES HiNT *Slackening the fork pinch bolts in the top yoke before slackening the fork top bolts releases pressure on the top bolt. This makes it much easier to remove and helps to preserve the threads.*

4 Note the position of the top of the fork tubes relative to the handlebar bracket so that they are installed in the same position (see illustration). Slacken but do not remove the fork clamp bolts in the bottom yoke, and remove the forks by twisting them and pulling them downwards (see illustration). Note how the forks pass through the headlight brackets.

 HAYNES HiNT *If the fork tubes are seized in the yokes, spray the area with penetrating fluid and allow time for it to soak in before trying again.*

Installation

5 Remove all traces of corrosion from the fork tubes and the yokes and slide the forks up through the bottom yoke, the headlight brackets, top yoke and handlebar bracket (see illustration)

6.4b Bottom yoke fork clamp bolt (arrow)

6.5 Install the fork up through the yokes and headlight bracket

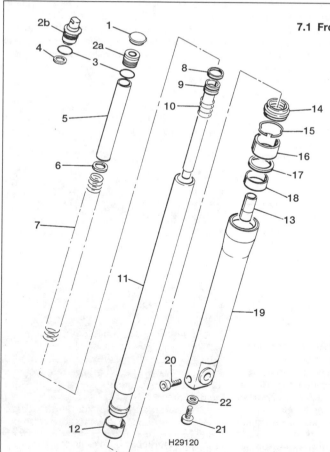

7.1 Front fork components

1 Top bolt cap (where fitted)
2a Top bolt – without pre-load adjuster
2b Top bolt – with pre-load adjuster
3 O-ring
4 Disc washer – models with pre-load adjuster
5 Spacer
6 Spring seat
7 Spring
8 Piston ring
9 Damper rod
10 Rebound spring
11 Fork tube
12 Bottom bush
13 Damper rod seat
14 Dust seal
15 Retaining clip
16 Oil seal
17 Washer
18 Top bush
19 Fork slider
20 Axle clamp bolt
21 Damper rod bolt
22 Sealing washer

H29120

7.8 Withdraw the damper rod and rebound spring from the tube

7.9 Prise out the dust seal using a flat-bladed screwdriver

7.10 Prise out the retaining clip using a flat-bladed screwdriver

so that they align with the handlebar bracket as noted on removal **(see illustration 6.4a)**.

6 Tighten the bottom yoke pinch bolts to the torque setting specified at the beginning of the Chapter **(see illustration 6.4b)**. If the fork legs have been dismantled or if the fork oil has been changed, the fork top bolts should now be tightened.

7 Tighten the top yoke pinch bolts to the specified torque setting **(see illustration 6.3)**. Fit the top bolt cap (where fitted) and install the handlebars if displaced.

8 Install the front brace and mudguard (see Chapter 7) and the front wheel (Chapter 6). Install the brake hose clamp onto the right-hand fork and tighten its bolt securely **(see illustration 6.2)**.

9 Check the operation of the front forks and brake before taking the machine out on the road. Where pre-load adjusters are fitted, set the pre-load as required (see Section 12).

7 Forks - disassembly, inspection and reassembly

Disassembly

1 Always dismantle the fork legs separately to avoid interchanging parts and thus causing an accelerated rate of wear. Store all components in separate, clearly marked containers **(see illustration)**.

2 Before dismantling the fork, it is advised that the damper rod bolt be slackened at this stage. Compress the fork tube in the slider so that the spring exerts maximum pressure on the damper rod head, then have an assistant slacken the damper rod bolt in the base of the fork slider.

3 If the fork top bolt was not slackened with the fork in situ, carefully clamp the fork tube in a vice, taking care not to overtighten or score its surface. Remove the top bolt cap (where fitted). On models with a pre-load adjuster incorporated in the fork top bolt, set the pre-load adjuster to its minimum setting (see Section 12).

4 Unscrew the fork top bolt from the top of the fork tube.

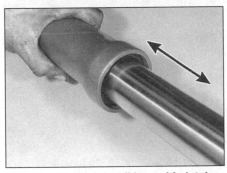

7.11 To separate the slider and fork tube, pull them apart firmly several times in a slide-hammer action

 Warning: The fork spring is pressing on the fork top bolt with considerable pressure. Unscrew the bolt very carefully, keeping a downward pressure on it and release it slowly as it is likely to spring clear. It is advisable to wear some form of eye and face protection when carrying out this operation.

5 Slide the fork tube down into the slider and withdraw the disc washer (where fitted), spacer, spring seat and the spring from the tube; note which way up they fit.

6 Invert the fork leg over a suitable container and pump the fork vigorously to expel as much fork oil as possible.

7 Remove the previously slackened damper rod bolt and its copper sealing washer from the bottom of the slider. Discard the sealing washer as a new one must be used on reassembly. If the damper rod bolt was not slackened before dismantling the fork, it may be necessary to re-install the spring, spring seat, spacer and top bolt to prevent the damper rod from turning. Alternatively, a broom handle pressed hard into the damper rod head quite often suffices.

8 Invert the fork and withdraw the damper rod from inside the fork tube. Remove the rebound spring from the damper rod **(see illustration)**.

9 Ease the fork protector off the top of the fork slider (K1 models onward), then prise out the dust seal from the top of the slider **(see illustration)**. Discard the dust seal as a new one must be used.

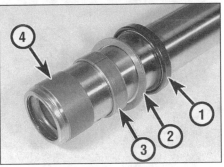

7.12 The oil seal (1), washer (2), top bush (3) and bottom bush (4) will come out with the fork tube

10 Carefully remove the retaining clip, taking care not to scratch the surface of the tube **(see illustration)**.

11 To separate the tube from the slider it will be necessary to displace the top bush and oil seal. The bottom bush should not pass through the top bush, and this can be used to good effect. Push the tube gently inwards until it stops against the damper rod seat. Take care not to do this forcibly or the seat may be damaged. Then pull the tube sharply outwards until the bottom bush strikes the top bush. Repeat this operation until the top bush and seal are tapped out of the slider **(see illustration)**.

12 With the tube removed, slide off the oil seal and its washer, noting which way up they fit **(see illustration)**. Discard the oil seal as a new one must be used. The top bush can then also be slid off its upper end.

Caution: Do not remove the bottom bush from the tube unless it is to be replaced.

13 Tip the damper rod seat out of the slider, noting which way up it fits.

Inspection

14 Clean all parts in solvent and blow them dry with compressed air, if available. Check the fork tube for score marks, scratches, flaking of the chrome finish and excessive or abnormal wear. Look for dents in the tube and replace the tube in both forks if any are found. Check the fork seal seat for nicks, gouges and scratches. If damage is evident, leaks will occur.

5

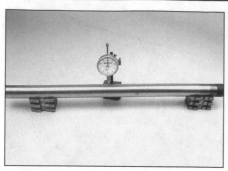

7.15 Check the fork tube for runout using V-blocks and a dial gauge

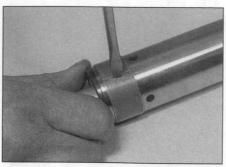

7.17 Prise off the bottom bush using a flat-bladed screwdriver

7.18 Replace the damper rod piston ring if it is worn or damaged

7.19a Slide the rebound spring onto the damper rod

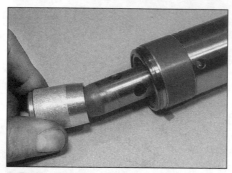

7.19b Fit the seat to the bottom of the damper rod

7.20a Slide the tube into the slider

7.20b Apply thread locking compound to the damper rod bolt and use a new sealing washer

7.21a Install the top bush . . .

7.21b . . . followed by the washer

15 Check the fork tube for runout using V-blocks and a dial gauge (see illustration).

 Warning: If it is bent, it should not be straightened; replace it with a new one.

16 Check the spring for cracks and other damage. Measure the spring free length and compare the measurement to the specifications at the beginning of the Chapter. If it is defective or sagged below the service limit, replace the springs in both forks with new ones. Never replace only one spring. Also check the rebound spring.

17 Examine the working surfaces of the two bushes; if worn or scuffed they must be replaced. Suzuki recommend that the bushes are replaced as a matter of course. To remove the bottom bush from the fork tube, prise it apart at the slit using a flat-bladed screwdriver

and slide it off (see illustration). Make sure the new one seats properly.

18 Check the damper rod and its piston ring for damage and wear, and replace them if necessary (see illustration).

Reassembly

19 If removed, install the piston ring into the groove in the damper rod head, then slide the rebound spring onto the rod (see illustration). Insert the damper rod into the fork tube and slide it into place so that it projects fully from the bottom of the tube, then install the seat on the bottom of the damper rod (see illustration).

20 Oil the fork tube and bottom bush with the specified fork oil and insert the assembly into the slider (see illustration). Fit a new copper sealing washer to the damper rod bolt and apply a few drops of a suitable non-permanent

thread locking compound, then install the bolt into the bottom of the slider (see illustration). Tighten the bolt to the specified torque setting. If the damper rod rotates inside the tube, temporarily install the fork spring and top bolt (see Steps 26 and 27) and compress the fork to hold the damper rod. Alternatively, a broom handle pressed hard into the damper rod head quite often suffices.

21 Push the fork tube fully into the slider, then oil the top bush and slide it down over the tube (see illustration). Press the bush squarely into its recess in the slider as far as possible, then install the oil seal washer (see illustration). Either use the service tool (Pt. No. 09940-50112) or a suitable piece of tubing to tap the bush fully into place; the tubing must be slightly larger in diameter than the fork tube and slightly smaller in diameter than the bush

7.22 Make sure the oil seal is the correct way up

7.23 Install the retaining clip . . .

7.24 . . . followed by the dust seal

7.25a Pour the oil into the top of the tube

7.25b Measure the oil level with the fork held vertical

the oil level should also be measured and adjustment made by adding or subtracting oil. Fully compress the fork tube into the slider and measure the fork oil level from the top of the tube **(see illustration)**. Add or subtract fork oil until the oil is at the level specified in the Specifications Section of this Chapter.

26 Clamp the slider very carefully in a vice, taking care not to overtighten and damage it. Pull the fork tube out of the slider as far as possible then install the spring, followed by the spring seat, with its shouldered side inserted into the spring, the spacer and the disc washer (where fitted) **(see illustrations)**.

27 Fit a new O-ring to the fork top bolt and thread the bolt into the top of the fork tube **(see illustration)**.

⚠ *Warning: It will be necessary to compress the spring by pressing it down using the top bolt to*

recess in the slider. Take care not to scratch the fork tube during this operation; it is best to make sure that the fork tube is pushed fully into the slider so that any accidental scratching is confined to the area above the oil seal.

22 When the bush is seated fully and squarely in its recess in the slider (remove the washer to check, wipe the recess clean, then reinstall the washer), install the new oil seal. Smear the seal's lips with fork oil and slide it over the tube so its markings face upwards and drive the seal into place as described in Step 21 until the retaining clip groove is visible above the seal **(see illustration)**.

23 Once the seal is correctly seated, fit the retaining clip, making sure it is correctly located in its groove **(see illustration)**.

24 Lubricate the lips of the new dust seal then slide it down the fork tube and press it into position **(see illustration)**. Install the fork protector (K1 models onward), positioning it

so that the tab on its inside edge engages the cutout in the fork slider and the protective shield faces forwards.

25 Slowly pour in the specified quantity of the specified grade of fork oil **(see illustration)**, and pump the fork to distribute the oil evenly;

7.26a Install the spring . . .

7.26b . . . followed by the spring seat (make sure its shouldered side fits into the top of the spring) . . .

7.26c . . . the spacer . . .

7.26d . . . and where fitted, the disc washer

7.27 Fit a new O-ring onto the top bolt and thread the bolt into the fork tube

5

8.3 Unscrew the bolts (arrows) and displace the clamp and guide/clip

8.7 Steering stem bolt (arrow)

engage the threads of the top bolt with the fork tube. This is a potentially dangerous operation and should be performed with care, using an assistant if necessary. Wipe off any excess oil before starting to prevent the possibility of slipping.
Keep the fork tube fully extended whilst pressing on the spring. Screw the top bolt carefully into the fork tube making sure it is not cross-threaded. Note: The top bolt can be tightened at this stage if the tube is held between the padded jaws of a vice, but do not risk distorting the tube by doing so. A better method is to tighten the top bolt when the fork has been installed in the bike and is securely held in the bottom yoke.

> **TOOL TiP** *Use a ratchet-type tool when installing the fork top bolt. This makes it unnecessary to remove the tool from the bolt whilst threading it in making it easier to maintain a downward pressure on the spring.*

28 Install the forks as described in Section 6.

8 Steering stem -
removal and installation

Caution: *Before removing the steering stem, it is recommended that the fuel tank be removed. This will prevent accidental damage to the paintwork.*

Removal

1 Remove the headlight (see Chapter 8).
2 Remove the instrument cluster (Chapter 8).
3 Unscrew the brake hose clamp bolts and the speedometer cable guide/ wiring loom clip to the bottom yoke **(see illustration)**.
4 Remove the handlebars, then remove the handlebar bracket from the top yoke (see Section 5).

5 Remove the front forks (see Section 6).
6 If the top yoke is to be removed from the bike altogether, trace the ignition switch wiring and disconnect it at its connector (see Chapter 8).
7 Remove the steering stem bolt and washer and lift the top yoke off the steering stem **(see**

illustration). Remove the headlight brackets with their rubber dampers, noting how they fit.
8 Supporting the bottom yoke, unscrew the adjuster nut using a suitable C-spanner, then remove the adjuster and the bearing cover from the steering stem **(see illustration)**.

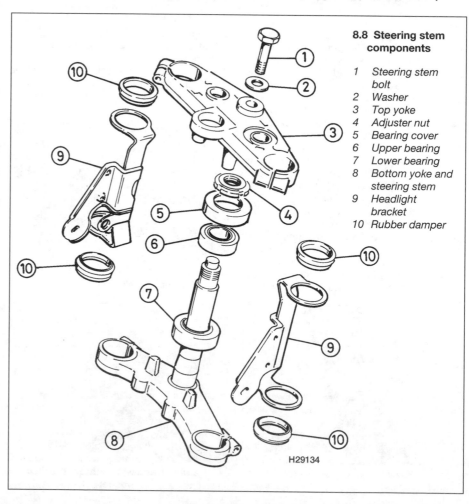

8.8 Steering stem components

1 Steering stem bolt
2 Washer
3 Top yoke
4 Adjuster nut
5 Bearing cover
6 Upper bearing
7 Lower bearing
8 Bottom yoke and steering stem
9 Headlight bracket
10 Rubber damper

H29134

8.13 Make sure the headlight brackets and their dampers are correctly installed

8.14 Tighten the steering stem bolt to the specified torque setting

9 Gently lower the bottom yoke and steering stem out of the frame.

10 Remove the upper bearing from the top of the steering head. Remove all traces of old grease from the bearings and races and check them for wear or damage (see Section 9). **Note:** *Do not attempt to remove the races from the frame or the lower bearing from the steering stem unless they are to be replaced.*

Installation

11 Smear a liberal quantity of grease on the bearing races in the frame. Work the grease well into both the upper and lower bearings.

12 Carefully lift the steering stem/bottom yoke up through the frame. Install the upper bearing in the top of the steering head. Install the bearing cover and thread the adjuster nut on the steering stem. Tighten the adjuster nut to the torque setting specified at the beginning of the Chapter, then turn the steering stem through its full lock five or six times, and then slacken the adjuster nut by 1/4 to 1/2 turn. If it is not possible to apply a torque wrench to the adjuster nut, tighten the nut and adjust the bearings as described in Chapter 1 after the installation procedure is complete.

Caution: Take great care not to apply excessive pressure because this will cause premature failure of the bearings.

13 Install the headlight brackets onto the bottom yoke, making sure the rubbers are in place. Install the top yoke onto the steering stem and make sure the top holes of the headlight brackets align with the holes in the top yoke and their rubbers are in place **(see illustration)**. Install the steering stem bolt and its washer and tighten it finger-tight at this stage. Temporarily install one of the forks to align the top and bottom yokes, and secure it by tightening the bottom yoke clamp bolt only.

14 Tighten the steering stem bolt to the specified torque setting **(see illustration)**. If disconnected, reconnect the ignition switch wiring connector.

15 Install the handlebar bracket and the handlebars (see Section 5).

16 Install the front forks (see Section 6).

17 Install the instrument cluster and the headlight (see Chapter 8).

18 Install the brake hose clamp and the speedometer guide/wiring loom clip onto the underside of the bottom yoke **(see illustration 8.3)**.

19 Carry out a check of the steering head bearing freeplay as described in Chapter 1, and if necessary re-adjust.

9 Steering head bearings - inspection and replacement

Inspection

1 Remove the steering stem (see Section 8).

2 Remove all traces of old grease from the bearings and races and check them for wear or damage. Also check the condition of the dust seal beneath the lower bearing.

3 The races should be polished and free from indentations. Inspect the bearing rollers for signs of wear, damage or discoloration, and examine the bearing roller retainer cage for signs of cracks or splits. Spin the bearings by hand. They should spin freely and smoothly. If there are any signs of wear on any of the above components both upper and lower bearing assemblies must be replaced as a set.

Replacement

4 The races are an interference fit in the steering head and can be tapped from position with a suitable drift. Tap firmly and evenly around each race to ensure that it is driven out squarely. It may prove advantageous to curve the end of the drift slightly to improve access.

5 Alternatively, the races can be removed using a slide-hammer type bearing extractor; these can often be hired from tool shops.

6 The new races can be pressed into the head using a drawbolt arrangement **(see illustration)**, or by using a large diameter tubular drift which bears only on the outer edge of the race. Ensure that the drawbolt washer or drift (as applicable) bears only on the outer edge of the race and does not contact the working surface. Alternatively, have the races installed by a Suzuki dealer with the bearing race installing tools.

> **HAYNES HiNT** *Installation of new head bearing races is made much easier if the races are left overnight in the freezer. This causes them to contract slightly making them a looser fit.*

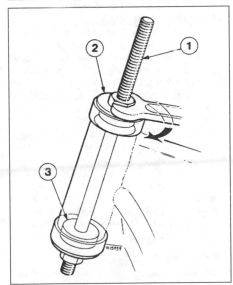

9.6 Drawbolt arrangement for fitting steering stem bearing races

1 *Long bolt or threaded bar*
2 *Thick washer*
3 *Guide for lower race*

5

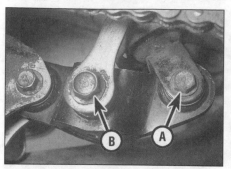

10.2 Shock absorber lower mounting bolt (A), suspension linkage rod bolt (B)

10.4a Remove the cap from the hole in the swingarm . . .

10.4b . . . then unscrew the bolt using a socket extension inserted through the hole

7 To remove the lower bearing from the steering stem, use two screwdrivers placed on opposite sides of the race to work it free. If the bearing is firmly in place it will be necessary to use a bearing puller, or in extreme circumstances to split the bearing's inner section.

8 Fit the new lower bearing onto the steering stem. A length of tubing with an internal diameter slightly larger than the steering stem will be needed to tap the new bearing into position. The drift must bear only on the inner edge of the bearing and not on the rollers.

9 Install the steering stem (see Section 8).

10 Rear shock absorber - removal, inspection and installation

Removal

1 Place the machine on its centre stand and position a support under the rear wheel so that it does not drop when the shock absorber is removed, but also making sure that the weight of the machine is off the rear suspension so that the shock is not compressed.

2 Unscrew the nut and withdraw the bolt securing the bottom of the shock absorber to the suspension linkage arm **(see illustration)**.

3 Unscrew the nut and withdraw the bolt securing the suspension linkage rods to the linkage arm, then swing the linkage arm down to provide clearance for removal of the shock absorber **(see illustration 10.2)**.

4 Access to the shock absorber upper mounting bolt is best achieved via the hole in the left-hand side of the frame. Remove the blanking cap, then counter-hold the nut and unscrew the bolt, using a socket extension inserted through the hole **(see illustrations)**. Support the shock absorber and withdraw the bolt, then manoeuvre the shock absorber out through the bottom of the swingarm.

Inspection

5 Inspect the shock absorber for obvious physical damage and the coil spring for looseness, cracks or signs of fatigue.

6 Inspect the damper rod for signs of bending, pitting and oil leakage.

7 Inspect the pivot hardware at the top and bottom of the shock for wear or damage.

8 If the shock absorber is damaged or worn it must be replaced. Individual replacement components are not available.

Installation

9 Installation is the reverse of removal, noting the following.

a) Apply multi-purpose lithium grease to the pivot points and to the bearings in the linkage arm.

b) Install the upper mounting bolt first, but do not tighten it until the lower mounting bolt and linkage rod bolt are installed.

c) Tighten all bolts to the specified torques.

d) Adjust the suspension pre-load as required (see Section 12).

11 Rear suspension linkage - removal, inspection and installation

Removal

1 Place the machine on its centre stand and position a support such as a block of wood under the rear wheel so that it does not drop when the shock absorber lower mounting bolt is removed, but also making sure that the weight of the machine is off the rear suspension so that the shock is not compressed.

2 Unscrew the nut and withdraw the bolt securing the linkage arm to the bottom of the shock absorber **(see illustrations)**.

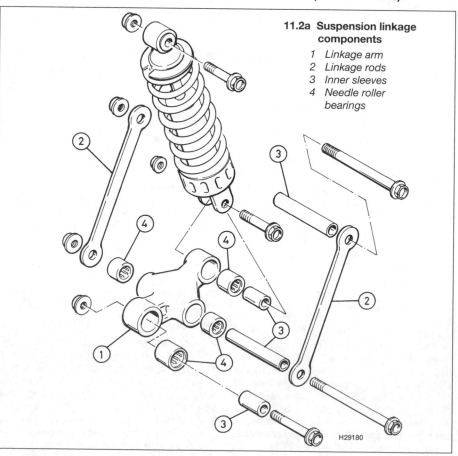

11.2a Suspension linkage components

1 Linkage arm
2 Linkage rods
3 Inner sleeves
4 Needle roller bearings

H29180

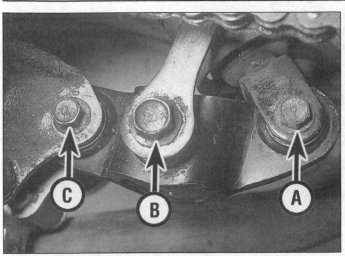

11.2b Shock absorber lower mounting bolt (A),
linkage rod bolt (B), linkage arm bolt (C)

11.4 Withdraw the linkage arm bolt and remove the arm
from the frame

3 Unscrew the nut and withdraw the bolt securing the linkage arm to the linkage rods (see illustration 11.2).

4 Unscrew the nut and withdraw the bolt securing the linkage arm to the frame, then remove the linkage arm from the frame, noting how it fits (see illustration).

5 Remove the chain guard (see Chapter 7). Unscrew the nut and withdraw the bolt securing the linkage rods to the top of the swingarm and remove the rods (see illustration).

Inspection

6 Withdraw the inner sleeves from the linkage arm, noting their different sizes (see illustration). Clean all components, removing all traces of dirt, corrosion and grease.

7 Inspect all components closely, looking for obvious signs of wear such as heavy scoring, or for damage such as cracks or distortion.

8 Check the condition of the needle roller bearings in the linkage arm and in the top of the swingarm (see illustration). If the linkage rod bearings in the swingarm need to be replaced, remove the swingarm (see Section 13).

9 Worn bearings can be driven out of their bores, but note that removal will destroy them; new bearings should be obtained before work commences. The new bearings should be pressed or drawn into their bores rather than driven into position. In the absence of a press, a suitable drawbolt arrangement can be made up - refer to *Bearings and bushes* in the Tools and Workshop tips section of Reference.

10 Lubricate the needle roller bearings and the inner sleeves with lithium-based grease (see illustration), then slip the inner sleeves into the bearings.

Installation

11 Installation is the reverse of removal, noting the following.

a) *Apply lithium-based grease to the bearings, inner sleeves and pivot bolts.*

b) *Do not fully tighten any of the bolts until they have all been installed.*

c) *Tighten the bolts to the torque setting specified at the beginning of the Chapter.*

d) *Check the operation of the rear suspension before taking the machine on the road.*

11.5 Unscrew the nut (arrow) and remove
the bolt to free the linkage rods

11.6 Linkage arm inner sleeves

12 Suspension - adjustments

Front forks

Note: *Pre-load adjusters are fitted to the top bolts on certain models.*

1 Place the machine on its centre stand and take the weight off the front forks, either by placing a support under the engine or by having an assistant press down on the rear of the machine.

2 Adjustment is made by turning the adjuster in the centre of the fork top bolt, using a spanner on the flats on the top of the adjuster

11.8 Check the needle roller bearings for
wear and damage

11.10 Lubricate all the bearings
with grease

5

12.2 Front fork pre-load adjuster – set to position 4

13.3a Release the brake hose from the front clamp (arrow) . . .

13.3b . . . and the rear clamp (arrow) on the swingarm

(see illustration). There are seven positions, indicated by lines on the adjuster. Position 7 (i.e. with 7 lines showing above the bolt hex) is the softest setting, position 1 (i.e. with 1 line showing) is the hardest. Align the setting line required with the top of the bolt hex. Position 4 is the standard setting.

3 To increase the pre-load, turn the adjuster clockwise. To decrease the pre-load, turn the adjuster anti-clockwise.

4 Ensure the setting line required is level with the top edge of the fork top bolt and that both adjusters are set to the same position.

Rear shock absorber

5 The rear shock absorber is adjustable for spring pre-load. Place the machine on its centre stand when making adjustments.

6 Adjustment is made using a suitable

C-spanner (one is provided in the toolkit) to turn the spring seat on the bottom of the shock absorber. There are seven positions. Position 1 is the softest setting, position 7 is the hardest. Align the setting number required with the adjustment stopper. Position 4 is the standard setting.

7 To increase the pre-load, turn the spring seat clockwise. To decrease the pre-load, turn the spring seat anti-clockwise.

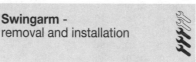

13 Swingarm -
removal and installation

Removal

Note: *Before removing the swingarm, it is*

advisable to perform the swingarm checks described in Chapter 1.

1 Remove the rear wheel (see Chapter 6).

2 Remove the rear shock absorber (Section 10).

3 Release the brake hose from its clamps and guide on the swingarm, using a screwdriver to prise open the clamps (see illustrations). Remove the split pin from the end of the bolt securing the brake torque arm to the brake caliper, then unscrew the nut, withdraw the bolt and remove the caliper from the torque arm (see illustrations). Move the caliper aside and support it so that no strain is placed on the hose.

4 Prise off the swingarm pivot pin caps on both sides of the swingarm (see illustration).

5 Before removing the swingarm it is advisable to re-check for play in the bearings. Any problems which may have been overlooked when checking with the wheel and shock absorber in place (see Chapter 1) are highlighted with these components removed.

6 Unscrew the nut and remove the washer on the right-hand end of the swingarm pivot bolt (see illustration). With the aid of an assistant to support the swingarm if required, drift the pivot bolt out and withdraw it from the left-hand side of the frame (see illustration). Note the positions of any breather and drain pipes and move them aside if necessary, then manoeuvre the swingarm out of the back of the machine.

13.3c Remove the split pin and unscrew the nut . . .

13.3d . . . then withdraw the bolt and separate the caliper from the torque arm

13.4 Remove the swingarm pivot caps

13.6a Unscrew the swingarm pivot nut (arrow) . . .

13.6b . . . and withdraw the swingarm pivot bolt

13.7 Note the brake hose guide fitted to the torque arm mounting

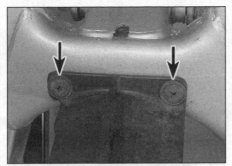

13.8 The mudflap is secured by two screws (arrows)

13.9 The chain slider is retained by the clip (arrow)

13.11a Tighten the swingarm nut to the specified torque setting

13.11b Fit a new split pin on each torque arm bolt

7 If required, remove the split pin from the end of the bolt securing the brake torque arm to the swingarm, then unscrew the nut, noting how the brake hose guide fits, withdraw the bolt and remove the torque arm **(see illustration)**.

8 If required, unscrew the two screws securing the mudflap to the underside of the swingarm and remove the flap **(see illustration)**.

9 Check the condition of the chain slider on the front of the swingarm and replace it if it is worn or damaged **(see illustration)**.

10 Inspect all parts for wear or damage (see Section 14).

Installation

11 Installation is the reverse of removal, noting the following.

a) *Remove the dust seal, washer and inner sleeve from each swingarm bearing, then lubricate the bearings and inner sleeves with lithium-based grease (see illustrations 14.3a and 14.3b). Fit the sleeves back into the bearings and install the washers and dust seals. Also lubricate the pivot bolt and the shock absorber pivot and suspension linkage bearings with lithium-based grease.*

b) *Loop the drive chain over the swingarm as it is offered up to the frame. Make sure that the chain slider is fitted to the swingarm.*

c) *Tighten the swingarm pivot bolt nut to the specified torque setting (see illustration).*

d) *Tighten the shock absorber and linkage bolts to the specified torque settings.*

e) *Tighten the brake torque arm nuts to the specified torque setting. Fit a new split pin onto the end of the bolt (see illustration)*

and bend its ends securely around the nut. Secure the brake hose in its clamps.

f) *Check the operation of the rear suspension before taking the machine on the road.*

---

14 Swingarm - inspection and bearing replacement

Inspection

1 Thoroughly clean all components, removing all traces of dirt, corrosion and grease **(see illustration)**.

2 Inspect all components closely, looking for obvious signs of wear such as heavy scoring, and cracks or distortion due to accident damage. Any damaged or worn component must be replaced.

Bearing replacement

3 Remove the dust seals, washers and the bearing inner sleeves and spacer, noting where

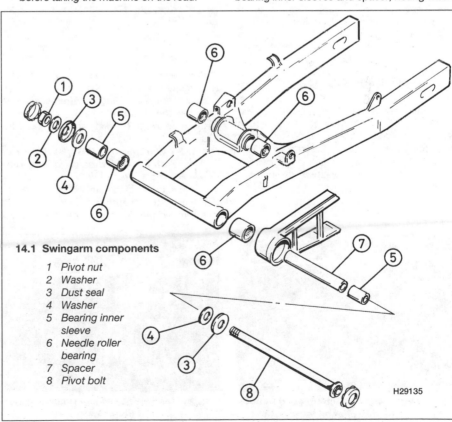

14.1 Swingarm components

1 Pivot nut
2 Washer
3 Dust seal
4 Washer
5 Bearing inner sleeve
6 Needle roller bearing
7 Spacer
8 Pivot bolt

H29135

5

14.3a Remove the dust seals and washers . . .

14.3b . . . then withdraw the inner sleeves . . .

14.3c . . . and spacer

14.3d Inspect the needle roller bearings in the swingarm

each one fits as they must be replaced in the same position **(see illustrations)**. Inspect them and the bearings for wear or damage and replace them if necessary **(see illustration)**.

4 Worn bearings can be driven out of their bores, but note that removal will destroy them; new bearings should be obtained before work commences. The new bearings should be pressed or drawn into their bores rather than driven into position. In the absence of a press, a suitable drawbolt arrangement can be made up - refer to *Tools* in the Reference section.

Note: *Install the bearings with their marked side facing outwards* **(see illustration 14.3d)**.

5 Apply lithium-based grease to the bearing, spacer, inner sleeves, washer and inside of the dust seal.

15 Drive chain - removal, cleaning and installation

Removal

Note: *The original equipment drive chain fitted to all models is an endless chain, which means it doesn't have a joining link. Removal either requires the removal of the swingarm as detailed below, or breaking and riveting of the chain.*

⚠️ **Warning: NEVER install a drive chain which uses a clip-type master (split) link.**

1 Remove the swingarm (see Section 13).

2 Unscrew the gearchange lever pinch bolt and remove the lever from the shaft, noting

any alignment marks on the lever and the shaft **(see illustration)**. If no marks are visible, make your own before removing the lever so that it can be correctly aligned with the shaft on installation. Unscrew the bolts securing the engine sprocket cover to the crankcase and move it aside **(see illustration)**. There is no need to detach the clutch cable from the cover.

3 Slip the chain off the front sprocket and remove it from the bike.

Cleaning

4 Soak the chain in paraffin (kerosene) for approximately five or six minutes.

Caution: Don't use petrol (gasoline), solvent or other cleaning fluids. Also don't use high-pressure water. Remove the chain, wipe it off, then blow dry it with compressed air immediately. The entire process shouldn't take longer than ten minutes - if it does, the O-rings in the chain rollers could be damaged.

Installation

5 Installation is the reverse of removal. On completion adjust and lubricate the chain following the procedures described in Chapter 1.

Caution: Use only the recommended lubricant.

16 Sprockets - check and replacement

Check

1 Unscrew the gearchange lever pinch bolt and remove the lever from its shaft, noting any alignment marks on the lever and the shaft **(see illustration 15.2a)**. If no marks are visible, make your own before removing the lever so that it can be correctly aligned with the shaft on installation. Unscrew the bolts securing the engine sprocket cover to the crankcase and move the cover aside **(see illustration 15.2b)**. There is no need to detach the clutch cable from the cover.

2 Check the wear pattern on both sprockets **(see illustration)**. If the sprocket teeth are

15.2a Unscrew the pinch bolt and remove the gearchange lever

15.2b The sprocket cover is secured by five bolts (arrows)

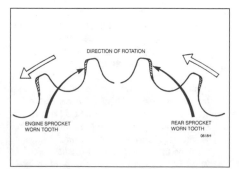

16.2 Check the sprocket teeth for wear in the areas indicated

worn excessively, replace the chain and both sprockets as a set. Whenever the sprockets are inspected, the drive chain should be inspected also (see Chapter 1). If you are replacing the chain, replace the sprockets as well.

3 Adjust and lubricate the chain following the procedures described in Chapter 1.
Caution: Use only the recommended lubricant.

Replacement

Front sprocket

4 Unscrew the gearchange lever pinch bolt and remove the lever from the shaft, noting any alignment marks on the lever and the shaft **(see illustration 15.2a)**. If no marks are visible, make your own before removing the lever so that it can be correctly aligned with the shaft on installation. Unscrew the bolts securing the engine sprocket cover to the crankcase and move the cover aside **(see illustration 15.2b)**. There is no need to detach the clutch cable from the cover.
5 Remove the circlip securing the sprocket to the end of the output shaft **(see illustration)**.
6 Slide the sprocket and chain off the shaft, then slip the sprocket out of the chain. If the chain is too tight to allow the sprocket to be slid off the shaft, slacken the chain adjusters to provide some freeplay (see Chapter 1), or, if the rear sprocket is being replaced as well, remove the rear wheel.
7 Engage the new sprocket with the chain

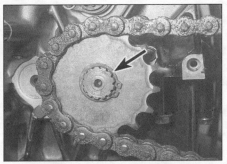
16.5 The sprocket is retained on the output shaft by a circlip (arrow)

and slide it on the shaft **(see illustrations)**. Secure the sprocket with its circlip, making sure it is properly seated in its groove **(see illustration)**.
8 Install the sprocket cover and the gearchange lever, aligning the punch marks. Adjust and lubricate the chain following the procedures described in Chapter 1.

Rear sprocket

9 Remove the rear wheel (see Chapter 6).
10 Unscrew the nuts securing the sprocket to the wheel coupling, then remove the sprocket, noting which way round it fits **(see illustration)**.
11 Before installing the new rear sprocket, check the wheel coupling and damper assembly components (see Section 17).
12 Install the sprocket onto the coupling with

the stamped mark facing out, then apply a suitable non-permanent thread locking compound to the stud threads and tighten the sprocket nuts to the torque setting specified at the beginning of the Chapter.
13 Install the rear wheel (see Chapter 6).
14 Adjust and lubricate the chain following the procedures described in Chapter 1.

17 Rear wheel coupling/ rubber dampers - check and replacement

1 Remove the rear wheel (see Chapter 6).
Caution: Do not lay the wheel down on the disc as it could become warped. Lay the wheel on wooden blocks so that the disc is off the ground.
2 Lift the sprocket coupling away from the wheel leaving the rubber dampers in position in the wheel **(see illustration)**. Note the spacer inside the coupling.
3 Lift the rubber damper segments from the wheel and check them for cracks, hardening and general deterioration **(see illustration)**. Replace the rubber dampers as a set if necessary.
4 Checking and replacement procedures for the sprocket coupling bearing are described in Section 16 of Chapter 6.
5 Installation is the reverse of removal. Make sure the spacer is correctly installed in the coupling.
6 Install the rear wheel (see Chapter 6).

16.7a Fit the sprocket into the chain . . .

16.7b . . . then slide the sprocket onto the shaft . . .

16.7c . . . and retain it with the circlip

16.10 The sprocket is secured by five nuts (arrows)

17.2 Lift the sprocket coupling out of the wheel . . .

17.3 . . . and check the damper segments for wear and deterioration

5

Notes

Chapter 6
Brakes, wheels and tyres

Contents

Degrees of difficulty

Easy, suitable for novice with little experience	**Fairly easy,** suitable for beginner with some experience	**Fairly difficult,** suitable for competent DIY mechanic	**Difficult,** suitable for experienced DIY mechanic	**Very difficult,** suitable for expert DIY or professional

Specifications

Brakes

Brake fluid type . . . . DOT 4

	Standard	Service limit
Disc minimum thickness		
Front	4.3 to 4.7 mm	4.0 mm
Rear	5.8 to 6.2 mm	5.5 mm
Disc maximum runout (front and rear)	0.3 mm	

Caliper bore ID
  Front
    EK to ES models
      Piston A . . . . 27.000 to 27.076 mm
      Piston B . . . . 33.960 to 34.036 mm
    ET to EY models and K1 models onward . . . . 30.230 to 30.306 mm
  Rear . . . . 38.180 to 38.256 mm
Caliper piston OD
  Front
    EK to ES models
      Piston A . . . . 26.920 to 26.970 mm
      Piston B . . . . 33.884 to 33.934 mm
    ET to EY models and K1 models onward . . . . 30.150 to 30.200 mm
  Rear . . . . 38.098 to 38.148 mm
Master cylinder bore ID (front and rear) . . . . 12.700 to 12.743 mm
Master cylinder piston OD (front and rear) . . . . 12.657 to 12.684 mm

Wheels

Maximum wheel runout (front and rear)
  Axial (side-to-side) . . . . 2.0 mm
  Radial (out-of-round) . . . . 2.0 mm
Maximum axle runout (front and rear) . . . . 0.25 mm

Tyres

Tyre pressures and tread depth . . . . see Chapter 1
Tyre sizes*
  Front 110/70-17 54H
  Rear 130/70-17 62H

*Refer to the owners handbook or the tyre information label on the drive chain guard for approved tyre brands.

6

Torque settings

Front brake caliper mounting bolts . . . . 30 to 48 Nm
Front brake disc retaining bolts . . . . 18 to 28 Nm
Front brake master cylinder clamp bolts . . . . 8 to 12 Nm
Rear brake caliper mounting bolts . . . . 20 to 31 Nm
Rear brake caliper body joining bolts . . . . 30 to 36 Nm
Rear brake torque arm nuts . . . . 22 to 35 Nm
Rear brake disc retaining bolts . . . . 18 to 28 Nm
Rear brake master cylinder mounting bolts . . . . 8 to 12 Nm
Brake caliper bleed valves . . . . 6 to 9 Nm
Brake hose banjo union bolts . . . . 15 to 20 Nm
Front axle nut
   Self-locking nut (UK models) . . . . 40 to 58 Nm
   Nut with split-pin (US models) . . . . 36 to 52 Nm
Front axle clamp bolt . . . . 18 to 28 Nm
Rear axle nut
   Self-locking nut (UK models) . . . . 60 to 96 Nm
   Nut with split-pin (US models) . . . . 50 to 80 Nm

1 General information

All models covered in this manual are fitted with cast alloy wheels designed for tubeless tyres only. Both front and rear brakes are single hydraulically operated disc brakes, the front being a sliding caliper design and the rear an opposed caliper design.

Caution: Disc brake components rarely require disassembly. Do not disassemble components unless absolutely necessary. If a hydraulic brake line is loosened, the entire system must be disassembled, drained, cleaned and then properly filled and bled upon reassembly. Do not use solvents on internal brake components. Solvents will cause the seals to swell and distort. Use only clean brake fluid or denatured alcohol for cleaning. Use care when working with brake fluid as it can injure your eyes and it will damage painted surfaces and plastic parts.

2 Front brake pads - replacement

⚠️ *Warning: The dust created by the brake system may contain asbestos, which is harmful to your health. Never blow it out with compressed air and don't inhale any of it. An approved filtering mask should be worn when working on the brakes.*

1 On EK to ES models, unscrew the brake caliper mounting bolts and slide the caliper off the disc **(see illustration 3.2a)**. Slide the caliper out on its sliders until the inner pad can be lifted off its guide pins on the caliper mounting bracket **(see illustration)**. Remove the outer pad from the caliper body, noting how the protrusion on each end of the pad locates against the guide. Also note how the pad spring is fitted and remove it if required.

2 On ET to EY models and K1 models onward, unscrew the brake caliper mounting bolts and slide the caliper off the disc. Remove the R-clip from the end of the pad retaining pin and withdraw the pin **(see illustrations)**. Rotate the inner pad on its guide pin and remove it **(see illustration)**. Remove the outer pad from the caliper body, noting how the protrusion on the upper end of the pad locates against the pad guide on the caliper bracket **(see illustration)**. Note the shim on the back of the outer pad.

3 Inspect the surface of each pad for contamination and check that the friction material has not worn beyond its wear limit. The original equipment pads feature wear indicators (see Chapter 1, Section 13). Replace both pads as a set if either pad has

2.1 Lift the inner pad until it clears its pins, then remove it from the caliper

2.2a Remove the R-clip (arrow) . . .

2.2d Note how the outer pad locates against the pad guide (arrow)

2.2b . . . and withdraw the pad retaining pin

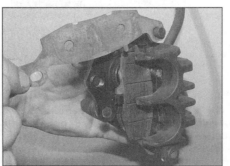
2.2c Rotate the inner pad and remove it . . .

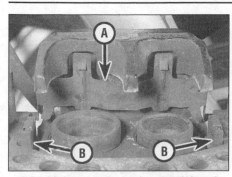

2.9a Make sure the pad spring (A) and outer pad guides (B) are correctly installed

2.9b Fit the inner pad onto its guide pins . . .

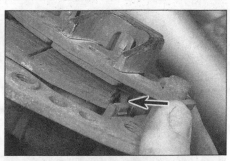

2.9c . . . and fit the outer pad so that the protrusion on each end locates on top of the guide

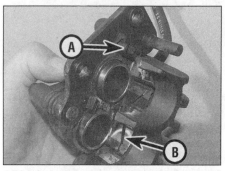

2.10a Location of pad guide (A) and spring (B)

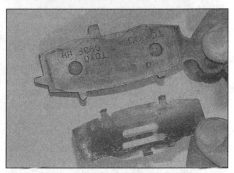

2.10b Shim is fitted to the back of the outer pad (K1 models onward)

worn down to, or beyond, the indicator. Additionally, renew the pads if they are fouled with grease, or heavily scored or damaged by dirt and debris. Note that it is not possible to degrease the friction material; if the pads are contaminated in any way they must be renewed.

4 If the pads are in good condition clean them carefully, using a fine wire brush which is completely free of oil and grease to remove all traces of road dirt and corrosion.

5 Check the condition of the brake disc (see Section 4).

6 On ET models onward, remove all traces of corrosion from the pad retaining pin. Inspect the pin for signs of damage and renew it if necessary.

7 Push the pistons as far back into the caliper as possible using hand pressure only. Due to the increased friction material thickness of new pads, it may be necessary to remove the master cylinder reservoir cover and diaphragm and siphon out some fluid.

8 Smear the backs of the pads and the shank of the pad retaining pin (ET to EY models and K1 models onwards) with copper-based grease, making sure that none gets on the front or sides of the pads.

9 On EK to ES models, installation of the pads is the reverse of removal. Make sure the pad spring and guides are correctly positioned **(see illustration)**. Insert the pads into the caliper so that the friction material of each pad will be facing the disc **(see illustration)**. Make sure the protrusion on each end of the outer pad locates correctly against its guide **(see illustration)**.

10 On ET to EY models and K1 models onward, installation of the pads and pad pin is the reverse of removal. Make sure the pad spring and guide are correctly positioned in the caliper **(see illustration)**. On K1 models onward, ensure the pad shim is correctly positioned on the back of the outer pad **(see illustration)**. Insert the pads in the caliper so that the friction material of each pad will be facing the disc. Make sure the protrusion on the outer pad locates correctly against the guide. Also make sure the pad pin passes through each pad, then secure it with the R-clip.

11 Install the caliper on the brake disc

making sure the pads sit squarely either side of the disc **(see illustration 3.13)**.

12 Apply a few drops of non-permanent locking compound to the threads of the caliper mounting bolts, then install and tighten them to the torque setting specified at the beginning of this Chapter **(see illustration 3.14a and 3.14b)**.

13 Top up the master cylinder reservoir if necessary (see *Daily (pre-ride) checks*), and replace the reservoir cover and diaphragm if removed.

14 Operate the brake lever several times to bring the pads into contact with the disc. Check the master cylinder fluid level in the reservoir and the operation of the brake before riding the motorcycle.

3 Front brake caliper - removal, overhaul and installation

> ⚠ **Warning: If the caliper indicates the need for an overhaul (usually due to leaking fluid or sticky operation), all old brake fluid should be flushed from the system. Also, the dust created by the brake system may contain asbestos, which is harmful to your health. Never blow it out with compressed air and don't inhale any of it. An approved filtering mask should be worn when working on the brakes. Do not use petroleum-based solvents to clean brake parts. Use clean brake fluid, brake cleaner or denatured alcohol only.**

Removal

1 Remove the brake hose banjo bolt, noting its position on the caliper and separate the hose from the caliper **(see illustration)**. Plug the hose end or wrap a plastic bag tightly around it to minimise fluid loss and prevent dirt entering the system. Discard the sealing washers as new ones must be used on installation. **Note:** *If you are planning to overhaul the caliper and don't have a source of compressed air to blow out the pistons, just loosen the banjo bolt at this stage and retighten it lightly. The bike's hydraulic system can then be used to force the pistons out of the body once the pads have been removed. Disconnect the hose once the pistons have been sufficiently displaced.*

2 Unscrew the caliper mounting bolts, and slide the caliper away from the disc (see

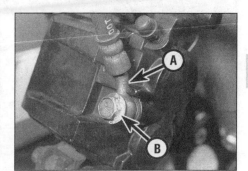

3.1 Note alignment of brake hose in slot (A) before unscrewing banjo bolt (B)

6

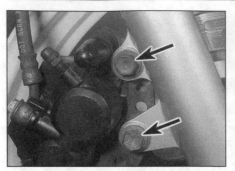

3.2a Caliper mounting bolts (arrows)

3.2b Remove the insulator piece from each piston

illustration). Remove the brake pads as described in Section 2. On EK to ES models, remove the insulator pieces from the pistons (see illustration).

Overhaul

3 Clean the exterior of the caliper with denatured alcohol or brake system cleaner (see illustration).

4 Remove the pistons from the caliper body, either by pumping them out by operating the front brake lever until the pistons are displaced, or by forcing them out using compressed air. Note that on EK to ES models, two sizes of piston are used (see Specifications), and that different size seals are used accordingly. Mark each piston head and caliper body with a felt marker to ensure that the pistons can be matched to their original bores on reassembly.

If the compressed air method is used, place a wad of rag between the pistons and the caliper to act as a cushion, then use compressed air directed into the fluid inlet to force the pistons out of the body. Use only low pressure to ease the pistons out and make sure both pistons are displaced at the same time. If the air pressure is too high and the pistons are forced out, the caliper and/or pistons may be damaged.

⚠️ **Warning: Never place your fingers in front of the pistons to catch or protect them when applying compressed air, as serious injury could result.**

5 Using a wooden or plastic tool, remove the dust seals from the caliper bores and discard them. New seals must be used on installation. If a metal tool is being used, take great care not to damage the caliper bores.

6 Remove and discard the piston seals in the same way.

7 Clean the pistons and bores with denatured alcohol, clean brake fluid or brake system cleaner. If compressed air is available, use it to dry the parts thoroughly (make sure it's filtered and unlubricated).
Caution: Do not use a petroleum-based solvent of any kind to clean brake parts.

8 Inspect the caliper bores and pistons for signs of corrosion, nicks and burrs and loss of plating. If surface defects are present, the caliper assembly must be replaced. If the necessary measuring equipment is available, compare the dimensions of the pistons and bores to those given in the Specifications Section of this Chapter, replacing any component that is worn beyond the service limit. Check that the caliper body is able to slide freely on the mounting bracket slider pins. If seized due to corrosion, separate the two components and clean off all traces of corrosion and hardened grease. Apply a smear of copper or silicone grease to the mounting bracket slider pins and reassemble the two components. Replace the rubber boots if they are damaged or deteriorated. If the caliper is in bad shape the master cylinder should also be checked.

9 Lubricate the new piston seals with clean brake fluid and install them in their grooves in the caliper bores. Note that on EK to ES models, two sizes of bore and piston are used (see Specifications), and care must therefore

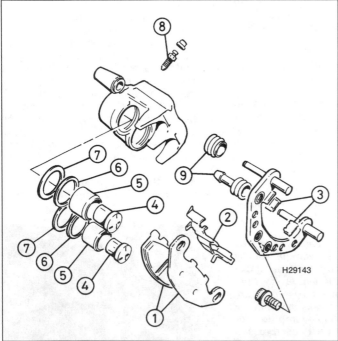

3.3a Front brake caliper components – EK to ES models

1 Brake pads	4 Piston insulator	7 Piston seal
2 Pad spring	5 Piston	8 Bleed valve
3 Outer pad guides	6 Dust seal	9 Rubber boot

3.3b Front brake caliper components – ET to EY models and K1 models onward

1 Brake pads	4 Piston seal	7 Pad spring	9 Outer pad
2 Pad pin	5 Dust seal	8 Rubber boot	guide
3 R-clip	6 Piston		10 Bleed valve

3.13 Slide the caliper onto the disc

3.14a Apply a thread locking compound to the caliper bolts . . .

3.14b . . . and tighten them to the specified torque setting

be taken to ensure that the correct size seals are fitted to the correct bores. The same applies when fitting the new dust seals and pistons.

10 Lubricate the new dust seals with clean brake fluid and install them in their grooves in the caliper bores.

11 Lubricate the pistons with clean brake fluid and install them closed-end first into the caliper bores. Using your thumbs, push the pistons all the way in, making sure they enter the bore squarely.

Installation

12 On EK to ES models, install the insulator pieces in the pistons **(see illustration 3.2b)**.

13 On all models, install the brake pads (see Section 2). Install the caliper on the brake disc making sure the pads sit squarely either side of the disc **(see illustration)**.

14 Apply a few drops of non-permanent locking compound to the threads of the caliper mounting bolts, then install and tighten them to the torque setting specified at the beginning of this **(see illustrations)**.

15 Connect the brake hose to the caliper, using new sealing washers on each side of the fitting. Position the hose so that it fits into its slot in the caliper **(see illustration 3.1)**. Tighten the banjo bolt to the torque setting specified at the beginning of the Chapter.

16 Fill the master cylinder with the recommended brake fluid (see Specifications) and bleed the hydraulic system as described in Section 11.

17 Check for leaks and thoroughly test the operation of the brake before riding the motorcycle.

---

4 Front brake disc - inspection, removal and installation

Inspection

1 Visually inspect the surface of the disc for score marks and other damage. Light scratches are normal after use and won't affect brake operation, but deep grooves and heavy score marks will reduce braking efficiency and accelerate pad wear. If a disc is

badly grooved it must be machined or replaced.

2 To check disc runout, position the bike on its centre stand and support it so that the front wheel is raised off the ground. Mount a dial gauge to a fork leg, with the plunger on the indicator touching the surface of the disc about 10 mm (1/2 inch) from the outer edge **(see illustration)**. Rotate the wheel and watch the indicator needle, comparing the reading with the limit listed in the Specifications at the beginning of the Chapter. If the runout is greater than the service limit, check the wheel bearings for play (see Chapter 1). If the bearings are worn, replace them (refer to Section 16) and repeat this check. If the disc runout is still excessive, it will have to be replaced, although machining by a competent engineering shop may be possible.

3 The disc must not be machined or allowed to wear down to a thickness less than the service

limit as listed in this Chapter's Specifications and as marked on the disc itself **(see illustration)**. The thickness of the disc can be checked with a micrometer **(see illustration)**. If the thickness of the disc is less than the service limit, it must be replaced.

Removal

4 Remove the wheel (see Section 14).

Caution: Do not lay the wheel down and allow it to rest on the disc - the disc could become warped. Set the wheel on wood blocks so the disc doesn't support the weight of the wheel.

5 Mark the relationship of the disc to the wheel, so it can be installed in the same position. Unscrew the disc retaining bolts, loosening them a little at a time in a criss-cross pattern to avoid distorting the disc, then remove the disc from the wheel **(see illustration)**.

4.2 Set up a dial gauge against the brake disc, then rotate wheel to check for runout

4.3a The minimum disc thickness is marked on the disc

4.3b Using a micrometer to measure disc thickness

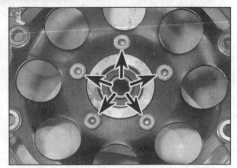

4.5 The disc is secured by five bolts (arrows)

6

5.4 Slacken the reservoir cover screws (arrows)

5.5 Disconnect the brake light switch electrical connectors (arrow)

5.6a Remove the locknut (arrow) . . .

5.6b . . . then unscrew the pivot bolt (arrow) and remove the lever

Installation

6 Install the disc on the wheel, aligning the previously applied matchmarks (if you're reinstalling the original disc).

7 Apply a suitable non-permanent thread locking compound to the disc mounting bolt threads, then install the bolts and tighten them in a criss-cross pattern evenly and progressively to the torque setting specified at the beginning of the Chapter. Clean off all grease from the brake disc using acetone or brake system cleaner. If a new brake disc has been installed, remove any protective coating from its working surfaces.

8 Install the front wheel (see Section 14).

9 Operate the brake lever several times to bring the pads into contact with the disc. Check the operation of the brake carefully before riding the bike.

5 Front brake master cylinder - removal, overhaul and installation

1 If the master cylinder is leaking fluid, or if the lever does not produce a firm feel when the brake is applied, and bleeding the brakes does not help (see Section 11), and the hydraulic hoses are all in good condition, then master cylinder overhaul is recommended.

2 Before disassembling the master cylinder, read through the entire procedure and make sure that you have the new seals required. Also, you will need some new, clean brake fluid of the recommended type, some clean rags and internal circlip pliers. **Note:** *To prevent damage to the paint from spilled brake fluid, always cover the fuel tank when working on the master cylinder.*

Caution: Disassembly, overhaul and reassembly of the brake master cylinder must be done in a spotlessly clean work area to avoid contamination and possible failure of the brake hydraulic system components.

Removal

3 If required, remove the rear view mirror (see Chapter 7).

4 Loosen, but do not remove, the screws holding the reservoir cover in place **(see illustration)**.

5 Disconnect the electrical connectors from the brake light switch **(see illustration)**.

6 Remove the locknut from the underside of the brake lever pivot bolt, then unscrew the bolt and remove the brake lever **(see illustrations)**.

7 Unscrew the brake hose banjo bolt and

5.8 Front brake master cylinder clamp bolts (arrows)

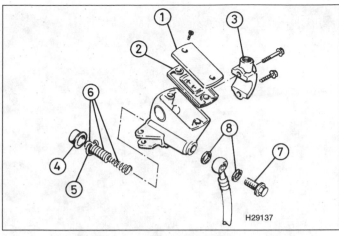

5.9 Front brake master cylinder components

1	Reservoir cover	4	Rubber dust boot
2	Rubber diaphragm and plate	5	Circlip
3	Clamp	6	Piston assembly and spring

7 Banjo bolt
8 Sealing washer

separate the hose from the master cylinder, noting its alignment. Discard the two sealing washers as they must be replaced with new ones. Wrap the end of the hose in a clean rag and suspend it in an upright position or bend it down carefully and place the open end in a clean container. The objective is to prevent excessive loss of brake fluid, fluid spills and system contamination.

8 Remove the master cylinder mounting bolts to free the clamp, noting how the mating surfaces of the clamp align with the punch mark on the handlebar, then lift the master cylinder and reservoir away from the handlebar (see illustration).
Caution: Do not tip the master cylinder upside down or brake fluid will run out.

Overhaul

9 Remove the reservoir cover retaining screws and lift off the cover, the diaphragm plate and the rubber diaphragm (see illustration). Drain the brake fluid from the reservoir into a suitable container. Wipe any remaining fluid out of the reservoir with a clean rag.
10 Remove the screw securing the brake light switch to the bottom of the master cylinder and remove the switch.
11 Carefully remove the dust boot from the end of the piston.
12 Using circlip pliers, remove the circlip and slide out the piston assembly and the spring, noting how they fit. Lay the parts out in the proper order to prevent confusion during reassembly.
13 Clean all parts with clean brake fluid or denatured alcohol. If compressed air is available, use it to dry the parts thoroughly (make sure it's filtered and unlubricated).
Caution: Do not, under any circumstances, use a petroleum-based solvent to clean brake parts.

14 Check the master cylinder bore for corrosion, scratches, nicks and score marks. If the necessary measuring equipment is available, compare the dimensions of the piston and bore to those given in the Specifications Section of this Chapter. If damage or wear is evident, the master cylinder must be replaced with a new one. If the master cylinder is in poor condition, then the caliper should be checked as well. Check that the fluid inlet and outlet ports in the master cylinder are clear.
15 The dust boot, circlip, piston and spring are only available as an assembly. Use all of the new parts, regardless of the apparent condition of the old ones.
16 Install the spring in the master cylinder so that its tapered (smaller) end faces the piston.
17 Lubricate the piston assembly components with clean brake fluid and install the assembly into the master cylinder, making sure all the components are the correct way round. Make sure the lips on the cup seals do not turn inside out when they are slipped into the bore. Depress the piston and install the new circlip, making sure that it locates in the master cylinder groove.
18 Install the rubber dust boot, making sure the lip is seated correctly in the piston groove.
19 Install the brake light switch.
20 Inspect the reservoir rubber diaphragm and replace if damaged or deteriorated.

Installation

21 Attach the master cylinder to the handlebar and fit the clamp. Align the mating surfaces of the clamp with the punch mark on the handlebar. Fully tighten the upper bolt first then the lower bolt to the torque setting specified at the beginning of the Chapter (see illustration).
22 Connect the brake hose to the master cylinder, using new sealing washers on each

side of the union, and aligning the hose as noted on removal. Tighten the banjo bolt to the torque setting specified at the beginning of this Chapter.
23 Install the brake lever into its bracket and secure it with its pivot bolt. Tighten the bolt then install the pivot bolt locknut (see illustrations 5.6b and 5.6a).
24 Connect the brake light switch wiring (see illustration 5.5) and install the rear view mirror if removed (see Chapter 7).
25 Fill the fluid reservoir with the specified brake fluid as described in Daily (pre-ride) checks. Refer to Section 11 of this Chapter and bleed the air from the system.
26 Fit the rubber diaphragm, making sure it is correctly folded, the diaphragm plate and the cover onto the master cylinder reservoir.

6 Rear brake pads - replacement

Warning: The dust created by the brake system may contain asbestos, which is harmful to your health. Never blow it out

5.21 Align the mating surfaces of the clamp with the punch mark (arrow)

6

6.2 Remove the pad pin clips . . .

6.3a . . . then press down on the pad spring ends and withdraw the pad pins . . .

6.3b . . . followed by the pad springs

6.4 Withdraw the pads and remove the anti-chatter shims

with compressed air and don't inhale any of it. An approved filtering mask should be worn when working on the brakes.

1 Prise off the brake pad cover using a flat-bladed screwdriver.

2 Remove the pad pin retaining clips, noting how they fit **(see illustration)**.

3 Withdraw the pad pins from the caliper using a suitable pair of pliers and remove the pad springs, noting how they fit **(see illustrations)**.

4 Withdraw the pads from the caliper body and remove the anti-chatter shim from the back of each pad, noting how it fits **(see illustration)**.

5 Inspect the surface of each pad for contamination and check that the friction material has not worn beyond its wear limit. The original equipment pads feature a wear indicator step or groove around the pad periphery. Refer to Chapter 1 *Brake pads - wear check* and replace both pads as a set if either pad has worn down to, or beyond, the limit. Additionally, replace the pads if they are fouled with oil or grease, or heavily scored or

damaged by dirt and debris. Note that it is not possible to degrease the friction material; if the pads are contaminated in any way they must be replaced.

6 If the pads are in good condition clean them carefully, using a fine wire brush which is completely free of oil and grease to remove all traces of road dirt and corrosion. Using a pointed instrument, clean out the groove in the friction material and dig out any embedded particles of foreign matter. Any areas of glazing may be removed using emery cloth.

7 Check the brake disc (see Section 8).

8 Push the pistons as far back into the caliper as possible using hand pressure only. Due to the friction material thickness of new pads, it may be necessary to remove the master cylinder reservoir cover and diaphragm and siphon out some fluid.

9 Smear the backs of the pads and the shank of each pad pin with copper-based grease, making sure that none gets on the front or sides of the pads.

10 Installation of the pads, anti-chatter shims, pad pins, springs and retaining clips is the reverse of removal. Install the anti-chatter shim on the back of each pad with its open end facing the rear of the motorcycle **(see illustration)**. Insert the pads into the caliper so that the friction material of each pad is facing the disc. Make sure the pad springs are

6.10a Make sure the anti-chatter shims are the right way round

6.10b Fit the clips into the hole in each pad pin

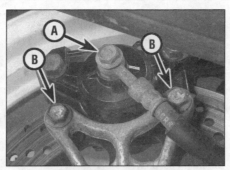

7.1 Brake hose banjo bolt (A), caliper mounting bolts (B)

7.2a Remove the split pin and unscrew the nut (arrow) . . .

correctly positioned, and the pins fit correctly through the holes in the pads **(see illustrations 6.3b and 6.3a)**. Secure the pins with the clips **(see illustration)**. Do not forget to install the pad cover.

11 Top up the master cylinder reservoir if necessary (see *Daily (pre-ride) checks*), and replace the reservoir cover and diaphragm if removed.

12 Operate the brake pedal several times to bring the pads into contact with the disc. Check the master cylinder reservoir fluid level and the operation of the brake before riding the motorcycle.

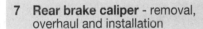

7 Rear brake caliper - removal, overhaul and installation

> ⚠ *Warning: If the caliper indicates the need for an overhaul (usually due to leaking fluid or sticky operation), all old brake fluid should be flushed from the system. Also, the dust created by the brake system may contain asbestos, which is harmful to your health. Never blow It out with compressed air and don't inhale any of it. An approved filtering mask should be worn when working on the brakes. Do not use petroleum-based solvents to clean brake parts. Use clean brake fluid, brake cleaner or denatured alcohol only.*

7.2b . . . then withdraw the bolt and lift the torque arm off the caliper

Removal

1 Remove the brake hose banjo bolt, noting its alignment on the caliper, and separate the hose from the caliper **(see illustration)**. Plug the hose end or wrap a plastic bag tightly around it to minimise fluid loss and prevent dirt entering the system. Discard the sealing washers as new ones must be used on installation. **Note:** *If you are planning to overhaul the caliper and don't have a source of compressed air to blow out the pistons, just loosen the banjo bolt at this stage and retighten it lightly. The bike's hydraulic system can then be used to force the pistons out of the body once the pads have been removed. Disconnect the hose once the pistons have been sufficiently displaced.*

7.2c Caliper body joining bolts

2 Remove the split pin from the end of the bolt securing the brake torque arm to the caliper, then unscrew the nut, withdraw the bolt and lift the arm off the caliper **(see illustrations)**. If the caliper body is to be split into its halves for seal replacement, it is advisable to slacken the caliper body joining bolts at this stage **(see illustration)**.

3 Unscrew the caliper mounting bolts, and slide the caliper away from the disc **(see illustration 7.1)**. Remove the brake pads as described in Section 6.

Overhaul

4 Clean the exterior of the caliper with denatured alcohol or brake system cleaner **(see illustration)**. Displace the pistons partway

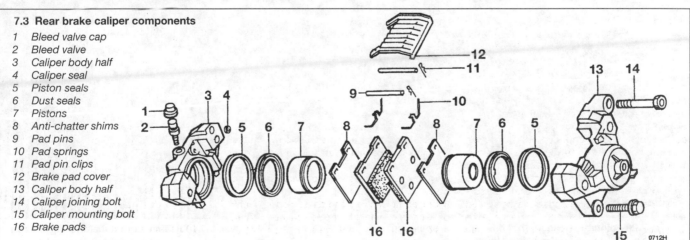

7.3 Rear brake caliper components

1 Bleed valve cap
2 Bleed valve
3 Caliper body half
4 Caliper seal
5 Piston seals
6 Dust seals
7 Pistons
8 Anti-chatter shims
9 Pad pins
10 Pad springs
11 Pad pin clips
12 Brake pad cover
13 Caliper body half
14 Caliper joining bolt
15 Caliper mounting bolt
16 Brake pads

6

out of the caliper bores, either by pumping them out by operating the rear brake pedal, or by forcing them out using compressed air. If the compressed air method is used, place a wad of rag between the pistons to act as a cushion, then use compressed air directed into the fluid inlet to force the pistons out of the body. Use only low pressure to ease the pistons out. If the air pressure is too high and the pistons are forced out, the caliper and/or pistons may be damaged.

 Warning: Never place your fingers in front of the piston in an attempt to catch or protect it when applying compressed air, as serious injury could result.

5 Unscrew the caliper body joining bolts and separate the body halves. Remove the piston from each half. Extract the caliper seal from whichever body half it is in and discard it as a new one must be used

6 Using a wooden or plastic tool, remove the dust seal from each caliper bore and discard them. New seals must be used on installation. If a metal tool is being used, take great care not to damage the caliper bore.

7 Remove and discard the piston seals in the same way.

8 Clean the pistons and bores with denatured alcohol, clean brake fluid or brake system cleaner. If compressed air is available, use it to dry the parts thoroughly (make sure it's filtered and unlubricated).

Caution: Do not, under any circumstances, use a petroleum-based solvent to clean brake parts.

9 Inspect the caliper bores and pistons for signs of corrosion, nicks and burrs and loss of plating. If surface defects are present, the caliper assembly must be replaced. If the necessary measuring equipment is available, compare the dimensions of the pistons and bores to those given in the Specifications Section of this Chapter, replacing any component that is worn beyond the service

limit. If the caliper is in bad shape the master cylinder should also be checked.

10 Lubricate the new piston seals with clean brake fluid and install each one in its groove in the caliper bore.

11 Lubricate the new dust seals with clean brake fluid and install each one in its groove in the caliper bore.

12 Lubricate the pistons with clean brake fluid and install each one closed-end first into its caliper bore. Using your thumbs, push the pistons all the way in, making sure they enter the bores squarely.

13 Lubricate the new caliper seal and install it into one half of the caliper body.

14 Join the two halves of the caliper body together, making sure that the caliper seal is correctly seated in its recess.

15 Install the caliper body joining bolts and tighten them to the torque setting specified at the beginning of the Chapter.

Installation

16 Install the brake pads as described in Section 6.

17 Install the caliper on the brake disc making sure the pads sit squarely either side of the disc.

18 Apply a suitable non-permanent thread locking compound to the caliper mounting bolts and tighten them to the torque setting specified at the beginning of the Chapter **(see illustration 7.1)**.

19 Lower the brake torque arm onto the caliper and secure it with its bolt **(see illustration 7.2b)**. Tighten the nut to the specified torque setting and secure it using a new split pin **(see illustration 7.2a)**.

20 Connect the brake hose to the caliper using new sealing washers on each side of the fitting. Position the hose so that it butts up against the lug on the caliper **(see illustration)**. Tighten the banjo bolt to the specified torque.

21 Fill the master cylinder with the recommended brake fluid (see *Daily (pre-ride)*

checks) and bleed the hydraulic system as described in Section 11.

22 Check for leaks and thoroughly test the operation of the brake before riding the motorcycle.

8 Rear brake disc - inspection, removal and installation

Inspection

1 Refer to Section 4 of this Chapter, noting that the dial indicator should be attached to the swingarm.

Removal

2 Remove the rear wheel (see Section 15).

3 Mark the relationship of the disc to the wheel so it can be installed in the same position. Unscrew the disc retaining bolts, loosening them a little at a time in a criss-cross pattern to avoid distorting the disc, and remove the disc **(see illustration)**.

Installation

4 Position the disc on the wheel, aligning the previously applied matchmarks (if you're reinstalling the original disc).

5 Apply a suitable non-permanent thread locking compound to the disc mounting bolts, then install the bolts and tighten them in a criss-cross pattern evenly and progressively to the torque setting specified at the beginning of this Chapter. Clean off all grease from the brake disc using acetone or brake system cleaner. If a new brake disc has been installed, remove any protective coating from its working surfaces.

6 Install the rear wheel (see Section 15).

7 Operate the brake pedal several times to bring the pads into contact with the disc. Check the operation of the brake carefully before riding the motorcycle.

7.20 Align the hose so that it butts against the lug on the caliper (arrow)

8.3 The disc is secured by four bolts (arrows)

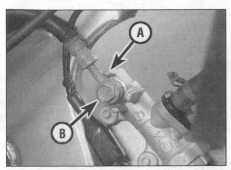

9.4 Note the alignment of the hose against the lug (A), then unscrew the banjo bolt (B)

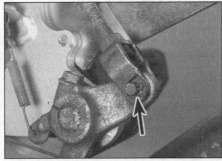

9.5 Remove the split pin (arrow) and withdraw the clevis pin from the outside

9.6 The master cylinder is secured by two bolts (arrows)

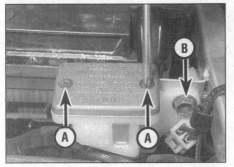

9.7 Reservoir cover screws (A) and mounting bolt (B)

9.8 Slacken the hose clamp screw (arrow) and pull the hose off its union

9 Rear brake master cylinder - removal, overhaul and installation

1 If the master cylinder is leaking fluid, or if the pedal does not produce a firm feel when the brake is applied, and bleeding the brake does not help (see Section 11), and the hydraulic hoses are all in good condition, then master cylinder overhaul is recommended.
2 Before disassembling the master cylinder, read through the entire procedure and make sure that you have the seals required. Also, you will need some new, clean brake fluid of the recommended type, some clean rags and internal circlip pliers.
Caution: Disassembly, overhaul and reassembly of the brake master cylinder must be done in a spotlessly clean work area to avoid contamination and possible failure of the brake hydraulic system components.

Removal

3 Remove the seat and right-hand side panel (see Chapter 7).
4 Unscrew the brake hose banjo bolt and separate the brake hose from the master cylinder, noting its alignment **(see illustration)**. Discard the two sealing washers as they must be replaced with new ones. Wrap the end of the hose in a clean rag and suspend the hose in an upright position or bend it down carefully and place the open end in a clean container. The objective is to prevent excessive loss of brake fluid, fluid spills and system contamination.

5 Remove the split pin from the clevis pin securing the actuating arm to the master cylinder pushrod **(see illustration)**. Withdraw the clevis pin and separate the arm from the pushrod. Discard the split pin as a new one must be used.
6 Unscrew the two bolts securing the master cylinder to the bracket **(see illustration)**.
7 Slacken the master cylinder fluid reservoir cover screws **(see illustration)**. Unscrew the nut and remove the bolt securing the reservoir to the frame, then remove the reservoir cover and pour the fluid into a container.
8 Separate the fluid reservoir hose from the elbow on the master cylinder by releasing the hose clamp **(see illustration)**.

Overhaul

9 If necessary, slacken the clevis locknut, then unscrew the clevis with its nut and locknut and remove them from the pushrod **(see illustration)**.
10 Dislodge the rubber dust boot from the

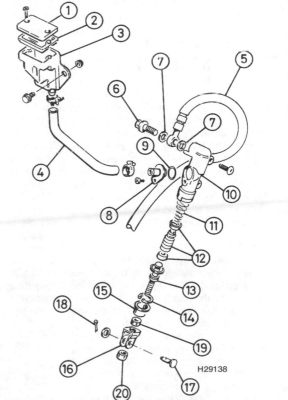

9.9 Rear brake master cylinder components

1 Reservoir cover
2 Rubber diaphragm
3 Reservoir
4 Reservoir hose
5 Brake hose
6 Banjo bolt
7 Sealing washer
8 Reservoir hose elbow
9 O-ring
10 Master cylinder
11 Spring
12 Piston assembly
13 Pushrod
14 Circlip
15 Rubber dust boot
16 Clevis
17 Clevis pin
18 Split pin
19 Clevis locknut
20 Clevis nut

H29138

6

base of the master cylinder to reveal the pushrod retaining circlip.

11 Depress the pushrod and, using circlip pliers, remove the circlip. Slide out the pushrod, piston assembly and spring. If they are difficult to remove, apply low pressure compressed air to the fluid outlet. Lay the parts out in the proper order to prevent confusion during reassembly.

12 Clean all of the parts with clean brake fluid or denatured alcohol. If compressed air is available, use it to dry the parts thoroughly (make sure it's filtered and unlubricated). *Caution: Do not, under any circumstances, use a petroleum-based solvent to clean brake parts.*

13 Check the master cylinder bore for corrosion, scratches, nicks and score marks. If the necessary measuring equipment is available, compare the dimensions of the piston and bore to those given in the Specifications Section of this Chapter. If damage is evident, the master cylinder must be replaced with a new one. If the master cylinder is in poor condition, then the caliper should be checked as well.

14 If required, unscrew the fluid reservoir hose union screw and detach the elbow from the master cylinder. Discard the O-ring as a new one must be fitted on installation. Inspect the reservoir hose for cracks or splits and replace if necessary.

15 The spring, piston and circlip are only supplied as an assembly which includes a new pushrod and dust boot. Use all the new parts, regardless of the condition of the old ones.

16 Install the spring in the master cylinder so that its tapered (smaller) end faces the piston.

17 Lubricate the piston assembly components with clean hydraulic fluid and install the assembly into the master cylinder, making sure all the components are the correct way round. Make sure the lips on the cup seals do not turn inside out when they are slipped into the bore.

18 Install and depress the pushrod, then install a new circlip, making sure it is properly seated in the groove.

19 Install the rubber dust boot, making sure the lip is seated properly in the groove.

20 If removed, fit a new O-ring to the fluid reservoir hose union, then install the union onto the master cylinder and secure it with its screw. Reconnect the fluid reservoir hose and secure it with its clamp.

Installation

21 Install the master cylinder onto the footrest bracket and tighten its mounting bolts to the torque setting specified at the beginning of the Chapter **(see illustration 9.6)**.

22 Secure the fluid reservoir to the frame with its retaining bolt and nut **(see illustration 9.7)**. Ensure that the hose is securely connected between the master cylinder and reservoir, correctly routed and secured by clamps at each end **(see illustration 9.8)**. If the clamps have weakened, use new ones.

23 Connect the brake hose banjo bolt to the master cylinder, using a new sealing washer on each side of the banjo union. Ensure that the hose is positioned so that it butts against the lug **(see illustration 9.4)** and tighten the banjo bolt to the specified torque setting.

24 If removed, install the clevis locknut, the clevis and its nut onto the master cylinder pushrod end, but do not yet tighten the locknut.

25 Align the pushrod actuating arm with the master cylinder pushrod clevis, then slide in the clevis pin and secure it using a new split pin **(see illustration 9.5)**.

26 If the clevis position on the pushrod was disturbed, re-set the brake pedal to its specified height (Chapter 1, Section 14).

27 Fill the fluid reservoir with the specified fluid (see Specifications) and bleed the system following the procedure in Section 11.

28 Check the operation of the brake carefully before riding the motorcycle.

10 Brake hoses and unions - inspection and replacement

Inspection

1 Brake hose condition should be checked regularly and the hoses replaced at the specified interval (see Chapter 1).

2 Twist and flex the rubber hoses while looking for cracks, bulges and seeping fluid. Check extra carefully around the areas where the hoses connect with the banjo fittings, as these are common areas for hose failure.

3 Inspect the metal banjo union fittings connected to the brake hoses. If the fittings are rusted, scratched or cracked, replace them.

Replacement

4 The brake hoses have banjo union fittings on each end. Cover the surrounding area with plenty of rags and unscrew the banjo bolt on each end of the hose. Detach the hose from any clips that may be present and remove the hose. Discard the sealing washers.

5 Position the new hose, making sure it isn't twisted or otherwise strained, and abut the tab on the hose union with the lug on the component casting. Install the banjo bolts, using new sealing washers on both sides of the unions, and tighten them to the torque setting specified at the beginning of this Chapter. Make sure they are correctly aligned and routed clear of all moving components.

6 Flush the old brake fluid from the system, refill with the recommended fluid (see Specifications) and bleed the air from the system (see Section 11). Check the operation of the brakes before riding the motorcycle.

11 Brake system bleeding

1 Bleeding the brakes is simply the process of removing all the air bubbles from the brake fluid reservoirs, the hoses and the brake calipers. Bleeding is necessary whenever a brake system hydraulic connection is loosened, when a component or hose is replaced, or when the master cylinder or caliper is overhauled. Leaks in the system may also allow air to enter, but leaking brake fluid will reveal their presence and warn you of the need for repair.

2 To bleed the brakes, you will need some new, clean brake fluid of the recommended type (see Specifications), a length of clear vinyl or plastic tubing, a small container partially filled with clean brake fluid, some rags and a spanner to fit the brake caliper bleed valves.

3 Cover the fuel tank and other painted components to prevent damage in the event that brake fluid is spilled.

4 If bleeding the rear brake, remove the seat for access to the fluid reservoir.

5 Remove the reservoir cover, diaphragm plate (front brake only) and diaphragm and slowly pump the brake lever or pedal a few times, until no air bubbles can be seen floating up from the holes in the bottom of the reservoir. Doing this bleeds the air from the master cylinder end of the line. Loosely refit the reservoir cover.

6 Pull the dust cap off the bleed valve **(see illustration)**. Attach one end of the clear vinyl or plastic tubing to the bleed valve and submerge the other end in the brake fluid in the container.

7 Remove the reservoir cover and check the fluid level. Do not allow the level to drop below the lower mark during the bleeding process.

8 Carefully pump the brake lever or pedal three or four times and hold it in (front) or down (rear) while opening the caliper bleed valve. When the valve is opened, brake fluid will flow out of the caliper into the clear tubing and the lever will move toward the handlebar or the pedal will move down.

9 Retighten the bleed valve, then release the brake lever or pedal gradually. Repeat the process until no air bubbles are visible in the brake fluid leaving the caliper and the lever or pedal is firm when applied. On completion, disconnect the bleeding equipment, then tighten the bleed valve to the torque setting specified at the beginning of the Chapter and install the dust cap.

10 Check the fluid level as described in *Daily (pre-ride) checks* and install the diaphragm,

11.6 Brake caliper bleed valve (arrow)

diaphragm plate (front brake) and cover. Wipe up any spilled brake fluid and check the entire system for leaks.

HAYNES HiNT *If it's not possible to produce a firm feel to the lever or pedal the fluid my be aerated. Let the brake fluid in the system stabilise for a few hours and then repeat the procedure when the tiny bubbles in the system have settled out.*

12 Wheels - inspection and repair

1 In order to carry out a proper inspection of the wheels, it is necessary to support the bike upright so that the wheel being inspected is raised off the ground. Position the motorcycle on its centre stand. Clean the wheels thoroughly to remove mud and dirt that may interfere with the inspection procedure or mask defects. Make a general check of the wheels and tyres as described in Chapter 1.
2 Attach a dial gauge to the fork slider or the swingarm and position its stem against the side of the rim **(see illustration)**. Spin the wheel slowly and check the axial (side-to-side) runout of the rim. In order to accurately check radial (out of round) runout with the dial gauge, the wheel would have to be removed from the machine, and the tyre from the wheel. With the axle clamped in a vice and the dial gauge positioned on the top of the rim, the wheel can be rotated to check the runout.
3 An easier, though slightly less accurate, method is to attach a stiff wire pointer to the fork slider or the swingarm and position the end a fraction of an inch from the wheel (where the wheel and tyre join). If the wheel is true, the distance from the pointer to the rim will be constant as the wheel is rotated. **Note:** *If wheel runout is excessive, check the wheel bearings very carefully before replacing the wheel.*

4 The wheels should also be visually inspected for cracks, flat spots on the rim and other damage. Look very closely for dents in the area where the tyre bead contacts the rim. Dents in this area may prevent complete sealing of the tyre against the rim, which leads to deflation of the tyre over a period of time. If damage is evident, or if runout in either direction is excessive, the wheel will have to be replaced with a new one. Never attempt to repair a damaged cast alloy wheel.

13 Wheels - alignment check

1 Misalignment of the wheels, which may be due to a cocked rear wheel or a bent frame or fork yokes, can cause strange and possibly serious handling problems. If the frame or yokes are at fault, repair by a frame specialist or replacement with new parts are the only alternatives.
2 To check the alignment you will need an assistant, a length of string or a perfectly straight piece of wood and a ruler. A plumb bob or other suitable weight will also be required.
3 In order to make a proper check of the wheels it is necessary to support the bike in an upright position, either on its centre stand or on an auxiliary stand. Measure the width of both tyres at their widest points. Subtract the smaller measurement from the larger measurement, then divide the difference by two. The result is the amount of offset that should exist between the front and rear tyres on both sides.
4 If a string is used, have your assistant hold one end of it about halfway between the floor and the rear axle, touching the rear sidewall of the tyre.
5 Run the other end of the string forward and pull it tight so that it is roughly parallel to the floor. Slowly bring the string into contact with the front sidewall of the rear tyre, then turn the front wheel until it is parallel with the

string. Measure the distance from the front tyre sidewall to the string.
6 Repeat the procedure on the other side of the motorcycle. The distance from the front tyre sidewall to the string should be equal on both sides.
7 As was previously pointed out, a perfectly straight length of wood may be substituted for the string - the procedure is the same.
8 If the distance between the string and tyre is greater on one side, or if the rear wheel appears to be cocked, refer to Chapter 1, Section 11 and make sure the drive chain adjusters are correctly aligned.
9 If the front-to-back alignment is correct, the wheels still may be out of alignment vertically.
10 Using the plumb bob, or other suitable weight, and a length of string, check the rear wheel to make sure it is vertical. To do this, hold the string against the tyre upper sidewall and allow the weight to settle just off the floor. When the string touches both the upper and lower tyre sidewalls and is perfectly straight, the wheel is vertical. If it is not, place thin spacers under one leg of the stand.
11 Once the rear wheel is vertical, check the front wheel in the same manner. If both wheels are not perfectly vertical, the frame and/or major suspension components are bent.

14 Front wheel - removal and installation

Removal

1 Position the motorcycle on its centre stand and support it under the crankcase so that the front wheel is off the ground. Always make sure the motorcycle is properly supported.
2 Remove the screw securing the speedometer cable on the left-hand side of the wheel hub and detach the cable from its drive unit **(see illustration)**.

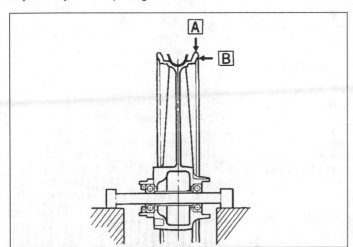

12.2 Check the wheel for radial (out-of-round) runout (A) and axial (side-to-side) runout (B)

14.2 Unscrew the speedometer cable retaining screw (arrow)

14.4a Slacken the axle clamp bolt (arrow) . . .

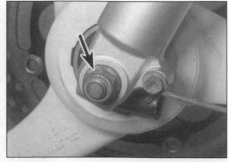

14.4b . . . then unscrew the axle nut (arrow)

14.5 Withdraw the axle and remove the wheel

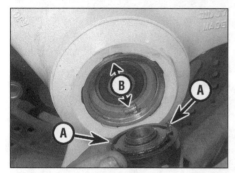

14.9 Make sure the drive gear tabs (A) fit into the wheel slots (B)

14.11a Install the wheel spacer as shown . . .

14.11b . . . and the axle spacer if removed

14.12 Abut the speedometer drive housing against the lug on the fork (arrow)

14.13a Install the axle nut . . .

14.13b . . . and tighten it to the specified torque setting

3 Remove the brake caliper mounting bolts and slide the caliper off the disc **(see illustration 3.2a)**. Support the caliper with a piece of wire or a bungee cord so that no strain is placed on its hydraulic hose. There is no need to disconnect the brake hose from the caliper.

4 Slacken the axle clamp bolt on the bottom of the right-hand side fork, then remove the split pin from the left-hand end of the axle (US models only) and unscrew the axle nut **(see illustrations)**.

5 Support the wheel, then withdraw the axle from the left-hand side and carefully lower the wheel **(see illustration)**.

6 Remove the wheel spacer from the right-hand side of the wheel, noting which way round it fits, and the speedometer drive housing from the left-hand side. Also remove the axle spacer from inside the eye of the right-hand fork slider, if it is loose. **Note:** *Do not operate the front brake lever with the wheel removed.*

Caution: Don't lay the wheel down resting on the disc - the disc may get warped. Set the wheel on wood blocks so the disc doesn't support the weight of the wheel.

7 Check the axle for straightness by rolling it on a flat surface such as a piece of plate glass (first wipe off all old grease and remove any corrosion using fine emery cloth). If the equipment is available, place the axle in V-blocks and measure the runout using a dial gauge. If the axle is bent or the runout exceeds the limit specified, replace it.

8 Check the condition of the wheel bearings (see Section 16).

Installation

9 Apply a smear of lithium-based grease to the speedometer drive components. Fit the speedometer drive to the wheel's left-hand side, aligning its drive gear tabs with the slots in the wheel hub **(see illustration)**.

10 Apply a smear of lithium-based grease to the inside of the axle spacer and the wheel spacer, and also to the inner face of the wheel spacer where it contacts the grease seal.

11 Manoeuvre the wheel into position. Apply a thin coat of grease to the axle. Fit the wheel spacer between the wheel and the fork, making sure it is the right way round **(see illustration)**. If removed, slide the axle spacer into the bottom of the fork **(see illustration)**.

12 Lift the wheel, making sure the spacers remain in place, and slide the axle into position from the left-hand side **(see illustration 14.5)**. Align the speedometer drive housing so that it butts against the lug on the fork slider and the cable socket faces rearwards **(see illustration)**.

13 Install the axle nut and tighten it to the torque setting specified at the beginning of the Chapter **(see illustrations)**. On US models, fit a new split pin to the end of the axle.

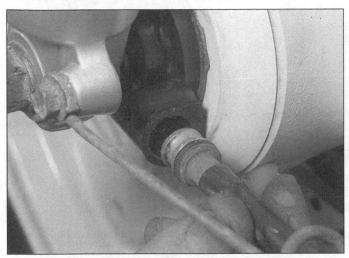

14.16a Fit the cable into the drive housing . . .

14.16b . . . and retain it with the screw

14 Tighten the axle clamp bolt on the right-hand side fork to the specified torque setting (see Illustration 14.4a).

15 Install the brake caliper, making sure the pads sit squarely on either side of the disc. Apply a suitable non-permanent thread locking compound to the caliper mounting bolts and tighten them to the torque setting specified at the beginning of the Chapter (see illustrations 3.14a and 3.14b).

16 Pass the speedometer cable through its guides (if withdrawn), then connect the cable to the drive housing, aligning the slot in the cable end with the drive tab, and securely tighten its screw (see illustrations).

17 Apply the front brake a few times to bring the pads back into contact with the discs. Move the motorcycle off its stand, apply the front brake and pump the front forks a few times to settle all components in position.

18 Check for correct operation of the front brake before riding the motorcycle.

15 Rear wheel -
removal and installation

Removal

1 Position the motorcycle on its centre stand. Remove the drive chain guard (see Chapter 7).

2 On US models, remove the split pin from the end of the axle. Unscrew the axle nut and remove the washer and the chain adjuster plate, noting how it fits (see illustration).

3 Support the wheel whilst withdrawing the axle from the right-hand side along with the adjuster plate, then lower the wheel to the ground. Raise the brake caliper to gain more clearance if required. Note how the axle passes through the caliper mounting bracket.

4 Disengage the chain from the sprocket and remove the wheel from the swingarm (see illustration). Remove the spacer from the right-hand side of the wheel, noting which

way round it fits (see illustration). If required, withdraw the chain adjusters from the ends of the swingarm.

Caution: Do not lay the wheel down and allow it to rest on the disc or the sprocket - they could become warped. Set the wheel on wood blocks so the disc or the sprocket doesn't support the weight of the wheel. Do not operate the brake pedal with the wheel removed.

5 Check the axle for straightness by rolling it on a flat surface such as a piece of plate glass (if the axle is corroded, first remove the corrosion with fine emery cloth). If the equipment is available, place the axle in

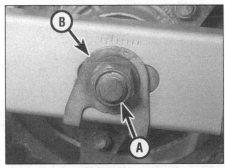

15.2 Unscrew the axle nut (A) and remove the adjuster plate (B)

15.4b Remove the spacer, noting how it fits

V-blocks and measure the runout using a dial gauge. If the axle is bent or the runout exceeds the limit specified at the beginning of the Chapter, replace it.

6 Check the condition of the wheel bearings (see Section 16).

Installation

7 Apply a thin coat of grease to the lips of the bearing seal on the outside of the sprocket coupling, and also to the inner face of the spacer where it contacts the bearing in the right-hand side of the wheel. If removed, install the chain adjusters into the ends of the swingarm (see illustration).

15.4a Slip the chain off the sprocket and remove the wheel

15.7 Install the chain adjusters into the swingarm

6

15.10a Install the axle through the wheel . . .

15.10b . . . then fit the left-hand adjuster plate . . .

15.10c . . . and the axle washer and nut

15.12 Tighten the axle nut to the specified torque setting

8 Position the wheel between the ends of the swingarm and apply a thin coat of grease to the axle. If raised, lower the brake caliper assembly so that it is roughly in position. Install the spacer between the caliper bracket and the wheel, with its wider end facing in **(see illustration 15.4b)**.

9 Engage the drive chain with the sprocket and lift the wheel into position. Make sure the spacer remains correctly in place and the disc fits correctly in the caliper, with the brake pads sitting squarely on each side of the disc. Make sure the caliper mounting bracket is correctly aligned for the axle to pass through it.

10 Slide the right-hand side adjuster plate onto the axle, making sure it is the right way round. Install the axle through the swingarm and chain adjuster, the caliper bracket and the spacer and into the wheel. Check that everything is correctly aligned, then fit the adjuster plate, washer and the axle nut, but do not tighten it yet **(see illustrations)**. If it is difficult to insert the axle due to the tension of the drive chain, slacken the chain adjusters (see Chapter 1).

11 Adjust the chain slack as described in Chapter 1.

12 Tighten the axle nut to the specified torque setting, counter-holding the axle head on the other side of the wheel if necessary **(see illustration)**. On US models, fit a new split pin to the end of the axle and bend its ends securely around the axle nut.

13 Operate the brake pedal several times to bring the pads into contact with the disc. Check the operation of the rear brake carefully before riding the bike.

16 Wheel bearings - removal, inspection and installation

Note: *Suzuki advise that the wheel bearings should be renewed if they are removed from the wheel. Always replace the wheel bearings in pairs. Never replace the bearings individually. Avoid using a high pressure cleaner on the wheel bearing area.*

Front wheel bearings

1 Remove the wheel (see Section 14).

2 Set the wheel on blocks so as not to allow the weight of the wheel to rest on the brake disc.

3 Remove the hub cover from the left-hand side of the wheel, noting how it fits **(see illustrations)**.

4 Using a metal rod (preferably a brass drift punch) inserted through the centre of the upper bearing, tap evenly around the inner race of the lower bearing to drive it from the hub **(see illustration)**. The bearing spacer will also come out.

5 Lay the wheel on its other side so that the remaining bearing faces down. Drive the bearing out of the wheel using the same technique as above.

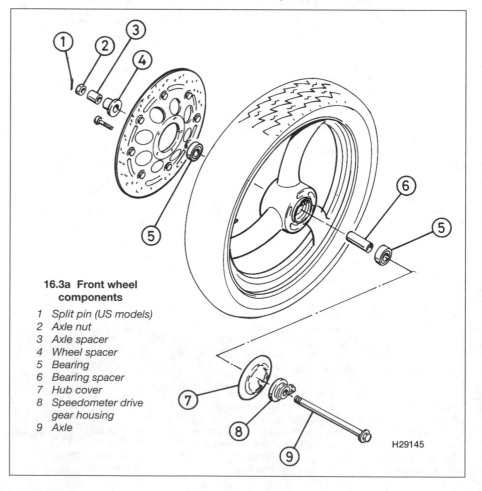

16.3a Front wheel components

1 *Split pin (US models)*
2 *Axle nut*
3 *Axle spacer*
4 *Wheel spacer*
5 *Bearing*
6 *Bearing spacer*
7 *Hub cover*
8 *Speedometer drive gear housing*
9 *Axle*

H29145

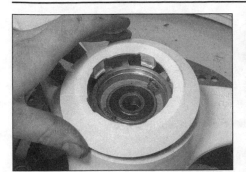

16.3b Prise the hub cover off the wheel

16.4 Using a drift to knock out the bearings

16.9 Using a bearing driver to install the bearings

6 If the bearings are of the unsealed type or are only sealed on one side, clean them with a high flash-point solvent (one which won't leave any residue) and blow them dry with compressed air (don't let the bearings spin as you dry them). Apply a few drops of oil to the bearing. **Note:** *If the bearing is sealed on both sides don't attempt to clean it.*

7 Hold the outer race of the bearing and rotate the inner race - if the bearing doesn't turn smoothly, has rough spots or is noisy, replace it with a new one.

8 If the bearing is good and can be re-used, wash it in solvent once again and dry it, then pack the bearing with high-quality lithium-based grease.

9 Thoroughly clean the hub area of the wheel. First install the left-hand side bearing into its recess in the hub, with the marked or sealed side facing outwards. Using a bearing driver or a socket large enough to contact the outer race of the bearing, drive it in until it's completely seated **(see illustration)**.

10 Turn the wheel over and install the bearing spacer. Drive the right-hand side bearing into place as described above.

11 Fit the hub cover onto the left-hand side of the wheel.

12 Clean off all grease from the brake disc using acetone or brake system cleaner then install the wheel (see Section 14).

Rear wheel bearings

13 Remove the rear wheel (see Section 15). Lift the rear sprocket and sprocket coupling assembly out of the wheel, noting how it fits **(see illustrations)**.

14 Set the wheel on blocks so the weight of the wheel is not resting on the brake disc.

15 Using a metal rod (preferably a brass drift punch) inserted through the centre of the upper bearing, tap evenly around the inner race of the lower bearing to drive it from the hub **(see illustration 16.4)**. The bearing spacer will also come out.

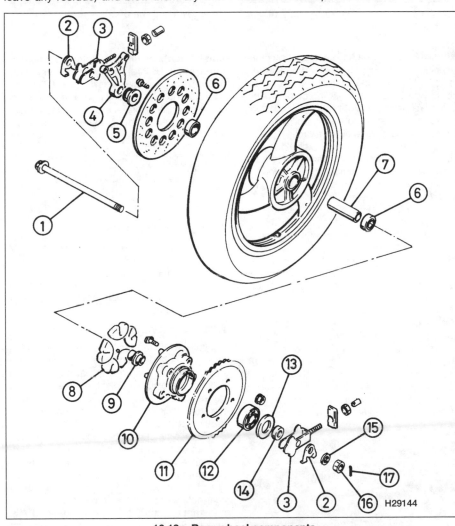

16.13a Rear wheel components

1	Axle	7	Bearing spacer	13	Bearing seal
2	Drive chain adjuster plate	8	Damper segments	14	Outer spacer
3	Drive chain adjuster	9	Inner spacer	15	Washer
4	Caliper bracket	10	Sprocket coupling	16	Axle nut
5	Spacer	11	Sprocket	17	Split pin (US models)
6	Bearing	12	Bearing		

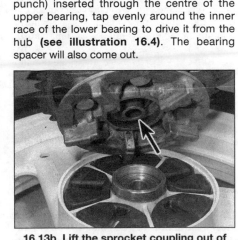

16.13b Lift the sprocket coupling out of the wheel, noting the inner spacer (arrow)

6

16.24a Remove the outer spacer . . .

16.24b . . . then lever out the bearing seal

16 Lay the wheel on its other side so that the remaining bearing faces down. Drive the bearing out of the wheel using the same technique as above.

17 If the bearings are of the unsealed type or are only sealed on one side, clean them with a high flash-point solvent (one which won't leave any residue) and blow them dry with compressed air (don't let the bearings spin as you dry them). Apply a few drops of oil to the bearing. **Note:** *If the bearing is sealed on both sides don't attempt to clean it.*

18 Hold the outer race of the bearing and rotate the inner race - if the bearing doesn't turn smoothly, has rough spots or is noisy, replace it with anew one.

19 If the bearing is good and can be re-used, wash it in solvent once again and dry it, then pack the bearing with high-quality lithium-based grease.

20 Thoroughly clean the hub area of the wheel. First install the right-hand side bearing into its recess in the hub, with the marked or sealed side facing outwards. Using a bearing driver or a socket large enough to contact the outer race of the bearing, drive it in squarely until it's completely seated **(see illustration 16.9)**.

21 Turn the wheel over and install the bearing spacer. Drive the left-hand side bearing into place as described above.

22 Clean off all grease from the brake disc using acetone or brake system cleaner. Install the rear sprocket and sprocket coupling assembly onto the wheel, then install the wheel (see Section 15).

Sprocket coupling bearing

23 Remove the rear wheel (see Section 15). Lift the sprocket and sprocket coupling assembly out of the wheel, noting how it fits **(see illustrations 16.13a and 16.13b)**.

24 Remove the spacers from the outside and inside of the coupling bearing **(see**

illustration). Using a flat-bladed screwdriver, lever out the bearing seal from the outside of the coupling **(see illustration)**.

25 Support the coupling on blocks of wood and drive the bearing out from the inside with a bearing driver or socket large enough to contact the outer race of the bearing.

26 Clean the bearing with a high flash-point solvent (one which won't leave any residue) and blow it dry with compressed air (don't let the bearing spin as you dry it). Apply a few drops of oil to the bearing.

27 Hold the outer race of the bearing and rotate the inner race - if the bearing doesn't turn smoothly, has rough spots or is noisy, replace it with a new one.

28 If the bearing is good and can be re-used, wash it in solvent once again and dry it, then pack the bearing with high-quality lithium-based grease.

29 Thoroughly clean the bearing recess then install the bearing into the recess in the coupling, with the marked side facing out. Using a bearing driver or a socket large enough to contact the outer race of the bearing, drive it in until it is completely seated.

30 Install a new bearing seal, using a seal or bearing driver, a suitable socket or a flat piece of wood to drive it into place **(see**

16.30 Drive the bearing seal onto the bearing

illustration). Install the outer spacer **(see illustration 16.24a)**. Install the inner spacer into the coupling **(see illustration 16.13b)**.

31 Clean off all grease from the brake disc using acetone or brake system cleaner. Install the sprocket coupling assembly onto the wheel, then install the wheel (see Section 15).

17 Tyres -
general information and fitting

General information

1 The wheels fitted to all models are designed to take tubeless tyres only.

2 Refer to the Daily (pre-ride) checks listed at the beginning of this manual, and to the scheduled checks in Chapter 1 for tyre and wheel maintenance.

Fitting new tyres

3 When selecting new tyres, refer to the tyre information and the tyre options listed in the owners handbook. Ensure that front and rear tyre types are compatible, the correct size and correct speed rating; if necessary seek advice from a Suzuki dealer or tyre fitting specialist **(see illustration)**.

4 It is recommended that tyres are fitted by a motorcycle tyre specialist rather than attempted in the home workshop. This is particularly relevant in the case of tubeless tyres because the force required to break the seal between the wheel rim and tyre bead is substantial, and is usually beyond the capabilities of an individual working with normal tyre levers. Additionally, the specialist will be able to balance the wheels after tyre fitting.

5 Note that punctured tubeless tyres can in some cases be repaired. Suzuki recommend that such repairs are carried out only by an authorised dealer.

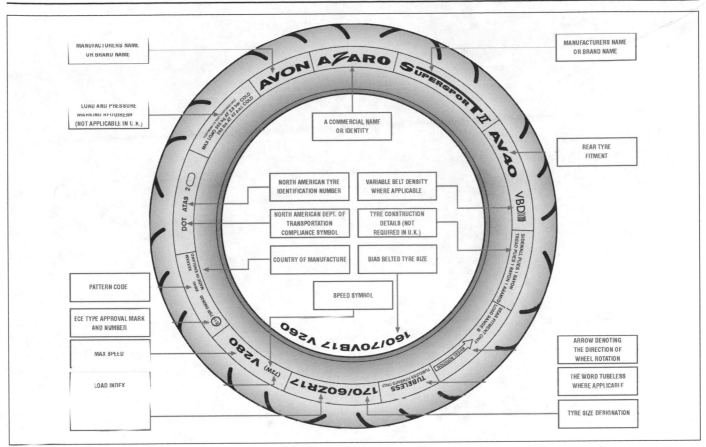

17.3 Common tyre sidewall markings

Notes

Chapter 7
Bodywork

Contents

Degrees of difficulty

Easy, suitable for novice with little experience	**Fairly easy,** suitable for beginner with some experience	**Fairly difficult,** suitable for competent DIY mechanic	**Difficult,** suitable for experienced DIY mechanic	**Very difficult,** suitable for expert DIY or professional

1 General information

This Chapter covers the procedures necessary to remove and install the body parts. Since many service and repair operations require the removal of the body parts, the procedures are grouped here and referred to from other Chapters.

In the case of damage to the body parts, it is usually necessary to remove the broken component and replace it with a new (or used) one. The material that the body panels are composed of doesn't lend itself to conventional repair techniques. There are however some shops that specialise in 'plastic welding', so it may be worthwhile seeking the advice of one of these specialists before consigning an expensive component to the bin.

When attempting to remove any body panel, first study it closely, noting any fasteners and associated fittings, to be sure of returning everything to its correct place on installation. In some cases the aid of an assistant will be required when removing panels, to help avoid the risk of damage to paintwork. Once the evident fasteners have been removed, try to withdraw the panel as described but DO NOT FORCE IT - if it will not release, check that all fasteners have been removed and try again. Where a panel engages another by means of tabs, be careful not to break the tab or its mating slot or to damage the paintwork. Remember that a few moments of patience at this stage will save you a lot of money in replacing broken fairing panels!

When installing a body panel, first study it closely, noting any fasteners and associated fittings removed with it, to be sure of returning everything to its correct place. Check that all fasteners are in good condition, including all trim nuts or clips and damping/rubber mounts; any of these must be replaced if faulty before the panel is reassembled. Check also that all mounting brackets are straight and repair or replace them if necessary before attempting to install the panel. Where assistance was required to remove a panel, make sure your assistant is on hand to install it.

Carefully settle the panel in place, following the instructions provided, and check that it engages correctly with its partners (where applicable) before tightening any of the fasteners. Where a panel engages another by means of tabs, be careful not to break the tab or its mating slot. Note that a small amount of lubricant (liquid soap or similar) applied to the mounting rubbers of the side panels will assist the panel retaining pegs to engage without the need for undue pressure.

Tighten the fasteners securely, but be careful not to overtighten any of them or the panel may break (not always immediately) due to the uneven stress.

Note: *A full fairing or quarter fairing and chin fairing may be fitted to certain models - these items are not standard equipment.*

2 Rear view mirrors - removal and installation

Removal

1 Slacken the locknut on the base of the mirror mounting damper, then unscrew the mirror and remove it from the handlebar **(see illustration)**.

Installation

2 Install the mirror into its mounting and screw it in until it is fully home. Adjust the position of the mirror until it is as required, then tighten the locknut against the mounting to secure it in position.

3 Seat - removal and installation

Removal

1 Insert the ignition key into the seat lock located under the left-hand side panel and turn it clockwise to unlock the seat **(see illustration)**.
2 Lift the rear of the seat and draw it back and away from the bike. Note how the tab at the front of the seat locates under the fuel tank mounting bracket, and how the seat locates onto the frame rail.

Installation

3 Locate the tab which is located at the front of the seat underneath the fuel tank mounting

2.1 Slacken the locknut (arrow), then unscrew the mirror

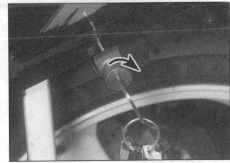
3.1 Turn the key clockwise to unlock the seat

7

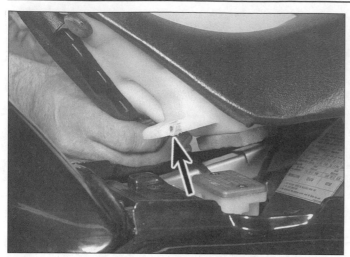

3.3 Locate the tab (arrow) under the fuel tank

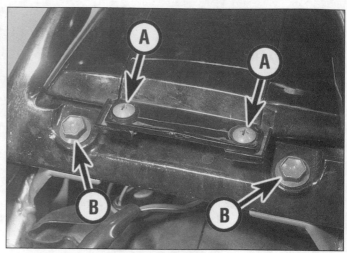

4.2 Tail light cover screws (A) and grab rail bolts (B) – EK to EY models

4.4a On EK to EY models, each side panel is secured by a bolt . . .

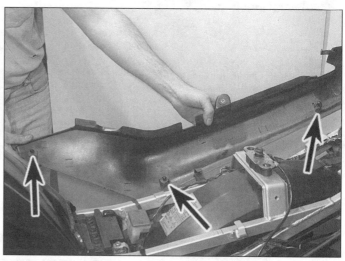

4.4b . . . and three pegs (arrows)

bracket **(see illustration)**. Align the seat at the rear and push down on it to engage the latches.

4 Side panels - removal and installation

Removal

1 Remove the seat (see Section 3).
2 On EK to EY models, unscrew the two screws securing the tail light cover to each side panel, then remove the cover, noting how it fits **(see illustration)**.
3 On all models, remove the two bolts securing the passenger grab-rail to the frame and remove the grab-rail, noting how it fits **(see illustration 4.2)**.
4 On EK to EY models, each side panel is secured by a bolt and three pegs which fit into

rubber grommets. Unscrew the bolt securing the panel to the frame, then gently pull the panel away from the frame to release the pegs **(see illustrations)**. Do not force or bend the panel while removing it.
5 On K1 models onward, the side panels

4.5a Unclip the outer cable and detach the cable end from the lock mechanism

must be removed as an assembly. First detach the seat lock cable from the lock mechanism, then unscrew the two screws securing the upper rear centre panel to the side panels **(see illustrations)**. The panels are retained by two bolts and two pegs which fit

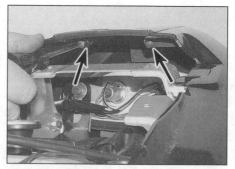

4.5b Location of upper rear centre panel screws (arrows)

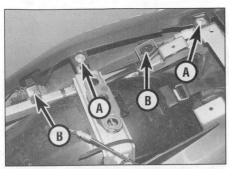

4.5c Each side is retained by two bolts (A) and two pegs (B)

4.5d Remove the panels as an assembly

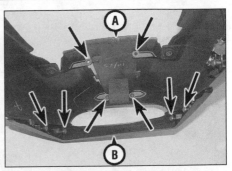

4.6 Location of screws securing the upper panel (A) and lower panel (B)

into rubber grommets on each side **(see illustration)**. Unscrew all four bolts then gently pull the panels away from the frame to release the pegs and draw the panel assembly rearwards off the bike **(see illustration)**.

6 If required, to separate the panels, unscrew the remaining two screws securing the upper centre panel and the four screws securing the lower centre panel **(see illustration)**.

Installation

7 Installation is the reverse of removal. On K1 models onward, ensure the seat lock cable is clipped securely in place before installing the seat.

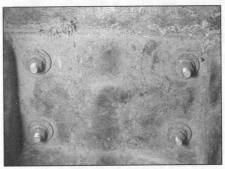

5.2a Counter-hold the nuts . . .

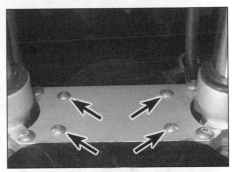

5.2b . . . then unscrew the four screws (arrows) . . .

5 Front mudguard and fork brace - removal and installation

Removal

1 Remove the front wheel (see Chapter 6). Withdraw the speedometer cable from its guides.

2 Counter-hold the nuts on the underside of the mudguard and unscrew the four screws securing the mudguard to its brace **(see illustrations)**. Lower the mudguard and carefully remove it from between the forks, noting how it fits **(see illustration)**.

3 Unscrew the four screws securing the brace to the forks, noting the cable guide

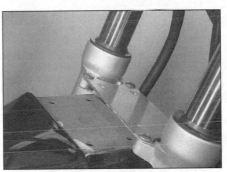

5.2c . . . to free the mudguard

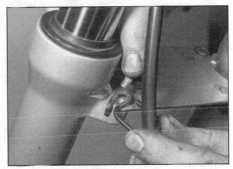

5.3 Note the position of the cable guide on the fork brace

secured by the rear left screw, and remove the brace **(see illustration)**.

Installation

4 Installation is the reverse of removal. Do not

forget to install the speedometer cable through its guides.

6 Drive chain guard - removal and installation

Removal

1 Remove the two screws securing the footguard to the footrest bracket and remove the guard **(see illustration)**.

2 Remove the two screws securing the chain guard to the swingarm and remove the guard, noting how it fits **(see illustration)**.

Installation

3 Installation is the reverse of removal.

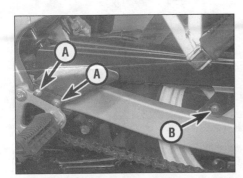

6.1 Unscrew the two footguard screws (A), the chain guard rear screw (B) . . .

6.2 . . . and the chain guard front screw

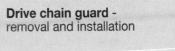

7

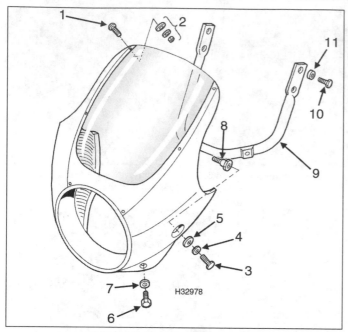

7.1 Fairing – EK and EL models

1 Screen fixing screw – 7 off
2 Plain washer, lock washer and nut – 7 off
3 Bolt – 2 off
4 Spring washer – 2 off
5 Plain washer – 4 off
6 Bolt – 2 off
7 Spring washer – 2 off
8 Headlight bolt – 2 off
9 Mounting bracket
10 Bolt – 4 off
11 Plain washer – 4 off

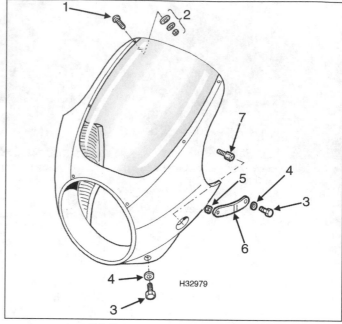

7.2 Fairing – EM models onward

1 Fixing screw – 7 off
2 Plain washer, lock washer and nut – 7 off
3 Bolt – 4 off
4 Spring washer – 4 off
5 Nut – 2 off
6 Mounting bracket – 2 off
7 Headlight bolt – 2 off

7 Fairing and belly pan – removal and installation (optional equipment)

Note: *Alternative aftermarket fairings may have different mountings to those described below.*

Removal

1 On EK and EL models the fairing is mounted on a U-shaped bracket which is bolted to the headlight bracket **(see illustration)**. Unscrew the four bolts securing the bracket to the bike and the two bolts which locate in the heads of the headlight mounting bolts, then lift the fairing assembly off. If required, unscrew the two lower bolts to detach the bracket from the fairing.

2 On all other models the fairing is mounted directly to the headlight bracket by two bolts and by two short brackets **(see illustration)**. Removal is the same as for EK and EL models.

3 The screen is secured to the fairing by seven screws and nuts. If the screen is removed, note the plain washers which fit on the outside of the screen and the lock washers which fit on the inside.

4 The belly pan is secured to the front frame tubes by four two-piece brackets **(see illustration)**. Unscrew the four mounting bolts

and remove the inner half of each bracket, then carefully draw the belly pan forwards off the bike. Note the washers fitted to each bolt and that the outer half of each bracket has an integral spacer which fits against the inside of the pan.

Installation

5 Installation is the reverse of removal. Take care not to overtighten the mounting bolts to avoid damaging the panels.

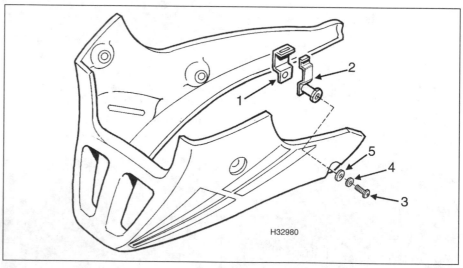

7.4 Belly pan

1 Inner mounting bracket
2 Outer mounting bracket
3 Mounting bolt
4 Spring washer
5 Plain washer

Chapter 8
Electrical system

Contents

Degrees of difficulty

Easy, suitable for novice with little experience	**Fairly easy,** suitable for beginner with some experience	**Fairly difficult,** suitable for competent DIY mechanic	**Difficult,** suitable for experienced DIY mechanic	**Very difficult,** suitable for expert DIY or professional

Specifications

Battery
Capacity .... 12 V, 11 Ah
Electrolyte specific gravity .... see Chapter 1

Alternator
Standard dc output .... 13.5 to 15.5 V at 5000 rpm
No-load ac output .... Min 75 V at 5000 rpm

Regulator/rectifier
Regulated voltage .... 13.5 to 15.5 V at 5000 rpm

Starter motor
Brush length (min) .... 9.0 mm
Starter relay coil resistance .... 3 to 5 ohms

Fuse .... 20 A

8

Bulbs

Headlight	60/55 W H4 halogen
Side light (UK only)	4.0 W
Brake/tail light	21/5 W
Turn signal lights	21 W
Tachometer light	3.4 W
Speedometer light	3.4 W
Turn signal indicator light	3.4 W
Neutral indicator light	3.4 W
Oil pressure indicator light	3.4 W
High beam indicator light	1.7 W

Torque setting

Alternator rotor bolt	110 to 130 Nm

1 General information

All models have a 12-volt electrical system. The components include a three-phase alternator unit and combined regulator/ rectifier unit.

The regulator maintains the charging system output within the specified range to prevent overcharging, and the rectifier converts the ac (alternating current) output of the alternator to dc (direct current) to power the lights and other components and to charge the battery. The alternator rotor is driven by the crankshaft.

The starter motor is mounted on the crankcase behind the cylinders. The starting system includes the starter motor, the battery, the relay and the various wires and switches. If the engine stop switch and the ignition (main) switch are both in the "Run" or "On" position, the starter relay allows the starter motor to operate only if the transmission is in neutral (neutral switch on) or, if the transmission is in gear, if the clutch lever is pulled into the handlebar (clutch switch on, where fitted) and the sidestand is up.

Note: *Keep in mind that electrical parts, once purchased, cannot be returned. To avoid unnecessary expense, make very sure the faulty component has been positively identified before buying a replacement part.*

2 Electrical troubleshooting

Warning: To prevent the risk of short circuits, the ignition (main) switch must always be OFF and the battery negative (-ve) terminal should be disconnected before any of the bike's other electrical components are disturbed. Don't forget to reconnect the terminal securely once work is finished or if battery power is needed for circuit testing.

1 A typical electrical circuit consists of an electrical component, the switches, relays, etc.

related to that component and the wiring and connectors that hook the component to both the battery and the frame. To aid in locating a problem in any electrical circuit, refer to the wiring diagrams at the end of this Chapter.

2 Before tackling any troublesome electrical circuit, first study the wiring diagram (see end of Chapter) thoroughly to get a complete picture of what makes up that individual circuit. Trouble spots, for instance, can often be narrowed down by noting if other components related to that circuit are operating properly or not. If several components or circuits fail at one time, chances are the fault lies in the fuse or earth (ground) connection, as several circuits often are routed through the same fuse and earth (ground) connections.

3 Electrical problems often stem from simple causes, such as loose or corroded connections or a blown fuse. Prior to any electrical troubleshooting, always visually check the condition of the fuse, wires and connections in the problem circuit. Intermittent failures can be especially frustrating, since you can't always duplicate the failure when it's convenient to test. In such situations, a good practice is to clean all connections in the affected circuit, whether or not they appear to be good. All of the connections and wires should also be wiggled to check for looseness which can cause intermittent failure.

4 If testing instruments are going to be utilised, use the wiring diagram to plan where

you will make the necessary connections in order to accurately pinpoint the trouble spot.

5 The basic tools needed for electrical fault finding include a battery and bulb test circuit, a continuity tester, a test light, and a jumper wire. A multimeter capable of reading volts, ohms and amps is also very useful as an alternative to the above, and is necessary for performing more extensive tests and checks. Full details on the use of this test equipment are given in *Fault Finding Equipment* in the Reference section of this manual.

3 Battery - removal, installation, inspection and maintenance

Caution: Be extremely careful when handling or working around the battery. The electrolyte is very caustic and an explosive gas (hydrogen) is given off when the battery is charging.

Removal and installation

1 Remove the seat (see Chapter 7). Unscrew the terminal screws and disconnect the leads from the battery, disconnecting the negative (-ve) terminal first, and noting that the positive (+ve) terminal has an insulating cover which must be pulled back **(see illustration)**. Pull the vent hose off its union on the side of the battery and lift the battery out of its box **(see illustrations)**.

3.1a Disconnect negative (-ve) terminal (A), then pull back the insulating cover (B) and disconnect the positive (+ve) terminal

3.1b Pull the vent hose off its union . . .

3.1c ... and remove the battery

3.2 Fit the insulating cover over the positive (+ve) terminal

2 On installation, clean the battery terminals and lead ends with a wire brush or knife and emery paper. Reconnect the leads, connecting the positive (+ve) terminal first, followed by its insulating cover **(see illustration)**, then connect the negative (-ve) terminal. Attach the vent hose to its union and install the seat (see Chapter 7).

HAYNES HINT *Battery corrosion can be kept to a minimum by applying a layer of petroleum jelly to the terminals after the cables have been connected.*

Inspection and maintenance

3 The battery fitted to the models covered in this manual is of the conventional lead/acid type, requiring regular checks of the electrolyte level (see *Daily (pre-ride) checks*) in addition to those detailed below.

4 Check the battery terminals and leads for tightness and corrosion. If necessary, disconnect and clean the terminals as described in Steps 1 and 2.

5 The battery case should be kept clean to prevent current leakage, which can discharge the battery over a period of time (especially when it sits unused). Wash the outside of the case with a solution of baking soda and water. Rinse the battery thoroughly, then dry it.

6 Look for cracks in the case and replace the battery if any are found. If acid has been spilled on the frame or battery holder, neutralise it with a baking soda and water solution, dry it thoroughly, then touch up any damaged paint. Make sure the battery vent hose is routed correctly and is not kinked or pinched.

7 If the motorcycle sits unused for long periods of time, disconnect the leads from the battery terminals, negative (-ve) terminal first. Refer to Section 4 and charge the battery once every month to six weeks.

8 The condition of the battery can be assessed by measuring the voltage present at the battery terminals. Connect the voltmeter positive (+ve) probe to the battery positive

(+ve) terminal and the negative (-ve) probe to the battery negative (-ve) terminal. When fully charged there should be approximately 13 volts present. If the voltage falls below 12.3 volts the battery must be removed and recharged as described below in Section 4.

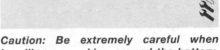
4 Battery - charging

Caution: Be extremely careful when handling or working around the battery. The electrolyte is very caustic and an explosive gas (hydrogen) is given off when the battery is charging.

1 Remove the battery (see Section 3). Connect the charger to the battery, making sure that the positive (+ve) lead on the charger is connected to the positive (+ve) terminal on the battery, and the negative (-ve) lead is connected to the negative (-ve) terminal.

2 Suzuki recommend that the battery is charged at a maximum rate of 1.1 amps for 10 hours. Exceeding this figure can cause the battery to overheat, buckling the plates and rendering it useless. Few owners will have access to an expensive current-controlled charger, so if a normal domestic charger is

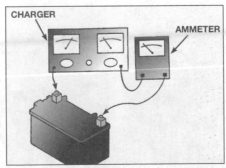

4.2 If the charger doesn't have ammeter built in, connect one in series as shown. **DO NOT** connect the ammeter between the battery terminals or it will be ruined

used check that after a possible initial peak, the charge rate falls to a safe level **(see illustration)**. **Note:** *In emergencies the battery can be charged at a higher rate of around 4.0 amps for a period of 1 hour. However, this is not recommended and the low amp charge is by far the safer method of charging the battery.* *Caution: Stop charging if the battery gets hot - further charging will cause damage.*

3 If the recharged battery discharges rapidly if left disconnected it is likely that an internal short caused by physical damage or sulphation has occurred. A new battery will be required. A sound item will tend to lose its charge at about 1% per day.

4 Install the battery (see Section 3).

5 If the motorcycle sits unused for long periods of time, charge the battery once every month to six weeks and leave it disconnected.

5 Fuse - check and replacement

1 The electrical system is protected by one 20 A fuse.

2 On EK models, the fuseholder is located under the seat behind the battery. On all other models, the fuse is located behind the right-hand side panel and is incorporated in the starter relay wiring connector **(see illustration)**.

5.2 Fuse location under the connector (A) on the starter relay. Note the spare fuse (B)

8

5.3a Disconnect the connector to access the fuse

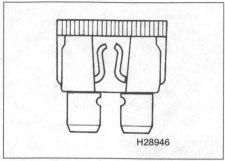

H28946

5.3b A blown fuse can be identified by a break in its element

3 The fuse can be removed and checked visually. On K models unclip the cover from the fuse holder and on all other models disconnect the starter relay wiring connector to access the fuse **(see illustration)**. If you can't pull the fuse out with your fingertips, use a pair of needle-nose pliers. A blown fuse is easily identified by a break in the element **(see illustration)**. The fuse is clearly marked with its rating and must only be replaced by a fuse of the correct rating. A spare fuse is located adjacent to the main fuse on EK models, and in the bottom of the starter relay on all other models **(see illustration 5.2)**. If the spare fuse is used, always replace it so that a spare is carried on the bike at all times.

Caution: Never put in a fuse of a higher rating or bridge the terminals with any other substitute, however temporary it may be. Serious damage may be done to the circuit, or a fire may start.

4 If the fuse blows, be sure to check the wiring circuit very carefully for evidence of a short-circuit. Look for bare wires and chafed, melted or burned insulation. If the fuse is replaced before the cause is located, the new fuse will blow immediately.

5 Occasionally the fuse will blow or cause an open-circuit for no obvious reason. Corrosion of the fuse ends and fusebox terminals may occur and cause poor fuse contact. If this happens, remove the corrosion with a wire brush or emery paper, then spray the fuse end and terminals with electrical contact cleaner.

---

6 Lighting system - check

1 The battery provides power for operation of the headlight, tail light, brake light and instrument cluster lights. If none of the lights operate, always check battery voltage before proceeding. Low battery voltage indicates either a faulty battery or a defective charging system. Refer to Section 3 for battery checks and Sections 31 and 32 for charging system tests. Also, check the condition of the fuse and replace it if it has blown.

Headlight

2 If the headlight fails to work, first check the fuse with the key ON (see Section 5), and then the bulb (see Section 7). If they are both good, use jumper wires to connect the bulb directly to the battery terminals. If the light comes on, the problem lies in the wiring or one of the switches in the circuit. Refer to Section 20 for the switch testing procedures, and also the wiring diagrams at the end of this Chapter.

Tail light

3 If the tail light fails to work, check the bulbs and the bulb terminals first, then the fuse, then check for battery voltage on the supply side of the tail light wiring connector. If voltage is present, check the earth (ground) circuit for an open or poor connection.
4 If no voltage is indicated, check the wiring between the tail light and the ignition switch,

then check the switch. Also check the lighting switch on UK models.

Brake light

5 See Section 14 for the brake light switch checking procedure.

Neutral indicator light

6 If the neutral light fails to operate when the transmission is in neutral, check the fuse and the bulb (see Sections 5 and 17). If they are in good condition, trace the neutral switch wiring back from the top of the engine sprocket cover and disconnect it at the connector behind the left-hand side panel. Check for battery voltage on the supply side of the connector. If battery voltage is present, refer to Section 22 for the neutral switch check and replacement procedures.
7 If no voltage is indicated, check the wiring between the switch and the bulb for open-circuits and poor connections.

Oil pressure warning light

8 See Section 18 for the oil pressure switch check.

---

7 Headlight bulb and side light bulb - replacement

Note: *The headlight bulb is of the quartz-halogen type. Do not touch the bulb glass as skin acids will shorten the bulb's service life. If the bulb is accidentally touched, it should be wiped carefully when cold with a rag soaked in methylated spirit (stoddard solvent) and dried before fitting.*

⚠️ **Warning: Allow the bulb time to cool before removing it if the headlight has just been on!**

Headlight

1 Remove the two screws securing the headlight rim to the headlight shell, and ease the rim out of the shell, noting how it fits **(see illustration)**.
2 Disconnect the wiring connector and remove the rubber dust cover, noting how it fits **(see illustration)**.

7.1 The headlight rim is secured by two screws, one on each side (arrow)

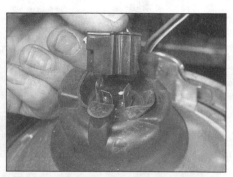

7.2 Disconnect the wiring connector and remove the rubber cover

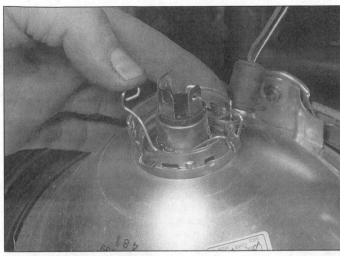

7.3a Release the bulb retaining clip . . .

7.3b . . . and remove the bulb

7.5 Fit the rubber cover with the TOP mark upwards

7.6 Ensure the rim fits correctly onto the tabs on the shell (arrows)

3 Release the bulb retaining clip, noting how it fits, then remove the bulb **(see illustrations)**.
4 Fit the new bulb, bearing in mind the information in the **Note** above. Make sure the tabs on the bulb fit correctly in the slots in the bulb housing, and secure it in position with the retaining clip.
5 Install the dust cover, making sure it is correctly seated and with the TOP mark facing

up, and connect the wiring connector **(see illustration)**.
6 Check the operation of the headlight, then install the rim into the shell and secure it with the screws **(see illustration)**.

Side light

7 Remove the two screws securing the headlight rim to the headlight shell, and ease

the rim out of the shell, noting how it fits **(see illustration 7.1)**.
8 Twist the bulbholder anti-clockwise to release it from the headlight **(see illustration)**. Push the bulb down and twist it anti-clockwise to release it from the bulbholder **(see illustration)**.
9 Install the new bulb in the bulbholder, then install the bulbholder by pressing it in and twisting it clockwise.
10 Check the operation of the side light, then install the headlight rim into the shell and secure it with the screws **(see illustration 7.6)**.

8 Headlight assembly - removal and installation

Removal

1 Remove the two screws securing the headlight rim to the headlight shell, and ease the rim out of the shell, noting how it fits **(see illustration 7.1)**.

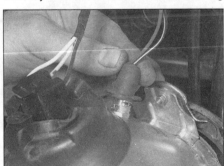

7.8a Remove the bulbholder from the headlight . . .

7.8b . . . and remove the bulb from the holder

8

8.3a Unscrew the nut (arrow) and remove the bolt

8.3b Headlight bracket bolts (arrows)

2 Disconnect the wiring connector from the headlight bulb and twist the side light bulbholder anti-clockwise to release it from the headlight **(see illustrations 7.2 and 7.8a).**
3 To remove the headlight shell, first free the wiring inside the shell from any clamps, then disconnect any wiring connectors necessary and ease the wiring out the back of the shell. Unscrew the nut and withdraw the bolt on the guide on the right-hand side of the headlight. Unscrew the nuts on the inside of the shell and remove the bolts securing the shell to the brackets **(see illustrations)**. If necessary, unscrew the bolts securing the brackets to the support frame and remove the brackets **(see illustration)**.

 When disconnecting wiring, label the connectors to avoid confusion on reconnection.

Installation

4 Installation is the reverse of removal. Make sure all the wiring is correctly connected and secured. Check the operation of the headlight and side light. Check the headlight aim (see Chapter 1).

9 Brake/tail light bulbs - replacement

EK to EY models

1 Remove the seat (see Chapter 7).
2 Turn the bulbholder anti-clockwise and withdraw it from the taillight **(see illustration)**.
3 Push the bulb into the holder and twist it anti-clockwise to remove it **(see illustration)**. Check the socket terminals for corrosion and clean them if necessary. Line up the pins of the new bulb with the slots in the socket, then push the bulb in and turn it clockwise until it

locks into place. **Note:** *The pins on the bulb are offset so it can only be installed one way. It is a good idea to use a paper towel or dry cloth when handling the new bulb to prevent injury if the bulb should break and to increase bulb life.*
4 Install the bulbholder into the tail light and turn it clockwise to secure it.
5 Install the seat (see Chapter 7).

K1 models onward

6 Remove the two screws securing the lens to the tail light and remove the lens **(see illustration)**. Note the sealing gasket between the lens and the body of the light unit. Push the bulb into the socket and twist it anti-clockwise to remove it. Check the socket terminals for corrosion and clean them if necessary. Line up the pins of the new bulb with the slots in the socket (see **Note** in Step 3), then push the bulb in and turn it clockwise until it locks into place **(see illustration)**.
7 Install the lens and secure it with the screws. Take care not to overtighten the screws.

10 Tail light assembly - removal and installation

Removal

1 Remove the seat (see Chapter 7).
2 Trace the tail light wiring back from the bulbholders and disconnect it at the connector **(see illustration)**.
3 Unscrew the two nuts securing the tail light to the frame and carefully withdraw it from the back of the bike **(see illustration)**. Note

9.2 On EK to EY models, twist the bulbholder anti-clockwise to release it ...

9.3 ... then push the bulb in gently and twist it anti-clockwise to remove it

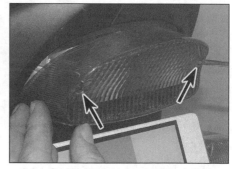

9.6a On K1 models onward the lens is secured by two screws

9.6b Line up the pins on the bulb with the slots in the socket

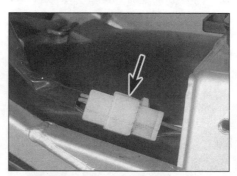

10.2 Disconnect the tail light wiring connector (arrow)

10.3 The tail light assembly is secured by two nuts (arrows)

10.4 On EK to EY models the lens is secured by tabs on the top and underside

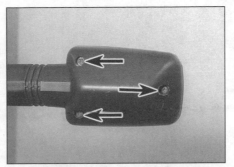

11.1a On EK to EY models, undo the three screws . . .

11.1b . . . and remove the signal lens . . .

11.2 . . . then push the bulb in and twist it anti-clockwise to release it

11.4a On K1 models onward, undo the single fixing screw . . .

11.4b . . . and note how the tab (arrow) locates inside the assembly

11.4c Turn the bulbholder anti-clockwise to release it . . .

11.4d . . . then push the bulb in and twist it anti-clockwise to release it

the fitting of the washers and rubber grommets.

4 On EK to EY models, if required, twist the bulbholders anti-clockwise and withdraw them from the tail light. To remove the lens, release its tabs from the slots in the shell rim and separate the lens from the shell, noting how it fits (see illustration).

Installation

5 Installation is the reverse of removal. Check the operation of the tail light and the brake light.

11 Turn signal bulbs - replacement

EK to EY models

1 Remove the three screws securing the lens to the turn signal assembly and remove the lens, noting which way round it fits (see illustrations).
2 Push the bulb into the holder and twist it anti-clockwise to remove it (see illustration). Check the socket terminals for corrosion and clean them if necessary. Line up the pins of the new bulb with the slots in the socket, then push the bulb in and turn it clockwise until it locks into place. Note: It is a good idea to use a paper towel or dry cloth when handling the new bulb to prevent injury if the bulb should break and to increase bulb life.
3 Install the lens back onto the turn signal

assembly, and tighten the three screws. Take care not to overtighten the screws as the assembly is easily cracked.

K1 models onward

4 Remove the screw securing the lens unit to the signal assembly and unclip the lens unit (see illustration). Note how the tab on the lens unit locates inside the signal assembly (see illustration). Turn the bulbholder anti-clockwise and withdraw it from the lens unit, then push the bulb into the holder and twist it anti-clockwise to remove it (see illustrations).
5 Check the socket terminals for corrosion and clean them if necessary. Line up the pins of the new bulb with the slots in the socket (see Note in Step 2), then push the bulb in and turn it clockwise until it locks into place.

HAYNES HINT *If the socket contacts are dirty or corroded, scrape them clean and spray with electrical contact cleaner before a new bulb is installed.*

12 Turn signal assemblies - removal and installation

Front

Removal

1 Remove the two screws securing the headlight rim to the headlight shell, and ease the rim out of the shell, noting how it fits (see illustration 7.1).
2 Trace the turn signal wiring back from the

8

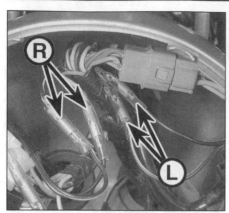

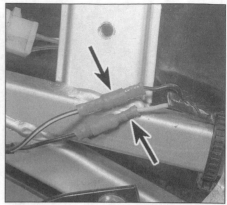

12.2 Front turn signal left (L) and right (R) wiring connectors inside headlight shell

12.3 Front turn signal mounting nut (arrow)

12.5 The rear turn signal wiring connectors are on each side of the frame (arrows)

turn signal and disconnect it at the connectors inside the headlight shell **(see illustration)**. Pull the wiring through to the turn signal mounting, noting its routing.

3 Unscrew the nut securing the turn signal to the support frame **(see illustration)** and carefully remove the assembly, taking care not to snag the wiring connectors as you draw them through the mounting hole.

Installation

4 Installation is the reverse of removal. Make sure the wiring is correctly routed and securely connected. Check the operation of the turn signals.

Rear

Removal

5 Remove the seat (see Chapter 7). Trace the turn signal wiring back from the turn signal and disconnect it at the connectors **(see illustration)**. Pull the wiring through to the

turn signal mounting, releasing it from any clips and noting its routing.

6 Unscrew the nut securing the turn signal assembly to the mudguard and carefully remove the assembly, taking care not to snag the wiring connectors as you draw them through the mounting hole **(see illustration)**.

Installation

7 Installation is the reverse of removal. Make sure the wiring is correctly routed and securely connected. Check the operation of the turn signals.

13 Turn signal circuit - check

1 The battery provides power for operation of the turn signal lights, so if they do not operate, always check the battery voltage first. Low battery voltage indicates either a faulty battery or a defective charging system. Refer to

Section 3 for battery checks and Sections 31 and 32 for charging system tests. Also, check the fuse (see Section 5) and the switch (see Section 20).

2 Most turn signal problems are the result of a burned out bulb or corroded socket. This is especially true when the turn signals function properly in one direction, but fail to flash in the other direction. Check the bulbs and the sockets (see Section 11).

3 If the bulbs and sockets are good, check for power at the turn signal relay orange wire with the ignition ON. The relay is mounted behind the right-hand side panel **(see illustration)**. Turn the ignition OFF when the check is complete. **Note:** *On K1 models onward, the turn signal relay is positioned to the right of the sidestand relay.*

4 If no power was present at the relay, check the wiring from the relay to the ignition (main) switch for continuity.

5 If power was present at the relay, using the appropriate wiring diagram at the end of this Chapter, check the wiring between the relay,

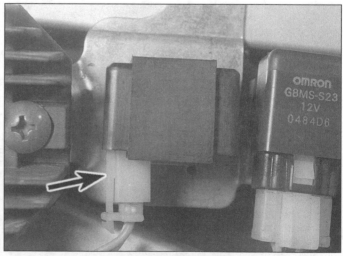

12.6 The rear turn signal assembly is secured to the mudguard by a single nut (arrow)

13.3 Disconnect the turn signal relay wiring connector (arrow) and check for power at the orange wire terminal

14.5 Front brake light switch wiring connectors (arrows)

14.6 The switch is secured by a single screw (arrow)

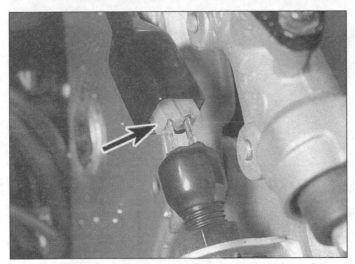

14.8 Rear brake light switch wiring connector (arrow)

14.9 Unhook the spring from the actuating arm (arrow)

turn signal switch and turn signal lights for continuity. If the wiring and switch are sound, replace the relay with a new one.

14 Brake light switches - check and replacement

Circuit check

1 Before checking any electrical circuit, check the bulb (see Section 9) and fuse (see Section 5).
2 Using a multimeter or test light connected to a good earth (ground), check for voltage at the brake light switch wiring connector **(see illustration 14.5 or 14.8)**. If there's no voltage present, check the wire between the switch and the ignition switch (see the *wiring diagrams* at the end of this Chapter).
3 If voltage is available, touch the probe of the test light to the other terminal of the switch, then pull the brake lever in or depress

the brake pedal. If no reading is obtained or the test light doesn't light up, replace the switch.
4 If a reading is obtained or the test light does light, check the wiring between the switch and the brake lights (see the *wiring diagrams* at the end of this Chapter).

Switch replacement

Front brake lever switch

5 Disconnect the wiring connectors from the switch **(see illustration)**.
6 Unscrew the single screw securing the switch to the bottom of the front brake master cylinder and remove the switch **(see illustration)**.
7 Installation is the reverse of removal. The switch isn't adjustable.

Rear brake pedal switch

8 The switch is mounted to the back of the right-hand footrest bracket. Pull the terminal

cover off the top of the switch and disconnect the wiring connector **(see illustration)**.
9 Detach the lower end of the switch spring from the brake actuating arm, then unscrew the switch **(see illustration)**.
10 Installation is the reverse of removal. Make sure the brake light is activated just before the rear brake pedal takes effect. For adjustment details, see Chapter 1, Section 14.

15 Instrument cluster, and speedometer/tachometer cables - removal and installation

Instrument cluster

Removal

1 Trace the wiring back from the instrument cluster and disconnect it at the connector inside the top of the headlight shell **(see illustration)**. It should be possible to withdraw the connector sufficiently from the hole in the headlight to be

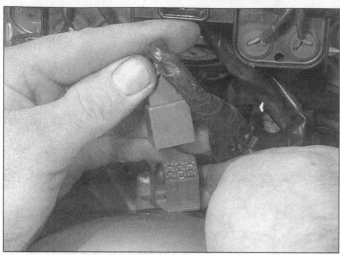

15.1 Disconnect the instrument cluster wiring connector

15.3a Unscrew the nut (arrow) . . .

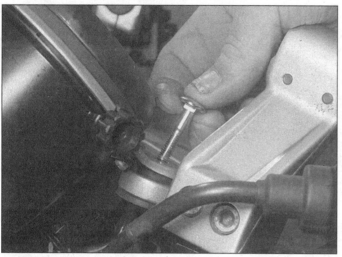

15.3b . . . and withdraw the bolt on each side of the cluster

15.5 Speedometer cable retaining ring (arrow)

able to disconnect it without having to access it from inside the shell. If not, unscrew the two screws securing the headlight rim to the headlight shell, and ease the rim out of the shell, noting how it fits **(see illustration 7.1)**.

2 Unscrew the speedometer and tachometer cable retaining rings from the rear of the instrument cluster and detach the cables **(see illustration 15.5)**.

3 Unscrew the two nuts from the instrument cluster mounting bolts and carefully lift the assembly off the top yoke, taking care not to snag the wiring and noting its routing **(see illustrations)**.

Installation

4 Installation is the reverse of removal. Make sure that the speedometer cable, tachometer cable and wiring connector are correctly routed and secured.

Speedometer cable

Removal

5 Unscrew the speedometer cable retaining

ring from the rear of the instrument cluster and detach the cable **(see illustration)**.

6 Remove the screw securing the lower end of the cable to the drive housing on the left-hand side of the front wheel **(see illustration)**.

7 Withdraw the cable from the guides on the front fork, front mudguard and fork brace, and remove it from the bike, noting its routing.

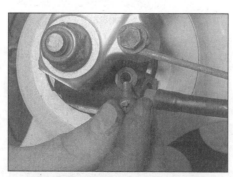

15.6 Remove the screw to free the speedometer cable from its drive housing

Installation

8 Route the cable correctly and install it in its retaining guides on the fork brace, front mudguard and the front fork **(see illustration)**.

9 Connect the cable upper end to the instrument cluster and tighten the retaining ring securely **(see illustration 15.5)**.

15.8 The speedometer cable passes through three guides (arrows)

15.13 Unscrew the ring (arrow) to release the tachometer cable from the cylinder head

15.17 Align the slot in the cable end so that it fits over the drive tab

10 Connect the cable lower end to the drive housing, aligning the slot in the cable end with the drive tab, and secure it with its screw **(see illustration 15.6)**.
11 Check that the cable doesn't restrict steering movement or interfere with any other components.

Tachometer cable

Removal

12 Unscrew the tachometer cable retaining ring from the rear of the instrument cluster and detach the cable.
13 Unscrew the retaining ring securing the lower end of the cable to the drive housing on the front of the cylinder head **(see illustration)**.
14 Withdraw the cable from its guides and remove it from the bike, noting its correct routing.

Installation

15 Route the cable correctly and install it in its retaining guides.
16 Connect the cable upper end to the instrument cluster and tighten the retaining ring securely.
17 Connect the cable lower end to the drive housing, aligning the slot in the cable end with the drive tab, and tighten the retaining ring securely **(see illustration)**.
18 Check that the cable doesn't restrict steering movement or interfere with any other components.

16 Instruments - check and replacement

Check

1 Special instruments are required to properly check the operation of the meters. If suspected to be faulty, take the motorcycle to a Suzuki dealer for assessment.

Replacement

2 The meters can be removed individually. Unscrew the cable retaining ring from the rear of the instrument cluster and detach the cable **(see illustration 15.5)**.
3 Unscrew the two nuts securing the meter to the instrument casing, noting the order of the washers **(see illustration)**. If removing the speedometer, remove the screw from the centre of the odometer trip knob and remove the knob **(see illustration)**.
4 Withdraw the speedometer from the casing, then remove the bulbholder **(see illustrations)**.

16.3a Unscrew the nuts to free the meter from the casing

16.4a Withdraw the instrument from the casing . . .

5 Install the meter by reversing the removal sequence. Make sure not to omit the large rubber sealing ring between the meter and instrument casing.

17 Instrument and warning light bulbs - replacement

1 To replace the instrument illumination bulbs, remove the relevant meter from the casing (see Section 16). Gently pull the bulb

16.3b Remove the screw (arrow) to release the trip knob

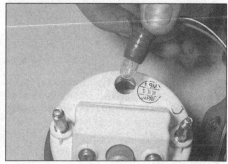

16.4b . . . and remove the bulbholder

8

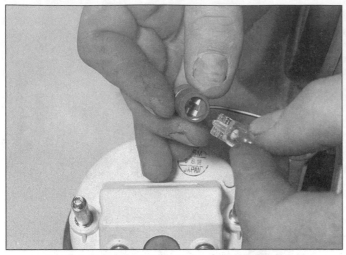

17.1 Carefully pull the bulb out of the holder

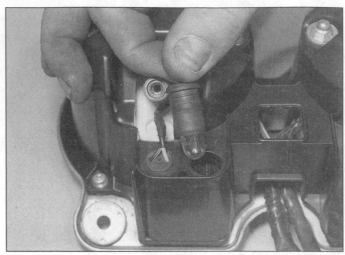

17.2a Pull the bulbholder out of the casing . . .

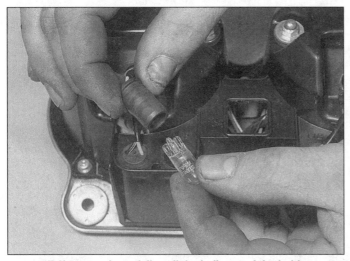

17.2b . . . and carefully pull the bulb out of the holder

18.3 Oil pressure switch wiring connector (arrow)

out of the bulbholder **(see illustration)**. If the socket contacts are dirty or corroded, scrape them clean and spray with electrical contact cleaner before a new bulb is installed. Carefully push the new bulb into the holder, then install the meter back into the casing (see Section 16).

2 To replace the warning light bulbs, pull the relevant bulbholder out of the back of the cluster **(see illustration)**. If access to the bulbholder is too restricted, unscrew the two nuts from the instrument cluster mounting bolts and carefully lift the assembly until sufficient clearance is obtained **(see illustration 15.3a)**. Gently pull the bulb out of the bulbholder **(see illustration)**. If the socket contacts are dirty or corroded, scrape them clean and spray with electrical contact cleaner before a new bulb is installed. Carefully push the new bulb into position, then push the bulbholder back into the rear of the cluster.

18 Oil pressure switch - check, removal and installation

Check

1 The oil pressure warning light should come on when the ignition (main) switch is turned ON and extinguish a few seconds after the engine is started. If the oil pressure light comes on whilst the engine is running, stop the engine immediately and carry out an oil pressure check as described in Chapter 1.

2 If the oil pressure warning light does not come on when the ignition is turned on, check the bulb (see Section 17) and fuse (see Section 5). If the bulb and fuse are in good order check the oil pressure switch as follows

3 The switch is screwed into the right-hand side crankcase cover and is accessed by unscrewing the three bolts securing the circular pulse generator assembly cover. Remove the cover and detach the wiring connector from the switch **(see illustration)**. With the ignition switched ON, earth (ground) the wire on the crankcase and check that the warning light comes on. If the light comes on, the switch is defective and must be replaced.

4 If the light still does not come on, check for voltage at the wire terminal using a test light. If there is no voltage present, check the wire between the switch, the instrument cluster and fusebox for continuity (see the *wiring diagrams* at the end of this Chapter).

5 If the warning light comes on whilst the engine is running, yet the oil pressure is satisfactory, remove the wire from the oil pressure switch. With the wire detached and the ignition switched ON the light should be out. If it comes on, the wire between the switch and instrument cluster must be earthed (grounded) at some point. If the wiring is good, the switch is faulty and should be replaced.

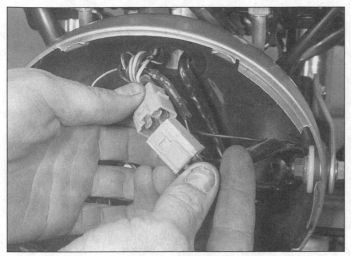

19.1 Disconnect the ignition (main) switch wiring connector

19.6 Ignition (main) switch bolts (arrows)

Removal

6 Drain the engine oil (see Chapter 1).
7 Remove the pulse generator coil assembly (see Chapter 4).
8 Unscrew the oil pressure switch and withdraw it from the crankcase.

Installation

9 Apply a suitable sealant (3-Bond or equivalent) to the threads of the switch, then install it in the crankcase and tighten it securely.
10 Install the pulse generator assembly (see Chapter 4).
11 Fill the engine with the correct type and quantity of oil as described in Chapter 1.

19 Ignition (main) switch - check, removal and installation

> **Warning: To prevent the risk of short circuits, disconnect the battery negative (-ve) lead before making any ignition (main) switch checks.**

Check

1 Remove the two headlight rim securing screws, and ease the rim out of the shell (see illustration 7.1). Trace the ignition (main) switch wiring back from the base of the switch and disconnect it at the connector in the headlight shell (see illustration).
2 Using an ohmmeter or a continuity tester, check the continuity of the terminal pairs (see the wiring diagrams at the end of this Chapter). Continuity should exist between the terminals connected by a solid line on the diagram when the switch is in the indicated position.
3 If the switch fails any of the tests, replace it.

Removal

4 Remove the instrument cluster (Section 15).
5 Remove the two screws securing the

headlight rim to the headlight shell, and ease the rim out of the shell (see illustration 7.1). Trace the ignition (main) switch wiring back from the base of the switch and disconnect it at the connector in the headlight shell.
6 Unscrew the two Torx bolts securing the switch to the underside of the top yoke and remove the switch (see illustration).

Installation

7 Installation is the reverse of removal. Tighten the switch mounting bolts securely.

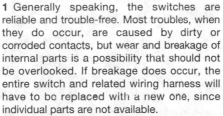

20 Handlebar switches - check

1 Generally speaking, the switches are reliable and trouble-free. Most troubles, when they do occur, are caused by dirty or corroded contacts, but wear and breakage of internal parts is a possibility that should not be overlooked. If breakage does occur, the entire switch and related wiring harness will have to be replaced with a new one, since individual parts are not available.
2 The switches can be checked for continuity using an ohmmeter or a continuity test light. Always disconnect the battery negative (-ve) lead, which will prevent the possibility of a short circuit, before making the checks.
3 Remove the two headlight rim securing screws, and ease the rim out of the shell (see illustration 7.1). Trace the wiring harness of the switch in question back to its connector(s) and disconnect it.
4 Using the ohmmeter or test light, check for continuity between the terminals of the switch harness with the switch in the various positions (ie switch off - no continuity, switch on - continuity) - see the wiring diagrams at the end of this Chapter.
5 If the continuity check indicates a problem exists, refer to Section 21, remove the switch and spray the switch contacts with electrical

contact cleaner. If they are accessible, the contacts can be scraped clean with a knife or polished with crocus cloth. If switch components are damaged or broken, it will be obvious when the switch is disassembled.

21 Handlebar switches - removal and installation

Right-hand handlebar switch

Removal

1 If the switch is to be removed from the bike, rather than just displaced from the handlebar, remove the two screws securing the headlight rim to the headlight shell, and ease the rim out of the shell (see illustration 7.1). Trace the wiring harness back from the switch to the wiring connector in the headlight housing and disconnect it. Work back along the harness, freeing it from all the relevant clips and ties, whilst noting its correct routing.
2 Disconnect the two wires from the brake light switch (see illustration 14.5). Unscrew the two handlebar switch retaining screws on the underside of the switch and remove the switch from the handlebar, noting how it fits (see illustration). Remove the throttle cable from the switch (see Chapter 4 if necessary).

21.2 The switch is secured by two screws

8

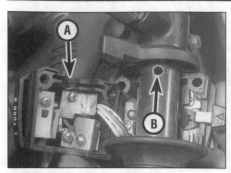

21.6 The switch pin (A) locates in the handlebar hole (B)

Installation

3 Installation is the reverse of removal. Make sure the locating pin in the upper half of the switch fits into hole in the top of the handlebar **(see illustration 21.6)**. If necessary, refer to Chapter 4 for installation of the throttle cable.

Left-hand handlebar switch

Removal

4 If the switch is to be removed from the bike, rather than just displaced from the handlebar, remove the two screws securing the headlight rim to the headlight shell, and ease the rim out of the shell **(see illustration 7.1)**. Work back along the harness, freeing it from all the relevant clips and ties, whilst noting its correct routing.

5 If fitted, disconnect the two wires from the clutch switch. Unscrew the two handlebar switch retaining screws on the underside of the switch and remove the switch from the

handlebar, noting how it fits. Remove the choke cable (see Chapter 3 if necessary).

Installation

6 Installation is the reverse of removal. Make sure the locating pin in the upper half of the switch fits into hole in the top of the handlebar **(see illustration)**. If necessary, refer to Chapter 3 for installation of the choke cable.

---

22 Neutral switch - check, removal and installation

Check

1 Before checking the electrical circuit, check the bulb (see Section 17) and fuse (see Section 5).

2 The switch is located in the left-hand side of the crankcase, behind the engine sprocket cover. Trace the switch wiring from the top of the engine sprocket cover and disconnect it at its connector behind the left-hand side panel **(see illustration)**. Make sure the transmission is in neutral.

3 With the connector disconnected and the ignition switched ON, the neutral light should be out. If not, the wire between the connector and instrument cluster must be earthed (grounded) at some point. Switch the ignition OFF.

4 Using an ohmmeter or continuity tester, check for continuity between the switch side of the wiring connector and the crankcase. With the transmission in neutral, there should be continuity. With the transmission in gear, there should be no continuity. If the tests

prove otherwise, then either the switch is faulty or the spring and plunger mechanism is faulty. Remove the switch and check the condition of the spring and plunger, and make sure that the plunger moves freely in its hole. If there is any sign of wear or damage, replace the spring and plunger and check the operation of the switch before buying a new switch.

5 If the continuity tests prove the switch is good, check for voltage at the wire terminal using a test light. If there's no voltage present, check the wire between the switch, diode, instrument cluster, ignition switch and fuse (see the *wiring diagrams* at the end of this Chapter). Also check the operation of the diode (see Section 26).

Removal

6 Unscrew the gearchange lever pinch bolt and remove the lever from the shaft, noting any alignment marks on the lever and the shaft. If no marks are visible, make your own before removing the lever so that it can be correctly aligned with the shaft on installation. Unscrew the bolts securing the engine sprocket cover to the crankcase and move the cover aside. There is no need to detach the clutch cable from the cover.

7 Trace the switch wiring from the top of the engine sprocket cover and disconnect it at its connector behind the left-hand side panel **(see illustration 22.2)**. Free the wiring from any clips or ties, noting its routing.

8 Remove the two screws securing the switch to the crankcase and carefully withdraw it, noting that the contact plunger is under spring pressure and is likely to eject itself out of its hole in the end of the selector drum **(see illustration)**. Discard the O-ring as a new one must be used.

Installation

9 Install the spring and plunger into the hole in the end of the selector drum, then install the switch using a new O-ring and tighten its screws securely **(see illustrations)**.

10 Route the wiring up to its connector behind the left-hand side panel and reconnect it. Secure the wiring with any clips or ties.

11 Check the operation of the neutral light.

12 Install the sprocket cover and the gearchange lever, aligning the marks made on removal.

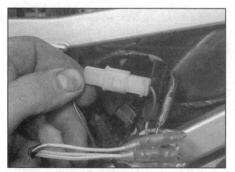

22.2 Neutral switch wiring connector

22.8 The neutral switch is secured by two screws (arrows)

22.9a Install the spring and plunger ...

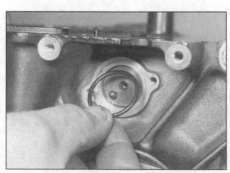

22.9b ... and a new O-ring ...

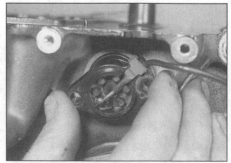

22.9c ... then install the switch

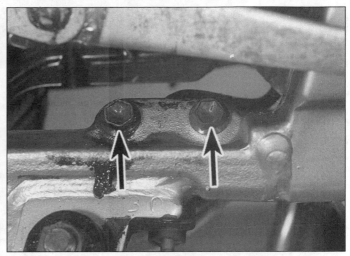

23.2 Sidestand switch wiring connectors

23.8 The sidestand switch is secured by two bolts (arrows)

23 Sidestand switch -
check and replacement

Check

1 The sidestand switch is mounted on the frame just behind the sidestand **(see illustration 23.8)**. The switch is part of the safety circuit which prevents or stops the engine running if the transmission is in gear whilst the sidestand is down, and prevents the engine from starting if the transmission is in gear unless the sidestand is up, and unless the clutch lever is pulled in (UK EV models onward and all US models – see Section 25). Before checking the electrical circuit, check the bulb (see Section 17) and fuse (see Section 5).
2 Trace the wiring back from the switch to its connectors behind the left-hand side panel and disconnect them **(see illustration)**.
3 Check the operation of the switch using an ohmmeter or continuity test light. Connect the meter to the black/white and green wires on the switch side of the connector. With the sidestand up there should be continuity (zero resistance) between the terminals, and with

the stand down there should be no continuity (infinite resistance).
4 If the switch does not perform as expected, it is defective and must be replaced. Check first that the fault is not caused by a sticking switch plunger due to the ingress of road dirt; spray the switch with a water dispersant aerosol.
5 If the switch is good, check the sidestand relay and other components in the starter circuit as described in the relevant sections of this Chapter. If all components are good, check the wiring between the various components (see the *wiring diagrams* at the end of this book).

Replacement

6 The sidestand switch is mounted on the frame just behind the sidestand. Trace the wiring back from the switch to its connectors behind the left-hand side panel and disconnect them **(see illustration 23.2)**.
7 Work back along the switch wiring, freeing it from any relevant retaining clips and ties, noting its correct routing.
8 Unscrew the two bolts securing the switch to the frame **(see illustration)**.
9 Fit the new switch to the frame and install the retaining bolts, tightening them securely.

10 Make sure the wiring is correctly routed up to the connectors and retained by all the necessary clips and ties.
11 Reconnect the wiring connectors and check the operation of the sidestand switch.

24 Sidestand relay -
check and replacement

Check

1 If the switch and wiring are good, the sidestand relay may be at fault. The relay is located behind the right-hand side panel.
2 Disconnect the relay wiring connector and remove the relay from its mounting **(see illustrations)**. Using an ohmmeter or continuity tester, connect the positive (+ve) lead to the No. 1 terminal on the relay and the negative (-ve) lead to the No. 2 terminal on the relay **(see illustration)**. There should be no continuity between these terminals. Using a spare 12 V battery and a set of insulated jumper leads, connect the battery positive (+ve) lead to the No. 3 terminal on the relay, and the battery negative (-ve) lead to the No. 4 terminal on the relay. With the battery connected, there should

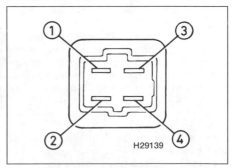

24.2a Disconnect the wire connector from the sidestand relay – EK to EY models

24.2b Sidestand relay (arrow) – K1 models onward

24.2c Sidestand relay terminal identification (see text)

8

25.2 Clutch switch wiring terminals (arrowed)

26.2 Diode location (arrow)

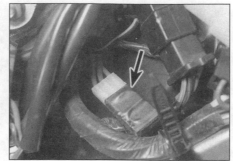

27.2 Disconnect the horn wiring connectors

be continuity (zero resistance) indicated on the ohmmeter on tester. If either of the above conditions do not exist, replace the relay.

3 If the relay is good, check the other components in the starter circuit as described in the relevant sections of this Chapter. If all components are good, check the wiring between the various components (see the *wiring diagrams* at the end of this book).

Replacement

4 Remove the right-hand side panel (see Chapter 7).

5 Disconnect the relay wiring connector and remove the relay from its mounting **(see illustration 24.2a or b)**.

6 Connect the wiring connector to the new relay and check the operation of the sidestand circuit.

25 Clutch switch – check and replacement

Note: *UK V models onward and all US models are fitted with a clutch switch.*

Check

1 The clutch switch is situated on the base of the clutch lever bracket. The switch is part of the safety circuit which prevents or stops the engine running if the transmission is in gear whilst the sidestand is down, and prevents the engine from starting if the transmission is in gear unless the sidestand is up, and unless the clutch is pulled in.

2 Disconnect the wiring connectors from the switch and connect the probes of an ohmmeter or a continuity tester to the two switch terminals **(see illustration)**. With the clutch lever pulled in, continuity should be indicated. With the clutch lever out, no continuity (infinite resistance) should be indicated.

3 If the switch is good, check the other components in the starter circuit as described in the relevant sections of this Chapter. If all components are good, check the wiring between the various components

(refer to the *wiring diagrams* at the end of this book).

Replacement

4 Disconnect the wiring connectors from the clutch switch. Remove the screw(s) securing the switch to the bottom of the clutch lever bracket and remove the switch.

5 Installation is the reverse of removal. Check for correct operation, as described above, on completion.

26 Diode – check and replacement

Check

1 Remove the seat (see Chapter 7).

2 The diode is a small block that plugs into a connector in the main wiring harness **(see illustration)**. The switch is part of the safety circuit which prevents or stops the engine running if the transmission is in gear whilst the sidestand is down, and prevents the engine from starting if the transmission is in gear unless the sidestand is up, and unless the clutch lever is pulled in (UK EV models onward and all US models). Disconnect the diode from the wire harness.

3 Using an ohmmeter or continuity tester, connect the positive (+ve) probe to one of the outer terminals of the diode and the negative (-ve) probe to the middle terminal of the diode. The diode should show continuity. Now reverse the probes. The diode should show no continuity (infinite resistance). Repeat the tests between the other outer terminal and the middle terminal. The same results should be achieved. If it doesn't behave as stated, replace the diode.

4 If the diode is good, check the other components in the starter circuit as described in the relevant sections of this Chapter. If all components are good, check the wiring between the various components (see the *wiring diagrams* at the end of this book).

Replacement

5 Remove the seat (see Chapter 7).

6 The diode is a small block that plugs into a connector in the main wiring harness **(see illustration 26.2)**. Disconnect the diode and connect the new one.

27 Horn - check and replacement

Check

1 The horn is mounted on the front of the frame below the steering head **(see illustration 27.4)**.

2 Unplug the wiring connectors from the horn **(see illustration)**. Using two insulated jumper wires, apply battery voltage directly to the terminals on the horn. If the horn sounds, check the switch (see Section 20) and the wiring between the switch and the horn (see the *wiring diagrams* at the end of this Chapter).

3 If the horn doesn't sound, replace it.

Replacement

4 The horn is mounted on the front of the frame below the steering head **(see illustration)**.

5 Unplug the wiring connectors from the horns **(see illustration 27.2)**, then unscrew the bolts securing the horn to the frame.

6 Install the horn and securely tighten the bolts. Connect the horn wiring connectors.

27.4 The horn is secured by two bolts (arrows)

28.2a Starter relay location

28.2b Pull back the rubber covers to expose the terminals

28 Starter relay -
check and replacement

Check

1 If the starter circuit is faulty, first check the fuse (see Section 5).

2 The starter relay is located behind the right-hand side panel (see illustration). Remove the side panel for access to the relay (Chapter 7). Pull back the rubber cover on the top of the relay, then unscrew the nut securing the starter motor lead to its terminal and disconnect the lead (see illustration). With the ignition switch ON, the engine kill switch in RUN, the transmission in neutral and the clutch pulled in (UK EV models onward and all US models), press the starter switch. The relay should be heard to click. If the relay doesn't click, switch off the ignition and remove the relay as described below; test it as follows.

3 With the relay removed from the bike, set a multimeter to the ohms x 1 scale and connect it across the relay's starter motor and battery lead terminals. Using a fully-charged 12 volt battery and two insulated jumper wires, connect the positive (+ve) terminal of the battery to the yellow/green wire terminal of

the relay, and the negative (-ve) terminal to the black/white wire terminal of the relay. At this point the relay should be heard to click and the multimeter read 0 ohms (continuity). If this is the case the relay is proved good. If the relay does not click when battery voltage is applied and indicates no continuity (infinite resistance) across its terminals, check its coil resistance as follows.

4 With the relay removed from the bike, connect a multimeter set to the ohms x 1 range across its yellow/green and black/white wire terminals. Relay coil resistance should fall within the specified figure (see Specifications). If an open circuit (infinite resistance) is shown, the relay is confirmed faulty and must be replaced with a new one.

5 If the relay is good, check for battery voltage between the yellow/green wire and the black/white wire when the starter button is pressed. Check the other components in the starter circuit as described in the relevant sections of this Chapter. If all components are good, check the wiring between the various components (see the *wiring diagrams* at the end of this book).

Replacement

6 Remove the right-hand side panel (see Chapter 7).

7 Disconnect the battery terminals, negative (-ve) terminal first.

8 Disconnect the relay wiring connector, then unscrew the two nuts securing the starter motor and battery leads to the relay and detach the leads (see illustration 28.2b). On EK models, unscrew the two screws securing the starter relay and remove the relay. On all other models, remove the relay with its rubber sleeve from its mounting lugs on the frame (see illustration).

9 Installation is the reverse of removal, ensuring the terminal nuts are securely tightened. Connect the negative (-ve) lead last when reconnecting the battery.

29 Starter motor -
removal and installation

Removal

1 Remove the seat (see Chapter 7). Disconnect the battery negative (-ve) lead.

2 Unscrew the two bolts securing the starter motor cover to the top of the crankcase behind the cylinder block and remove the cover (see illustration).

3 Peel back the rubber cover and unscrew the nut securing the starter cable to the motor (see illustration).

28.8 The relay's rubber sleeve mounts onto lugs on the frame

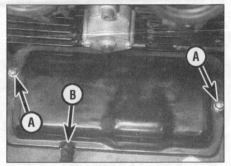

29.2 The starter motor cover is secured by two bolts (A). Note cutout for the wiring (B)

29.3 Peel back the cover to expose the terminal

8

29.4 The starter motor is secured by two bolts (arrows)

29.7 Fit a new O-ring onto the starter motor

29.8 Fit the starter motor into the crankcase

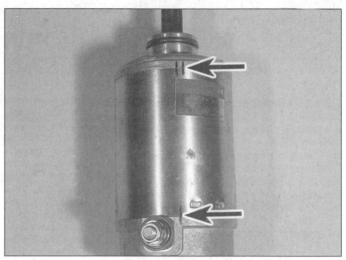

30.2 Make alignment marks (arrows) across both end covers

4 Unscrew the two bolts securing the starter motor to the crankcase **(see illustration)**.
5 Slide the starter motor out from the crankcase and remove it from the machine.
6 Remove the O-ring on the end of the starter motor and discard it as a new one must be used.

Installation

7 Install a new O-ring on the end of the starter motor and ensure it is seated in its groove **(see illustration)**. Apply a smear of engine oil to the O-ring to aid installation.
8 Manoeuvre the motor into position and slide it into the crankcase **(see illustration)**. Ensure that the starter motor teeth mesh correctly with those of the starter idle/reduction gear.
9 Install the retaining bolts and tighten them securely **(see illustration 29.4)**.
10 Connect the starter cable to the motor and secure it with the nut **(see illustration 29.3)**. Make sure the rubber cover is correctly seated over the terminal.

11 Install the starter motor cover, making sure the starter lead is channelled correctly in its slot, and tighten the cover bolts securely **(see illustration 29.2)**.
12 Connect the battery negative (-ve) lead and install the seat.

30 Starter motor - disassembly, inspection and reassembly

Disassembly

1 Remove the starter motor (see Section 29).
2 Make alignment marks between the main housing and the front and rear covers **(see illustration)**.
3 Unscrew the two long bolts and withdraw them from the starter motor. Discard their O-rings as new ones must be used. Remove the right-hand end cover from the motor along with its O-ring and the brushplate assembly. Discard the O-ring as a new one must be

used. Remove the shim from the end of the armature shaft or from inside the right-hand end cover after the brushplate assembly has been removed.
4 Wrap some insulating tape around the teeth on the end of the starter motor shaft - this will protect the oil seal from damage as the left-hand end cover is removed. Remove the end cover from the motor along with its O-ring. Discard the O-ring as a new one must be used. Remove the shims from the end of the armature shaft or the inside of the left-hand end cover, noting their correct fitted locations.
5 Withdraw the armature from the main housing.
6 Noting the correct fitted location of each component, unscrew the terminal nut and withdraw the terminal bolt and brushplate assembly from the right-hand end cover.
7 Lift the brush springs and slide the brushes out from their holders.

Inspection

8 The parts of the starter motor that are most

30.8 Measure the length of each brush

30.9 Check the commutator bars
as described

30.10a Continuity should exist between
the commutator bars

30.10b There should be no continuity
between the commutator bars and the
armature shaft

30.14 Check the oil seal in the
left-hand end cover

30.16 Fit the brushes back into their
holders

30.17 Fit a new O-ring around the cover

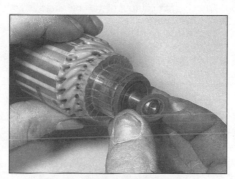

30.18a Fit the shim onto the
armature shaft . . .

30.18b . . . then install the armature into
the right-hand end cover . . .

likely to require attention are the brushes. Measure the length of the brushes and compare the results to the brush length listed in this Chapter's Specifications **(see illustration)**. If any of the brushes are worn beyond the service limit, replace the brush assembly with a new one. If the brushes are not worn excessively, nor cracked, chipped, or otherwise damaged, they may be re-used.

9 Inspect the commutator bars on the armature for scoring, scratches and discoloration **(see illustration)**. The commutator can be cleaned and polished with crocus cloth, but do not use sandpaper or emery paper. After cleaning, wipe away any residue with a cloth soaked in electrical system cleaner or denatured alcohol.

10 Using an ohmmeter or a continuity test light, check for continuity between the commutator bars **(see illustration)**. Continuity should exist between each bar and all of the others. Also, check for continuity between the commutator bars and the armature shaft **(see illustration)**. There should be no continuity (infinite resistance) between the commutator and the shaft. If the checks indicate otherwise, the armature is defective.

11 Check for continuity between each brush and the terminal bolt. There should be continuity (zero resistance). Check for continuity between the terminal bolt and the housing (when assembled). There should be no continuity (infinite resistance).

12 Check the end of the armature shaft for worn, cracked, chipped and broken teeth. If the shaft is damaged or worn, replace the armature.

13 Inspect the end covers for signs of cracks or wear. Inspect the magnets in the main housing and the housing itself for cracks.

14 Inspect the insulating washers and left-

hand end cover oil seal for signs of damage and replace them if necessary **(see illustration)**.

Reassembly

15 Ensure that the inner rubber insulator is in place on the terminal bolt, then insert the bolt through the right-hand end cover. Fit the O-ring and the outer rubber insulator over the terminal and secure it with the nut.

16 Slide the brushes back into position in their holders and place the brush spring ends onto the brushes **(see illustration)**.

17 Install the brushplate assembly in the right-hand end cover making sure its tab is correctly located in the slot in the cover. Fit a new O-ring onto the cover **(see illustration)**.

18 Slide the shim over the end of the armature shaft, then insert the armature into the right-hand end cover taking care not to damage the brushes **(see illustrations)**. As it

8

30.19 . . . and the main housing over the armature

30.20a Fit a new O-ring around the left-hand end cover

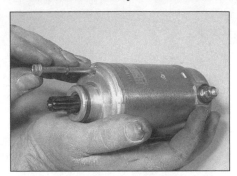

30.20b Fit the outer shim, making sure its tabs locate correctly in the cover . . .

30.20c . . . and the inner shim

30.20d Slide the left-hand end cover onto the motor

30.21 Install the long bolts using new O-rings

is inserted, locate the brushes on the commutator bars. Check that each brush is securely pressed against the commutator by its spring and is free to move easily in its holder.

19 Fit the main housing over the armature, aligning the marks made on removal **(see illustration)**.

20 Apply a smear of grease to the lips of the left-hand end cover oil seal and fit a new O-ring onto the cover **(see illustration)**. Fit the shims onto the cover, making sure that the tabs on the outer shim locate correctly **(see illustrations)**. Install the end cover, aligning the marks made on removal **(see illustration)**. Remove the protective tape from the shaft end.

21 Slide a new O-ring onto each of the long bolts. Check the marks made on removal are correctly aligned, then apply a suitable non-permanent thread locking compound to the threads of the long bolts and tighten them securely **(see illustration)**.

22 Install the starter motor (see Section 29).

31 Charging system testing - general information and precautions

1 If the performance of the charging system is suspect, the system as a whole should be checked first, followed by testing of the individual components. **Note:** *Before beginning the checks, make sure the battery is fully charged and that all system connections are clean and tight.*

2 Checking the output of the charging system and the performance of the various components within the charging system requires the use of a multimeter (with voltage, current and resistance checking facilities).

3 When making the checks, follow the procedures carefully to prevent incorrect connections or short circuits, as irreparable damage to electrical system components may result if short circuits occur.

4 If a multimeter is not available, the job of checking the charging system should be left to a Suzuki dealer.

32 Charging system - leakage and output test

1 If the charging system is thought to be faulty, remove the seat (see Chapter 7) and perform the following checks.

Leakage test

2 Turn the ignition switch OFF and disconnect the lead from the battery negative (-ve) terminal.

3 Set the multimeter to the mA (milli Amps) function and connect its negative (-ve) probe to the battery negative (-ve) terminal, and its positive (+ve) probe to the disconnected negative (-ve) lead **(see illustration)**. With the meter connected like this the reading should not exceed 0.1 mA.

4 If the reading exceeds the specified amount it is likely that there is a short circuit in the wiring. Thoroughly check the wiring between

the various components (see the *wiring diagrams* at the end of this book).

5 If the reading is below the specified amount, the leakage rate is satisfactory. Disconnect the meter and connect the negative (-) lead to the battery, tightening it securely, Check the alternator output as described below.

Output test - under load

6 Start the engine and warm it up to normal operating temperature. Turn the lighting switch on (UK models) and switch it to high beam (all models).

7 Allow the engine to idle and connect a multimeter set to the 0 - 20 volts dc scale (voltmeter) across the terminals of the battery

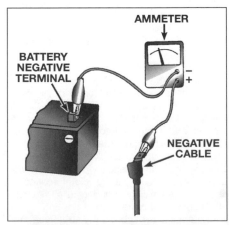

32.3 Checking the charging system leakage rate. Connect the meter as shown

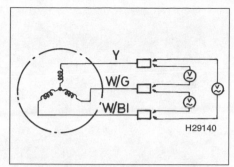

32.9 Alternator no-load voltage test connections

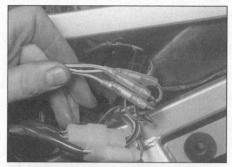

33.1 Disconnect the alternator wiring connectors

(positive (+ve) lead to battery positive (+ve) terminal, negative (-ve) lead to battery negative (-ve) terminal. Slowly increase the engine speed to 5000 rpm and note the reading obtained. At this speed the voltage should be 13.5 to 15.5 volts. Stop the engine and turn off the lights. If the voltage is outside these limits, perform a no-load output check as described in the following Step, and also check the regulator/rectifier (see Section 35). **Note:** *If the voltage is below 13.5 volts, then it is more likely that the alternator is faulty. If the voltage is above 15.5 volts, it is more likely that the regulator is faulty.*

 Clues to a faulty regulator are constantly blowing bulbs, with brightness varying greatly with engine speed, and battery overheating, necessitating frequent topping up of the electrolyte.

Output test - no-load

 Warning: If in any doubt about your ability to carry out this test, entrust it to a Suzuki dealer.

8 Remove the left-hand side panel (see Chapter 7). Trace the alternator wiring back from the top of the engine sprocket cover and disconnect it at the connector. Start the engine and increase the engine speed to 5000 rpm by adjusting the throttle stop screw underneath the carburettors. **Caution: Do not run the engine at this speed for any longer than is necessary to take this reading, otherwise it will overheat and engine damage may result.**

9 Using a multimeter set to the 0 - 100 volts ac scale (voltmeter), measure the voltage between each of the wires on the alternator side of the connector, so that three separate readings are taken in all **(see illustration)**. Compare the readings taken to the minimum no-load voltage specified at the beginning of the Chapter. If any of the readings are below the minimum specified, check the stator coil resistance (see Section 34).

10 On completion of the test, re-set the engine idle speed (see Chapter 1). Stop the engine and reconnect the alternator wiring.

33 Alternator - removal and installation

Removal

1 Remove the left-hand side panel (Chapter 7). Trace the alternator wiring back from the top of the engine sprocket cover and disconnect it at the connectors **(see illustration)**. Release the wiring from any clips or ties.

2 Unscrew the gearchange lever pinch bolt and remove the lever from the shaft, noting any alignment marks on the lever and the shaft. If no marks are visible, make your own before removing the lever so that it can be correctly aligned with the shaft on installation. Unscrew the bolts securing the engine sprocket cover to the crankcase and move the cover aside. There is no need to detach the clutch cable from the cover. Release the alternator wiring from the clamp next to the neutral switch.

3 Working in a criss-cross pattern, evenly slacken the left-hand side crankcase cover retaining bolts **(see illustration)**. Lift the cover away from the engine, being prepared to catch any residual oil which may be released as the cover is removed. Remove the gasket and discard it. Note the position of the locating dowel fitted to the crankcase and remove it for safe-keeping if it is loose. Note that the starter idle/reduction gear shaft locates into the crankcase cover and acts as a second locating dowel. **Note:** *If only the stator coils require attention, refer to Step 7.*

4 To remove the rotor bolt it is necessary to stop the rotor from rotating. If a rotor holding strap or tool is not available, place the transmission in gear and have an assistant apply the rear brake, or alternatively use a suitable spanner on the flats of the middle section of the rotor. Unscrew the bolt **(see illustration)**.

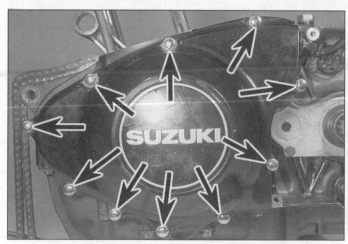

33.3 The cover is secured by ten bolts (arrows)

33.4 Alternator rotor bolt (arrow)

33.6a Insert the spacer . . .

33.6b . . . and the bolt . . .

33.6c . . . and tighten it until the rotor is displaced

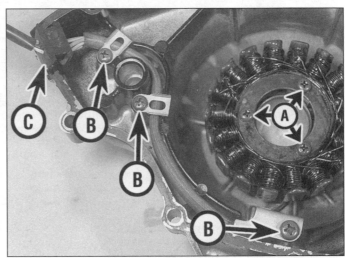

33.7 Stator screws (A), wiring clamp screws (B), wiring grommet (C)

5 The rotor will be a tight fit on the crankshaft taper, requiring a puller to draw it off. The Suzuki special tool (Pt. Nos. 09930-30102 and 09930-33710) consists of a slide-hammer and adapter which threads into the rotor. Commercial slide-hammer equivalents can be used, but make sure the adapter is the correct thread size. Screw the adapter into the rotor thread and attach the slide-hammer. Operate the slide-hammer to draw the rotor off the crankshaft.

6 Alternatively, it is possible to thread an M14 x 1.5 bolt into the rotor (or use the swingarm bolt, which has the same thread size) and tighten it down so that its bears on the end of the crankshaft and pulls the rotor off. This method requires a short spacer (36 mm long) to be inserted between the bolt and crankshaft end **(see illustration)**. Thread the bolt into the rotor and tighten it down whilst preventing the crankshaft from turning as

described above **(see illustrations)**. **Note:** A smart tap on the head of the bolt will help jar the taper free.

Caution: If the swingarm bolt is used, refer to Chapter 5 for details of its removal and support the swingarm in place using a block or a long bar inserted through the frame and swingarm.

7 To remove the stator from the crankcase cover, remove the six screws securing the stator and wiring clamps, then remove the assembly from the cover, noting the routing of the wiring and how the rubber grommet fits **(see illustration)**.

Installation

8 De-grease the tapered portion of the crankshaft and the corresponding surface in the rotor using a suitable solvent. Make sure that no metal objects have attached themselves to the magnets on the inside of

the rotor then install the rotor onto the crankshaft, making sure the teeth of the starter driven gear mesh correctly with those of the idle/reduction gear **(see illustration)**. Apply a suitable non-permanent thread locking compound to the threads of the rotor

33.8a Make sure all the pinions mesh correctly

33.8b Install the rotor bolt . . .

33.8c . . . and tighten it to the specified torque setting

33.10a Fit a new gasket . . .

33.10b . . . then install the cover

bolt, then install the bolt and tighten it to the torque setting specified at the beginning of the Chapter **(see illustrations)**. Use the method employed on removal to stop the rotor from turning.

9 Install the stator into the cover, aligning the rubber wiring grommet with the groove in the cover **(see illustration 33.7)**. Apply a suitable non-permanent thread locking compound to the stator bolt threads, then install the bolts and tighten them securely. Route the wiring around the casing, then apply thread locking compound to the threads of the wiring clamp screws and install the clamps. Apply a suitable sealant to the wiring grommet, then install it into the cut-out in the cover.

10 If removed, insert the dowel in the crankcase. Install the crankcase cover using a new gasket, making sure it locates correctly onto the dowel and the idle/reduction gear shaft **(see illustrations)**. Tighten the cover bolts evenly in a criss-cross sequence.

11 Reconnect the wiring at the connectors, making sure it is correctly routed, and secure it with any clips or ties, not forgetting the one next to the neutral switch.

12 Install the sprocket cover and the gear lever, aligning the marks made on removal.

13 Install the side panel (see Chapter 7).

34 Alternator stator coils - check

1 Remove the left-hand side panel (see Chapter 7).

2 Trace the alternator wiring back from the top of the engine sprocket cover and disconnect it at the connectors **(see illustration 33.1)**.

3 Using an ohmmeter or continuity test light, check for continuity between each of the wires on the alternator side of the connector,

taking a total of three readings, then check for continuity between each terminal and earth (ground). If the stator coil windings are in good condition there should be continuity (zero resistance) between each of the terminals, and no continuity (infinite resistance) between any of the terminals and earth (ground). If not, the alternator stator coil assembly is at fault and should be replaced. **Note:** *Before condemning the stator coils, check the fault is not due to damaged wiring between the connectors and coils.*

35 Regulator/rectifier unit - check and replacement

⚠️ *Warning: Always disconnect the battery negative (-ve) lead before checking or removing the regulator/rectifier.*

8

- +	Y1	Y2	Y3	R	B/W
Y1		infinity	infinity	6 ohms	infinity
Y2	infinity		infinity	6 ohms	infinity
Y3	infinity	infinity		6 ohms	infinity
R	infinity	infinity	infinity		infinity
B/W	6 ohms	6 ohms	6 ohms	40 ohms	

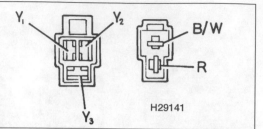

35.1a Regulator/rectifier test table

Check

1 Remove the right-hand side panel (see Chapter 7). Trace the wiring back from the regulator/rectifier unit and disconnect it at the connectors. Using a multimeter set to the appropriate resistance scale, measure the resistance between the terminal pairs of the regulator/rectifier connectors indicated in the table **(see illustrations)**.

2 If the readings do not compare closely with those shown the regulator/rectifier unit can be considered faulty. **Note:** *The use of certain multimeters could lead to false readings being obtained. Therefore, if the above check shows the regulator/rectifier unit to be faulty take the unit to a Suzuki dealer for confirmation of its condition before replacing it.*

Replacement

3 Remove the right-hand side panel (see

35.1b Regulator/rectifier wiring connectors

Chapter 7). Trace the wiring back from the regulator/rectifier unit and disconnect it at the connectors **(see illustration 35.1b)**.

4 Unscrew the two screws securing the unit to its bracket and remove it **(see illustration)**.

35.4 The regulator/rectifier is secured by two screws (arrows)

5 Install the new unit and tighten its screws securely. Connect the wiring at the connectors.

6 Install the right-hand side panel (see Chapter 7).

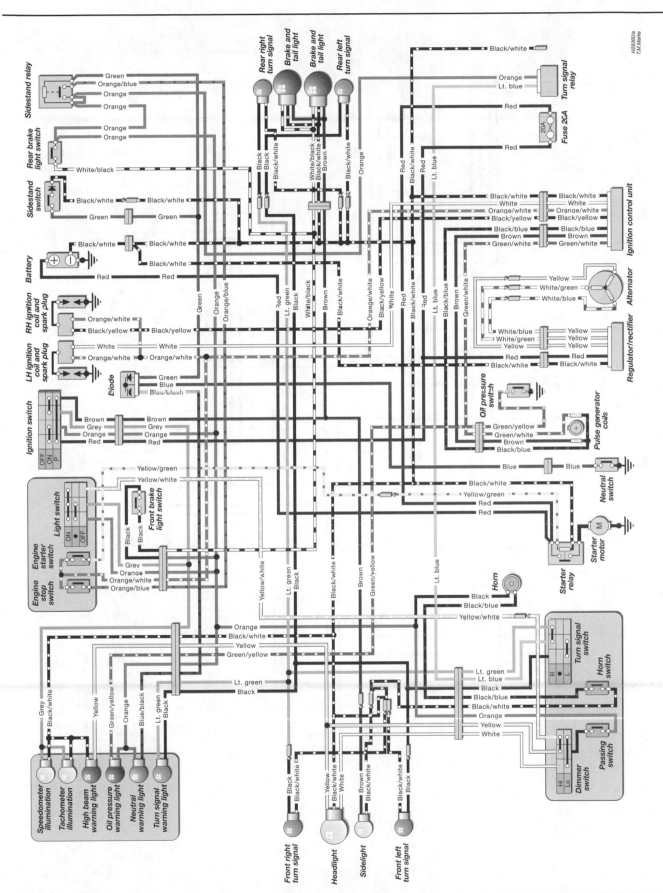

Wiring diagram - UK GS500 EK model

8

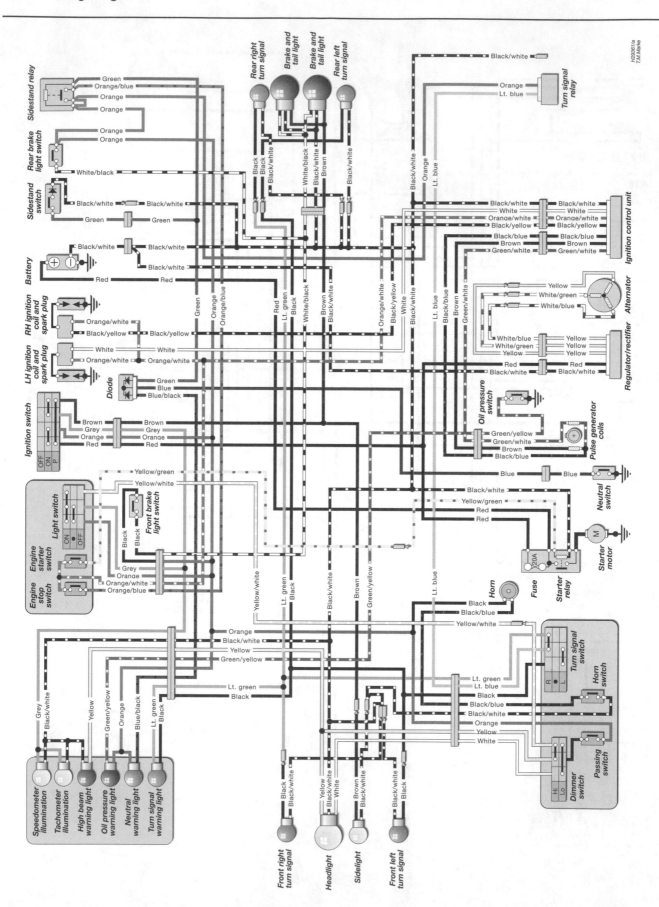

Wiring diagram - UK GS500 EL, M, N, P, R, S and T models

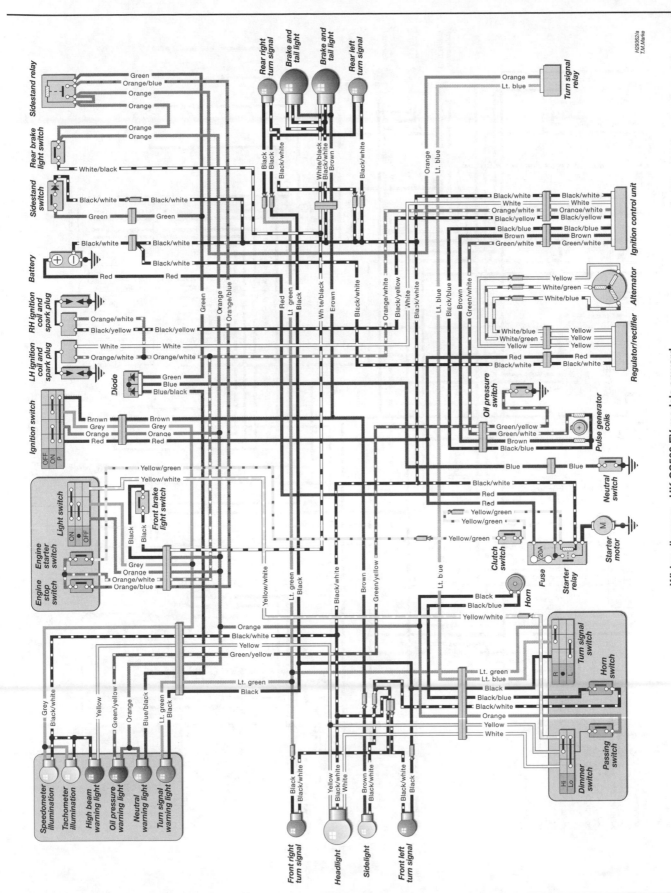

Wiring diagram - UK GS500 EV models onward

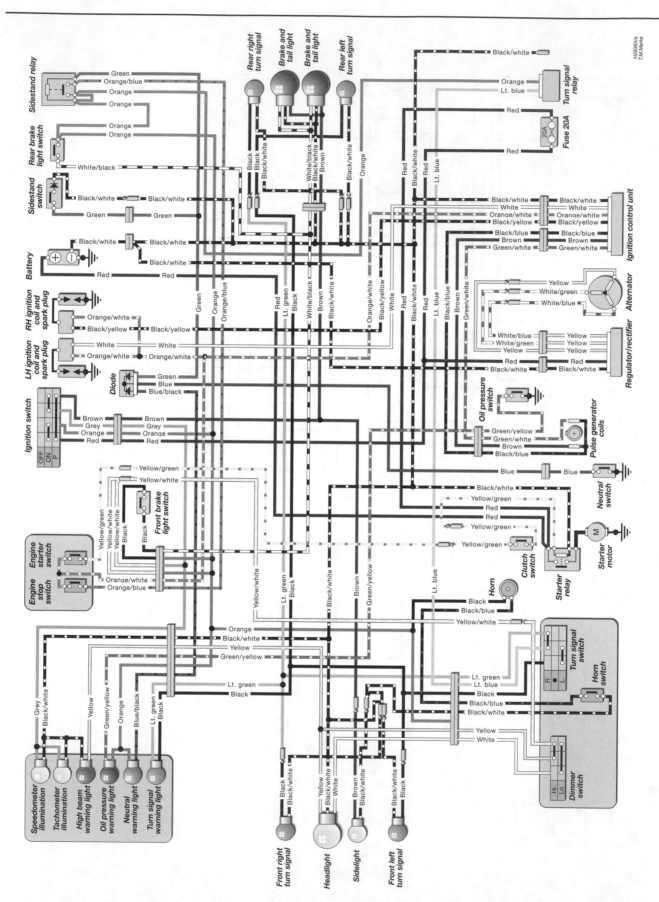

Wiring diagram - US GS500 EK model

Rear right turn signal
Brake and tail light
Brake and tail light
Rear left turn signal

H29363/a
T.M.Marke

Sidestand relay
Green
Orange/blue
Orange
Orange

Rear brake light switch
Orange
Orange

White/black

Sidestand switch
Black/white — Black/white
Green — Green

Battery
Black/white — Black/white
Black/white
Red — Red

RH ignition coil and spark plug
Orange/white
Black/yellow — Black/yellow

LH ignition coil and spark plug
White — White
Orange/white — Orange/white

Diode
Green
Blue
Blue/black

Ignition switch
Brown — Brown
Grey — Grey
Orange — Orange
Red — Red
OFF
ON
P

Engine stop switch
Engine starter switch
Yellow/green
Yellow/white
Yellow/white
Orange/white
Orange/blue

Front brake light switch
Yellow/green
Yellow/white
Yellow/white
Black — Black

Black/white
Green
Orange
Orange/blue
Red
Lt. green
Black
White/black
Brown
Black/white
Orange/white
Black/yellow
White
Red
Black/white
Red
Lt. blue
Brown
Green/white

Black/white
Orange
White
Red
Black/white

Orange
Black/white
Yellow
Green/yellow
Lt. green
Black

Grey
Black/white
Yellow
Green/yellow
Orange
Blue/black
Lt. green
Black

Speedometer illumination
Tachometer illumination
High beam warning light
Oil pressure warning light
Neutral warning light
Turn signal warning light

Front right turn signal
Black
Black/white

Headlight
Yellow
Black/white
White

Sidelight
Brown
Black/white

Front left turn signal
Black/white
Black

Black/white
Orange
Lt. blue
Red
Red
Black/white
White
Orange/white
Black/yellow
Black/blue
Brown
Green/white
Ignition control unit

Turn signal relay
Orange
Lt. blue
Red
Fuse 20A
20A
Red

Alternator
Yellow
White/green
White/blue

Regulator/rectifier
White/blue — Yellow
White/green — Yellow
Yellow — Yellow
Red — Red
Black/white — Black/white

Oil pressure switch

Pulse generator coils
Green/yellow
Green/white
Brown
Black/blue

Blue — Blue
Neutral switch

Black/white
Yellow/green
Red
Red
Yellow/green
Yellow/green
Starter motor
M

Clutch switch
Starter relay

Horn
Black
Black/blue
Yellow/white

Turn signal switch
R L
Horn switch

Lt. green
Lt. blue
Black
Black/blue
Black/white
Yellow
White
Dimmer switch
Hi
Lo

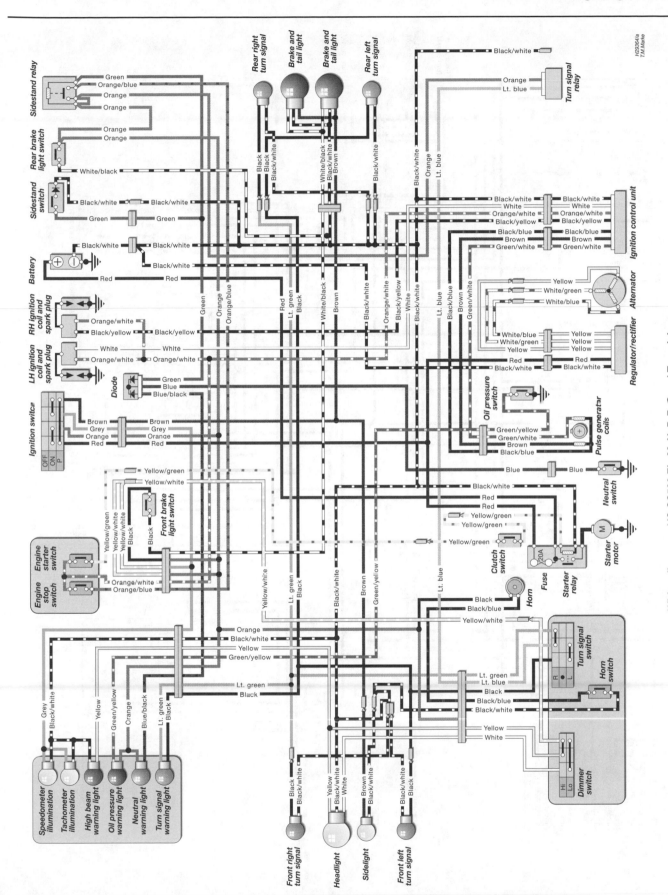

Wiring diagram - US GS500 EL, M, N, P, R, S and T models

Wiring diagram - US GS500 EV models onward

Reference

Tools and Workshop Tips

● Building up a tool kit and equipping your workshop ● Using tools ● Understanding bearing, seal, fastener and chain sizes and markings ● Repair techniques

Security

● Locks and chains ● U-locks ● Disc locks ● Alarms and immobilisers ● Security marking systems ● Tips on how to prevent bike theft

Lubricants and fluids REF•23

● Engine oils ● Transmission (gear) oils ● Coolant/anti-freeze ● Fork oils and suspension fluids ● Brake/clutch fluids ● Spray lubes, degreasers and solvents

Conversion Factors REF•26

$$34\ Nm \times 0.738 = 25\ lbf\ ft$$

● Formulae for conversion of the metric (SI) units used throughout the manual into Imperial measures

MOT Test Checks

● A guide to the UK MOT test ● Which items are tested ● How to prepare your motorcycle for the test and perform a pre-test check

Storage

● How to prepare your motorcycle for going into storage and protect essential systems ● How to get the motorcycle back on the road

Fault Finding

● Common faults and their likely causes ● How to check engine cylinder compression ● How to make electrical tests and use test meters

Technical Terms Explained REF•49

● Component names, technical terms and common abbreviations explained

Index REF•53

Buying tools

A toolkit is a fundamental requirement for servicing and repairing a motorcycle. Although there will be an initial expense in building up enough tools for servicing, this will soon be offset by the savings made by doing the job yourself. As experience and confidence grow, additional tools can be added to enable the repair and overhaul of the motorcycle. Many of the specialist tools are expensive and not often used so it may be preferable to hire them, or for a group of friends or motorcycle club to join in the purchase.

As a rule, it is better to buy more expensive, good quality tools. Cheaper tools are likely to wear out faster and need to be renewed more often, nullifying the original saving.

> ⚠️ **Warning: To avoid the risk of a poor quality tool breaking in use, causing injury or damage to the component being worked on, always aim to purchase tools which meet the relevant national safety standards.**

The following lists of tools do not represent the manufacturer's service tools, but serve as a guide to help the owner decide which tools are needed for this level of work. In addition, items such as an electric drill, hacksaw, files, soldering iron and a workbench equipped with a vice, may be needed. Although not classed as tools, a selection of bolts, screws, nuts, washers and pieces of tubing always come in useful.

For more information about tools, refer to the Haynes *Motorcycle Workshop Practice TechBook* (Bk. No. 3470).

Manufacturer's service tools

Inevitably certain tasks require the use of a service tool. Where possible an alternative tool or method of approach is recommended, but sometimes there is no option if personal injury or damage to the component is to be avoided. Where required, service tools are referred to in the relevant procedure.

Service tools can usually only be purchased from a motorcycle dealer and are identified by a part number. Some of the commonly-used tools, such as rotor pullers, are available in aftermarket form from mail-order motorcycle tool and accessory suppliers.

Maintenance and minor repair tools

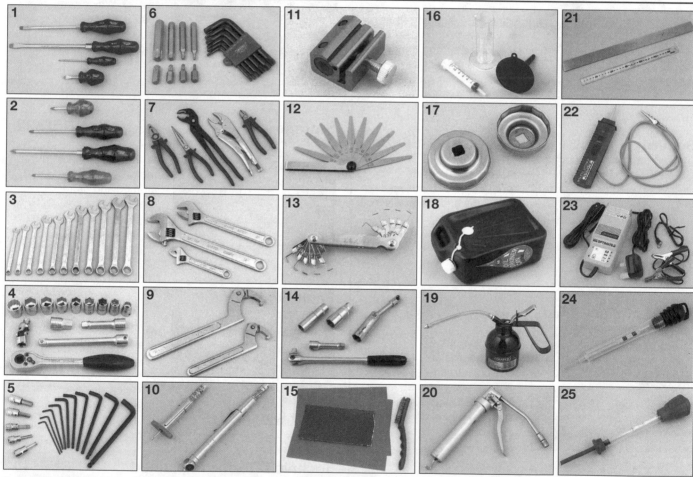

1 Set of flat-bladed screwdrivers
2 Set of Phillips head screwdrivers
3 Combination open-end and ring spanners
4 Socket set (3/8 inch or 1/2 inch drive)
5 Set of Allen keys or bits
6 Set of Torx keys or bits
7 Pliers, cutters and self-locking grips (Mole grips)
8 Adjustable spanners
9 C-spanners
10 Tread depth gauge and tyre pressure gauge
11 Cable oiler clamp
12 Feeler gauges
13 Spark plug gap measuring tool
14 Spark plug spanner or deep plug sockets
15 Wire brush and emery paper
16 Calibrated syringe, measuring vessel and funnel
17 Oil filter adapters
18 Oil drainer can or tray
19 Pump type oil can
20 Grease gun
21 Straight-edge and steel rule
22 Continuity tester
23 Battery charger
24 Hydrometer (for battery specific gravity check)
25 Anti-freeze tester (for liquid-cooled engines)

Repair and overhaul tools

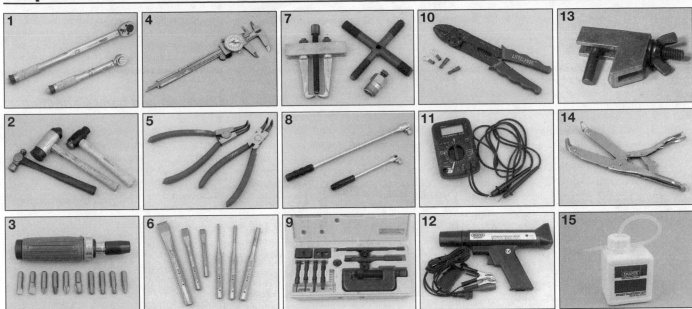

1 Torque wrench
  (small and mid-ranges)
2 Conventional, plastic or
  soft-faced hammers
3 Impact driver set

4 Vernier gauge
5 Circlip pliers (internal and
  external, or combination)
6 Set of cold chisels
  and punches

7 Selection of pullers
8 Breaker bars
9 Chain breaking/
  riveting tool set

10 Wire stripper and
   crimper tool
11 Multimeter (measures
   amps, volts and ohms)
12 Stroboscope (for
   dynamic timing checks)

13 Hose clamp
   (wingnut type shown)
14 Clutch holding tool
15 One-man brake/clutch
   bleeder kit

Specialist tools

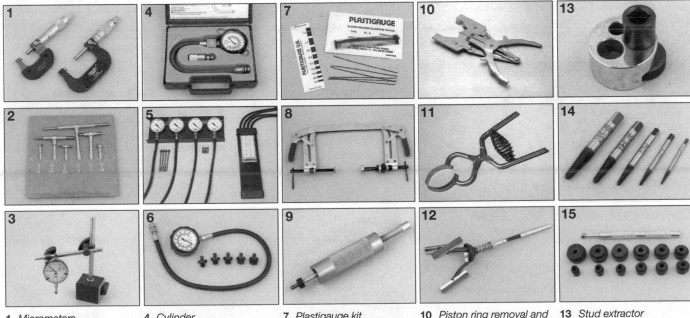

1 Micrometers
  (external type)
2 Telescoping gauges
3 Dial gauge

4 Cylinder
  compression gauge
5 Vacuum gauges (left) or
  manometer (right)
6 Oil pressure gauge

7 Plastigauge kit
8 Valve spring compressor
  (4-stroke engines)
9 Piston pin drawbolt tool

10 Piston ring removal and
   installation tool
11 Piston ring clamp
12 Cylinder bore hone
   (stone type shown)

13 Stud extractor
14 Screw extractor set
15 Bearing driver set

1 Workshop equipment and facilities

The workbench

● Work is made much easier by raising the bike up on a ramp - components are much more accessible if raised to waist level. The hydraulic or pneumatic types seen in the dealer's workshop are a sound investment if you undertake a lot of repairs or overhauls (see illustration 1.1).

1.1 Hydraulic motorcycle ramp

● If raised off ground level, the bike must be supported on the ramp to avoid it falling. Most ramps incorporate a front wheel locating clamp which can be adjusted to suit different diameter wheels. When tightening the clamp, take care not to mark the wheel rim or damage the tyre - use wood blocks on each side to prevent this.
● Secure the bike to the ramp using tie-downs (see illustration 1.2). If the bike has only a sidestand, and hence leans at a dangerous angle when raised, support the bike on an auxiliary stand.

1.2 Tie-downs are used around the passenger footrests to secure the bike

● Auxiliary (paddock) stands are widely available from mail order companies or motorcycle dealers and attach either to the wheel axle or swingarm pivot (see illustration 1.3). If the motorcycle has a centrestand, you can support it under the crankcase to prevent it toppling whilst either wheel is removed (see illustration 1.4).

1.3 This auxiliary stand attaches to the swingarm pivot

1.4 Always use a block of wood between the engine and jack head when supporting the engine in this way

Fumes and fire

● Refer to the Safety first! page at the beginning of the manual for full details. Make sure your workshop is equipped with a fire extinguisher suitable for fuel-related fires (Class B fire - flammable liquids) - it is not sufficient to have a water-filled extinguisher.
● Always ensure adequate ventilation is available. Unless an exhaust gas extraction system is available for use, ensure that the engine is run outside of the workshop.
● If working on the fuel system, make sure the workshop is ventilated to avoid a build-up of fumes. This applies equally to fume build-up when charging a battery. Do not smoke or allow anyone else to smoke in the workshop.

Fluids

● If you need to drain fuel from the tank, store it in an approved container marked as suitable for the storage of petrol (gasoline) (see illustration 1.5). Do not store fuel in glass jars or bottles.

1.5 Use an approved can only for storing petrol (gasoline)

● Use proprietary engine degreasers or solvents which have a high flash-point, such as paraffin (kerosene), for cleaning off oil, grease and dirt - never use petrol (gasoline) for cleaning. Wear rubber gloves when handling solvent and engine degreaser. The fumes from certain solvents can be dangerous - always work in a well-ventilated area.

Dust, eye and hand protection

● Protect your lungs from inhalation of dust particles by wearing a filtering mask over the nose and mouth. Many frictional materials still contain asbestos which is dangerous to your health. Protect your eyes from spouts of liquid and sprung components by wearing a pair of protective goggles (see illustration 1.6).

1.6 A fire extinguisher, goggles, mask and protective gloves should be at hand in the workshop

● Protect your hands from contact with solvents, fuel and oils by wearing rubber gloves. Alternatively apply a barrier cream to your hands before starting work. If handling hot components or fluids, wear suitable gloves to protect your hands from scalding and burns.

What to do with old fluids

● Old cleaning solvent, fuel, coolant and oils should not be poured down domestic drains or onto the ground. Package the fluid up in old oil containers, label it accordingly, and take it to a garage or disposal facility. Contact your local authority for location of such sites or ring the oil care hotline.

OIL CARE
FOLLOW THE CODE
OIL BANK LINE
0800 66 33 66
www.oilbankline.org.uk

Note: It is antisocial and illegal to dump oil down the drain. To find the location of your local oil recycling bank, call this number free.

In the USA, note that any oil supplier must accept used oil for recycling.

2 Fasteners -
screws, bolts and nuts

Fastener types and applications

Bolts and screws

● Fastener head types are either of hexagonal, Torx or splined design, with internal and external versions of each type (see illustrations 2.1 and 2.2); splined head fasteners are not in common use on motorcycles. The conventional slotted or Phillips head design is used for certain screws. Bolt or screw length is always measured from the underside of the head to the end of the item (see illustration 2.11).

2.1 Internal hexagon/Allen (A), Torx (B) and splined (C) fasteners, with corresponding bits

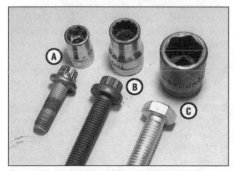

2.2 External Torx (A), splined (B) and hexagon (C) fasteners, with corresponding sockets

● Certain fasteners on the motorcycle have a tensile marking on their heads, the higher the marking the stronger the fastener. High tensile fasteners generally carry a 10 or higher marking. Never replace a high tensile fastener with one of a lower tensile strength.

Washers (see illustration 2.3)

● Plain washers are used between a fastener head and a component to prevent damage to the component or to spread the load when torque is applied. Plain washers can also be used as spacers or shims in certain assemblies. Copper or aluminium plain washers are often used as sealing washers on drain plugs.

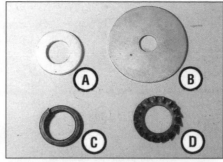

2.3 Plain washer (A), penny washer (B), spring washer (C) and serrated washer (D)

● The split-ring spring washer works by applying axial tension between the fastener head and component. If flattened, it is fatigued and must be renewed. If a plain (flat) washer is used on the fastener, position the spring washer between the fastener and the plain washer.

● Serrated star type washers dig into the fastener and component faces, preventing loosening. They are often used on electrical earth (ground) connections to the frame.

● Cone type washers (sometimes called Belleville) are conical and when tightened apply axial tension between the fastener head and component. They must be installed with the dished side against the component and often carry an OUTSIDE marking on their outer face. If flattened, they are fatigued and must be renewed.

● Tab washers are used to lock plain nuts or bolts on a shaft. A portion of the tab washer is bent up hard against one flat of the nut or bolt to prevent it loosening. Due to the tab washer being deformed in use, a new tab washer should be used every time it is disturbed.

● Wave washers are used to take up endfloat on a shaft. They provide light springing and prevent excessive side-to-side play of a component. Can be found on rocker arm shafts.

Nuts and split pins

● Conventional plain nuts are usually six-sided (see illustration 2.4). They are sized by thread diameter and pitch. High tensile nuts carry a number on one end to denote their tensile strength.

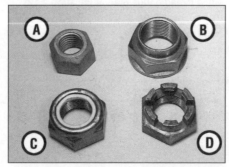

2.4 Plain nut (A), shouldered locknut (B), nylon insert nut (C) and castellated nut (D)

● Self-locking nuts either have a nylon insert, or two spring metal tabs, or a shoulder which is staked into a groove in the shaft - their advantage over conventional plain nuts is a resistance to loosening due to vibration. The nylon insert type can be used a number of times, but must be renewed when the friction of the nylon insert is reduced, ie when the nut spins freely on the shaft. The spring tab type can be reused unless the tabs are damaged. The shouldered type must be renewed every time it is disturbed.

● Split pins (cotter pins) are used to lock a castellated nut to a shaft or to prevent slackening of a plain nut. Common applications are wheel axles and brake torque arms. Because the split pin arms are deformed to lock around the nut a new split pin must always be used on installation - always fit the correct size split pin which will fit snugly in the shaft hole. Make sure the split pin arms are correctly located around the nut (see illustrations 2.5 and 2.6).

2.5 Bend split pin (cotter pin) arms as shown (arrows) to secure a castellated nut

2.6 Bend split pin (cotter pin) arms as shown to secure a plain nut

Caution: If the castellated nut slots do not align with the shaft hole after tightening to the torque setting, tighten the nut until the next slot aligns with the hole - never slacken the nut to align its slot.

● R-pins (shaped like the letter R), or slip pins as they are sometimes called, are sprung and can be reused if they are otherwise in good condition. Always install R-pins with their closed end facing forwards (see illustration 2.7).

2.7 Correct fitting of R-pin. Arrow indicates forward direction

Circlips (see illustration 2.8)

● Circlips (sometimes called snap-rings) are used to retain components on a shaft or in a housing and have corresponding external or internal ears to permit removal. Parallel-sided (machined) circlips can be installed either way round in their groove, whereas stamped circlips (which have a chamfered edge on one face) must be installed with the chamfer facing away from the direction of thrust load **(see illustration 2.9)**.

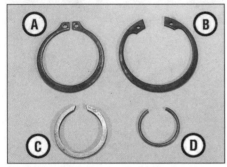

2.8 External stamped circlip (A), internal stamped circlip (B), machined circlip (C) and wire circlip (D)

● Always use circlip pliers to remove and install circlips; expand or compress them just enough to remove them. After installation, rotate the circlip in its groove to ensure it is securely seated. If installing a circlip on a splined shaft, always align its opening with a shaft channel to ensure the circlip ends are well supported and unlikely to catch **(see illustration 2.10)**.

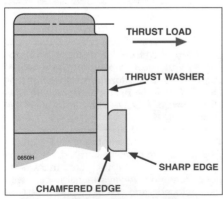

THRUST LOAD

THRUST WASHER

SHARP EDGE

CHAMFERED EDGE

2.9 Correct fitting of a stamped circlip

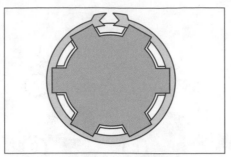

2.10 Align circlip opening with shaft channel

● Circlips can wear due to the thrust of components and become loose in their grooves, with the subsequent danger of becoming dislodged in operation. For this reason, renewal is advised every time a circlip is disturbed.
● Wire circlips are commonly used as piston pin retaining clips. If a removal tang is provided, long-nosed pliers can be used to dislodge them, otherwise careful use of a small flat-bladed screwdriver is necessary. Wire circlips should be renewed every time they are disturbed.

Thread diameter and pitch

● Diameter of a male thread (screw, bolt or stud) is the outside diameter of the threaded portion **(see illustration 2.11)**. Most motorcycle manufacturers use the ISO (International Standards Organisation) metric system expressed in millimetres, eg M6 refers to a 6 mm diameter thread. Sizing is the same for nuts, except that the thread diameter is measured across the valleys of the nut.
● Pitch is the distance between the peaks of the thread **(see illustration 2.11)**. It is expressed in millimetres, thus a common bolt size may be expressed as 6.0 x 1.0 mm (6 mm thread diameter and 1 mm pitch). Generally pitch increases in proportion to thread diameter, although there are always exceptions.
● Thread diameter and pitch are related for conventional fastener applications and the accompanying table can be used as a guide. Additionally, the AF (Across Flats), spanner or socket size dimension of the bolt or nut **(see illustration 2.11)** is linked to thread and pitch specification. Thread pitch can be measured with a thread gauge **(see illustration 2.12)**.

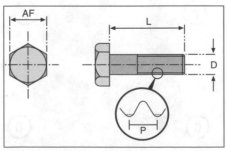

AF

L

D

P

2.11 Fastener length (L), thread diameter (D), thread pitch (P) and head size (AF)

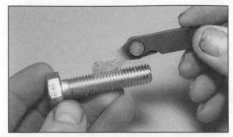

2.12 Using a thread gauge to measure pitch

AF size	Thread diameter x pitch (mm)
8 mm	M5 x 0.8
8 mm	M6 x 1.0
10 mm	M6 x 1.0
12 mm	M8 x 1.25
14 mm	M10 x 1.25
17 mm	M12 x 1.25

● The threads of most fasteners are of the right-hand type, ie they are turned clockwise to tighten and anti-clockwise to loosen. The reverse situation applies to left-hand thread fasteners, which are turned anti-clockwise to tighten and clockwise to loosen. Left-hand threads are used where rotation of a component might loosen a conventional right-hand thread fastener.

Seized fasteners

● Corrosion of external fasteners due to water or reaction between two dissimilar metals can occur over a period of time. It will build up sooner in wet conditions or in countries where salt is used on the roads during the winter. If a fastener is severely corroded it is likely that normal methods of removal will fail and result in its head being ruined. When you attempt removal, the fastener thread should be heard to crack free and unscrew easily - if it doesn't, stop there before damaging something.
● A smart tap on the head of the fastener will often succeed in breaking free corrosion which has occurred in the threads **(see illustration 2.13)**.
● An aerosol penetrating fluid (such as WD-40) applied the night beforehand may work its way down into the thread and ease removal. Depending on the location, you may be able to make up a Plasticine well around the fastener head and fill it with penetrating fluid.

2.13 A sharp tap on the head of a fastener will often break free a corroded thread

● If you are working on an engine internal component, corrosion will most likely not be a problem due to the well lubricated environment. However, components can be very tight and an impact driver is a useful tool in freeing them (see illustration 2.14).

2.14 Using an impact driver to free a fastener

● Where corrosion has occurred between dissimilar metals (eg steel and aluminium alloy), the application of heat to the fastener head will create a disproportionate expansion rate between the two metals and break the seizure caused by the corrosion. Whether heat can be applied depends on the location of the fastener - any surrounding components likely to be damaged must first be removed (see illustration 2.15). Heat can be applied using a paint stripper heat gun or clothes iron, or by immersing the component in boiling water - wear protective gloves to prevent scalding or burns to the hands.

2.15 Using heat to free a seized fastener

● As a last resort, it is possible to use a hammer and cold chisel to work the fastener head unscrewed (see illustration 2.16). This will damage the fastener, but more importantly extreme care must be taken not to damage the surrounding component.

> *Caution: Remember that the component being secured is generally of more value than the bolt, nut or screw - when the fastener is freed, do not unscrew it with force, instead work the fastener back and forth when resistance is felt to prevent thread damage.*

2.16 Using a hammer and chisel to free a seized fastener

Broken fasteners and damaged heads

● If the shank of a broken bolt or screw is accessible you can grip it with self-locking grips. The knurled wheel type stud extractor tool or self-gripping stud puller tool is particularly useful for removing the long studs which screw into the cylinder mouth surface of the crankcase or bolts and screws from which the head has broken off (see illustration 2.17). Studs can also be removed by locking two nuts together on the threaded end of the stud and using a spanner on the lower nut (see illustration 2.18).

2.17 Using a stud extractor tool to remove a broken crankcase stud

2.18 Two nuts can be locked together to unscrew a stud from a component

● A bolt or screw which has broken off below or level with the casing must be extracted using a screw extractor set. Centre punch the fastener to centralise the drill bit, then drill a hole in the fastener (see illustration 2.19). Select a drill bit which is approximately half to three-quarters the

2.19 When using a screw extractor, first drill a hole in the fastener . . .

diameter of the fastener and drill to a depth which will accommodate the extractor. Use the largest size extractor possible, but avoid leaving too small a wall thickness otherwise the extractor will merely force the fastener walls outwards wedging it in the casing thread.

● If a spiral type extractor is used, thread it anti-clockwise into the fastener. As it is screwed in, it will grip the fastener and unscrew it from the casing (see illustration 2.20).

2.20 . . . then thread the extractor anti-clockwise into the fastener

● If a taper type extractor is used, tap it into the fastener so that it is firmly wedged in place. Unscrew the extractor (anti-clockwise) to draw the fastener out.

> ⚠️ *Warning: Stud extractors are very hard and may break off in the fastener if care is not taken - ask an engineer about spark erosion if this happens.*

● Alternatively, the broken bolt/screw can be drilled out and the hole retapped for an oversize bolt/screw or a diamond-section thread insert. It is essential that the drilling is carried out squarely and to the correct depth, otherwise the casing may be ruined - if in doubt, entrust the work to an engineer.

● Bolts and nuts with rounded corners cause the correct size spanner or socket to slip when force is applied. Of the types of spanner/socket available always use a six-point type rather than an eight or twelve-point type - better grip

2.21 Comparison of surface drive ring spanner (left) with 12-point type (right)

is obtained. Surface drive spanners grip the middle of the hex flats, rather than the corners, and are thus good in cases of damaged heads **(see illustration 2.21).**

● Slotted-head or Phillips-head screws are often damaged by the use of the wrong size screwdriver. Allen-head and Torx-head screws are much less likely to sustain damage. If enough of the screw head is exposed you can use a hacksaw to cut a slot in its head and then use a conventional flat-bladed screwdriver to remove it. Alternatively use a hammer and cold chisel to tap the head of the fastener around to slacken it. Always replace damaged fasteners with new ones, preferably Torx or Allen-head type.

HAYNES
HiNT

A dab of valve grinding compound between the screw head and screw-driver tip will often give a good grip.

Thread repair

● Threads (particularly those in aluminium alloy components) can be damaged by overtightening, being assembled with dirt in the threads, or from a component working loose and vibrating. Eventually the thread will fail completely, and it will be impossible to tighten the fastener.

● If a thread is damaged or clogged with old locking compound it can be renovated with a thread repair tool (thread chaser) **(see illustrations 2.22 and 2.23);** special thread

2.22 A thread repair tool being used to correct an internal thread

2.23 A thread repair tool being used to correct an external thread

chasers are available for spark plug hole threads. The tool will not cut a new thread, but clean and true the original thread. Make sure that you use the correct diameter and pitch tool. Similarly, external threads can be cleaned up with a die or a thread restorer file **(see illustration 2.24).**

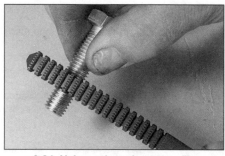

2.24 Using a thread restorer file

● It is possible to drill out the old thread and retap the component to the next thread size. This will work where there is enough surrounding material and a new bolt or screw can be obtained. Sometimes, however, this is not possible - such as where the bolt/screw passes through another component which must also be suitably modified, also in cases where a spark plug or oil drain plug cannot be obtained in a larger diameter thread size.

● The diamond-section thread insert (often known by its popular trade name of Heli-Coil) is a simple and effective method of renewing the thread and retaining the original size. A kit can be purchased which contains the tap, insert and installing tool **(see illustration 2.25).** Drill out the damaged thread with the size drill specified **(see illustration 2.26).** Carefully retap the thread **(see illustration 2.27).** Install the

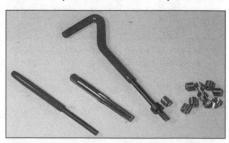

2.25 Obtain a thread insert kit to suit the thread diameter and pitch required

2.26 To install a thread insert, first drill out the original thread . . .

2.27 . . . tap a new thread . . .

2.28 . . . fit insert on the installing tool . . .

2.29 . . . and thread into the component . . .

2.30 . . . break off the tang when complete

insert on the installing tool and thread it slowly into place using a light downward pressure **(see illustrations 2.28 and 2.29).** When positioned between a 1/4 and 1/2 turn below the surface withdraw the installing tool and use the break-off tool to press down on the tang, breaking it off **(see illustration 2.30).**

● There are epoxy thread repair kits on the market which can rebuild stripped internal threads, although this repair should not be used on high load-bearing components.

Thread locking and sealing compounds

● Locking compounds are used in locations where the fastener is prone to loosening due to vibration or on important safety-related items which might cause loss of control of the motorcycle if they fail. It is also used where important fasteners cannot be secured by other means such as lockwashers or split pins.

● Before applying locking compound, make sure that the threads (internal and external) are clean and dry with all old compound removed. Select a compound to suit the component being secured - a non-permanent general locking and sealing type is suitable for most applications, but a high strength type is needed for permanent fixing of studs in castings. Apply a drop or two of the compound to the first few threads of the fastener, then thread it into place and tighten to the specified torque. Do not apply excessive thread locking compound otherwise the thread may be damaged on subsequent removal.

● Certain fasteners are impregnated with a dry film type coating of locking compound on their threads. Always renew this type of fastener if disturbed.

● Anti-seize compounds, such as copper-based greases, can be applied to protect threads from seizure due to extreme heat and corrosion. A common instance is spark plug threads and exhaust system fasteners.

3 Measuring tools and gauges

Feeler gauges

● Feeler gauges (or blades) are used for measuring small gaps and clearances (see illustration 3.1). They can also be used to measure endfloat (sideplay) of a component on a shaft where access is not possible with a dial gauge.

● Feeler gauge sets should be treated with care and not bent or damaged. They are etched with their size on one face. Keep them clean and very lightly oiled to prevent corrosion build-up.

3.1 Feeler gauges are used for measuring small gaps and clearances - thickness is marked on one face of gauge

● When measuring a clearance, select a gauge which is a light sliding fit between the two components. You may need to use two gauges together to measure the clearance accurately.

Micrometers

● A micrometer is a precision tool capable of measuring to 0.01 or 0.001 of a millimetre. It should always be stored in its case and not in the general toolbox. It must be kept clean and never dropped, otherwise its frame or measuring anvils could be distorted resulting in inaccurate readings.

● External micrometers are used for measuring outside diameters of components and have many more applications than internal micrometers. Micrometers are available in different size ranges, eg 0 to 25 mm, 25 to 50 mm, and upwards in 25 mm steps; some large micrometers have interchangeable anvils to allow a range of measurements to be taken. Generally the largest precision measurement you are likely to take on a motorcycle is the piston diameter.

● Internal micrometers (or bore micrometers) are used for measuring inside diameters, such as valve guides and cylinder bores. Telescoping gauges and small hole gauges are used in conjunction with an external micrometer, whereas the more expensive internal micrometers have their own measuring device.

External micrometer

Note: *The conventional analogue type instrument is described. Although much easier to read, digital micrometers are considerably more expensive.*

● Always check the calibration of the micrometer before use. With the anvils closed (0 to 25 mm type) or set over a test gauge (for

3.2 Check micrometer calibration before use

the larger types) the scale should read zero (see illustration 3.2); make sure that the anvils (and test piece) are clean first. Any discrepancy can be adjusted by referring to the instructions supplied with the tool. Remember that the micrometer is a precision measuring tool - don't force the anvils closed, use the ratchet (4) on the end of the micrometer to close it. In this way, a measured force is always applied.

● To use, first make sure that the item being measured is clean. Place the anvil of the micrometer (1) against the item and use the thimble (2) to bring the spindle (3) lightly into contact with the other side of the item (see illustration 3.3). Don't tighten the thimble down because this will damage the micrometer - instead use the ratchet (4) on the end of the micrometer. The ratchet mechanism applies a measured force preventing damage to the instrument.

● The micrometer is read by referring to the linear scale on the sleeve and the annular scale on the thimble. Read off the sleeve first to obtain the base measurement, then add the fine measurement from the thimble to obtain the overall reading. The linear scale on the sleeve represents the measuring range of the micrometer (eg 0 to 25 mm). The annular scale

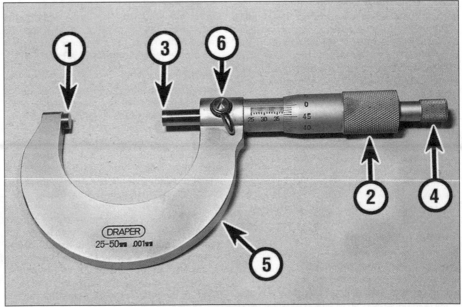

3.3 Micrometer component parts

1 Anvil	3 Spindle	5 Frame
2 Thimble	4 Ratchet	6 Locking lever

on the thimble will be in graduations of 0.01 mm (or as marked on the frame) - one full revolution of the thimble will move 0.5 mm on the linear scale. Take the reading where the datum line on the sleeve intersects the thimble's scale. Always position the eye directly above the scale otherwise an inaccurate reading will result.

In the example shown the item measures 2.95 mm (see illustration 3.4):

Linear scale	2.00 mm
Linear scale	0.50 mm
Annular scale	0.45 mm
Total figure	**2.95 mm**

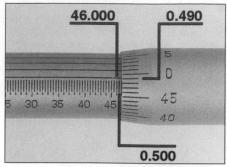

3.5 Micrometer reading of 46.99 mm on linear and annular scales . . .

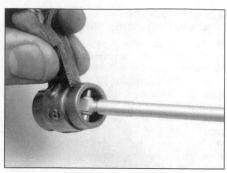

3.7 Expand the telescoping gauge in the bore, lock its position . . .

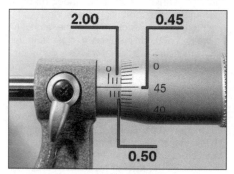

3.4 Micrometer reading of 2.95 mm

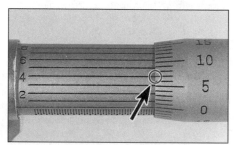

3.6 . . . and 0.004 mm on vernier scale

3.8 . . . then measure the gauge with a micrometer

Most micrometers have a locking lever (6) on the frame to hold the setting in place, allowing the item to be removed from the micrometer.
● Some micrometers have a vernier scale on their sleeve, providing an even finer measurement to be taken, in 0.001 increments of a millimetre. Take the sleeve and thimble measurement as described above, then check which graduation on the vernier scale aligns with that of the annular scale on the thimble **Note:** *The eye must be perpendicular to the scale when taking the vernier reading - if necessary rotate the body of the micrometer to ensure this.* Multiply the vernier scale figure by 0.001 and add it to the base and fine measurement figures.

In the example shown the item measures 46.994 mm (see illustrations 3.5 and 3.6):

Linear scale (base)	46.000 mm
Linear scale (base)	00.500 mm
Annular scale (fine)	00.490 mm
Vernier scale	00.004 mm
Total figure	**46.994 mm**

Internal micrometer

● Internal micrometers are available for measuring bore diameters, but are expensive and unlikely to be available for home use. It is suggested that a set of telescoping gauges and small hole gauges, both of which must be used with an external micrometer, will suffice for taking internal measurements on a motorcycle.
● Telescoping gauges can be used to

measure internal diameters of components. Select a gauge with the correct size range, make sure its ends are clean and insert it into the bore. Expand the gauge, then lock its position and withdraw it from the bore (see illustration 3.7). Measure across the gauge ends with a micrometer (see illustration 3.8).
● Very small diameter bores (such as valve guides) are measured with a small hole gauge. Once adjusted to a slip-fit inside the component, its position is locked and the gauge withdrawn for measurement with a micrometer (see illustrations 3.9 and 3.10).

Vernier caliper
Note: *The conventional linear and dial gauge type instruments are described. Digital types are easier to read, but are far more expensive.*
● The vernier caliper does not provide the precision of a micrometer, but is versatile in being able to measure internal and external diameters. Some types also incorporate a depth gauge. It is ideal for measuring clutch plate friction material and spring free lengths.
● To use the conventional linear scale vernier, slacken off the vernier clamp screws (1) and set its jaws over (2), or inside (3), the item to be measured (see illustration 3.11). Slide the jaw into contact, using the thumbwheel (4) for fine movement of the sliding scale (5) then tighten the clamp screws (1). Read off the main scale (6) where the zero on the sliding scale (5) intersects it, taking the whole number to the left of the zero; this provides the base measurement. View along the sliding scale and select the division which

3.9 Expand the small hole gauge in the bore, lock its position . . .

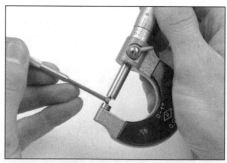

3.10 . . . then measure the gauge with a micrometer

lines up exactly with any of the divisions on the main scale, noting that the divisions usually represents 0.02 of a millimetre. Add this fine measurement to the base measurement to obtain the total reading.

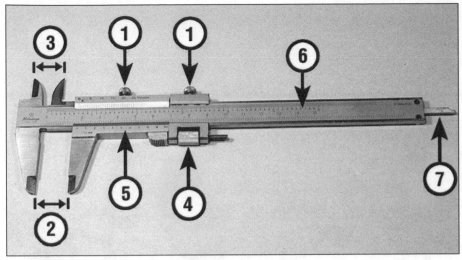

3.11 Vernier component parts (linear gauge)

1 Clamp screws	3 Internal jaws	5 Sliding scale	7 Depth gauge
2 External jaws	4 Thumbwheel	6 Main scale	

In the example shown the item measures 55.92 mm **(see illustration 3.12)**:

Base measurement	55.00 mm
Fine measurement	00.92 mm
Total figure	**55.92 mm**

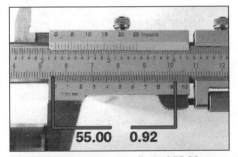

3.12 Vernier gauge reading of 55.92 mm

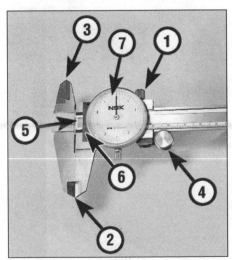

3.13 Vernier component parts (dial gauge)

1 Clamp screw	5 Main scale
2 External jaws	6 Sliding scale
3 Internal jaws	7 Dial gauge
4 Thumbwheel	

● Some vernier calipers are equipped with a dial gauge for fine measurement. Before use, check that the jaws are clean, then close them fully and check that the dial gauge reads zero. If necessary adjust the gauge ring accordingly. Slacken the vernier clamp screw (1) and set its jaws over (2), or inside (3), the item to be measured **(see illustration 3.13)**. Slide the jaws into contact, using the thumbwheel (4) for fine movement. Read off the main scale (5) where the edge of the sliding scale (6) intersects it, taking the whole number to the left of the zero; this provides the base measurement. Read off the needle position on the dial gauge (7) scale to provide the fine measurement; each division represents 0.05 of a millimetre. Add this fine measurement to the base measurement to obtain the total reading.

In the example shown the item measures 55.95 mm **(see illustration 3.14)**:

Base measurement	55.00 mm
Fine measurement	00.95 mm
Total figure	**55.95 mm**

3.14 Vernier gauge reading of 55.95 mm

Plastigauge

● Plastigauge is a plastic material which can be compressed between two surfaces to measure the oil clearance between them. The width of the compressed Plastigauge is measured against a calibrated scale to determine the clearance.

● Common uses of Plastigauge are for measuring the clearance between crankshaft journal and main bearing inserts, between crankshaft journal and big-end bearing inserts, and between camshaft and bearing surfaces. The following example describes big-end oil clearance measurement.

● Handle the Plastigauge material carefully to prevent distortion. Using a sharp knife, cut a length which corresponds with the width of the bearing being measured and place it carefully across the journal so that it is parallel with the shaft **(see illustration 3.15)**. Carefully install both bearing shells and the connecting rod. Without rotating the rod on the journal tighten its bolts or nuts (as applicable) to the specified torque. The connecting rod and bearings are then disassembled and the crushed Plastigauge examined.

3.15 Plastigauge placed across shaft journal

● Using the scale provided in the Plastigauge kit, measure the width of the material to determine the oil clearance **(see illustration 3.16)**. Always remove all traces of Plastigauge after use using your fingernails.

Caution: Arriving at the correct clearance demands that the assembly is torqued correctly, according to the settings and sequence (where applicable) provided by the motorcycle manufacturer.

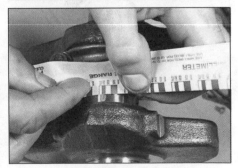

3.16 Measuring the width of the crushed Plastigauge

Dial gauge or DTI (Dial Test Indicator)

● A dial gauge can be used to accurately measure small amounts of movement. Typical uses are measuring shaft runout or shaft endfloat (sideplay) and setting piston position for ignition timing on two-strokes. A dial gauge set usually comes with a range of different probes and adapters and mounting equipment.

● The gauge needle must point to zero when at rest. Rotate the ring around its periphery to zero the gauge.

● Check that the gauge is capable of reading the extent of movement in the work. Most gauges have a small dial set in the face which records whole millimetres of movement as well as the fine scale around the face periphery which is calibrated in 0.01 mm divisions. Read off the small dial first to obtain the base measurement, then add the measurement from the fine scale to obtain the total reading.

In the example shown the gauge reads 1.48 mm **(see illustration 3.17)**:

Base measurement	1.00 mm
Fine measurement	0.48 mm
Total figure	**1.48 mm**

3.17 Dial gauge reading of 1.48 mm

● If measuring shaft runout, the shaft must be supported in vee-blocks and the gauge mounted on a stand perpendicular to the shaft. Rest the tip of the gauge against the centre of the shaft and rotate the shaft slowly whilst watching the gauge reading **(see illustration 3.18)**. Take several measurements along the length of the shaft and record the

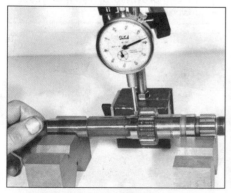

3.18 Using a dial gauge to measure shaft runout

maximum gauge reading as the amount of runout in the shaft. **Note:** *The reading obtained will be total runout at that point - some manufacturers specify that the runout figure is halved to compare with their specified runout limit.*

● Endfloat (sideplay) measurement requires that the gauge is mounted securely to the surrounding component with its probe touching the end of the shaft. Using hand pressure, push and pull on the shaft noting the maximum endfloat recorded on the gauge **(see illustration 3.19)**.

3.19 Using a dial gauge to measure shaft endfloat

● A dial gauge with suitable adapters can be used to determine piston position BTDC on two-stroke engines for the purposes of ignition timing. The gauge, adapter and suitable length probe are installed in the place of the spark plug and the gauge zeroed at TDC. If the piston position is specified as 1.14 mm BTDC, rotate the engine back to 2.00 mm BTDC, then slowly forwards to 1.14 mm BTDC.

Cylinder compression gauges

● A compression gauge is used for measuring cylinder compression. Either the rubber-cone type or the threaded adapter type can be used. The latter is preferred to ensure a perfect seal against the cylinder head. A 0 to 300 psi (0 to 20 Bar) type gauge (for petrol/gasoline engines) will be suitable for motorcycles.

● The spark plug is removed and the gauge either held hard against the cylinder head (cone type) or the gauge adapter screwed into the cylinder head (threaded type) **(see illustration 3.20)**. Cylinder compression is measured with the engine turning over, but not running - carry out the compression test as described in

3.20 Using a rubber-cone type cylinder compression gauge

Fault Finding Equipment. The gauge will hold the reading until manually released.

Oil pressure gauge

● An oil pressure gauge is used for measuring engine oil pressure. Most gauges come with a set of adapters to fit the thread of the take-off point **(see illustration 3.21)**. If the take-off point specified by the motorcycle manufacturer is an external oil pipe union, make sure that the specified replacement union is used to prevent oil starvation.

3.21 Oil pressure gauge and take-off point adapter (arrow)

● Oil pressure is measured with the engine running (at a specific rpm) and often the manufacturer will specify pressure limits for a cold and hot engine.

Straight-edge and surface plate

● If checking the gasket face of a component for warpage, place a steel rule or precision straight-edge across the gasket face and measure any gap between the straight-edge and component with feeler gauges **(see illustration 3.22)**. Check diagonally across the component and between mounting holes **(see illustration 3.23)**.

3.22 Use a straight-edge and feeler gauges to check for warpage

3.23 Check for warpage in these directions

● Checking individual components for warpage, such as clutch plain (metal) plates, requires a perfectly flat plate or piece or plate glass and feeler gauges.

4 Torque and leverage

What is torque?

● Torque describes the twisting force about a shaft. The amount of torque applied is determined by the distance from the centre of the shaft to the end of the lever and the amount of force being applied to the end of the lever; distance multiplied by force equals torque.
● The manufacturer applies a measured torque to a bolt or nut to ensure that it will not slacken in use and to hold two components securely together without movement in the joint. The actual torque setting depends on the thread size, bolt or nut material and the composition of the components being held.
● Too little torque may cause the fastener to loosen due to vibration, whereas too much torque will distort the joint faces of the component or cause the fastener to shear off. Always stick to the specified torque setting.

Using a torque wrench

● Check the calibration of the torque wrench and make sure it has a suitable range for the job. Torque wrenches are available in Nm (Newton-metres), kgf m (kilograms-force metre), lbf ft (pounds-feet), lbf in (inch-pounds). Do not confuse lbf ft with lbf in.
● Adjust the tool to the desired torque on the scale (see illustration 4.1). If your torque wrench is not calibrated in the units specified, carefully convert the figure (see Conversion Factors). A manufacturer sometimes gives a torque setting as a range (8 to 10 Nm) rather than a single figure - in this case set the tool midway between the two settings. The same torque may be expressed as 9 Nm ± 1 Nm. Some torque wrenches have a method of locking the setting so that it isn't inadvertently altered during use.

4.1 Set the torque wrench index mark to the setting required, in this case 12 Nm

● Install the bolts/nuts in their correct location and secure them lightly. Their threads must be clean and free of any old locking compound. Unless specified the threads and flange should be dry - oiled threads are necessary in certain circumstances and the manufacturer will take this into account in the specified torque figure. Similarly, the manufacturer may also specify the application of thread-locking compound.
● Tighten the fasteners in the specified sequence until the torque wrench clicks, indicating that the torque setting has been reached. Apply the torque again to double-check the setting. Where different thread diameter fasteners secure the component, as a rule tighten the larger diameter ones first.
● When the torque wrench has been finished with, release the lock (where applicable) and fully back off its setting to zero - do not leave the torque wrench tensioned. Also, do not use a torque wrench for slackening a fastener.

Angle-tightening

● Manufacturers often specify a figure in degrees for final tightening of a fastener. This usually follows tightening to a specific torque setting.
● A degree disc can be set and attached to the socket (see illustration 4.2) or a protractor can be used to mark the angle of movement on the bolt/nut head and the surrounding casting (see illustration 4.3).

4.2 Angle tightening can be accomplished with a torque-angle gauge . . .

4.3 . . . or by marking the angle on the surrounding component

Loosening sequences

● Where more than one bolt/nut secures a component, loosen each fastener evenly a little at a time. In this way, not all the stress of the joint is held by one fastener and the components are not likely to distort.
● If a tightening sequence is provided, work in the REVERSE of this, but if not, work from the outside in, in a criss-cross sequence (see illustration 4.4).

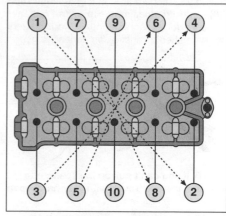
4.4 When slackening, work from the outside inwards

Tightening sequences

● If a component is held by more than one fastener it is important that the retaining bolts/nuts are tightened evenly to prevent uneven stress build-up and distortion of sealing faces. This is especially important on high-compression joints such as the cylinder head.
● A sequence is usually provided by the manufacturer, either in a diagram or actually marked in the casting. If not, always start in the centre and work outwards in a criss-cross pattern (see illustration 4.5). Start off by securing all bolts/nuts finger-tight, then set the torque wrench and tighten each fastener by a small amount in sequence until the final torque is reached. By following this practice,

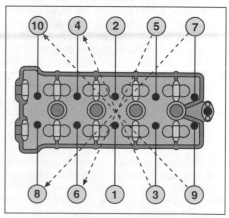
4.5 When tightening, work from the inside outwards

the joint will be held evenly and will not be distorted. Important joints, such as the cylinder head and big-end fasteners often have two- or three-stage torque settings.

Applying leverage

● Use tools at the correct angle. Position a socket wrench or spanner on the bolt/nut so that you pull it towards you when loosening. If this can't be done, push the spanner without curling your fingers around it **(see illustration 4.6)** - the spanner may slip or the fastener loosen suddenly, resulting in your fingers being crushed against a component.

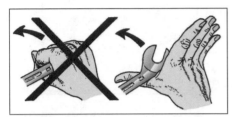

4.6 If you can't pull on the spanner to loosen a fastener, push with your hand open

● Additional leverage is gained by extending the length of the lever. The best way to do this is to use a breaker bar instead of the regular length tool, or to slip a length of tubing over the end of the spanner or socket wrench.
● If additional leverage will not work, the fastener head is either damaged or firmly corroded in place (see *Fasteners*).

5 Bearings

Bearing removal and installation

Drivers and sockets

● Before removing a bearing, always inspect the casing to see which way it must be driven out - some casings will have retaining plates or a cast step. Also check for any identifying markings on the bearing and if installed to a certain depth, measure this at this stage. Some roller bearings are sealed on one side - take note of the original fitted position.
● Bearings can be driven out of a casing using a bearing driver tool (with the correct size head) or a socket of the correct diameter. Select the driver head or socket so that it contacts the outer race of the bearing, not the balls/rollers or inner race. Always support the casing around the bearing housing with wood blocks, otherwise there is a risk of fracture. The bearing is driven out with a few blows on the driver or socket from a heavy mallet. Unless access is severely restricted (as with wheel bearings), a pin-punch is not recommended unless it is moved around the bearing to keep it square in its housing.

● The same equipment can be used to install bearings. Make sure the bearing housing is supported on wood blocks and line up the bearing in its housing. Fit the bearing as noted on removal - generally they are installed with their marked side facing outwards. Tap the bearing squarely into its housing using a driver or socket which bears only on the bearing's outer race - contact with the bearing balls/rollers or inner race will destroy it **(see illustrations 5.1 and 5.2)**.
● Check that the bearing inner race and balls/rollers rotate freely.

5.1 Using a bearing driver against the bearing's outer race

5.2 Using a large socket against the bearing's outer race

Pullers and slide-hammers

● Where a bearing is pressed on a shaft a puller will be required to extract it **(see illustration 5.3)**. Make sure that the puller clamp or legs fit securely behind the bearing and are unlikely to slip out. If pulling a bearing

5.3 This bearing puller clamps behind the bearing and pressure is applied to the shaft end to draw the bearing off

off a gear shaft for example, you may have to locate the puller behind a gear pinion if there is no access to the race and draw the gear pinion off the shaft as well **(see illustration 5.4)**.

> *Caution: Ensure that the puller's centre bolt locates securely against the end of the shaft and will not slip when pressure is applied. Also ensure that puller does not damage the shaft end.*

5.4 Where no access is available to the rear of the bearing, it is sometimes possible to draw off the adjacent component

● Operate the puller so that its centre bolt exerts pressure on the shaft end and draws the bearing off the shaft.
● When installing the bearing on the shaft, tap only on the bearing's inner race - contact with the balls/rollers or outer race with destroy the bearing. Use a socket or length of tubing as a drift which fits over the shaft end **(see illustration 5.5)**.

5.5 When installing a bearing on a shaft use a piece of tubing which bears only on the bearing's inner race

● Where a bearing locates in a blind hole in a casing, it cannot be driven or pulled out as described above. A slide-hammer with knife-edged bearing puller attachment will be required. The puller attachment passes through the bearing and when tightened expands to fit firmly behind the bearing **(see illustration 5.6)**. By operating the slide-hammer part of the tool the bearing is jarred out of its housing **(see illustration 5.7)**.
● It is possible, if the bearing is of reasonable weight, for it to drop out of its housing if the casing is heated as described opposite. If this

5.6 Expand the bearing puller so that it locks behind the bearing . . .

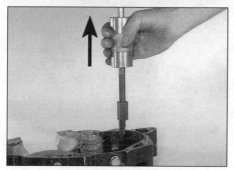

5.7 . . . attach the slide hammer to the bearing puller

method is attempted, first prepare a work surface which will enable the casing to be tapped face down to help dislodge the bearing - a wood surface is ideal since it will not damage the casing's gasket surface. Wearing protective gloves, tap the heated casing several times against the work surface to dislodge the bearing under its own weight **(see illustration 5.8)**.

5.8 Tapping a casing face down on wood blocks can often dislodge a bearing

● Bearings can be installed in blind holes using the driver or socket method described above.

Drawbolts

● Where a bearing or bush is set in the eye of a component, such as a suspension linkage arm or connecting rod small-end, removal by drift may damage the component. Furthermore, a rubber bushing in a shock absorber eye cannot successfully be driven out of position. If access is available to a engineering press, the task is straightforward. If not, a drawbolt can be fabricated to extract the bearing or bush.

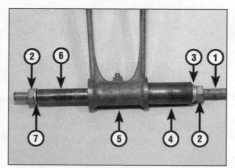

5.9 Drawbolt component parts assembled on a suspension arm

1 Bolt or length of threaded bar
2 Nuts
3 Washer (external diameter greater than tubing internal diameter)
4 Tubing (internal diameter sufficient to accommodate bearing)
5 Suspension arm with bearing
6 Tubing (external diameter slightly smaller than bearing)
7 Washer (external diameter slightly smaller than bearing)

5.10 Drawing the bearing out of the suspension arm

● To extract the bearing/bush you will need a long bolt with nut (or piece of threaded bar with two nuts), a piece of tubing which has an internal diameter larger than the bearing/bush, another piece of tubing which has an external diameter slightly smaller than the bearing/ bush, and a selection of washers **(see illustrations 5.9 and 5.10)**. Note that the pieces of tubing must be of the same length, or longer, than the bearing/bush.
● The same kit (without the pieces of tubing) can be used to draw the new bearing/bush back into place **(see illustration 5.11)**.

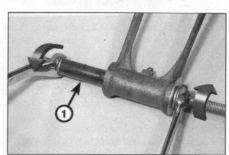

5.11 Installing a new bearing (1) in the suspension arm

Temperature change

● If the bearing's outer race is a tight fit in the casing, the aluminium casing can be heated to release its grip on the bearing. Aluminium will expand at a greater rate than the steel bearing outer race. There are several ways to do this, but avoid any localised extreme heat (such as a blow torch) - aluminium alloy has a low melting point.
● Approved methods of heating a casing are using a domestic oven (heated to 100°C) or immersing the casing in boiling water **(see illustration 5.12)**. Low temperature range localised heat sources such as a paint stripper heat gun or clothes iron can also be used **(see illustration 5.13)**. Alternatively, soak a rag in boiling water, wring it out and wrap it around the bearing housing.

> ⚠ **Warning: All of these methods require care in use to prevent scalding and burns to the hands. Wear protective gloves when handling hot components.**

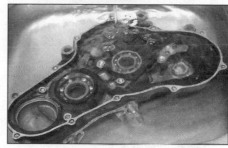

5.12 A casing can be immersed in a sink of boiling water to aid bearing removal

5.13 Using a localised heat source to aid bearing removal

● If heating the whole casing note that plastic components, such as the neutral switch, may suffer - remove them beforehand.
● After heating, remove the bearing as described above. You may find that the expansion is sufficient for the bearing to fall out of the casing under its own weight or with a light tap on the driver or socket.
● If necessary, the casing can be heated to aid bearing installation, and this is sometimes the recommended procedure if the motorcycle manufacturer has designed the housing and bearing fit with this intention.

● Installation of bearings can be eased by placing them in a freezer the night before installation. The steel bearing will contract slightly, allowing easy insertion in its housing. This is often useful when installing steering head outer races in the frame.

Bearing types and markings

● Plain shell bearings, ball bearings, needle roller bearings and tapered roller bearings will all be found on motorcycles (see illustrations 5.14 and 5.15). The ball and roller types are usually caged between an inner and outer race, but uncaged variations may be found.

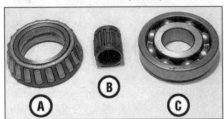

5.14 Shell bearings are either plain or grooved. They are usually identified by colour code (arrow)

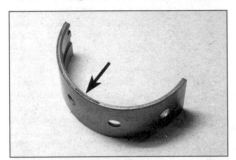

5.15 Tapered roller bearing (A), needle roller bearing (B) and ball journal bearing (C)

● Shell bearings (often called inserts) are usually found at the crankshaft main and connecting rod big-end where they are good at coping with high loads. They are made of a phosphor-bronze material and are impregnated with self-lubricating properties.
● Ball bearings and needle roller bearings consist of a steel inner and outer race with the balls or rollers between the races. They require constant lubrication by oil or grease and are good at coping with axial loads. Taper roller bearings consist of rollers set in a tapered cage set on the inner race; the outer race is separate. They are good at coping with axial loads and prevent movement along the shaft - a typical application is in the steering head.
● Bearing manufacturers produce bearings to ISO size standards and stamp one face of the bearing to indicate its internal and external diameter, load capacity and type (see illustration 5.16).
● Metal bushes are usually of phosphor-bronze material. Rubber bushes are used in suspension mounting eyes. Fibre bushes have also been used in suspension pivots.

5.16 Typical bearing marking

Bearing fault finding

● If a bearing outer race has spun in its housing, the housing material will be damaged. You can use a bearing locking compound to bond the outer race in place if damage is not too severe.
● Shell bearings will fail due to damage of their working surface, as a result of lack of lubrication, corrosion or abrasive particles in the oil (see illustration 5.17). Small particles of dirt in the oil may embed in the bearing material whereas larger particles will score the bearing and shaft journal. If a number of short journeys are made, insufficient heat will be generated to drive off condensation which has built up on the bearings.

5.17 Typical bearing failures

● Ball and roller bearings will fail due to lack of lubrication or damage to the balls or rollers. Tapered-roller bearings can be damaged by overloading them. Unless the bearing is sealed on both sides, wash it in paraffin (kerosene) to remove all old grease then allow it to dry. Make a visual inspection looking to dented balls or rollers, damaged cages and worn or pitted races (see illustration 5.18).
● A ball bearing can be checked for wear by listening to it when spun. Apply a film of light oil to the bearing and hold it close to the ear - hold the outer race with one hand and spin the inner

5.18 Example of ball journal bearing with damaged balls and cages

5.19 Hold outer race and listen to inner race when spun

race with the other hand (see illustration 5.19). The bearing should be almost silent when spun; if it grates or rattles it is worn.

6 Oil seals

Oil seal removal and installation

● Oil seals should be renewed every time a component is dismantled. This is because the seal lips will become set to the sealing surface and will not necessarily reseal.
● Oil seals can be prised out of position using a large flat-bladed screwdriver (see illustration 6.1). In the case of crankcase seals, check first that the seal is not lipped on the inside, preventing its removal with the crankcases joined.

6.1 Prise out oil seals with a large flat-bladed screwdriver

● New seals are usually installed with their marked face (containing the seal reference code) outwards and the spring side towards the fluid being retained. In certain cases, such as a two-stroke engine crankshaft seal, a double lipped seal may be used due to there being fluid or gas on each side of the joint.

● Use a bearing driver or socket which bears only on the outer hard edge of the seal to install it in the casing - tapping on the inner edge will damage the sealing lip.

Oil seal types and markings

● Oil seals are usually of the single-lipped type. Double-lipped seals are found where a liquid or gas is on both sides of the joint.
● Oil seals can harden and lose their sealing ability if the motorcycle has been in storage for a long period - renewal is the only solution.
● Oil seal manufacturers also conform to the ISO markings for seal size - these are moulded into the outer face of the seal (see illustration 6.2).

6.2 These oil seal markings indicate inside diameter, outside diameter and seal thickness

7 Gaskets and sealants

Types of gasket and sealant

● Gaskets are used to seal the mating surfaces between components and keep lubricants, fluids, vacuum or pressure contained within the assembly. Aluminium gaskets are sometimes found at the cylinder joints, but most gaskets are paper-based. If the mating surfaces of the components being joined are undamaged the gasket can be installed dry, although a dab of sealant or grease will be useful to hold it in place during assembly.
● RTV (Room Temperature Vulcanising) silicone rubber sealants cure when exposed to moisture in the atmosphere. These sealants are good at filling pits or irregular gasket faces, but will tend to be forced out of the joint under very high torque. They can be used to replace a paper gasket, but first make sure that the width of the paper gasket is not essential to the shimming of internal components. RTV sealants should not be used on components containing petrol (gasoline).
● Non-hardening, semi-hardening and hard setting liquid gasket compounds can be used with a gasket or between a metal-to-metal joint. Select the sealant to suit the application: universal non-hardening sealant can be used on virtually all joints; semi-hardening on joint faces which are rough or damaged; hard setting sealant on joints which require a permanent bond and are subjected to high temperature and pressure. **Note:** Check first if the paper gasket has a bead of sealant

impregnated in its surface before applying additional sealant.
● When choosing a sealant, make sure it is suitable for the application, particularly if being applied in a high-temperature area or in the vicinity of fuel. Certain manufacturers produce sealants in either clear, silver or black colours to match the finish of the engine. This has a particular application on motorcycles where much of the engine is exposed.
● Do not over-apply sealant. That which is squeezed out on the outside of the joint can be wiped off, whereas an excess of sealant on the inside can break off and clog oilways.

Breaking a sealed joint

● Age, heat, pressure and the use of hard setting sealant can cause two components to stick together so tightly that they are difficult to separate using finger pressure alone. Do not resort to using levers unless there is a pry point provided for this purpose (see illustration 7.1) or else the gasket surfaces will be damaged.
● Use a soft-faced hammer (see illustration 7.2) or a wood block and conventional hammer to strike the component near the mating surface. Avoid hammering against cast extremities since they may break off. If this method fails, try using a wood wedge between the two components.

> **Caution:** If the joint will not separate, double-check that you have removed all the fasteners.

7.1 If a pry point is provided, apply gently pressure with a flat-bladed screwdriver

7.2 Tap around the joint with a soft-faced mallet if necessary - don't strike cooling fins

Removal of old gasket and sealant

● Paper gaskets will most likely come away complete, leaving only a few traces stuck on

Most components have one or two hollow locating dowels between the two gasket faces. If a dowel cannot be removed, do not resort to gripping it with pliers - it will almost certainly be distorted. Install a close-fitting socket or Phillips screwdriver into the dowel and then grip the outer edge of the dowel to free it.

the sealing faces of the components. It is imperative that all traces are removed to ensure correct sealing of the new gasket.
● Very carefully scrape all traces of gasket away making sure that the sealing surfaces are not gouged or scored by the scraper (see illustrations 7.3, 7.4 and 7.5). Stubborn deposits can be removed by spraying with an aerosol gasket remover. Final preparation of

7.3 Paper gaskets can be scraped off with a gasket scraper tool . . .

7.4 . . . a knife blade . . .

7.5 . . . or a household scraper

7.6 Fine abrasive paper is wrapped around a flat file to clean up the gasket face

7.7 A kitchen scourer can be used on stubborn deposits

the gasket surface can be made with very fine abrasive paper or a plastic kitchen scourer **(see illustrations 7.6 and 7.7)**.

● Old sealant can be scraped or peeled off components, depending on the type originally used. Note that gasket removal compounds are available to avoid scraping the components clean; make sure the gasket remover suits the type of sealant used.

8 Chains

Breaking and joining final drive chains

● Drive chains for all but small bikes are continuous and do not have a clip-type connecting link. The chain must be broken using a chain breaker tool and the new chain securely riveted together using a new soft rivet-type link. Never use a clip-type connecting link instead of a rivet-type link, except in an emergency. Various chain breaking and riveting tools are available, either as separate tools or combined as illustrated in the accompanying photographs - read the instructions supplied with the tool carefully.

⚠ **Warning: The need to rivet the new link pins correctly cannot be overstressed - loss of control of the motorcycle is very likely to result if the chain breaks in use.**

● Rotate the chain and look for the soft link. The soft link pins look like they have been

8.1 Tighten the chain breaker to push the pin out of the link . . .

8.2 . . . withdraw the pin, remove the tool . . .

8.3 . . . and separate the chain link

deeply centre-punched instead of peened over like all the other pins **(see illustration 8.9)** and its sideplate may be a different colour. Position the soft link midway between the sprockets and assemble the chain breaker tool over one of the soft link pins **(see illustration 8.1)**. Operate the tool to push the pin out through the chain **(see illustration 8.2)**. On an O-ring chain, remove the O-rings **(see illustration 8.3)**. Carry out the same procedure on the other soft link pin.

Caution: Certain soft link pins (particularly on the larger chains) may require their ends to be filed or ground off before they can be pressed out using the tool.

● Check that you have the correct size and strength (standard or heavy duty) new soft link - do not reuse the old link. Look for the size marking on the chain sideplates **(see illustration 8.10)**.

● Position the chain ends so that they are engaged over the rear sprocket. On an O-ring

8.4 Insert the new soft link, with O-rings, through the chain ends . . .

8.5 . . . install the O-rings over the pin ends . . .

8.6 . . . followed by the sideplate

chain, install a new O-ring over each pin of the link and insert the link through the two chain ends **(see illustration 8.4)**. Install a new O-ring over the end of each pin, followed by the sideplate (with the chain manufacturer's marking facing outwards) **(see illustrations 8.5 and 8.6)**. On an unsealed chain, insert the link through the two chain ends, then install the sideplate with the chain manufacturer's marking facing outwards.

● Note that it may not be possible to install the sideplate using finger pressure alone. If using a joining tool, assemble it so that the plates of the tool clamp the link and press the sideplate over the pins **(see illustration 8.7)**. Otherwise, use two small sockets placed over

8.7 Push the sideplate into position using a clamp

8.8 Assemble the chain riveting tool over one pin at a time and tighten it fully

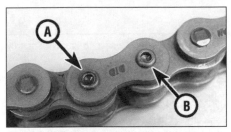

8.9 Pin end correctly riveted (A), pin end unriveted (B)

the rivet ends and two pieces of the wood between a G-clamp. Operate the clamp to press the sideplate over the pins.

● Assemble the joining tool over one pin (following the maker's instructions) and tighten the tool down to spread the pin end securely **(see illustrations 8.8 and 8.9)**. Do the same on the other pin.

> ⚠ **Warning: Check that the pin ends are secure and that there is no danger of the sideplate coming loose. If the pin ends are cracked the soft link must be renewed.**

Final drive chain sizing

● Chains are sized using a three digit number, followed by a suffix to denote the chain type **(see illustration 8.10)**. Chain type is either standard or heavy duty (thicker sideplates), and also unsealed or O-ring/X-ring type.

● The first digit of the number relates to the pitch of the chain, ie the distance from the centre of one pin to the centre of the next pin **(see illustration 8.11)**. Pitch is expressed in eighths of an inch, as follows:

8.10 Typical chain size and type marking

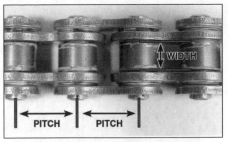

8.11 Chain dimensions

Sizes commencing with a 4 (eg 428) have a pitch of 1/2 inch (12.7 mm)

Sizes commencing with a 5 (eg 520) have a pitch of 5/8 inch (15.9 mm)

Sizes commencing with a 6 (eg 630) have a pitch of 3/4 inch (19.1 mm)

● The second and third digits of the chain size relate to the width of the rollers, again in imperial units, eg the 525 shown has 5/16 inch (7.94 mm) rollers **(see illustration 8.11)**.

9 Hoses

Clamping to prevent flow

● Small-bore flexible hoses can be clamped to prevent fluid flow whilst a component is worked on. Whichever method is used, ensure that the hose material is not permanently distorted or damaged by the clamp.

a) A brake hose clamp available from auto accessory shops **(see illustration 9.1)**.

b) A wingnut type hose clamp **(see illustration 9.2)**.

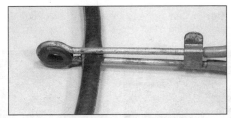

9.1 Hoses can be clamped with an automotive brake hose clamp . . .

9.2 . . . a wingnut type hose clamp . . .

c) Two sockets placed each side of the hose and held with straight-jawed self-locking grips **(see illustration 9.3)**.

d) Thick card each side of the hose held between straight-jawed self-locking grips **(see illustration 9.4)**.

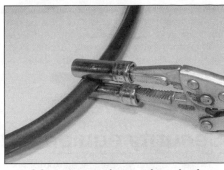

9.3 . . . two sockets and a pair of self-locking grips . . .

9.4 . . . or thick card and self-locking grips

Freeing and fitting hoses

● Always make sure the hose clamp is moved well clear of the hose end. Grip the hose with your hand and rotate it whilst pulling it off the union. If the hose has hardened due to age and will not move, slit it with a sharp knife and peel its ends off the union **(see illustration 9.5)**.

● Resist the temptation to use grease or soap on the unions to aid installation; although it helps the hose slip over the union it will equally aid the escape of fluid from the joint. It is preferable to soften the hose ends in hot water and wet the inside surface of the hose with water or a fluid which will evaporate.

9.5 Cutting a coolant hose free with a sharp knife

Introduction

In less time than it takes to read this introduction, a thief could steal your motorcycle. Returning only to find your bike has gone is one of the worst feelings in the world. Even if the motorcycle is insured against theft, once you've got over the initial shock, you will have the inconvenience of dealing with the police and your insurance company.

The motorcycle is an easy target for the professional thief and the joyrider alike and

the official figures on motorcycle theft make for depressing reading; on average a motorcycle is stolen every 16 minutes in the UK!

Motorcycle thefts fall into two categories, those stolen 'to order' and those taken by opportunists. The thief stealing to order will be on the look out for a specific make and model and will go to extraordinary lengths to obtain that motorcycle. The opportunist thief on the other hand will look for easy targets which can be stolen with the minimum of effort and risk.

Whilst it is never going to be possible to make your machine 100% secure, it is estimated that around half of all stolen motorcycles are taken by opportunist thieves. Remember that the opportunist thief is always on the look out for the easy option: if there are two similar motorcycles parked side-by-side, they will target the one with the lowest level of security. By taking a few precautions, you can reduce the chances of your motorcycle being stolen.

Security equipment

There are many specialised motorcycle security devices available and the following text summarises their applications and their good and bad points.

Once you have decided on the type of security equipment which best suits your needs, we recommended that you read one of the many equipment tests regularly carried

Ensure the lock and chain you buy is of good quality and long enough to shackle your bike to a solid object

out by the motorcycle press. These tests compare the products from all the major manufacturers and give impartial ratings on their effectiveness, value-for-money and ease of use.

No one item of security equipment can provide complete protection. It is highly recommended that two or more of the items described below are combined to increase the security of your motorcycle (a lock and chain plus an alarm system is just about ideal). The more security measures fitted to the bike, the less likely it is to be stolen.

Lock and chain

Pros: *Very flexible to use; can be used to secure the motorcycle to almost any immovable object. On some locks and chains, the lock can be used on its own as a disc lock (see below).*

Cons: *Can be very heavy and awkward to carry on the motorcycle, although some types*

will be supplied with a carry bag which can be strapped to the pillion seat.

● Heavy-duty chains and locks are an excellent security measure **(see illustration 1)**. Whenever the motorcycle is parked, use the lock and chain to secure the machine to a solid, immovable object such as a post or railings. This will prevent the machine from being ridden away or being lifted into the back of a van.

● When fitting the chain, always ensure the chain is routed around the motorcycle frame or swingarm **(see illustrations 2 and 3)**. Never merely pass the chain around one of the wheel rims; a thief may unbolt the wheel and lift the rest of the machine into a van, leaving you with just the wheel! Try to avoid having excess chain free, thus making it difficult to use cutting tools, and keep the chain and lock off the ground to prevent thieves attacking it with a cold chisel. Position the lock so that its lock barrel is facing downwards; this will make it harder for the thief to attack the lock mechanism.

Pass the chain through the bike's frame, rather than just through a wheel . . .

. . . and loop it around a solid object

U-locks

Pros: *Highly effective deterrent which can be used to secure the bike to a post or railings. Most U-locks come with a carrier which allows the lock to be easily carried on the bike.*

Cons: *Not as flexible to use as a lock and chain.*

● These are solid locks which are similar in use to a lock and chain. U-locks are lighter than a lock and chain but not so flexible to use. The length and shape of the lock shackle limit the objects to which the bike can be secured **(see illustration 4)**.

U-locks can be used to secure the bike to a solid object – ensure you purchase one which is long enough

Disc locks

Pros: *Small, light and very easy to carry; most can be stored underneath the seat.*

Cons: *Does not prevent the motorcycle being lifted into a van. Can be very embarrassing if you*

A typical disc lock attached through one of the holes in the disc

forget to remove the lock before attempting to ride off!

● Disc locks are designed to be attached to the front brake disc. The lock passes through one of the holes in the disc and prevents the wheel rotating by jamming against the fork/brake caliper **(see illustration 5)**. Some are equipped with an alarm siren which sounds if the disc lock is moved; this not only acts as a theft deterrent but also as a handy reminder if you try to move the bike with the lock still fitted.

● Combining the disc lock with a length of cable which can be looped around a post or railings provides an additional measure of security **(see illustration 6)**.

Alarms and immobilisers

Pros: *Once installed it is completely hassle-free to use. If the system is 'Thatcham' or 'Sold Secure-approved', insurance companies may give you a discount.*

Cons: *Can be expensive to buy and complex to install. No system will prevent the motorcycle from being lifted into a van and taken away.*

● Electronic alarms and immobilisers are available to suit a variety of budgets. There are three different types of system available: pure alarms, pure immobilisers, and the more expensive systems which are combined alarm/immobilisers **(see illustration 7)**.
● An alarm system is designed to emit an audible warning if the motorcycle is being tampered with.
● An immobiliser prevents the motorcycle being started and ridden away by disabling its electrical systems.
● When purchasing an alarm/immobiliser system, check the cost of installing the system unless you are able to do it yourself. If the motorcycle is not used regularly, another consideration is the current drain of the system. All alarm/immobiliser systems are powered by the motorcycle's battery; purchasing a system with a very low current drain could prevent the battery losing its charge whilst the motorcycle is not being used.

A disc lock combined with a security cable provides additional protection

A typical alarm/immobiliser system

Indelible markings can be applied to most areas of the bike – always apply the manufacturer's sticker to warn off thieves

Chemically-etched code numbers can be applied to main body panels . . .

. . . again, always ensure that the kit manufacturer's sticker is applied in a prominent position

Security marking kits

Pros: *Very cheap and effective deterrent. Many insurance companies will give you a discount on your insurance premium if a recognised security marking kit is used on your motorcycle.*

Cons: *Does not prevent the motorcycle being stolen by joyriders.*

● There are many different types of security marking kits available. The idea is to mark as many parts of the motorcycle as possible with a unique security number **(see illustrations 8, 9 and 10)**. A form will be included with the kit to register your personal details and those of the motorcycle with the kit manufacturer. This register is made available to the police to help them trace the rightful owner of any motorcycle or components which they recover should all other forms of identification have been removed. Always apply the warning stickers provided with the kit to deter thieves.

Ground anchors, wheel clamps and security posts

Pros: *An excellent form of security which will deter all but the most determined of thieves.*

Cons: *Awkward to install and can be expensive.*

● Whilst the motorcycle is at home, it is a good idea to attach it securely to the floor or a solid wall, even if it is kept in a securely locked garage. Various types of ground anchors, security posts and wheel clamps are available for this purpose **(see illustration 11)**. These security devices are either bolted to a solid concrete or brick structure or can be cemented into the ground.

Permanent ground anchors provide an excellent level of security when the bike is at home

Security at home

A high percentage of motorcycle thefts are from the owner's home. Here are some things to consider whenever your motorcycle is at home:

✔ Where possible, always keep the motorcycle in a securely locked garage. Never rely solely on the standard lock on the garage door, these are usual hopelessly inadequate. Fit an additional locking mechanism to the door and consider having the garage alarmed. A security light, activated by a movement sensor, is also a good investment.

✔ Always secure the motorcycle to the ground or a wall, even if it is inside a securely locked garage.
✔ Do not regularly leave the motorcycle outside your home, try to keep it out of sight wherever possible. If a garage is not available, fit a motorcycle cover over the bike to disguise its true identity.
✔ It is not uncommon for thieves to follow a motorcyclist home to find out where the bike is kept. They will then return at a later date. Be aware of this whenever you are returning

home on your motorcycle. If you suspect you are being followed, do not return home, instead ride to a garage or shop and stop as a precaution.
✔ When selling a motorcycle, do not provide your home address or the location where the bike is normally kept. Arrange to meet the buyer at a location away from your home. Thieves have been known to pose as potential buyers to find out where motorcycles are kept and then return later to steal them.

Security away from the home

As well as fitting security equipment to your motorcycle here are a few general rules to follow whenever you park your motorcycle.
✔ Park in a busy, public place.
✔ Use car parks which incorporate security features, such as CCTV.

✔ At night, park in a well-lit area, preferably directly underneath a street light.
✔ Engage the steering lock.
✔ Secure the motorcycle to a solid, immovable object such as a post or railings with an additional lock. If this is not possible,

secure the bike to a friend's motorcycle. Some public parking places provide security loops for motorcycles.
✔ Never leave your helmet or luggage attached to the motorcycle. Take them with you at all times.

Lubricants and fluids

A wide range of lubricants, fluids and cleaning agents is available for motor-cycles. This is a guide as to what is available, its applications and properties.

Four-stroke engine oil

● Engine oil is without doubt the most important component of any four-stroke engine. Modern motorcycle engines place a lot of demands on their oil and choosing the right type is essential. Using an unsuitable oil will lead to an increased rate of engine wear and could result in serious engine damage. Before purchasing oil, always check the recommended oil specification given by the manufacturer. The manufacturer will state a recommended 'type or classification' and also a specific 'viscosity' range for engine oil.

● The oil 'type or classification' is identified by its API (American Petroleum Institute) rating. The API rating will be in the form of two letters, e.g. SG. The S identifies the oil as being suitable for use in a petrol (gasoline) engine (S stands for spark ignition) and the second letter, ranging from A to J, identifies the oil's performance rating. The later this letter, the higher the specification of the oil; for example API SG oil exceeds the requirements of API SF oil. **Note:** *On some oils there may also be a second rating consisting of another two letters, the first letter being C, e.g. API SF/CD. This rating indicates the oil is also suitable for use in a diesel engines (the C stands for compression ignition) and is thus of no relevance for motorcycle use.*

● The 'viscosity' of the oil is identified by its SAE (Society of Automotive Engineers) rating. All modern engines require multigrade oils and the SAE rating will consist of two numbers, the first followed by a W, e.g.

10W/40. The first number indicates the viscosity rating of the oil at low temperatures (W stands for winter – tested at –20ºC) and the second number represents the viscosity of the oil at high temperatures (tested at 100ºC). The lower the number, the thinner the oil. For example an oil with an SAE 10W/40 rating will give better cold starting and running than an SAE 15W/40 oil.

● As well as ensuring the 'type' and 'viscosity' of the oil match the recommendations, another consideration to make when buying engine oil is whether to purchase a standard mineral-based oil, a semi-synthetic oil (also known as a synthetic blend or synthetic-based oil) or a fully-synthetic oil. Although all oils will have a similar rating and viscosity, their cost will vary considerably; mineral-based oils are the cheapest, the fully-synthetic oils the most expensive with the semi-synthetic oils falling somewhere in-between. This decision is very much up to the owner, but it should be noted that modern synthetic oils have far better lubricating and cleaning qualities than traditional mineral-based oils and tend to retain these properties for far longer. Bearing in mind the operating conditions inside a modern, high-revving motorcycle engine it is highly recommended that a fully synthetic oil is used. The extra expense at each service could save you money in the long term by preventing premature engine wear.

● As a final note always ensure that the oil is specifically designed for use in motorcycle engines. Engine oils designed primarily for use in car engines sometimes contain additives or friction modifiers which could cause clutch slip on a motorcycle fitted with a wet-clutch.

Two-stroke engine oil

● Modern two-stroke engines, with their high power outputs, place high demands on their oil. If engine seizure is to be avoided it is essential that a high-quality oil is used. Two-stroke oils differ hugely from four-stroke oils. The oil lubricates only the crankshaft and piston(s) (the transmission has its own lubricating oil) and is used on a total-loss basis where it is burnt completely during the combustion process.

● The Japanese have recently introduced a classification system for two-stroke oils, the JASO rating. This rating is in the form of two letters, either FA, FB or FC – FA is the lowest classification and FC the highest. Ensure the oil being used meets or exceeds the recommended rating specified by the manufacturer.

● As well as ensuring the oil rating matches the recommendation, another consideration to make when buying engine oil is whether to purchase a standard mineral-based oil, a semi-synthetic oil (also known as a synthetic blend or synthetic-based oil) or a fully-synthetic oil. The cost of each type of oil varies considerably; mineral-based oils are the cheapest, the fully-synthetic oils the most expensive with the semi-synthetic oils falling somewhere in-between. This decision is very much up to the owner, but it should be noted that modern synthetic oils have far better lubricating properties and burn cleaner than traditional mineral-based oils. It is therefore recommended that a fully synthetic oil is used. The extra expense could save you money in the long term by preventing premature engine wear, engine performance will be improved, carbon deposits and exhaust smoke will be reduced.

● Always ensure that the oil is specifically designed for use in an injector system. Many high quality two-stroke oils are designed for competition use and need to be pre-mixed with fuel. These oils are of a much higher viscosity and are not designed to flow through the injector pumps used on road-going two-stroke motorcycles.

Transmission (gear) oil

● On a two-stroke engine, the transmission and clutch are lubricated by their own separate oil bath which must be changed in accordance with the Maintenance Schedule.
● Although the engine and transmission units of most four-strokes use a common lubrication supply, there are some exceptions where the engine and gearbox have separate oil reservoirs and a dry clutch is used.
● Motorcycle manufacturers will either recommend a monograde transmission oil or a four-stroke multigrade engine oil to lubricate the transmission.
● Transmission oils, or gear oils as they are often called, are designed specifically for use in transmission systems. The viscosity of these oils is represented by an SAE number, but the scale of measurement applied is different to that used to grade engine oils. As a rough guide a SAE90 gear oil will be of the same viscosity as an SAE50 engine oil.

Shaft drive oil

● On models equipped with shaft final drive, the shaft drive gears are will have their own oil supply. The manufacturer will state a recommended 'type or classification' and also a specific 'viscosity' range in the same manner as for four-stroke engine oil.
● Gear oil classification is given by the number which follows the API GL (GL standing for gear lubricant) rating, the higher the number, the higher the specification of the oil, e.g. API GL5 oil is a higher specification than API GL4 oil. Ensure the oil meets or

exceeds the classification specified and is of the correct viscosity. The viscosity of gear oils is also represented by an SAE number but the scale of measurement used is different to that used to grade engine oils. As a rough guide an SAE90 gear oil will be of the same viscosity as an SAE50 engine oil.
● If the use of an EP (Extreme Pressure) gear oil is specified, ensure the oil purchased is suitable.

Fork oil and suspension fluid

● Conventional telescopic front forks are hydraulic and require fork oil to work. To ensure the forks function correctly, the fork oil must be changed in accordance with the Maintenance Schedule.
● Fork oil is available in a variety of viscosities, identified by their SAE rating; fork oil ratings vary from light (SAE 5) to heavy (SAE 30). When purchasing fork oil, ensure the viscosity rating matches that specified by the manufacturer.
● Some lubricant manufacturers also produce a range of high-quality suspension fluids which are very similar to fork oil but are designed mainly for competition use. These fluids may have a different viscosity rating system which is not to be confused with the SAE rating of normal fork oil. Refer to the manufacturer's instructions if in any doubt.

Brake and clutch fluid

● All disc brake systems and some clutch systems are hydraulically operated. To ensure correct operation, the hydraulic fluid must be changed in accordance with the Maintenance Schedule.
● Brake and clutch fluid is classified by its DOT rating with most motorcycle manufacturers specifying DOT 3 or 4 fluid. Both fluid types are glycol-based and can be mixed together without adverse effect; DOT 4 fluid exceeds the requirements of DOT 3

fluid. Although it is safe to use DOT 4 fluid in a system designed for use with DOT 3 fluid, never use DOT 3 fluid in a system which specifies the use of DOT 4 as this will adversely affect the system's performance. The type required for the system will be marked on the fluid reservoir cap.
● Some manufacturers also produce a DOT 5 hydraulic fluid. DOT 5 hydraulic fluid is silicone-based and is not compatible with the glycol-based DOT 3 and 4 fluids. Never mix DOT 5 fluid with DOT 3 or 4 fluid as this will seriously affect the performance of the hydraulic system.

Coolant/antifreeze

● When purchasing coolant/antifreeze, always ensure it is suitable for use in an aluminium engine and contains corrosion inhibitors to prevent possible blockages of the internal coolant passages of the system. As a general rule, most coolants are designed to be used neat and should not be diluted whereas antifreeze can be mixed with distilled water to provide a coolant solution of the required strength. Refer to the manufacturer's instructions on the bottle.
● Ensure the coolant is changed in accordance with the Maintenance Schedule.

Chain lube

● Chain lube is an aerosol-type spray lubricant specifically designed for use on motorcycle final drive chains. Chain lube has two functions, to minimise friction between the final drive chain and sprockets and to prevent corrosion of the chain. Regular use of a good-quality chain lube will extend the life of the drive chain and sprockets and thus maximise the power being transmitted from the transmission to the rear wheel.
● When using chain lube, always allow some time for the solvents in the lube to evaporate before riding the motorcycle. This will minimise the amount of lube which will

'fling' off from the chain when the motorcycle is used. If the motorcycle is equipped with an 'O-ring' chain, ensure the chain lube is labelled as being suitable for use on 'O-ring' chains.

Degreasers and solvents

● There are many different types of solvents and degreasers available to remove the grime and grease which accumulate around the motorcycle during normal use. Degreasers and solvents are usually available as an aerosol-type spray or as a liquid which you apply with a brush. Always closely follow the manufacturer's instructions and wear eye protection during use. Be aware that many solvents are flammable and may give off noxious fumes; take adequate precautions when using them (see Safety First!).

● For general cleaning, use one of the many solvents or degreasers available from most motorcycle accessory shops. These solvents are usually applied then left for a certain time before being washed off with water.

Brake cleaner is a solvent specifically designed to remove all traces of oil, grease and dust from braking system components. Brake cleaner is designed to evaporate quickly and leaves behind no residue.

Carburettor cleaner is an aerosol-type solvent specifically designed to clear carburettor blockages and break down the hard deposits and gum often found inside carburettors during overhaul.

Contact cleaner is an aerosol-type solvent designed for cleaning electrical components. The cleaner will remove all traces of oil and dirt from components such as switch contacts or fouled spark plugs and then dry, leaving behind no residue.

Gasket remover is an aerosol-type solvent designed for removing stubborn gaskets from engine components during overhaul. Gasket remover will minimise the amount of scraping required to remove the gasket and therefore reduce the risk of damage to the mating surface.

Spray lubricants

● Aerosol-based spray lubricants are widely available and are excellent for lubricating lever pivots and exposed cables and switches. Try to use a lubricant which is of the dry-film type as the fluid evaporates, leaving behind a dry-film of lubricant. Lubricants which leave behind an oily residue will attract dust and dirt which will increase the rate of wear of the cable/lever.

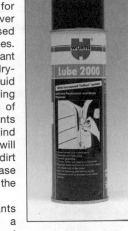

● Most lubricants also act as a moisture dispersant and a penetrating fluid. This means they can also be used to 'dry out' electrical components such as wiring connectors or switches as well as helping to free seized fasteners.

Greases

● Grease is used to lubricate many of the pivot-points. A good-quality multi-purpose grease is suitable for most applications but some manufacturers will specify the use of specialist greases for use on components such as swingarm and suspension linkage bushes. These specialist greases can be purchased from most motorcycle (or car) accessory shops; commonly specified types include molybdenum disulphide grease, lithium-based grease, graphite-based grease, silicone-based grease and high-temperature copper-based grease.

Gasket sealing compounds

● Gasket sealing compounds can be used in conjunction with gaskets, to improve their sealing capabilities, or on their own to seal metal-to-metal joints. Depending on their type, sealing compounds either set hard or stay relatively soft and pliable.

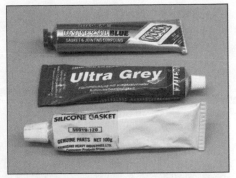

● When purchasing a gasket sealing compound, ensure that it is designed specifically for use on an internal combustion engine. General multi-purpose sealants available from DIY stores may appear visibly similar but they are not designed to withstand the extreme heat or contact with fuel and oil encountered when used on an engine (see 'Tools and Workshop Tips' for further information).

Thread locking compound

● Thread locking compounds are used to secure certain threaded fasteners in position to prevent them from loosening due to vibration. Thread locking compounds can be purchased from most motorcycle (and car) accessory shops. Ensure the threads of the both components are completely clean and dry before sparingly applying the locking compound (see 'Tools and Workshop Tips' for further information).

Fuel additives

● Fuel additives which protect and clean the fuel system components are widely available. These additives are designed to remove all traces of deposits that build up on the carburettors/injectors and prevent wear, helping the fuel system to operate more efficiently. If a fuel additive is being used, check that it is suitable for use with your motorcycle, especially if your motorcycle is equipped with a catalytic converter.

● Octane boosters are also available. These additives are designed to improve the performance of highly-tuned engines being run on normal pump-fuel and are of no real use on standard motorcycles.

Length (distance)

Inches (in)	x 25.4	= Millimetres (mm)	x 0.0394	=	Inches (in)
Feet (ft)	x 0.305	= Metres (m)	x 3.281	=	Feet (ft)
Miles	x 1.609	= Kilometres (km)	x 0.621	=	Miles

Volume (capacity)

Cubic inches (cu in; in^3)	x 16.387	= Cubic centimetres (cc; cm^3)	x 0.061	=	Cubic inches (cu in; in^3)
Imperial pints (Imp pt)	x 0.568	= Litres (l)	x 1.76	=	Imperial pints (Imp pt)
Imperial quarts (Imp qt)	x 1.137	= Litres (l)	x 0.88	=	Imperial quarts (Imp qt)
Imperial quarts (Imp qt)	x 1.201	= US quarts (US qt)	x 0.833	=	Imperial quarts (Imp qt)
US quarts (US qt)	x 0.946	= Litres (l)	x 1.057	=	US quarts (US qt)
Imperial gallons (Imp gal)	x 4.546	= Litres (l)	x 0.22	=	Imperial gallons (Imp gal)
Imperial gallons (Imp gal)	x 1.201	= US gallons (US gal)	x 0.833	=	Imperial gallons (Imp gal)
US gallons (US gal)	x 3.785	= Litres (l)	x 0.264	=	US gallons (US gal)

Mass (weight)

Ounces (oz)	x 28.35	= Grams (g)	x 0.035	=	Ounces (oz)
Pounds (lb)	x 0.454	= Kilograms (kg)	x 2.205	=	Pounds (lb)

Force

Ounces-force (ozf; oz)	x 0.278	= Newtons (N)	x 3.6	=	Ounces-force (ozf; oz)
Pounds-force (lbf; lb)	x 4.448	= Newtons (N)	x 0.225	=	Pounds-force (lbf; lb)
Newtons (N)	x 0.1	= Kilograms-force (kgf; kg)	x 9.81	=	Newtons (N)

Pressure

Pounds-force per square inch (psi; lbf/in^2; lb/in^2)	x 0.070	= Kilograms-force per square centimetre (kgf/cm^2; kg/cm^2)	x 14.223	=	Pounds-force per square inch (psi; lbf/in^2; lb/in^2)
Pounds-force per square inch (psi; lbf/in^2; lb/in^2)	x 0.068	= Atmospheres (atm)	x 14.696	=	Pounds-force per square inch (psi; lbf/in^2; lb/in^2)
Pounds-force per square inch (psi; lbf/in^2; lb/in^2)	x 0.069	= Bars	x 14.5	=	Pounds-force per square inch (psi; lbf/in^2; lb/in^2)
Pounds-force per square inch (psi; lbf/in^2; lb/in^2)	x 6.895	= Kilopascals (kPa)	x 0.145	=	Pounds-force per square inch (psi; lbf/in^2; lb/in^2)
Kilopascals (kPa)	x 0.01	= Kilograms-force per square centimetre (kgf/cm^2; kg/cm^2)	x 98.1	=	Kilopascals (kPa)
Millibar (mbar)	x 100	= Pascals (Pa)	x 0.01	=	Millibar (mbar)
Millibar (mbar)	x 0.0145	= Pounds-force per square inch (psi; lbf/in^2; lb/in^2)	x 68.947	=	Millibar (mbar)
Millibar (mbar)	x 0.75	= Millimetres of mercury (mmHg)	x 1.333	=	Millibar (mbar)
Millibar (mbar)	x 0.401	= Inches of water (inH$_2$O)	x 2.491	=	Millibar (mbar)
Millimetres of mercury (mmHg)	x 0.535	= Inches of water (inH$_2$O)	x 1.868	=	Millimetres of mercury (mmHg)
Inches of water (inH$_2$O)	x 0.036	= Pounds-force per square inch (psi; lbf/in^2; lb/in^2)	x 27.68	=	Inches of water (inH$_2$O)

Torque (moment of force)

Pounds-force inches (lbf in; lb in)	x 1.152	= Kilograms-force centimetre (kgf cm; kg cm)	x 0.868	=	Pounds-force inches (lbf in; lb in)
Pounds-force inches (lbf in; lb in)	x 0.113	= Newton metres (Nm)	x 8.85	=	Pounds-force inches (lbf in; lb in)
Pounds-force inches (lbf in; lb in)	x 0.083	= Pounds-force feet (lbf ft; lb ft)	x 12	=	Pounds-force inches (lbf in; lb in)
Pounds-force feet (lbf ft; lb ft)	x 0.138	= Kilograms-force metres (kgf m; kg m)	x 7.233	=	Pounds-force feet (lbf ft; lb ft)
Pounds-force feet (lbf ft; lb ft)	x 1.356	= Newton metres (Nm)	x 0.738	=	Pounds-force feet (lbf ft; lb ft)
Newton metres (Nm)	x 0.102	= Kilograms-force metres (kgf m; kg m)	x 9.804	=	Newton metres (Nm)

Power

Horsepower (hp)	x 745.7	= Watts (W)	x 0.0013	=	Horsepower (hp)

Velocity (speed)

Miles per hour (miles/hr; mph)	x 1.609	= Kilometres per hour (km/hr; kph)	x 0.621	=	Miles per hour (miles/hr; mph)

Fuel consumption*

Miles per gallon (mpg)	x 0.354	= Kilometres per litre (km/l)	x 2.825	=	Miles per gallon (mpg)

Temperature

Degrees Fahrenheit = (°C x 1.8) + 32   Degrees Celsius (Degrees Centigrade; °C) = (°F - 32) x 0.56

It is common practice to convert from miles per gallon (mpg) to litres/100 kilometres (l/100km), where mpg x l/100 km = 282

About the MOT Test

In the UK, all vehicles more than three years old are subject to an annual test to ensure that they meet minimum safety requirements. A current test certificate must be issued before a machine can be used on public roads, and is required before a road fund licence can be issued. Riding without a current test certificate will also invalidate your insurance.

For most owners, the MOT test is an annual cause for anxiety, and this is largely due to owners not being sure what needs to be checked prior to submitting the motorcycle for testing. The simple answer is that a fully roadworthy motorcycle will have no difficulty in passing the test.

This is a guide to getting your motorcycle through the MOT test. Obviously it will not be possible to examine the motorcycle to the same standard as the professional MOT tester, particularly in view of the equipment required for some of the checks. However, working through the following procedures will enable you to identify any problem areas before submitting the motorcycle for the test.

It has only been possible to summarise the test requirements here, based on the regulations in force at the time of printing. Test standards are becoming increasingly stringent, although there are some exemptions for older vehicles. More information about the MOT test can be obtained from the TSO publications, *How Safe is your Motorcycle* and *The MOT Inspection Manual for Motorcycle Testing*.

Many of the checks require that one of the wheels is raised off the ground. If the motorcycle doesn't have a centre stand, note that an auxiliary stand will be required. Additionally, the help of an assistant may prove useful.

Certain exceptions apply to machines under 50 cc, machines without a lighting system, and Classic bikes - if in doubt about any of the requirements listed below seek confirmation from an MOT tester prior to submitting the motorcycle for the test.

Check that the frame number is clearly visible.

HAYNES HINT *If a component is in borderline condition, the tester has discretion in deciding whether to pass or fail it. If the motorcycle presented is clean and evidently well cared for, the tester may be more inclined to pass a borderline component than if the motorcycle is scruffy and apparently neglected.*

Electrical System

Lights, turn signals, horn and reflector

✔ With the ignition on, check the operation of the following electrical components. **Note:** *The electrical components on certain small-capacity machines are powered by the generator, requiring that the engine is run for this check.*

a) *Headlight and tail light. Check that both illuminate in the low and high beam switch positions.*
b) *Position lights. Check that the front position (or sidelight) and tail light illuminate in this switch position.*
c) *Turn signals. Check that all flash at the correct rate, and that the warning light(s) function correctly. Check that the turn signal switch works correctly.*
d) *Hazard warning system (where fitted). Check that all four turn signals flash in this switch position.*
e) *Brake stop light. Check that the light comes on when the front and rear brakes are independently applied. Models first used on or after 1st April 1986 must have a brake light switch on each brake.*
f) *Horn. Check that the sound is continuous and of reasonable volume.*

✔ Check that there is a red reflector on the rear of the machine, either mounted separately or as part of the tail light lens.
✔ Check the condition of the headlight, tail light and turn signal lenses.

Headlight beam height

✔ The MOT tester will perform a headlight beam height check using specialised beam setting equipment **(see illustration 1)**. This equipment will not be available to the home mechanic, but if you suspect that the headlight is incorrectly set or may have been maladjusted in the past, you can perform a rough test as follows.
✔ Position the bike in a straight line facing a brick wall. The bike must be off its stand, upright and with a rider seated. Measure the height from the ground to the centre of the headlight and mark a horizontal line on the wall at this height. Position the motorcycle 3.8 metres from the wall and draw a vertical

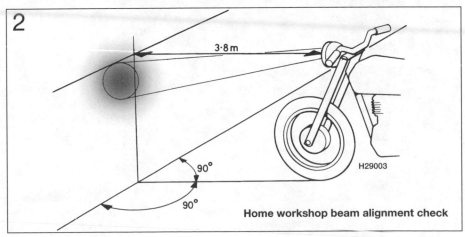

Headlight beam height checking equipment

line up the wall central to the centreline of the motorcycle. Switch to dipped beam and check that the beam pattern falls slightly lower than the horizontal line and to the left of the vertical line **(see illustration 2)**.

Home workshop beam alignment check

Exhaust System and Final Drive

Exhaust

✔ Check that the exhaust mountings are secure and that the system does not foul any of the rear suspension components.
✔ Start the motorcycle. When the revs are increased, check that the exhaust is neither holed nor leaking from any of its joints. On a linked system, check that the collector box is not leaking due to corrosion.

✔ Note that the exhaust decibel level ("loudness" of the exhaust) is assessed at the discretion of the tester. If the motorcycle was first used on or after 1st January 1985 the silencer must carry the BSAU 193 stamp, or a marking relating to its make and model, or be of OE (original equipment) manufacture. If the silencer is marked NOT FOR ROAD USE, RACING USE ONLY or similar, it will fail the MOT.

Final drive

✔ On chain or belt drive machines, check that the chain/belt is in good condition and does not have excessive slack. Also check that the sprocket is securely mounted on the rear wheel hub. Check that the chain/belt guard is in place.
✔ On shaft drive bikes, check for oil leaking from the drive unit and fouling the rear tyre.

Steering and Suspension

Steering

✔ With the front wheel raised off the ground, rotate the steering from lock to lock. The handlebar or switches must not contact the fuel tank or be close enough to trap the rider's hand. Problems can be caused by damaged lock stops on the lower yoke and frame, or by the fitting of non-standard handlebars.
✔ When performing the lock to lock check, also ensure that the steering moves freely without drag or notchiness. Steering movement can be impaired by poorly routed cables, or by overtight head bearings or worn bearings. The tester will perform a check of the steering head bearing lower race by mounting the front wheel on a surface plate, then performing a lock to

lock check with the weight of the machine on the lower bearing (see illustration 3).
✔ Grasp the fork sliders (lower legs) and attempt to push and pull on the forks (see

Front wheel mounted on a surface plate for steering head bearing lower race check

illustration 4). Any play in the steering head bearings will be felt. Note that in extreme cases, wear of the front fork bushes can be misinterpreted for head bearing play.
✔ Check that the handlebars are securely mounted.
✔ Check that the handlebar grip rubbers are secure. They should by bonded to the bar left end and to the throttle cable pulley on the right end.

Front suspension

✔ With the motorcycle off the stand, hold the front brake on and pump the front forks up and down (see illustration 5). Check that they are adequately damped.

Checking the steering head bearings for freeplay

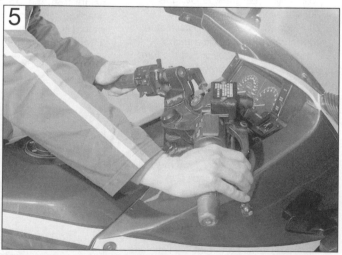

Hold the front brake on and pump the front forks up and down to check operation

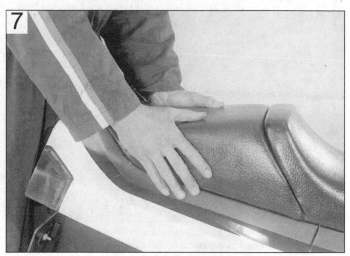

Inspect the area around the fork dust seal for oil leakage (arrow)

Bounce the rear of the motorcycle to check rear suspension operation

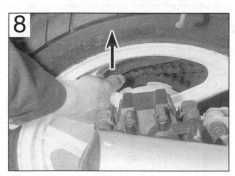

Checking for rear suspension linkage play

✔ Inspect the area above and around the front fork oil seals **(see illustration 6)**. There should be no sign of oil on the fork tube (stanchion) nor leaking down the slider (lower leg). On models so equipped, check that there is no oil leaking from the anti-dive units.

✔ On models with swingarm front suspension, check that there is no freeplay in the linkage when moved from side to side.

Rear suspension

✔ With the motorcycle off the stand and an assistant supporting the motorcycle by its handlebars, bounce the rear suspension **(see illustration 7)**. Check that the suspension components do not foul on any of the cycle parts and check that the shock absorber(s) provide adequate damping.

✔ Visually inspect the shock absorber(s) and check that there is no sign of oil leakage from its damper. This is somewhat restricted on certain single shock models due to the location of the shock absorber.

✔ With the rear wheel raised off the ground, grasp the wheel at the highest point and attempt to pull it up **(see illustration 8)**. Any play in the swingarm pivot or suspension linkage bearings will be felt as movement. **Note:** *Do not confuse play with actual suspension movement.* Failure to lubricate suspension linkage bearings can lead to bearing failure **(see illustration 9)**.

✔ With the rear wheel raised off the ground, grasp the swingarm ends and attempt to move the swingarm from side to side and forwards and backwards - any play indicates wear of the swingarm pivot bearings **(see illustration 10)**.

Worn suspension linkage pivots (arrows) are usually the cause of play in the rear suspension

Grasp the swingarm at the ends to check for play in its pivot bearings

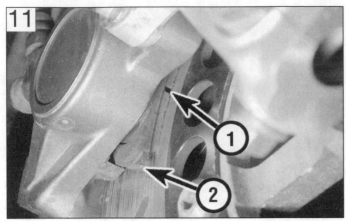

Brake pad wear can usually be viewed without removing the caliper. Most pads have wear indicator grooves (1) and some also have indicator tangs (2)

On drum brakes, check the angle of the operating lever with the brake fully applied. Most drum brakes have a wear indicator pointer and scale.

Brakes, Wheels and Tyres

Brakes

✔ With the wheel raised off the ground, apply the brake then free it off, and check that the wheel is about to revolve freely without brake drag.

✔ On disc brakes, examine the disc itself. Check that it is securely mounted and not cracked.

✔ On disc brakes, view the pad material through the caliper mouth and check that the pads are not worn down beyond the limit **(see illustration 11)**.

✔ On drum brakes, check that when the brake is applied the angle between the operating lever and cable or rod is not too great **(see illustration 12)**. Check also that the operating lever doesn't foul any other components.

✔ On disc brakes, examine the flexible hoses from top to bottom. Have an assistant hold the brake on so that the fluid in the hose is under pressure, and check that there is no sign of fluid leakage, bulges or cracking. If there are any metal brake pipes or unions, check that these are free from corrosion and damage. Where a brake-linked anti-dive system is fitted, check the hoses to the anti-dive in a similar manner.

✔ Check that the rear brake torque arm is secure and that its fasteners are secured by self-locking nuts or castellated nuts with split-pins or R-pins **(see illustration 13)**.

✔ On models with ABS, check that the self-check warning light in the instrument panel works.

✔ The MOT tester will perform a test of the motorcycle's braking efficiency based on a calculation of rider and motorcycle weight. Although this cannot be carried out at home, you can at least ensure that the braking systems are properly maintained. For hydraulic disc brakes, check the fluid level, lever/pedal feel (bleed of air if its spongy) and pad material. For drum brakes, check adjustment, cable or rod operation and shoe lining thickness.

Wheels and tyres

✔ Check the wheel condition. Cast wheels should be free from cracks and if of the built-up design, all fasteners should be secure. Spoked wheels should be checked for broken, corroded, loose or bent spokes.

✔ With the wheel raised off the ground, spin the wheel and visually check that the tyre and wheel run true. Check that the tyre does not foul the suspension or mudguards.

✔ With the wheel raised off the ground, grasp the wheel and attempt to move it about the axle (spindle) **(see illustration 14)**. Any play felt here indicates wheel bearing failure.

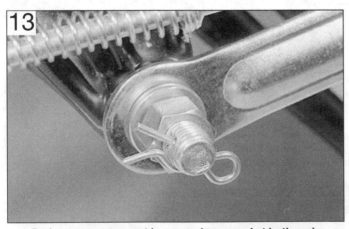

Brake torque arm must be properly secured at both ends

Check for wheel bearing play by trying to move the wheel about the axle (spindle)

Checking the tyre tread depth

Tyre direction of rotation arrow can be found on tyre sidewall

Castellated type wheel axle (spindle) nut must be secured by a split pin or R-pin

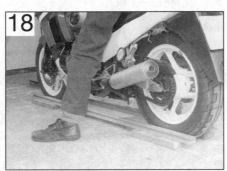

Two straightedges are used to check wheel alignment

✔ Check the tyre tread depth, tread condition and sidewall condition (see illustration 15).
✔ Check the tyre type. Front and rear tyre types must be compatible and be suitable for road use. Tyres marked NOT FOR ROAD USE, COMPETITION USE ONLY or similar, will fail the MOT.

✔ If the tyre sidewall carries a direction of rotation arrow, this must be pointing in the direction of normal wheel rotation (see illustration 16).
✔ Check that the wheel axle (spindle) nuts (where applicable) are properly secured. A self-locking nut or castellated nut with a split-pin or R-pin can be used (see illustration 17).
✔ Wheel alignment is checked with the motorcycle off the stand and a rider seated. With the front wheel pointing straight ahead, two perfectly straight lengths of metal or wood and placed against the sidewalls of both tyres (see illustration 18). The gap each side of the front tyre must be equidistant on both sides. Incorrect wheel alignment may be due to a cocked rear wheel (often as the result of poor chain adjustment) or in extreme cases, a bent frame.

General checks and condition

✔ Check the security of all major fasteners, bodypanels, seat, fairings (where fitted) and mudguards.

✔ Check that the rider and pillion footrests, handlebar levers and brake pedal are securely mounted.

✔ Check for corrosion on the frame or any load-bearing components. If severe, this may affect the structure, particularly under stress.

Sidecars

A motorcycle fitted with a sidecar requires additional checks relating to the stability of the machine and security of attachment and swivel joints, plus specific wheel alignment (toe-in) requirements. Additionally, tyre and lighting requirements differ from conventional motorcycle use. Owners are advised to check MOT test requirements with an official test centre.

Preparing for storage

Before you start

If repairs or an overhaul is needed, see that this is carried out now rather than left until you want to ride the bike again.

Give the bike a good wash and scrub all dirt from its underside. Make sure the bike dries completely before preparing for storage.

Engine

● Remove the spark plug(s) and lubricate the cylinder bores with approximately a teaspoon of motor oil using a spout-type oil can **(see illustration 1)**. Reinstall the spark plug(s). Crank the engine over a couple of times to coat the piston rings and bores with oil. If the bike has a kickstart, use this to turn the engine over. If not, flick the kill switch to the OFF position and crank the engine over on the starter **(see illustration 2)**. If the nature on the ignition system prevents the starter operating with the kill switch in the OFF position,

remove the spark plugs and fit them back in their caps; ensure that the plugs are earthed (grounded) against the cylinder head when the starter is operated **(see illustration 3)**.

⚠ *Warning: It is important that the plugs are earthed (grounded) away from the spark plug holes otherwise there is a risk of atomised fuel from the cylinders igniting.*

HAYNES HiNT *On a single cylinder four-stroke engine, you can seal the combustion chamber completely by positioning the piston at TDC on the compression stroke.*

● Drain the carburettor(s) otherwise there is a risk of jets becoming blocked by gum deposits from the fuel **(see illustration 4)**.

● If the bike is going into long-term storage, consider adding a fuel stabiliser to the fuel in the tank. If the tank is drained completely, corrosion of its internal surfaces may occur if left unprotected for a long period. The tank can be treated with a rust preventative especially for this purpose. Alternatively, remove the tank and pour half a litre of motor oil into it, install the filler cap and shake the tank to coat its internals with oil before draining off the excess. The same effect can also be achieved by spraying WD40 or a similar water-dispersant around the inside of the tank via its flexible nozzle.

● Make sure the cooling system contains the correct mix of antifreeze. Antifreeze also contains important corrosion inhibitors.

● The air intakes and exhaust can be sealed off by covering or plugging the openings. Ensure that you do not seal in any condensation; run the engine until it is hot,

Squirt a drop of motor oil into each cylinder

Flick the kill switch to OFF . . .

. . . and ensure that the metal bodies of the plugs (arrows) are earthed against the cylinder head

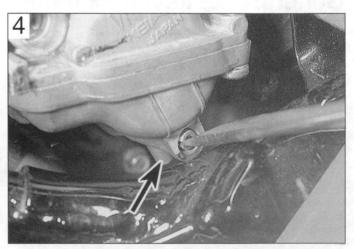

Connect a hose to the carburettor float chamber drain stub (arrow) and unscrew the drain screw

Exhausts can be sealed off with a plastic bag

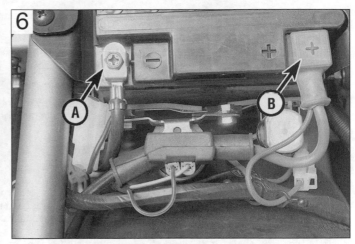

Disconnect the negative lead (A) first, followed by the positive lead (B)

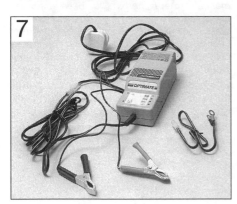

Use a suitable battery charger - this kit also assess battery condition

then switch off and allow to cool. Tape a piece of thick plastic over the silencer end(s) **(see illustration 5)**. Note that some advocate pouring a tablespoon of motor oil into the silencer(s) before sealing them off.

Battery

● Remove it from the bike - in extreme cases of cold the battery may freeze and crack its case **(see illustration 6)**.

● Check the electrolyte level and top up if necessary (conventional refillable batteries). Clean the terminals.
● Store the battery off the motorcycle and away from any sources of fire. Position a wooden block under the battery if it is to sit on the ground.
● Give the battery a trickle charge for a few hours every month **(see illustration 7)**.

Tyres

● Place the bike on its centrestand or an auxiliary stand which will support the motorcycle in an upright position. Position wood blocks under the tyres to keep them off the ground and to provide insulation from damp. If the bike is being put into long-term storage, ideally both tyres should be off the ground; not only will this protect the tyres, but will also ensure that no load is placed on the steering head or wheel bearings.
● Deflate each tyre by 5 to 10 psi, no more or the beads may unseat from the rim, making subsequent inflation difficult on tubeless tyres.

Pivots and controls

● Lubricate all lever, pedal, stand and footrest pivot points. If grease nipples are fitted to the rear suspension components, apply lubricant to the pivots.
● Lubricate all control cables.

Cycle components

● Apply a wax protectant to all painted and plastic components. Wipe off any excess, but don't polish to a shine. Where fitted, clean the screen with soap and water.
● Coat metal parts with Vaseline (petroleum jelly). When applying this to the fork tubes, do not compress the forks otherwise the seals will rot from contact with the Vaseline.
● Apply a vinyl cleaner to the seat.

Storage conditions

● Aim to store the bike in a shed or garage which does not leak and is free from damp.
● Drape an old blanket or bedspread over the bike to protect it from dust and direct contact with sunlight (which will fade paint). This also hides the bike from prying eyes. Beware of tight-fitting plastic covers which may allow condensation to form and settle on the bike.

Getting back on the road

Engine and transmission

● Change the oil and replace the oil filter. If this was done prior to storage, check that the oil hasn't emulsified - a thick whitish substance which occurs through condensation.
● Remove the spark plugs. Using a spout-type oil can, squirt a few drops of oil into the cylinder(s). This will provide initial lubrication as the piston rings and bores comes back into contact. Service the spark plugs, or fit new ones, and install them in the engine.

● Check that the clutch isn't stuck on. The plates can stick together if left standing for some time, preventing clutch operation. Engage a gear and try rocking the bike back and forth with the clutch lever held against the handlebar. If this doesn't work on cable-operated clutches, hold the clutch lever back against the handlebar with a strong elastic band or cable tie for a couple of hours **(see illustration 8)**.
● If the air intakes or silencer end(s) were blocked off, remove the bung or cover used.
● If the fuel tank was coated with a rust

Hold clutch lever back against the handlebar with elastic bands or a cable tie

preventative, oil or a stabiliser added to the fuel, drain and flush the tank and dispose of the fuel sensibly. If no action was taken with the fuel tank prior to storage, it is advised that the old fuel is disposed of since it will go off over a period of time. Refill the fuel tank with fresh fuel.

Frame and running gear

● Oil all pivot points and cables.
● Check the tyre pressures. They will definitely need inflating if pressures were reduced for storage.
● Lubricate the final drive chain (where applicable).
● Remove any protective coating applied to the fork tubes (stanchions) since this may well destroy the fork seals. If the fork tubes weren't protected and have picked up rust spots, remove them with very fine abrasive paper and refinish with metal polish.
● Check that both brakes operate correctly. Apply each brake hard and check that it's not possible to move the motorcycle forwards, then check that the brake frees off again once released. Brake caliper pistons can stick due to corrosion around the piston head, or on the sliding caliper types, due to corrosion of the slider pins. If the brake doesn't free after repeated operation, take the caliper off for examination. Similarly drum brakes can stick due to a seized operating cam, cable or rod linkage.
● If the motorcycle has been in long-term storage, renew the brake fluid and clutch fluid (where applicable).
● Depending on where the bike has been stored, the wiring, cables and hoses may have been nibbled by rodents. Make a visual check and investigate disturbed wiring loom tape.

Battery

● If the battery has been previously removal and given top up charges it can simply be reconnected. Remember to connect the positive cable first and the negative cable last.
● On conventional refillable batteries, if the battery has not received any attention, remove it from the motorcycle and check its electrolyte level. Top up if necessary then charge the battery. If the battery fails to hold a charge and a visual checks show heavy white sulphation of the plates, the battery is probably defective and must be renewed. This is particularly likely if the battery is old. Confirm battery condition with a specific gravity check.
● On sealed (MF) batteries, if the battery has not received any attention, remove it from the motorcycle and charge it according to the information on the battery case - if the battery fails to hold a charge it must be renewed.

Starting procedure

● If a kickstart is fitted, turn the engine over a couple of times with the ignition OFF to distribute oil around the engine. If no kickstart is fitted, flick the engine kill switch OFF and the ignition ON and crank the engine over a couple of times to work oil around the upper cylinder components. If the nature of the ignition system is such that the starter won't work with the kill switch OFF, remove the spark plugs, fit them back into their caps and earth (ground) their bodies on the cylinder head. Reinstall the spark plugs afterwards.
● Switch the kill switch to RUN, operate the choke and start the engine. If the engine won't start don't continue cranking the engine - not only will this flatten the battery, but the starter motor will overheat. Switch the ignition off and try again later. If the engine refuses to start, go through the fault finding procedures in this manual. **Note:** *If the bike has been in storage for a long time, old fuel or a carburettor blockage may be the problem. Gum deposits in carburettors can block jets - if a carburettor cleaner doesn't prove successful the carburettors must be dismantled for cleaning.*

● Once the engine has started, check that the lights, turn signals and horn work properly.
● Treat the bike gently for the first ride and check all fluid levels on completion. Settle the bike back into the maintenance schedule.

This Section provides an easy reference-guide to the more common faults that are likely to afflict your machine. Obviously, the opportunities are almost limitless for faults to occur as a result of obscure failures, and to try and cover all eventualities would require a book. Indeed, a number have been written on the subject.

Successful troubleshooting is not a mysterious 'black art' but the application of a bit of knowledge combined with a systematic and logical approach to the problem. Approach any troubleshooting by first accurately identifying the symptom and then checking through the list of possible causes, starting with the simplest or most obvious and progressing in stages to the most complex.

Take nothing for granted, but above all apply liberal quantities of common sense.

The main symptom of a fault is given in the text as a major heading below which are listed the various systems or areas which may contain the fault. Details of each possible cause for a fault and the remedial action to be taken are given, in brief, in the paragraphs below each heading. Further information should be sought in the relevant Chapter.

1 Engine doesn't start or is difficult to start
- [ ] Starter motor doesn't rotate
- [ ] Starter motor rotates but engine does not turn over
- [ ] Starter works but engine won't turn over (seized)
- [ ] No fuel flow
- [ ] Engine flooded
- [ ] No spark or weak spark
- [ ] Compression low
- [ ] Stalls after starting
- [ ] Rough idle

2 Poor running at low speed
- [ ] Spark weak
- [ ] Fuel/air mixture incorrect
- [ ] Compression low
- [ ] Poor acceleration

3 Poor running or no power at high speed
- [ ] Firing incorrect
- [ ] Fuel/air mixture incorrect
- [ ] Compression low
- [ ] Knocking or pinging
- [ ] Miscellaneous causes

4 Overheating
- [ ] Engine overheats
- [ ] Firing incorrect
- [ ] Fuel/air mixture incorrect
- [ ] Compression too high
- [ ] Engine load excessive
- [ ] Lubrication inadequate
- [ ] Miscellaneous causes

5 Clutch problems
- [ ] Clutch slipping
- [ ] Clutch not disengaging completely

6 Gear shifting problems
- [ ] Doesn't go into gear, or lever doesn't return
- [ ] Jumps out of gear
- [ ] Overshifts

7 Abnormal engine noise
- [ ] Knocking or pinging
- [ ] Piston slap or rattling
- [ ] Valve noise
- [ ] Other noise

8 Abnormal driveline noise
- [ ] Clutch noise
- [ ] Transmission noise
- [ ] Final drive noise

9 Abnormal frame and suspension noise
- [ ] Front end noise
- [ ] Shock absorber noise
- [ ] Brake noise

10 Oil pressure indicator light comes on
- [ ] Engine lubrication system
- [ ] Electrical system

11 Excessive exhaust smoke
- [ ] White smoke
- [ ] Black smoke
- [ ] Brown smoke

12 Poor handling or stability
- [ ] Handlebar hard to turn
- [ ] Handlebar shakes or vibrates excessively
- [ ] Handlebar pulls to one side
- [ ] Poor shock absorbing qualities

13 Braking problems
- [ ] Brakes are spongy, don't hold
- [ ] Brake lever or pedal pulsates
- [ ] Brakes drag

14 Electrical problems
- [ ] Battery dead or weak
- [ ] Battery overcharged

1 Engine doesn't start or is difficult to start

Starter motor doesn't rotate

☐ Engine kill switch OFF.
☐ Fuse blown. Check fuse (Chapter 8).
☐ Battery voltage low. Check and recharge battery (Chapter 8).
☐ Starter motor defective. Make sure the wiring to the starter is secure. Make sure the starter relay clicks when the start button is pushed. If the relay clicks, then the fault is in the wiring or motor.
☐ Starter relay faulty. Check it according to the procedure in Chapter 8.
☐ Starter switch not contacting. The contacts could be wet, corroded or dirty. Disassemble and clean the switch (Chapter 8).
☐ Wiring open or shorted. Check all wiring connections and harnesses to make sure that they are dry, tight and not corroded. Also check for broken or frayed wires that can cause a short to ground (earth) (see wiring diagram, Chapter 8).
☐ Ignition (main) switch defective. Check the switch according to the procedure in Chapter 8. Replace the switch with a new one if it is defective.
☐ Engine kill switch defective. Check for wet, dirty or corroded contacts. Clean or replace the switch as necessary (Chapter 8).
☐ Faulty neutral or side stand switch. Check the wiring to each switch and the switch itself according to the procedures in Chapter 8.
☐ Faulty sidestand relay or diode. Check according to the procedure in Chapter 8.

Starter motor rotates but engine does not turn over

☐ Starter clutch defective. Inspect and repair or replace (Chapter 2).
☐ Damaged idle/reduction gear or starter gears. Inspect and replace the damaged parts (Chapter 2).

Starter works but engine won't turn over (seized)

☐ Seized engine caused by one or more internally damaged components. Failure due to wear, abuse or lack of lubrication. Damage can include seized valves, followers, camshafts, pistons, crankshaft, connecting rod bearings, or transmission gears or bearings. Refer to Chapter 2 for engine disassembly.

No fuel flow

☐ No fuel in tank.
☐ Main fuel cock filter clogged. Remove the fuel cock and clean it and the filter (Chapter 3).
☐ Fuel line clogged. Pull the fuel line loose and carefully blow through it.
☐ Float needle valve clogged. For both of the valves to be clogged, either a very bad batch of fuel with an unusual additive has been used, or some other foreign material has entered the tank. Many times after a machine has been stored for many months without running, the fuel turns to a varnish-like liquid and forms deposits on the inlet needle valves and jets. The carburettors should be removed and overhauled if draining the float chambers doesn't solve the problem (Chapter 3).

Engine flooded

☐ Float height incorrect. Check and adjust as necessary (Chapter 3).
☐ Float needle valve worn or stuck open. A piece of dirt, rust or other debris can cause the valve to seat improperly, causing excess fuel to be admitted to the float chamber. In this case, the float chamber should be cleaned and the needle valve and seat inspected. If the needle and seat are worn, then the leaking will persist and the parts should be replaced with new ones (Chapter 3).

☐ Starting technique incorrect. Under normal circumstances (i.e., if all the carburettor functions are sound) the machine should start with little or no throttle. When the engine is cold, the choke should be operated and the engine started without opening the throttle. When the engine is at operating temperature, only a very slight amount of throttle should be necessary. If the engine is flooded hold the throttle open while cranking the engine. This will allow additional air to reach the cylinders.

No spark or weak spark

☐ Ignition switch OFF.
☐ Engine kill switch turned to the OFF position.
☐ Battery voltage low. Check and recharge the battery as necessary (Chapter 8).
☐ Spark plugs dirty, defective or worn out. Locate reason for fouled plugs using spark plug condition chart and follow the plug maintenance procedures (Chapter 1).
☐ Spark plug caps or secondary (HT) wiring faulty. Check condition. Replace either or both components if cracks or deterioration are evident (Chapter 4).
☐ Spark plug caps not making good contact. Make sure that the plug caps fit snugly over the plug ends.
☐ Ignition control unit defective. Check the unit, referring to Chapter 4 for details.
☐ Pulse generator coils defective. Check the coils, referring to Chapter 4 for details.
☐ Ignition HT coils defective. Check the coils, referring to Chapter 4 for details.
☐ Ignition or kill switch shorted. This is usually caused by water, corrosion, damage or excessive wear. The switches can be disassembled and cleaned with electrical contact cleaner. If cleaning does not help, replace the switches (Chapter 8).
☐ Wiring shorted or broken between:
  a) *Ignition (main) switch and engine kill switch (or blown fuse)*
  b) *Ignition control unit and engine kill switch*
  c) *Ignition control unit and ignition HT coils*
  d) *Ignition HT coils and spark plugs*
  e) *Ignition control unit and pulse generator coils*
☐ Make sure that all wiring connections are clean, dry and tight. Look for chafed and broken wires (Chapters 4 and 8).

Compression low

☐ Spark plugs loose. Remove the plugs and inspect their threads. Reinstall and tighten to the specified torque (Chapter 1).
☐ Cylinder head not sufficiently tightened down. If the cylinder head is suspected of being loose, then there's a chance that the gasket or head is damaged if the problem has persisted for any length of time. The head bolts should be tightened to the proper torque in the correct sequence (Chapter 2).
☐ Improper valve clearance. This means that the valve is not closing completely and compression pressure is leaking past the valve. Check and adjust the valve clearances (Chapter 1).
☐ Cylinder and/or piston worn. Excessive wear will cause compression pressure to leak past the rings. This is usually accompanied by worn rings as well. A top-end overhaul is necessary (Chapter 2).
☐ Piston rings worn, weak, broken, or sticking. Broken or sticking piston rings usually indicate a lubrication or carburation problem that causes excess carbon deposits or seizures to form on the pistons and rings. Top-end overhaul is necessary (Chapter 2).

1 Engine doesn't start or is difficult to start (continued)

- ☐ Piston ring-to-groove clearance excessive. This is caused by excessive wear of the piston ring lands. Piston replacement is necessary (Chapter 2).
- ☐ Cylinder head gasket damaged. If the head is allowed to become loose, or if excessive carbon build-up on the piston crown and combustion chamber causes extremely high compression, the head gasket may leak. Retorquing the head is not always sufficient to restore the seal, so gasket replacement is necessary (Chapter 2).
- ☐ Cylinder head warped. This is caused by overheating or improperly tightened head bolts. Machine shop resurfacing or head replacement is necessary (Chapter 2).
- ☐ Valve spring broken or weak. Caused by component failure or wear; the springs must be replaced (Chapter 2).
- ☐ Valve not seating properly. This is caused by a bent valve (from over-revving or improper valve adjustment), burned valve or seat (improper carburation) or an accumulation of carbon deposits on the seat (from carburation or lubrication problems). The valves must be cleaned and/or replaced and the seats serviced if possible (Chapter 2).

Stalls after starting

- ☐ Improper choke action. Make sure the choke linkage shaft is getting a full stroke and staying in the out position (Chapter 3).
- ☐ Ignition malfunction (Chapter 4).

- ☐ Carburettor malfunction (Chapter 3).
- ☐ Fuel contaminated. The fuel can be contaminated with either dirt or water, or can change chemically if the machine is allowed to sit for several months or more. Drain the tank and float chambers (Chapter 3).
- ☐ Intake air leak. Check for loose carburettor-to-intake manifold connections, loose or missing vacuum gauge adapter caps, or loose carburettor tops (Chapter 3).
- ☐ Engine idle speed incorrect. Turn idle adjusting screw until the engine idles at the specified rpm (Chapter 1).

Rough idle

- ☐ Ignition malfunction (Chapter 4).
- ☐ Idle speed incorrect (Chapter 1).
- ☐ Carburettors not synchronised. Adjust carburettors with vacuum gauge or manometer set (Chapter 1).
- ☐ Carburettor malfunction (Chapter 3).
- ☐ Fuel contaminated. The fuel can be contaminated with either dirt or water, or can change chemically if the machine is allowed to sit for several months or more. Drain the tank and float chambers (Chapter 3).
- ☐ Intake air leak. Check for loose carburettor-to-intake manifold connections, loose or missing vacuum gauge adapter caps, or loose carburettor tops (Chapter 3).
- ☐ Air filter clogged. Replace the air filter element (Chapter 1).

2 Poor running at low speeds

Spark weak

- ☐ Battery voltage low. Check and recharge battery (Chapter 8).
- ☐ Spark plugs fouled, defective or worn out (Chapter 1)
- ☐ Spark plug cap or HT wiring defective (Chapters 1 and 4).
- ☐ Spark plug caps not making contact. Make sure they are properly connected.
- ☐ Incorrect spark plugs. Wrong type, heat range or cap configuration. Check and install correct plugs (Chapter 1).
- ☐ Ignition control defective (Chapter 4).
- ☐ Pulse generator coils defective (Chapter 4).
- ☐ Ignition HT coils defective (Chapter 4).

Fuel/air mixture incorrect

- ☐ Pilot screws out of adjustment (Chapter 3).
- ☐ Pilot jet or air passage clogged. Remove and overhaul the carburettors (Chapter 3).
- ☐ Air bleed holes clogged. Remove carburettor and blow out all passages (Chapter 3).
- ☐ Air filter clogged, poorly sealed or missing (Chapter 1).
- ☐ Air filter housing poorly sealed. Look for cracks, holes or loose clamps and replace or repair defective parts (Chapter 3).
- ☐ Fuel level too high or too low. Check the float height (Chapter 3).
- ☐ Carburettor intake manifolds loose. Check for cracks, breaks, tears or loose clamps. Replace the rubber intake manifold joints if split or perished (Chapter 3).

Compression low

- ☐ Spark plugs loose. Remove the plugs and inspect their threads. Reinstall and tighten to the specified torque (Chapter 1).
- ☐ Cylinder head not sufficiently tightened down. If the cylinder head is suspected of being loose, then there's a chance that the gasket or head is damaged if the problem has persisted for any length of time. The head bolts should be tightened to the proper torque in the correct sequence (Chapter 2).

- ☐ Improper valve clearance. This means that the valve is not closing completely and compression pressure is leaking past the valve. Check and adjust the valve clearances (Chapter 1).
- ☐ Cylinder and/or piston worn. Excessive wear will cause compression pressure to leak past the rings. This is usually accompanied by worn rings as well. A top-end overhaul is necessary (Chapter 2).
- ☐ Piston rings worn, weak, broken, or sticking. Broken or sticking piston rings usually indicate a lubrication or carburation problem that causes excess carbon deposits or seizures to form on the pistons and rings. Top-end overhaul is necessary (Chapter 2).
- ☐ Piston ring-to-groove clearance excessive. This is caused by excessive wear of the piston ring lands. Piston replacement is necessary (Chapter 2).
- ☐ Cylinder head gasket damaged. If the head is allowed to become loose, or if excessive carbon build-up on the piston crown and combustion chamber causes extremely high compression, the head gasket may leak. Retorquing the head is not always sufficient to restore the seal, so gasket replacement is necessary (Chapter 2).
- ☐ Cylinder head warped. This is caused by overheating or improperly tightened head bolts. Machine shop resurfacing or head replacement is necessary (Chapter 2).
- ☐ Valve spring broken or weak. Caused by component failure or wear; the springs must be replaced (Chapter 2).
- ☐ Valve not seating properly. This is caused by a bent valve (from over-revving or improper valve adjustment), burned valve or seat (improper carburation) or an accumulation of carbon deposits on the seat (from carburation or lubrication problems). The valves must be cleaned and/or replaced and the seats serviced if possible (Chapter 2).

2 Poor running at low speeds (continued)

Poor acceleration

☐ Carburettors leaking or dirty. Overhaul the carburettors (Chapter 3).
☐ Timing not advancing. Faulty pick-up coils or ignitor unit (Chapter 4).
☐ Carburettors not synchronised. Adjust them with a vacuum gauge set or manometer (Chapter 1).

☐ Engine oil viscosity too high. Using a heavier oil than that recommended in Chapter 1 can damage the oil pump or lubrication system and cause drag on the engine.
☐ Brakes dragging. Usually caused by debris which has entered the brake piston seals, or from a warped disc or bent axle. Repair as necessary (Chapter 6).

3 Poor running or no power at high speed

Firing incorrect

☐ Air filter restricted. Clean or replace filter (Chapter 1).
☐ Spark plugs fouled, defective or worn out (Chapter 1).
☐ Spark plug cap or HT wiring defective (Chapters 1 and 4).
☐ Spark plug caps not making contact. Make sure they are properly connected.
☐ Incorrect spark plugs. Wrong type, heat range or cap configuration. Check and install correct plugs (Chapter 1).
☐ Ignition control unit defective (Chapter 4).
☐ Pulse generator coils defective (Chapter 4).
☐ Ignition HT coils defective (Chapter 4).

Fuel/air mixture incorrect

☐ Air bleed holes clogged. Remove carburettor and blow out all passages (Chapter 3).
☐ Air filter clogged, poorly sealed or missing (Chapter 1).
☐ Air filter housing poorly sealed. Look for cracks, holes or loose clamps and replace or repair defective parts (Chapter 3).
☐ Fuel level too high or too low. Check the float height (Chapter 3).
☐ Carburettor intake manifolds loose. Check for cracks, breaks, tears or loose clamps. Replace the rubber intake manifold joints if split or perished (Chapter 3).
☐ Jet needle incorrectly positioned or worn Check and adjust or replace (Chapter 3).
☐ Main jet clogged. Dirt, water or other contaminants can clog the main jets. Clean the fuel tap filter, the in-line filter, the float chamber area, and the jets and carburettor orifices (Chapter 3).
☐ Main jet wrong size. The standard jetting is for sea level atmospheric pressure and oxygen content. Check jet size (Chapter 3).
☐ Throttle shaft-to-carburettor body clearance excessive. Overhaul carburettors, replacing worn parts or complete carburettor if necessary (Chapter 3).

Compression low

☐ Spark plugs loose. Remove the plugs and inspect their threads. Reinstall and tighten to the specified torque (Chapter 1).
☐ Cylinder head not sufficiently tightened down. If the cylinder head is suspected of being loose, then there's a chance that the gasket or head is damaged if the problem has persisted for any length of time. The head bolts should be tightened to the proper torque in the correct sequence (Chapter 2).
☐ Improper valve clearance. This means that the valve is not closing completely and compression pressure is leaking past the valve. Check and adjust the valve clearances (Chapter 1).
☐ Cylinder and/or piston worn. Excessive wear will cause compression pressure to leak past the rings. This is usually accompanied by worn rings as well. A top-end overhaul is necessary (Chapter 2).
☐ Piston rings worn, weak, broken, or sticking. Broken or sticking piston rings usually indicate a lubrication or carburation problem that causes excess carbon deposits or seizures to form on the pistons and rings. Top-end overhaul is necessary (Chapter 2).

☐ Piston ring-to-groove clearance excessive. This is caused by excessive wear of the piston ring lands. Piston replacement is necessary (Chapter 2).
☐ Cylinder head gasket damaged. If the head is allowed to become loose, or if excessive carbon build-up on the piston crown and combustion chamber causes extremely high compression, the head gasket may leak. Retorquing the head is not always sufficient to restore the seal, so gasket replacement is necessary (Chapter 2).
☐ Cylinder head warped. This is caused by overheating or improperly tightened head bolts. Machine shop resurfacing or head replacement is necessary (Chapter 2).
☐ Valve spring broken or weak. Caused by component failure or wear; the springs must be replaced (Chapter 2).
☐ Valve not seating properly. This is caused by a bent valve (from over-revving or improper valve adjustment), burned valve or seat (improper carburation) or an accumulation of carbon deposits on the seat (from carburation or lubrication problems). The valves must be cleaned and/or replaced and the seats serviced if possible (Chapter 2).

Knocking or pinging

☐ Carbon build-up in combustion chamber. Use of a fuel additive that will dissolve the adhesive bonding the carbon particles to the crown and chamber is the easiest way to remove the build-up. Otherwise, the cylinder head will have to be removed and decarbonized (Chapter 2).
☐ Incorrect or poor quality fuel. Old or improper grades of fuel can cause detonation. This causes the piston to rattle, thus the knocking or pinging sound. Drain old fuel and always use the recommended fuel grade (Chapter 3).
☐ Spark plug heat range incorrect. Uncontrolled detonation indicates the plug heat range is too hot. The plug in effect becomes a glow plug, raising cylinder temperatures. Install the proper heat range plug (Chapter 1).
☐ Improper air/fuel mixture. This will cause the cylinder to run hot, which leads to detonation. Clogged jets or an air leak can cause this imbalance (Chapter 3).

Miscellaneous causes

☐ Throttle valve doesn't open fully. Adjust the throttle grip freeplay (Chapter 1).
☐ Clutch slipping. May be caused by loose or worn clutch components. Overhaul clutch (Chapter 2).
☐ Timing not advancing. Ignition control unit faulty (Chapter 4).
☐ Engine oil viscosity too high. Using a heavier oil than the one recommended in Chapter 1 can damage the oil pump or lubrication system and cause drag on the engine.
☐ Brakes dragging. Usually caused by debris which has entered the brake piston seals, or from a warped disc or bent axle. Repair as necessary.

4 Overheating

Firing incorrect

☐ Spark plugs fouled, defective or worn out (Chapter 1).
☐ Incorrect spark plugs (Chapter 1).
☐ Faulty ignition HT coils (Chapter 4).

Fuel/air mixture incorrect

☐ Main jet clogged. Dirt, water and other contaminants can clog the main jets. Clean the fuel tap filter, the fuel pump in-line filter, the float chamber area and the jets and carburettor orifices (Chapter 3).
☐ Main jet wrong size. The standard jetting is for sea level atmospheric pressure and oxygen content. Check jet size (Chapter 3).
☐ Air filter clogged, poorly sealed or missing (Chapter 1).
☐ Air filter housing poorly sealed. Look for cracks, holes or loose clamps and replace or repair (Chapter 3).
☐ Fuel level too low. Check float height (Chapter 3).
☐ Carburettor intake manifolds loose. Check for cracks, breaks, tears or loose clamps. Replace the rubber intake manifold joints if split or perished (Chapter 3).

Compression too high

☐ Carbon build-up in combustion chamber. Use of a fuel additive that will dissolve the adhesive bonding the carbon particles to the piston crown and chamber is the easiest way to remove the build-up. Otherwise, the cylinder head will have to be removed and decarbonized (Chapter 2).
☐ Improperly machined head surface or installation of incorrect gasket during engine assembly (Chapter 2).

Engine load excessive

☐ Clutch slipping. Can be caused by damaged, loose or worn clutch components. Overhaul clutch (Chapter 2).

☐ Engine oil level too high. The addition of too much oil will cause pressurisation of the crankcase and inefficient engine operation. Check Specifications and drain to proper level (Chapter 1).
☐ Engine oil viscosity too high. Using a heavier oil than the one recommended in Chapter 1 can damage the oil pump or lubrication system as well as cause drag on the engine.
☐ Brakes dragging. Usually caused by debris which has entered the brake piston seals, or from a warped disc or bent axle. Repair as necessary.
☐ Excessive friction in moving engine parts due to inadequate lubrication, worn bearings or incorrect assembly. Overhaul engine (Chapter 2).

Lubrication inadequate

☐ Engine oil level too low. Friction caused by intermittent lack of lubrication or from oil that is overworked can cause overheating. The oil provides a definite cooling function in the engine. Check the oil level (Chapter 1).
☐ Poor quality engine oil or incorrect viscosity or type. Oil is rated not only according to viscosity but also according to type. Some oils are not rated high enough for use in this engine. Check the Specifications section and change to the correct oil (Chapter 1).
☐ Worn oil pump or clogged oil passages. Check oil pump and clean passages (Chapter 2).

Miscellaneous causes

☐ Engine cooling fins clogged with debris.
☐ Modification to exhaust system. Most aftermarket exhaust systems cause the engine to run leaner, which make them run hotter. When installing an accessory exhaust system, always rejet the carburettors.

5 Clutch problems

Clutch slipping

☐ Cable freeplay insufficient. Check and adjust cable (Chapter 1).
☐ Friction plates worn or warped. Overhaul the clutch assembly (Chapter 2).
☐ Plain plates warped (Chapter 2).
☐ Clutch springs broken or weak. Old or heat-damaged (from slipping clutch) springs should be replaced with new ones (Chapter 2).
☐ Clutch release mechanism defective. Replace any defective parts (Chapter 2).
☐ Clutch centre or housing unevenly worn. This causes improper engagement of the plates. Replace the damaged or worn parts (Chapter 2).

Clutch not disengaging completely

☐ Cable freeplay excessive. Check and adjust cable (Chapter 1).
☐ Clutch plates warped or damaged. This will cause clutch drag, which in turn will cause the machine to creep. Overhaul the clutch assembly (Chapter 2).

☐ Clutch spring tension uneven. Usually caused by a sagged or broken spring. Check and replace the springs as a set (Chapter 2).
☐ Engine oil deteriorated. Old, thin, worn out oil will not provide proper lubrication for the plates, causing the clutch to drag. Replace the oil and filter (Chapter 1).
☐ Engine oil viscosity too high. Using a heavier oil than recommended in Chapter 1 can cause the plates to stick together, putting a drag on the engine. Change to the correct weight oil (Chapter 1).
☐ Clutch housing seized on mainshaft. Lack of lubrication, severe wear or damage can cause the guide to seize on the shaft. Overhaul of the clutch, and perhaps transmission, may be necessary to repair the damage (Chapter 2).
☐ Clutch release mechanism defective. Overhaul the clutch cover components (Chapter 2).
☐ Loose clutch centre nut. Causes drum and centre misalignment putting a drag on the engine. Engagement adjustment continually varies. Overhaul the clutch assembly (Chapter 2).

6 Gear shifting problems

Doesn't go into gear or lever doesn't return

- ☐ Clutch not disengaging. See above.
- ☐ Selector fork(s) bent or seized. Often caused by dropping the machine or from lack of oil. Overhaul the transmission (Chapter 2).
- ☐ Gear(s) stuck on shaft. Most often caused by a lack of lubrication or excessive wear in transmission bearings and bushings. Overhaul the transmission (Chapter 2).
- ☐ Gear selector drum binding. Caused by lubrication failure or excessive wear. Replace the drum and bearing (Chapter 2).
- ☐ Gearchange lever return spring weak or broken (Chapter 2).
- ☐ Gearchange lever broken. Splines stripped out of lever or shaft, caused by allowing the lever to get loose or from dropping the machine. Replace necessary parts (Chapter 2).

- ☐ Gearchange mechanism stopper arm broken or worn. Full engagement and rotary movement of shift drum results. Replace the arm (Chapter 2).
- ☐ Stopper arm spring broken. Allows arm to float, causing sporadic shift operation. Replace spring (Chapter 2).

Jumps out of gear

- ☐ Selector fork(s) worn. Overhaul the transmission (Chapter 2).
- ☐ Gear groove(s) worn. Overhaul the transmission (Chapter 2).
- ☐ Gear dogs or dog slots worn or damaged. The gears should be inspected and replaced. Don't service the worn parts (Chapter 2).

Overshifts

- ☐ Stopper arm spring weak or broken (Chapter 2).
- ☐ Gearchange shaft return spring post broken or distorted (Chapter 2).

7 Abnormal engine noise

Knocking or pinging

- ☐ Carbon build-up in combustion chamber. Use of a fuel additive that will dissolve the adhesive bonding the carbon particles to the piston crown and chamber is the easiest way to remove the build-up. Otherwise, the cylinder head will have to be removed and decarbonized (Chapter 2).
- ☐ Incorrect or poor quality fuel. Old or improper fuel can cause detonation. This causes the pistons to rattle, thus the knocking or pinging sound. Drain the old fuel and always use the recommended grade fuel (Chapter 3).
- ☐ Spark plug heat range incorrect. Uncontrolled detonation indicates that the plug heat range is too hot. The plug in effect becomes a glow plug, raising cylinder temperatures. Install the proper heat range plug (Chapter 1).
- ☐ Improper air/fuel mixture. This will cause the cylinders to run hot and lead to detonation. Clogged jets or an air leak can cause this imbalance (Chapter 3).

Piston slap or rattling

- ☐ Cylinder-to-piston clearance excessive. Caused by improper assembly. Inspect and overhaul top-end parts (Chapter 2).
- ☐ Connecting rod bent. Caused by over-revving, trying to start a badly flooded engine or from ingesting a foreign object into the combustion chamber. Replace the damaged parts (Chapter 2).
- ☐ Piston pin or piston pin bore worn or seized from wear or lack of lubrication. Replace damaged parts (Chapter 2).
- ☐ Piston ring(s) worn, broken or sticking. Overhaul the top-end (Chapter 2).
- ☐ Piston seizure damage. Usually from lack of lubrication or overheating. Replace the pistons and bore the cylinders, as necessary (Chapter 2).

- ☐ Connecting rod upper or lower end clearance excessive. Caused by excessive wear or lack of lubrication. Replace worn parts (Chapter 2).

Valve noise

- ☐ Incorrect valve clearances. Adjust the clearances (Chapter 1).
- ☐ Valve spring broken or weak. Check and replace weak valve springs (Chapter 2).
- ☐ Camshaft or cylinder head worn or damaged. Lack of lubrication at high rpm is usually the cause of damage. Insufficient oil or failure to change the oil at the recommended intervals are the chief causes. Since there are no replaceable bearings in the head, the head itself will have to be replaced if there is excessive wear or damage (Chapter 2).

Other noise

- ☐ Cylinder head gasket leaking (Chapter 1).
- ☐ Exhaust pipe leaking at cylinder head connection. Caused by improper fit of pipe(s) or loose exhaust flange. All exhaust fasteners should be tightened evenly and carefully. Failure to do this will lead to a leak (Chapter 3).
- ☐ Crankshaft runout excessive. Caused by a bent crankshaft (from over-revving) or damage from an upper cylinder component failure. Can also be attributed to dropping the machine on either of the crankshaft ends (Chapter 2).
- ☐ Engine mounting bolts loose. Tighten all engine mount bolts (Chapter 2).
- ☐ Crankshaft bearings worn (Chapter 2).
- ☐ Cam chain tensioner defective. Replace (Chapter 2).
- ☐ Cam chain, sprockets or guides worn (Chapter 2).

8 Abnormal driveline noise

Clutch noise

- ☐ Clutch housing/friction plate clearance excessive (Chapter 2).
- ☐ Loose or damaged clutch pressure plate and/or bolts (Chapter 2).

Transmission noise

- ☐ Bearings worn. Also includes the possibility that the shafts are worn. Overhaul the transmission (Chapter 2).
- ☐ Gears worn or chipped (Chapter 2).
- ☐ Metal chips jammed in gear teeth. Probably pieces from a broken component picked up by the gears. This will cause early bearing

failure (Chapter 2).
- ☐ Engine oil level too low. Causes a howl from transmission. Also affects engine power and clutch operation (Chapter 1).

Final drive noise

- ☐ Chain not adjusted properly (Chapter 1).
- ☐ Front or rear sprocket loose. Tighten fasteners (Chapter 5).
- ☐ Sprockets worn. Replace sprockets (Chapter 5).
- ☐ Rear sprocket warped. Replace sprockets (Chapter 5).
- ☐ Wheel coupling damper worn. Replace damper (Chapter 5).

9 Abnormal frame and suspension noise

Front end noise

- [ ] Low fluid level or improper viscosity oil in forks. This can sound like spurting and is usually accompanied by irregular fork action (Chapter 5).
- [ ] Spring weak or broken. Makes a clicking or scraping sound. Fork oil, when drained, will have a lot of metal particles in it (Chapter 5).
- [ ] Steering head bearings loose or damaged. Clicks when braking. Check and adjust or replace as necessary (Chapters 1 and 5).
- [ ] Fork yokes loose. Make sure all clamp pinch bolts are tight (Chapter 5).
- [ ] Fork tube bent. Good possibility if machine has been dropped. Replace tube with a new one (Chapter 5).
- [ ] Front axle or axle clamp bolt loose. Tighten them to the specified torque (Chapter 6).

Shock absorber noise

- [ ] Fluid level incorrect. Indicates a leak caused by defective seal. Shock will be covered with oil. Replace shock or seek advice on repair from a Suzuki dealer (Chapter 5).
- [ ] Defective shock absorber with internal damage. This is in the body of the shock and can't be remedied. The shock must be replaced with a new one (Chapter 5).

- [ ] Bent or damaged shock body. Replace the shock with a new one (Chapter 5).
- [ ] Loose or worn linkage components. Check and replace as needed (Chapter 5).

Brake noise

- [ ] Squeal caused by pad shim not installed or positioned correctly (Chapter 6).
- [ ] Squeal caused by dust on brake pads. Usually found in combination with glazed pads. Clean using brake cleaning solvent (Chapter 6).
- [ ] Contamination of brake pads. Oil, brake fluid or dirt causing brake to chatter or squeal. Clean or replace pads (Chapter 6).
- [ ] Pads glazed. Caused by excessive heat from prolonged use or from contamination. Do not use sandpaper, emery cloth, carborundum cloth or any other abrasive to roughen the pad surfaces as abrasives will stay in the pad material and damage the disc. A very fine flat file can be used, but pad replacement is suggested as a cure (Chapter 6).
- [ ] Disc warped. Can cause a chattering, clicking or intermittent squeal. Usually accompanied by a pulsating lever and uneven braking. Replace the disc (Chapter 6).
- [ ] Loose or worn wheel bearings. Check and replace as needed (Chapter 6).

10 Oil pressure light comes on

Engine lubrication system

- [ ] Engine oil pump defective, blocked oil strainer gauze or failed relief valve. Carry out oil pressure check (Chapter 2).
- [ ] Engine oil level low. Inspect for leak or other problem causing low oil level and add recommended oil (Chapter 1).
- [ ] Engine oil viscosity too low. Very old, thin oil or an improper weight of oil used in the engine. Change to correct oil (Chapter 1).
- [ ] Camshaft or journals worn. Excessive wear causing drop in oil pressure. Replace cam and/or cylinder head. Abnormal wear could be caused by oil starvation at high rpm from low oil level or improper weight or type of oil (Chapter 1).

- [ ] Crankshaft and/or bearings worn. Same problems as paragraph 4. Check and replace crankshaft and/or bearings (Chapter 2).

Electrical system

- [ ] Oil pressure switch defective. Check the switch according to the procedure in Chapter 8. Replace it if it is defective.
- [ ] Oil pressure indicator light circuit defective. Check for pinched, shorted, disconnected or damaged wiring (Chapter 8).

11 Excessive exhaust smoke

White smoke

- [ ] Piston oil ring worn. The ring may be broken or damaged, causing oil from the crankcase to be pulled past the piston into the combustion chamber. Replace the rings with new ones (Chapter 2).
- [ ] Cylinders worn, cracked, or scored. Caused by overheating or oil starvation. The cylinders will have to be rebored and new pistons installed (Chapter 2).
- [ ] Valve oil seal damaged or worn. Replace oil seals with new ones (Chapter 2).
- [ ] Valve guide worn. Perform a complete valve job (Chapter 2).
- [ ] Engine oil level too high, which causes the oil to be forced past the rings. Drain oil to the proper level (Chapter 1).
- [ ] Head gasket broken between oil return and cylinder. Causes oil to be pulled into the combustion chamber. Replace the head gasket and check the head for warpage (Chapter 2).
- [ ] Abnormal crankcase pressurisation, which forces oil past the rings. Clogged ventilation system or breather hose (Chapter 2).

Black smoke

- [ ] Air filter clogged. Clean or replace the element (Chapter 1).

- [ ] Main jet too large or loose. Compare jet size with the Specifications (Chapter 3).
- [ ] Choke cable or linkage shaft stuck, causing fuel to be pulled through choke circuit (Chapter 3).
- [ ] Fuel level too high. Check and adjust the float height(s) as necessary (Chapter 3).
- [ ] Float needle valve held off needle seat. Clean the float chambers and fuel line and replace the needles and seats if necessary (Chapter 3).

Brown smoke

- [ ] Main jet too small or clogged. Lean condition caused by wrong size main jet or by a restricted orifice. Clean float chambers and jets and compare jet size to Specifications (Chapter 3).
- [ ] Fuel flow insufficient. Float needle valve stuck closed due to chemical reaction with old fuel. Float height incorrect. Restricted fuel line. Clean line and float chamber and adjust floats if necessary (Chapter 3).
- [ ] Carburettor intake manifold clamps loose (Chapter 3).
- [ ] Air filter poorly sealed or not installed (Chapter 1).

12 Poor handling or stability

Handlebar hard to turn

- [ ] Steering head bearing adjuster nut too tight. Check adjustment (Chapter 1).
- [ ] Bearings damaged. Roughness can be felt as the bars are turned from side-to-side. Replace bearings and races (Chapter 5).
- [ ] Races dented or worn. Denting results from wear in only one position (e.g., straight ahead), from a collision or hitting a pothole or from dropping the machine. Replace races and bearings (Chapter 5).
- [ ] Steering stem lubrication inadequate. Causes are grease getting hard from age or being washed out by high pressure car washes. Disassemble steering head and repack bearings (Chapter 5).
- [ ] Steering stem bent. Caused by a collision, hitting a pothole or by dropping the machine. Replace damaged part. Don't try to straighten the steering stem (Chapter 5).
- [ ] Front tire air pressure too low (Chapter 1).

Handlebar shakes or vibrates excessively

- [ ] Tyres worn or out of balance (Chapter 6).
- [ ] Swingarm bearings worn. Replace worn bearings (Chapter 5).
- [ ] Rim(s) warped or damaged. Inspect wheels for runout (Chapter 6).
- [ ] Wheel bearings worn. Worn front or rear wheel bearings can cause poor tracking. Worn front bearings will cause wobble (Chapter 6).
- [ ] Handlebar clamp bolts loose (Chapter 5).
- [ ] Fork yoke bolts loose. Tighten them to the specified torque (Chapter 5).
- [ ] Engine mounting bolts loose. Will cause excessive vibration with increased engine rpm (Chapter 2).

Handlebar pulls to one side

- [ ] Frame bent. Definitely suspect this if the machine has been dropped. May or may not be accompanied by cracking near the bend. Replace the frame (Chapter 5).
- [ ] Wheels out of alignment. Caused by improper location of axle spacers or from bent steering stem or frame (Chapter 5).
- [ ] Swingarm bent or twisted. Caused by age (metal fatigue) or impact damage. Replace the arm (Chapter 5).
- [ ] Steering stem bent. Caused by impact damage or by dropping the motorcycle. Replace the steering stem (Chapter 5).
- [ ] Fork tube bent. Disassemble the forks and replace the damaged parts (Chapter 5).
- [ ] Fork oil level uneven. Check and add or drain as necessary (Chapter 5).

Poor shock absorbing qualities

- [ ] Too hard:
  - a) *Fork oil level excessive (Chapter 5).*
  - b) *Fork oil viscosity too high. Use a lighter oil (see the Specifications in Chapter 5).*
  - c) *Fork tube bent. Causes a harsh, sticking feeling (Chapter 5).*
  - d) *Shock shaft or body bent or damaged (Chapter 5).*
  - e) *Fork internal damage (Chapter 5).*
  - f) *Shock internal damage.*
  - g) *Tire pressure too high (Chapter 1).*
- [ ] Too soft:
  - a) *Fork or shock oil insufficient and/or leaking (Chapter 5).*
  - b) *Fork oil level too low (Chapter 5).*
  - c) *Fork oil viscosity too light (Chapter 5).*
  - d) *Fork springs weak or broken (Chapter 5).*
  - e) *Shock internal damage or leakage (Chapter 5).*

13 Braking problems

Brakes are spongy, don't hold

- [ ] Air in brake line. Caused by inattention to master cylinder fluid level or by leakage. Locate problem and bleed brakes (Chapter 6).
- [ ] Pad or disc worn (Chapters 1 and 6).
- [ ] Brake fluid leak. Causes air in brake line. Locate problem and bleed brakes (Chapter 6).
- [ ] Contaminated pads. Caused by contamination with oil, grease, brake fluid, etc. Clean or replace pads. Clean disc thoroughly with brake cleaner (Chapter 6).
- [ ] Brake fluid deteriorated. Fluid is old or contaminated. Drain system, replenish with new fluid and bleed the system (Chapter 6).
- [ ] Master cylinder internal parts worn or damaged causing fluid to bypass (Chapter 6).
- [ ] Master cylinder bore scratched by foreign material or broken spring. Repair or replace master cylinder (Chapter 6).
- [ ] Disc warped. Replace disc (Chapter 6).

Brake lever or pedal pulsates

- [ ] Disc warped. Replace disc (Chapter 6).
- [ ] Axle bent. Replace axle (Chapter 6).

- [ ] Brake caliper bolts loose (Chapter 6).
- [ ] Brake caliper sliders damaged or sticking (rear caliper), causing caliper to bind. Lubricate the sliders or replace them if they are corroded or bent (Chapter 6).
- [ ] Wheel warped or otherwise damaged (Chapter 6).
- [ ] Wheel bearings damaged or worn (Chapter 6).

Brakes drag

- [ ] Master cylinder piston seized. Caused by wear or damage to piston or cylinder bore (Chapter 6).
- [ ] Lever balky or stuck. Check pivot and lubricate (Chapter 6).
- [ ] Brake caliper binds. Caused by inadequate lubrication or damage to caliper sliders (Chapter 6).
- [ ] Brake caliper piston seized in bore. Caused by wear or ingestion of dirt past deteriorated seal (Chapter 6).
- [ ] Brake pad damaged. Pad material separated from backing plate. Usually caused by faulty manufacturing process or from contact with chemicals. Replace pads (Chapter 6).
- [ ] Pads improperly installed (Chapter 6).

14 Electrical problems

Battery dead or weak

☐ Battery faulty. Caused by sulphated plates which are shorted through sedimentation. Also, broken battery terminal making only occasional contact (Chapter 8).

☐ Battery cables making poor contact (Chapter 1).

☐ Load excessive. Caused by addition of high wattage lights or other electrical accessories.

☐ Ignition (main) switch defective. Switch either grounds (earths) internally or fails to shut off system. Replace the switch (Chapter 8).

☐ Regulator/rectifier defective (Chapter 8).

☐ Alternator stator coil open or shorted (Chapter 8).

☐ Wiring faulty. Wiring grounded (earthed) or connections loose in ignition, charging or lighting circuits (Chapter 8).

Battery overcharged

☐ Regulator/rectifier defective. Overcharging is noticed when battery gets excessively warm (Chapter 8).

☐ Battery defective. Replace battery with a new one (Chapter 8).

☐ Battery amperage too low, wrong type or size. Install manufacturer's specified amp-hour battery to handle charging load (Chapter 8).

Checking engine compression

● Low compression will result in exhaust smoke, heavy oil consumption, poor starting and poor performance. A compression test will provide useful information about an engine's condition and if performed regularly, can give warning of trouble before any other symptoms become apparent.

● A compression gauge will be required, along with an adapter to suit the spark plug hole thread size. Note that the screw-in type gauge/adapter set up is preferable to the rubber cone type.

● Before carrying out the test, first check the valve clearances as described in Chapter 1.

1 Run the engine until it reaches normal operating temperature, then stop it and remove the spark plug(s), taking care not to scald your hands on the hot components.

2 Install the gauge adapter and compression gauge in No. 1 cylinder spark plug hole **(see Illustration 1)**.

Screw the compression gauge adapter into the spark plug hole, then screw the gauge into the adapter

3 On kickstart-equipped motorcycles, make sure the ignition switch is OFF, then open the throttle fully and kick the engine over a couple of times until the gauge reading stabilises.

4 On motorcycles with electric start only, the procedure will differ depending on the nature of the ignition system. Flick the engine kill switch (engine stop switch) to OFF and turn the ignition switch ON; open the throttle fully and crank the engine over on the starter motor for a couple of revolutions until the gauge reading stabilises. If the starter will not operate with the kill switch OFF, turn the ignition switch OFF and refer to the next paragraph.

5 Install the spark plugs back into their suppressor caps and arrange the plug electrodes so that their metal bodies are earthed (grounded) against the cylinder head; this is essential to prevent damage to the ignition system as the engine is spun over **(see illustration 2)**. Position the plugs well

All spark plugs must be earthed (grounded) against the cylinder head

away from the plug holes otherwise there is a risk of atomised fuel escaping from the combustion chambers and igniting. As a safety precaution, cover the top of the valve cover with rag. Now turn the ignition switch ON and kill switch ON, open the throttle fully and crank the engine over on the starter motor for a couple of revolutions until the gauge reading stabilises.

6 After one or two revolutions the pressure should build up to a maximum figure and then stabilise. Take a note of this reading and on multi-cylinder engines repeat the test on the remaining cylinders.

7 The correct pressures are given in Chapter 1 Specifications. If the results fall within the specified range and on multi-cylinder engines all are relatively equal, the engine is in good condition. If there is a marked difference between the readings, or if the readings are lower than specified, inspection of the top-end components will be required.

8 Low compression pressure may be due to worn cylinder bores, pistons or rings, failure of the cylinder head gasket, worn valve seals, or poor valve seating.

9 To distinguish between cylinder/piston wear and valve leakage, pour a small quantity of oil into the bore to temporarily seal the piston rings, then repeat the compression tests **(see illustration 3)**. If the readings show

Bores can be temporarily sealed with a squirt of motor oil

a noticeable increase in pressure this confirms that the cylinder bore, piston, or rings are worn. If, however, no change is indicated, the cylinder head gasket or valves should be examined.

10 High compression pressure indicates excessive carbon build-up in the combustion chamber and on the piston crown. If this is the case the cylinder head should be removed and the deposits removed. Note that excessive carbon build-up is less likely with the used on modern fuels.

Checking battery open-circuit voltage

 Warning: The gases produced by the battery are explosive - never smoke or create any sparks in the vicinity of the battery. Never allow the electrolyte to contact your skin or clothing - if it does, wash it off and seek immediate medical attention.

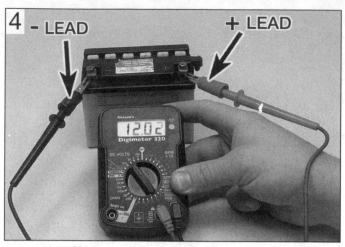

Measuring open-circuit battery voltage

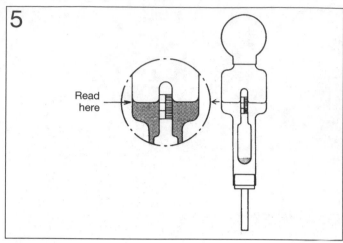

Float-type hydrometer for measuring battery specific gravity

● Before any electrical fault is investigated the battery should be checked.

● You'll need a dc voltmeter or multimeter to check battery voltage. Check that the leads are inserted in the correct terminals on the meter, red lead to positive (+ve), black lead to negative (-ve). Incorrect connections can damage the meter.

● A sound fully-charged 12 volt battery should produce between 12.3 and 12.6 volts across its terminals (12.8 volts for a maintenance-free battery). On machines with a 6 volt battery, voltage should be between 6.1 and 6.3 volts.

1 Set a multimeter to the 0 to 20 volts dc range and connect its probes across the battery terminals. Connect the meter's positive (+ve) probe, usually red, to the battery positive (+ve) terminal, followed by the meter's negative (-ve) probe, usually black, to the battery negative terminal (-ve) **(see illustration 4)**.

2 If battery voltage is low (below 10 volts on a 12 volt battery or below 4 volts on a six volt battery), charge the battery and test the voltage again. If the battery repeatedly goes flat, investigate the motorcycle's charging system.

Checking battery specific gravity (SG)

 Warning: The gases produced by the battery are explosive - never smoke or create any sparks in the vicinity of the battery. Never allow the electrolyte to contact your skin or clothing - if it does, wash it off and seek immediate medical attention.

● The specific gravity check gives an indication of a battery's state of charge.

● A hydrometer is used for measuring specific gravity. Make sure you purchase one

which has a small enough hose to insert in the aperture of a motorcycle battery.

● Specific gravity is simply a measure of the electrolyte's density compared with that of water. Water has an SG of 1.000 and fully-charged battery electrolyte is about 26% heavier, at 1.260.

● Specific gravity checks are not possible on maintenance-free batteries. Testing the open-circuit voltage is the only means of determining their state of charge.

1 To measure SG, remove the battery from the motorcycle and remove the first cell cap. Draw

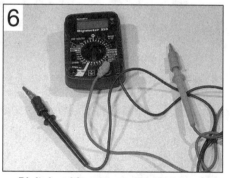

Digital multimeter can be used for all electrical tests

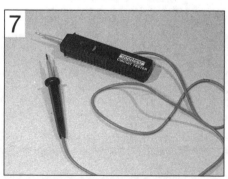

Battery-powered continuity tester

some electrolyte into the hydrometer and note the reading **(see illustration 5)**. Return the electrolyte to the cell and install the cap.

2 The reading should be in the region of 1.260 to 1.280. If SG is below 1.200 the battery needs charging. Note that SG will vary with temperature; it should be measured at 20°C (68°F). Add 0.007 to the reading for every 10°C above 20°C, and subtract 0.007 from the reading for every 10°C below 20°C. Add 0.004 to the reading for every 10°F above 68°F, and subtract 0.004 from the reading for every 10°F below 68°F.

3 When the check is complete, rinse the hydrometer thoroughly with clean water.

Checking for continuity

● The term continuity describes the uninterrupted flow of electricity through an electrical circuit. A continuity check will determine whether an **open-circuit** situation exists.

● Continuity can be checked with an ohmmeter, multimeter, continuity tester or battery and bulb test circuit **(see illustrations 6, 7 and 8)**.

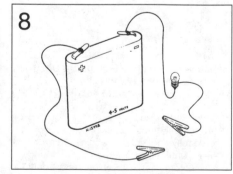

Battery and bulb test circuit

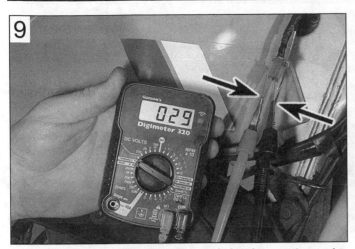

Continuity check of front brake light switch using a meter - note split pins used to access connector terminals

Continuity check of rear brake light switch using a continuity tester

● All of these instruments are self-powered by a battery, therefore the checks are made with the ignition OFF.

● As a safety precaution, always disconnect the battery negative (-ve) lead before making checks, particularly if ignition switch checks are being made.

● If using a meter, select the appropriate ohms scale and check that the meter reads infinity (∞). Touch the meter probes together and check that meter reads zero; where necessary adjust the meter so that it reads zero.

● After using a meter, always switch it OFF to conserve its battery.

Switch checks

1 If a switch is at fault, trace its wiring up to the wiring connectors. Separate the wire connectors and inspect them for security and condition. A build-up of dirt or corrosion here will most likely be the cause of the problem - clean up and apply a water dispersant such as WD40.

2 If using a test meter, set the meter to the ohms x 10 scale and connect its probes across the wires from the switch (see illustration 9). Simple ON/OFF type switches, such as brake light switches, only have two

wires whereas combination switches, like the ignition switch, have many internal links. Study the wiring diagram to ensure that you are connecting across the correct pair of wires. Continuity (low or no measurable resistance - 0 ohms) should be indicated with the switch ON and no continuity (high resistance) with it OFF.

3 Note that the polarity of the test probes doesn't matter for continuity checks, although care should be taken to follow specific test procedures if a diode or solid-state component is being checked.

4 A continuity tester or battery and bulb circuit can be used in the same way. Connect its probes as described above (see illustration 10). The light should come on to indicate continuity in the ON switch position, but should extinguish in the OFF position.

Wiring checks

● Many electrical faults are caused by damaged wiring, often due to incorrect routing or chaffing on frame components.
● Loose, wet or corroded wire connectors can also be the cause of electrical problems, especially in exposed locations.

1 A continuity check can be made on a single length of wire by disconnecting it at each end

and connecting a meter or continuity tester across both ends of the wire (see illustration 11).

2 Continuity (low or no resistance - 0 ohms) should be indicated if the wire is good. If no continuity (high resistance) is shown, suspect a broken wire.

Checking for voltage

● A voltage check can determine whether current is reaching a component.
● Voltage can be checked with a dc voltmeter, multimeter set on the dc volts scale, test light or buzzer (see illustrations 12 and 13). A meter has the advantage of being able to measure actual voltage.
● When using a meter, check that its leads are inserted in the correct terminals on the meter, red to positive (+ve), black to negative (-ve). Incorrect connections can damage the meter.
● A voltmeter (or multimeter set to the dc volts scale) should always be connected in parallel (across the load). Connecting it in series will destroy the meter.
● Voltage checks are made with the ignition ON.

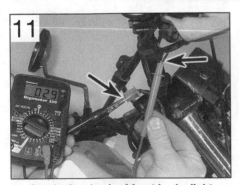

Continuity check of front brake light switch sub-harness

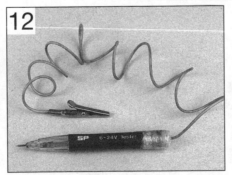

A simple test light can be used for voltage checks

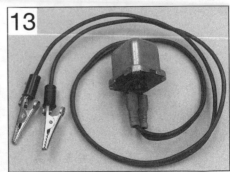

A buzzer is useful for voltage checks

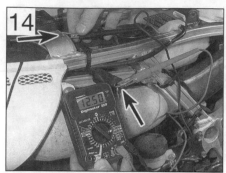

Checking for voltage at the rear brake light power supply wire using a meter . . .

1 First identify the relevant wiring circuit by referring to the wiring diagram at the end of this manual. If other electrical components share the same power supply (ie are fed from the same fuse), take note whether they are working correctly - this is useful information in deciding where to start checking the circuit.

2 If using a meter, check first that the meter leads are plugged into the correct terminals on the meter (see above). Set the meter to the dc volts function, at a range suitable for the battery voltage. Connect the meter red probe (+ve) to the power supply wire and the black probe to a good metal earth (ground) on the motorcycle's frame or directly to the battery negative (-ve) terminal **(see illustration 14)**. Battery voltage should be shown on the meter

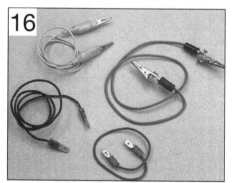

A selection of jumper wires for making earth (ground) checks

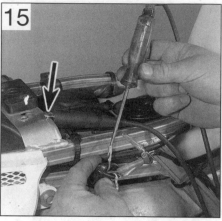

. . . or a test light - note the earth connection to the frame (arrow)

with the ignition switched ON.

3 If using a test light or buzzer, connect its positive (+ve) probe to the power supply terminal and its negative (-ve) probe to a good earth (ground) on the motorcycle's frame or directly to the battery negative (-ve) terminal **(see illustration 15)**. With the ignition ON, the test light should illuminate or the buzzer sound.

4 If no voltage is indicated, work back towards the fuse continuing to check for voltage. When you reach a point where there is voltage, you know the problem lies between that point and your last check point.

Checking the earth (ground)

● Earth connections are made either directly to the engine or frame (such as sensors, neutral switch etc. which only have a positive feed) or by a separate wire into the earth circuit of the wiring harness. Alternatively a short earth wire is sometimes run directly from the component to the motorcycle's frame.

● Corrosion is often the cause of a poor earth connection.

● If total failure is experienced, check the security of the main earth lead from the negative (-ve) terminal of the battery and also the main earth (ground) point on the wiring harness. If corroded, dismantle the connection and clean all surfaces back to bare metal.

1 To check the earth on a component, use an insulated jumper wire to temporarily bypass its earth connection **(see illustration 16)**. Connect one end of the jumper wire between the earth terminal or metal body of the component and the other end to the motorcycle's frame.

2 If the circuit works with the jumper wire installed, the original earth circuit is faulty. Check the wiring for open-circuits or poor connections. Clean up direct earth connections, removing all traces of corrosion and remake the joint. Apply petroleum jelly to the joint to prevent future corrosion.

Tracing a short-circuit

● A short-circuit occurs where current shorts to earth (ground) bypassing the circuit components. This usually results in a blown fuse.

● A short-circuit is most likely to occur where the insulation has worn through due to wiring chafing on a component, allowing a direct path to earth (ground) on the frame.

1 Remove any bodypanels necessary to access the circuit wiring.

2 Check that all electrical switches in the circuit are OFF, then remove the circuit fuse and connect a test light, buzzer or voltmeter (set to the dc scale) across the fuse terminals. No voltage should be shown.

3 Move the wiring from side to side whilst observing the test light or meter. When the test light comes on, buzzer sounds or meter shows voltage, you have found the cause of the short. It will usually shown up as damaged or burned insulation.

4 Note that the same test can be performed on each component in the circuit, even the switch.

A

ABS (Anti-lock braking system) A system, usually electronically controlled, that senses incipient wheel lockup during braking and relieves hydraulic pressure at wheel which is about to skid.

Aftermarket Components suitable for the motorcycle, but not produced by the motorcycle manufacturer.

Allen key A hexagonal wrench which fits into a recessed hexagonal hole.

Alternating current (ac) Current produced by an alternator. Requires converting to direct current by a rectifier for charging purposes.

Alternator Converts mechanical energy from the engine into electrical energy to charge the battery and power the electrical system.

Ampere (amp) A unit of measurement for the flow of electrical current. Current = Volts ÷ Ohms.

Ampere-hour (Ah) Measure of battery capacity.

Angle-tightening A torque expressed in degrees. Often follows a conventional tightening torque for cylinder head or main bearing fasteners **(see illustration)**.

Angle-tightening cylinder head bolts

Antifreeze A substance (usually ethylene glycol) mixed with water, and added to the cooling system, to prevent freezing of the coolant In winter. Antifreeze also contains chemicals to inhibit corrosion and the formation of rust and other deposits that would tend to clog the radiator and coolant passages and reduce cooling efficiency.

Anti-dive System attached to the fork lower leg (slider) to prevent fork dive when braking hard.

Anti-seize compound A coating that reduces the risk of seizing on fasteners that are subjected to high temperatures, such as exhaust clamp bolts and nuts.

API American Petroleum Institute. A quality standard for 4-stroke motor oils.

Asbestos A natural fibrous mineral with great heat resistance, commonly used in the composition of brake friction materials. Asbestos is a health hazard and the dust created by brake systems should never be inhaled or ingested.

ATF Automatic Transmission Fluid. Often used in front forks.

ATU Automatic Timing Unit. Mechanical device for advancing the ignition timing on early engines.

ATV All Terrain Vehicle. Often called a Quad.

Axial play Side-to-side movement.

Axle A shaft on which a wheel revolves. Also known as a spindle.

B

Backlash The amount of movement between meshed components when one component is held still. Usually applies to gear teeth.

Ball bearing A bearing consisting of a hardened inner and outer race with hardened steel balls between the two races.

Bearings Used between two working surfaces to prevent wear of the components and a build-up of heat. Four types of bearing are commonly used on motorcycles: plain shell bearings, ball bearings, tapered roller bearings and needle roller bearings.

Bevel gears Used to turn the drive through 90°. Typical applications are shaft final drive and camshaft drive **(see illustration)**.

Bevel gears are used to turn the drive through 90°

BHP Brake Horsepower. The British measurement for engine power output. Power output is now usually expressed in kilowatts (kW).

Bias-belted tyre Similar construction to radial tyre, but with outer belt running at an angle to the wheel rim.

Big-end bearing The bearing in the end of the connecting rod that's attached to the crankshaft.

Bleeding The process of removing air from an hydraulic system via a bleed nipple or bleed screw.

Bottom-end A description of an engine's crankcase components and all components contained there-in.

BTDC Before Top Dead Centre in terms of piston position. Ignition timing is often expressed in terms of degrees or millimetres BTDC.

Bush A cylindrical metal or rubber component used between two moving parts.

Burr Rough edge left on a component after machining or as a result of excessive wear.

C

Cam chain The chain which takes drive from the crankshaft to the camshaft(s).

Canister The main component in an evaporative emission control system (California market only); contains activated charcoal granules to trap vapours from the fuel system rather than allowing them to vent to the atmosphere.

Castellated Resembling the parapets along the top of a castle wall. For example, a castellated wheel axle or spindle nut.

Catalytic converter A device in the exhaust system of some machines which converts certain pollutants in the exhaust gases into less harmful substances.

Charging system Description of the components which charge the battery, ie the alternator, rectifer and regulator.

Circlip A ring-shaped clip used to prevent endwise movement of cylindrical parts and shafts. An internal circlip is installed in a groove in a housing; an external circlip fits into a groove on the outside of a cylindrical piece such as a shaft. Also known as a snap-ring.

Clearance The amount of space between two parts. For example, between a piston and a cylinder, between a bearing and a journal, etc.

Coil spring A spiral of elastic steel found in various sizes throughout a vehicle, for example as a springing medium in the suspension and in the valve train.

Compression Reduction in volume, and increase in pressure and temperature, of a gas, caused by squeezing it into a smaller space.

Compression damping Controls the speed the suspension compresses when hitting a bump.

Compression ratio The relationship between cylinder volume when the piston is at top dead centre and cylinder volume when the piston is at bottom dead centre.

Continuity The uninterrupted path in the flow of electricity. Little or no measurable resistance.

Continuity tester Self-powered bleeper or test light which indicates continuity.

Cp Candlepower. Bulb rating commonly found on US motorcycles.

Crossply tyre Tyre plies arranged in a criss-cross pattern. Usually four or six plies used, hence 4PR or 6PR in tyre size codes.

Cush drive Rubber damper segments fitted between the rear wheel and final drive sprocket to absorb transmission shocks **(see illustration)**.

Cush drive rubbers dampen out transmission shocks

D

Degree disc Calibrated disc for measuring piston position. Expressed in degrees.

Dial gauge Clock-type gauge with adapters for measuring runout and piston position. Expressed in mm or inches.

Diaphragm The rubber membrane in a master cylinder or carburettor which seals the upper chamber.

Diaphragm spring A single sprung plate often used in clutches.

Direct current (dc) Current produced by a dc generator.

Decarbonisation The process of removing carbon deposits - typically from the combustion chamber, valves and exhaust port/system.

Detonation Destructive and damaging explosion of fuel/air mixture in combustion chamber instead of controlled burning.

Diode An electrical valve which only allows current to flow in one direction. Commonly used in rectifiers and starter interlock systems.

Disc valve (or rotary valve) A induction system used on some two-stroke engines.

Double-overhead camshaft (DOHC) An engine that uses two overhead camshafts, one for the intake valves and one for the exhaust valves.

Drivebelt A toothed belt used to transmit drive to the rear wheel on some motorcycles. A drivebelt has also been used to drive the camshafts. Drivebelts are usually made of Kevlar.

Driveshaft Any shaft used to transmit motion. Commonly used when referring to the final driveshaft on shaft drive motorcycles.

E

Earth return The return path of an electrical circuit, utilising the motorcycle's frame.

ECU (Electronic Control Unit) A computer which controls (for instance) an ignition system, or an anti-lock braking system.

EGO Exhaust Gas Oxygen sensor. Sometimes called a Lambda sensor.

Electrolyte The fluid in a lead-acid battery.

EMS (Engine Management System) A computer controlled system which manages the fuel injection and the ignition systems in an integrated fashion.

Endfloat The amount of lengthways movement between two parts. As applied to a crankshaft, the distance that the crankshaft can move side-to-side in the crankcase.

Endless chain A chain having no joining link. Common use for cam chains and final drive chains.

EP (Extreme Pressure) Oil type used in locations where high loads are applied, such as between gear teeth.

Evaporative emission control system Describes a charcoal filled canister which stores fuel vapours from the tank rather than allowing them to vent to the atmosphere. Usually only fitted to California models and referred to as an EVAP system.

Expansion chamber Section of two-stroke engine exhaust system so designed to improve engine efficiency and boost power.

F

Feeler blade or gauge A thin strip or blade of hardened steel, ground to an exact thickness, used to check or measure clearances between parts.

Final drive Description of the drive from the transmission to the rear wheel. Usually by chain or shaft, but sometimes by belt.

Firing order The order in which the engine cylinders fire, or deliver their power strokes, beginning with the number one cylinder.

Flooding Term used to describe a high fuel level in the carburettor float chambers, leading to fuel overflow. Also refers to excess fuel in the combustion chamber due to incorrect starting technique.

Free length The no-load state of a component when measured. Clutch, valve and fork spring lengths are measured at rest, without any preload.

Freeplay The amount of travel before any action takes place. The looseness in a linkage, or an assembly of parts, between the initial application of force and actual movement. For example, the distance the rear brake pedal moves before the rear brake is actuated.

Fuel injection The fuel/air mixture is metered electronically and directed into the engine intake ports (indirect injection) or into the cylinders (direct injection). Sensors supply information on engine speed and conditions.

Fuel/air mixture The charge of fuel and air going into the engine. See **Stoichiometric ratio**.

Fuse An electrical device which protects a circuit against accidental overload. The typical fuse contains a soft piece of metal which is calibrated to melt at a predetermined current flow (expressed as amps) and break the circuit.

G

Gap The distance the spark must travel in jumping from the centre electrode to the side electrode in a spark plug. Also refers to the distance between the ignition rotor and the pickup coil in an electronic ignition system.

Gasket Any thin, soft material - usually cork, cardboard, asbestos or soft metal - installed between two metal surfaces to ensure a good seal. For instance, the cylinder head gasket seals the joint between the block and the cylinder head.

Gauge An instrument panel display used to monitor engine conditions. A gauge with a movable pointer on a dial or a fixed scale is an analogue gauge. A gauge with a numerical readout is called a digital gauge.

Gear ratios The drive ratio of a pair of gears in a gearbox, calculated on their number of teeth.

Glaze-busting see **Honing**

Grinding Process for renovating the valve face and valve seat contact area in the cylinder head.

Gudgeon pin The shaft which connects the connecting rod small-end with the piston. Often called a piston pin or wrist pin.

H

Helical gears Gear teeth are slightly curved and produce less gear noise that straight-cut gears. Often used for primary drives.

Installing a Helicoil thread insert in a cylinder head

Helicoil A thread insert repair system. Commonly used as a repair for stripped spark plug threads **(see illustration)**.

Honing A process used to break down the glaze on a cylinder bore (also called glaze-busting). Can also be carried out to roughen a rebored cylinder to aid ring bedding-in.

HT (High Tension) Description of the electrical circuit from the secondary winding of the ignition coil to the spark plug.

Hydraulic A liquid filled system used to transmit pressure from one component to another. Common uses on motorcycles are brakes and clutches.

Hydrometer An instrument for measuring the specific gravity of a lead-acid battery.

Hygroscopic Water absorbing. In motorcycle applications, braking efficiency will be reduced if DOT 3 or 4 hydraulic fluid absorbs water from the air - care must be taken to keep new brake fluid in tightly sealed containers.

I

lbf ft Pounds-force feet. An imperial unit of torque. Sometimes written as ft-lbs.

lbf in Pound-force inch. An imperial unit of torque, applied to components where a very low torque is required. Sometimes written as in-lbs.

IC Abbreviation for Integrated Circuit.

Ignition advance Means of increasing the timing of the spark at higher engine speeds. Done by mechanical means (ATU) on early engines or electronically by the ignition control unit on later engines.

Ignition timing The moment at which the spark plug fires, expressed in the number of crankshaft degrees before the piston reaches the top of its stroke, or in the number of millimetres before the piston reaches the top of its stroke.

Infinity (∞) Description of an open-circuit electrical state, where no continuity exists.

Inverted forks (upside down forks) The sliders or lower legs are held in the yokes and the fork tubes or stanchions are connected to the wheel axle (spindle). Less unsprung weight and stiffer construction than conventional forks.

J

JASO Quality standard for 2-stroke oils.

Joule The unit of electrical energy.

Journal The bearing surface of a shaft.

K

Kickstart Mechanical means of turning the engine over for starting purposes. Only usually fitted to mopeds, small capacity motorcycles and off-road motorcycles.

Kill switch Handebar-mounted switch for emergency ignition cut-out. Cuts the ignition circuit on all models, and additionally prevent starter motor operation on others.

km Symbol for kilometre.

kmh Abbreviation for kilometres per hour.

L

Lambda (λ) sensor A sensor fitted in the exhaust system to measure the exhaust gas oxygen content (excess air factor).

Lapping see **Grinding**.
LCD Abbreviation for Liquid Crystal Display.
LED Abbreviation for Light Emitting Diode.
Liner A steel cylinder liner inserted in a aluminium alloy cylinder block.
Locknut A nut used to lock an adjustment nut, or other threaded component, in place.
Lockstops The lugs on the lower triple clamp (yoke) which abut those on the frame, preventing handlebar-to-fuel tank contact.
Lockwasher A form of washer designed to prevent an attaching nut from working loose.
LT Low Tension Description of the electrical circuit from the power supply to the primary winding of the ignition coil.

M

Main bearings The bearings between the crankshaft and crankcase.
Maintenance-free (MF) battery A sealed battery which cannot be topped up.
Manometer Mercury-filled calibrated tubes used to measure intake tract vacuum. Used to synchronise carburettors on multi-cylinder engines.
Micrometer A precision measuring instrument that measures component outside diameters **(see illustration)**.

Tappet shims are measured with a micrometer

MON (Motor Octane Number) A measure of a fuel's resistance to knock.
Monograde oil An oil with a single viscosity, eg SAE80W.
Monoshock A single suspension unit linking the swingarm or suspension linkage to the frame.
mph Abbreviation for miles per hour.
Multigrade oil Having a wide viscosity range (eg 10W40). The W stands for Winter, thus the viscosity ranges from SAE10 when cold to SAE40 when hot.
Multimeter An electrical test instrument with the capability to measure voltage, current and resistance. Some meters also incorporate a continuity tester and buzzer.

N

Needle roller bearing Inner race of caged needle rollers and hardened outer race. Examples of uncaged needle rollers can be found on some engines. Commonly used in rear suspension applications and in two-stroke engines.
Nm Newton metres.
NOx Oxides of Nitrogen. A common toxic pollutant emitted by petrol engines at higher temperatures.

O

Octane The measure of a fuel's resistance to knock.
OE (Original Equipment) Relates to components fitted to a motorcycle as standard or replacement parts supplied by the motorcycle manufacturer.
Ohm The unit of electrical resistance. Ohms = Volts ÷ Current.
Ohmmeter An instrument for measuring electrical resistance.
Oil cooler System for diverting engine oil outside of the engine to a radiator for cooling purposes.
Oil injection A system of two-stroke engine lubrication where oil is pump-fed to the engine in accordance with throttle position.
Open-circuit An electrical condition where there is a break in the flow of electricity - no continuity (high resistance).
O-ring A type of sealing ring made of a special rubber-like material; in use, the O-ring is compressed into a groove to provide the sealing action.
Oversize (OS) Term used for piston and ring size options fitted to a rebored cylinder.
Overhead cam (sohc) engine An engine with single camshaft located on top of the cylinder head.
Overhead valve (ohv) engine An engine with the valves located in the cylinder head, but with the camshaft located in the engine block or crankcase.
Oxygen sensor A device installed in the exhaust system which senses the oxygen content in the exhaust and converts this information into an electric current. Also called a Lambda sensor.

P

Plastigauge A thin strip of plastic thread, available in different sizes, used for measuring clearances. For example, a strip of Plastigauge is laid across a bearing journal. The parts are assembled and dismantled; the width of the crushed strip indicates the clearance between journal and bearing.
Polarity Either negative or positive earth (ground), determined by which battery lead is connected to the frame (earth return). Modern motorcycles are usually negative earth.
Pre-ignition A situation where the fuel/air mixture ignites before the spark plug fires. Often due to a hot spot in the combustion chamber caused by carbon build-up. Engine has a tendency to 'run-on'.
Pre-load (suspension) The amount a spring is compressed when in the unloaded state. Preload can be applied by gas, spacer or mechanical adjuster.
Premix The method of engine lubrication on older two-stroke engines. Engine oil is mixed with the petrol in the fuel tank in a specific ratio. The fuel/oil mix is sometimes referred to as "petroil".
Primary drive Description of the drive from the crankshaft to the clutch. Usually by gear or chain.
PS Pfedestärke - a German interpretation of BHP.
PSI Pounds-force per square inch. Imperial measurement of tyre pressure and cylinder pressure measurement.
PTFE Polytetrafluoroethylene. A low friction substance.

Pulse secondary air injection system A process of promoting the burning of excess fuel present in the exhaust gases by routing fresh air into the exhaust ports.

Q

Quartz halogen bulb Tungsten filament surrounded by a halogen gas. Typically used for the headlight **(see illustration)**.

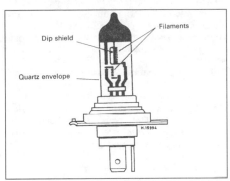

Quartz halogen headlight bulb construction

R

Rack-and-pinion A pinion gear on the end of a shaft that mates with a rack (think of a geared wheel opened up and laid flat). Sometimes used in clutch operating systems.
Radial play Up and down movement about a shaft.
Radial ply tyres Tyre plies run across the tyre (from bead to bead) and around the circumference of the tyre. Less resistant to tread distortion than other tyre types.
Radiator A liquid-to-air heat transfer device designed to reduce the temperature of the coolant in a liquid cooled engine.
Rake A feature of steering geometry - the angle of the steering head in relation to the vertical **(see illustration)**.

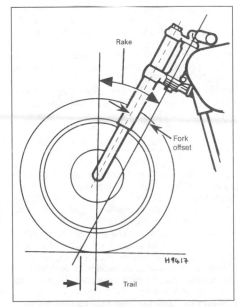

Steering geometry

Rebore Providing a new working surface to the cylinder bore by boring out the old surface. Necessitates the use of oversize piston and rings.

Rebound damping A means of controlling the oscillation of a suspension unit spring after it has been compressed. Resists the spring's natural tendency to bounce back after being compressed.

Rectifier Device for converting the ac output of an alternator into dc for battery charging.

Reed valve An induction system commonly used on two-stroke engines.

Regulator Device for maintaining the charging voltage from the generator or alternator within a specified range.

Relay A electrical device used to switch heavy current on and off by using a low current auxiliary circuit.

Resistance Measured in ohms. An electrical component's ability to pass electrical current.

RON (Research Octane Number) A measure of a fuel's resistance to knock.

rpm revolutions per minute.

Runout The amount of wobble (in-and-out movement) of a wheel or shaft as it's rotated. The amount a shaft rotates 'out-of-true'. The out-of-round condition of a rotating part.

S

SAE (Society of Automotive Engineers) A standard for the viscosity of a fluid.

Sealant A liquid or paste used to prevent leakage at a joint. Sometimes used in conjunction with a gasket.

Service limit Term for the point where a component is no longer useable and must be renewed.

Shaft drive A method of transmitting drive from the transmission to the rear wheel.

Shell bearings Plain bearings consisting of two shell halves. Most often used as big-end and main bearings in a four-stroke engine. Often called bearing inserts.

Shim Thin spacer, commonly used to adjust the clearance or relative positions between two parts. For example, shims inserted into or under tappets or followers to control valve clearances. Clearance is adjusted by changing the thickness of the shim.

Short-circuit An electrical condition where current shorts to earth (ground) bypassing the circuit components.

Skimming Process to correct warpage or repair a damaged surface, eg on brake discs or drums.

Slide-hammer A special puller that screws into or hooks onto a component such as a shaft or bearing; a heavy sliding handle on the shaft bottoms against the end of the shaft to knock the component free.

Small-end bearing The bearing in the upper end of the connecting rod at its joint with the gudgeon pin.

Spalling Damage to camshaft lobes or bearing journals shown as pitting of the working surface.

Specific gravity (SG) The state of charge of the electrolyte in a lead-acid battery. A measure of the electrolyte's density compared with water.

Straight-cut gears Common type gear used on gearbox shafts and for oil pump and water pump drives.

Stanchion The inner sliding part of the front forks, held by the yokes. Often called a fork tube.

Stoichiometric ratio The optimum chemical air/fuel ratio for a petrol engine, said to be 14.7 parts of air to 1 part of fuel.

Sulphuric acid The liquid (electrolyte) used in a lead-acid battery. Poisonous and extremely corrosive.

Surface grinding (lapping) Process to correct a warped gasket face, commonly used on cylinder heads.

T

Tapered-roller bearing Tapered inner race of caged needle rollers and separate tapered outer race. Examples of taper roller bearings can be found on steering heads.

Tappet A cylindrical component which transmits motion from the cam to the valve stem, either directly or via a pushrod and rocker arm. Also called a cam follower.

TCS Traction Control System. An electronically-controlled system which senses wheel spin and reduces engine speed accordingly.

TDC Top Dead Centre denotes that the piston is at its highest point in the cylinder.

Thread-locking compound Solution applied to fastener threads to prevent slackening. Select type to suit application.

Thrust washer A washer positioned between two moving components on a shaft. For example, between gear pinions on gearshaft.

Timing chain See **Cam Chain.**

Timing light Stroboscopic lamp for carrying out ignition timing checks with the engine running.

Top-end A description of an engine's cylinder block, head and valve gear components.

Torque Turning or twisting force about a shaft.

Torque setting A prescribed tightness specified by the motorcycle manufacturer to ensure that the bolt or nut is secured correctly. Undertightening can result in the bolt or nut coming loose or a surface not being sealed. Overtightening can result in stripped threads, distortion or damage to the component being retained.

Torx key A six-point wrench.

Tracer A stripe of a second colour applied to a wire insulator to distinguish that wire from another one with the same colour insulator. For example, Br/W is often used to denote a brown insulator with a white tracer.

Trail A feature of steering geometry. Distance from the steering head axis to the tyre's central contact point.

Triple clamps The cast components which extend from the steering head and support the fork stanchions or tubes. Often called fork yokes.

Turbocharger A centrifugal device, driven by exhaust gases, that pressurises the intake air. Normally used to increase the power output from a given engine displacement.

TWI Abbreviation for Tyre Wear Indicator. Indicates the location of the tread depth indicator bars on tyres.

U

Universal joint or U-joint (UJ) A double-pivoted connection for transmitting power from a driving to a driven shaft through an angle. Typically found in shaft drive assemblies.

Unsprung weight Anything not supported by the bike's suspension (ie the wheel, tyres, brakes, final drive and bottom (moving) part of the suspension).

V

Vacuum gauges Clock-type gauges for measuring intake tract vacuum. Used for carburettor synchronisation on multi-cylinder engines.

Valve A device through which the flow of liquid, gas or vacuum may be stopped, started or regulated by a moveable part that opens, shuts or partially obstructs one or more ports or passageways. The intake and exhaust valves in the cylinder head are of the poppet type.

Valve clearance The clearance between the valve tip (the end of the valve stem) and the rocker arm or tappet/follower. The valve clearance is measured when the valve is closed. The correct clearance is important - if too small the valve won't close fully and will burn out, whereas if too large noisy operation will result.

Valve lift The amount a valve is lifted off its seat by the camshaft lobe.

Valve timing The exact setting for the opening and closing of the valves in relation to piston position.

Vernier caliper A precision measuring instrument that measures inside and outside dimensions. Not quite as accurate as a micrometer, but more convenient.

VIN Vehicle Identification Number. Term for the bike's engine and frame numbers.

Viscosity The thickness of a liquid or its resistance to flow.

Volt A unit for expressing electrical "pressure" in a circuit. Volts = current x ohms.

W

Water pump A mechanically-driven device for moving coolant around the engine.

Watt A unit for expressing electrical power. Watts = volts x current.

Wear limit see **Service limit**

Wet liner A liquid-cooled engine design where the pistons run in liners which are directly surrounded by coolant **(see illustration)**.

Wet liner arrangement

Wheelbase Distance from the centre of the front wheel to the centre of the rear wheel.

Wiring harness or loom Describes the electrical wires running the length of the motorcycle and enclosed in tape or plastic sheathing. Wiring coming off the main harness is usually referred to as a sub harness.

Woodruff key A key of semi-circular or square section used to locate a gear to a shaft. Often used to locate the alternator rotor on the crankshaft.

Wrist pin Another name for gudgeon or piston pin.

Note: *References throughout this index are in the form – "Chapter number" • "page number"*

Haynes Motorcycle Manuals – The Complete List

Title	Book No
BMW	
BMW 2-valve Twins (70 - 96)	0249
BMW K100 & 75 2-valve Models (83 - 96)	1373
BMW R850 & R1100 4-valve Twins (93 - 97)	3466
BSA	
BSA Bantam (48 - 71)	0117
BSA Unit Singles (58 - 72)	0127
BSA Pre-unit Singles (54 - 61)	0326
BSA A7 & A10 Twins (47 - 62)	0121
BSA A50 & A65 Twins (62 - 73)	0155
DUCATI	
Ducati MK III & Desmo Singles (69 - 76)	0445
Ducati 600, 750 & 900 2-valve V-Twins (91 - 96)	3290
Ducati 748, 916 & 996 4-valve V-Twins (94 - 01)	3756
HARLEY-DAVIDSON	
Harley-Davidson Sportsters (70 - 01)	0702
Harley-Davidson Big Twins (70 - 99)	0703
Harley-Davidson Twin Cam 88 (99 - 03)	2478
HONDA	
Honda NB, ND, NP & NS50 Melody (81 - 85)	◇ 0622
Honda NE/NB50 Vision & SA50 Vision Met-in (85 - 95)	◇ 1278
Honda MB, MBX, MT & MTX50 (80 - 93)	0731
Honda C50, C70 & C90 (67 - 99)	0324
Honda XR80R & XR100R (85 - 96)	2218
Honda XL/XR 80, 100, 125, 185 & 200 2-valve Models (78 - 87)	0566
Honda H100 & H100S Singles (80 - 92)	◇ 0734
Honda CB/CD125T & CM125C Twins (77 - 88)	◇ 0571
Honda CG125 (76 - 00)	◇ 0433
Honda NS125 (86 - 93)	◇ 3056
Honda MBX/MTX125 & MTX200 (83 - 93)	◇ 1132
Honda CD/CM185 200T & CM250C 2-valve Twins (77 - 85)	0572
Honda XL/XR 250 & 500 (78 - 84)	0567
Honda XR250L, XR250R & XR400R (86 - 03)	2219
Honda CB250 & CB400N Super Dreams (78 - 84)	◇ 0540
Honda CR Motocross Bikes (86 - 01)	2222
Honda CBR400RR Fours (88 - 99)	3552
Honda VFR400 (NC30) & RVF400 (NC35) V-Fours (89 - 98)	3496
Honda CB500 (93 - 01)	3753
Honda CB400 & CB550 Fours (73 - 77)	0262
Honda CX/GL500 & 650 V-Twins (78 - 86)	0442
Honda CBX550 Four (82 - 86)	◇ 0940
Honda XL600R & XR600R (83 - 00)	2183
Honda XL600/650V Transalp & XRV750 Africa Twin (87 - 02)	3919
Honda CBR600F1 & 1000F Fours (87 - 96)	1730
Honda CBR600F2 & F3 Fours (91 - 98)	2070
Honda CBR600F4 (99 - 02)	3911
Honda CB600F Hornet (98 - 02)	3915
Honda CB650 sohc Fours (78 - 84)	0665
Honda NTV600 Revere, NTV650 & NT650V Deauville (88 - 01)	3243
Honda Shadow VT600 & 750 (USA) (88 - 00)	2312
Honda CB750 sohc Four (69 - 79)	0131
Honda V45/65 Sabre & Magna (82 - 88)	0820
Honda VFR750 & 700 V-Fours (86 - 97)	2101
Honda VFR800 V-Fours (97 - 01)	3703
Honda VTR1000 (FireStorm, Super Hawk) & XL1000V (Varadero) (97 - 00)	3744
Honda CB750 & CB900 dohc Fours (78 - 84)	0535
Honda CBR900RR FireBlade (92 - 99)	2161
Honda CBR900RR FireBlade (00 - 03)	4060
Honda CBR1100XX Super Blackbird (97 - 02)	3901
Honda ST1100 Pan European V-Fours (90 - 01)	3384
Honda Shadow VT1100 (USA) (85 - 98)	2313
Honda GL1000 Gold Wing (75 - 79)	0309
Honda GL1100 Gold Wing (79 - 81)	0669
Honda Gold Wing 1200 (USA) (84 - 87)	2199
Honda Gold Wing 1500 (USA) (88 - 00)	2225

Title	Book No
KAWASAKI	
Kawasaki AE/AR 50 & 80 (81 - 95)	1007
Kawasaki KC, KE & KH100 (75 - 99)	1371
Kawasaki KMX125 & 200 (86 - 02)	◇ 3046
Kawasaki 250, 350 & 400 Triples (72 - 79)	0134
Kawasaki 400 & 440 Twins (74 - 81)	0281
Kawasaki 400, 500 & 550 Fours (79 - 91)	0910
Kawasaki EN450 & 500 Twins (Ltd/Vulcan) (85 - 93)	2053
Kawasaki EX & ER500 (GPZ500S & ER-5) Twins (87 - 99)	2052
Kawasaki ZX600 (Ninja ZX-6, ZZ-R600) Fours (90 - 00)	2146
Kawasaki ZX-6R Ninja Fours (95 - 02)	3541
Kawasaki ZX600 (GPZ600R, GPX600R, Ninja 600R & RX) & ZX750 (GPX750R, Ninja 750R) Fours (85 - 97)	1780
Kawasaki 650 Four (76 - 78)	0373
Kawasaki Vulcan 700/750 & 800 (85 - 01)	2457
Kawasaki 750 Air-cooled Fours (80 - 91)	0574
Kawasaki ZR550 & 750 Zephyr Fours (90 - 97)	3382
Kawasaki ZX750 (Ninja ZX-7 & ZXR750) Fours (89 - 96)	2054
Kawasaki Ninja ZX-7R & ZX-9R (ZX750P, ZX900B/C/D/E) (94 - 00)	3721
Kawasaki 900 & 1000 Fours (73 - 77)	0222
Kawasaki ZX900, 1000 & 1100 Liquid-cooled Fours (83 - 97)	1681
MOTO GUZZI	
Moto Guzzi 750, 850 & 1000 V-Twins (74 - 78)	0339
MZ	
MZ ETZ Models (81 - 95)	◇ 1680
NORTON	
Norton 500, 600, 650 & 750 Twins (57 - 70)	0187
Norton Commando (68 - 77)	0125
PEUGEOT	
Peugeot Speedfight, Trekker & Vivacity Scooters (96 - 02)	3920
PIAGGIO	
Piaggio (Vespa) Scooters (91 - 98)	3492
SUZUKI	
Suzuki GT, ZR & TS50 (77 - 90)	◇ 0799
Suzuki TS50X (84 - 00)	◇ 1599
Suzuki 100, 125, 185 & 250 Air-cooled Trail bikes (79 - 89)	0797
Suzuki GP100 & 125 Singles (78 - 93)	◇ 0576
Suzuki GS, GN, GZ & DR125 Singles (82 - 99)	◇ 0888
Suzuki 250 & 350 Twins (68 - 78)	0120
Suzuki GT250X7, GT200X5 & SB200 Twins (78 - 83)	◇ 0469
Suzuki GS/GSX250, 400 & 450 Twins (79 - 85)	0736
Suzuki GS500 Twin (89 - 02)	3238
Suzuki GS550 (77 - 82) & GS750 Fours (76 - 79)	0363
Suzuki GS/GSX550 4-valve Fours (83 - 88)	1133
Suzuki SV650 (99 - 02)	3912
Suzuki GSX-R600 & 750 (96 - 00)	3553
Suzuki GSX-R600 (01 - 02), GSX-R750 (00 - 02) & GSX-R1000 (01 - 02)	3986
Suzuki GSF600 & 1200 Bandit Fours (95 - 01)	3367
Suzuki GS850 Fours (78 - 88)	0536
Suzuki GS1000 Four (77 - 79)	0484
Suzuki GSX-R750, GSX-R1100 (85 - 92), GSX600F, GSX750F, GSX1100F (Katana) Fours (88 - 96)	2055
Suzuki GSX600/750F & GSX750 (98 - 02)	3987
Suzuki GS/GSX1000, 1100 & 1150 4-valve Fours (79 - 88)	0737
Suzuki TL1000S/R & DL1000	4083
TRIUMPH	
Triumph Tiger Cub & Terrier (52 - 68)	0414
Triumph 350 & 500 Unit Twins (58 - 73)	0137
Triumph Pre-Unit Twins (47 - 62)	0251
Triumph 650 & 750 2-valve Unit Twins (63 - 83)	0122
Triumph Trident & BSA Rocket 3 (69 - 75)	0136
Triumph Fuel Injected Triples (97 - 00)	3755
Triumph Triples & Fours (carburettor engines) (91 - 99)	2162
VESPA	
Vespa P/PX125, 150 & 200 Scooters (78 - 95)	0707
Vespa Scooters (59 - 78)	0126

Title	Book No
YAMAHA	
Yamaha DT50 & 80 Trail Bikes (78 - 95)	◇ 0800
Yamaha T50 & 80 Townmate (83 - 95)	◇ 1247
Yamaha YB100 Singles (73 - 91)	◇ 0474
Yamaha RS/RXS100 & 125 Singles (74 - 95)	0331
Yamaha RD & DT125LC (82 - 87)	0887
Yamaha TZR125 (87 - 93) & DT125R (88 - 02)	1655
Yamaha TY50, 80, 125 & 175 (74 - 84)	0464
Yamaha XT & SR125 (82 - 02)	1021
Yamaha Trail Bikes (81 - 00)	2350
Yamaha 250 & 350 Twins (70 - 79)	0040
Yamaha XS250, 360 & 400 sohc Twins (75 - 84)	0378
Yamaha RD250 & 350LC Twins (80 - 82)	0803
Yamaha RD350 YPVS Twins (83 - 95)	1158
Yamaha RD400 Twin (75 - 79)	0333
Yamaha XT, TT & SR500 Singles (75 - 83)	0342
Yamaha XZ550 Vision V-Twins (82 - 85)	0821
Yamaha FJ, FZ, XJ & YX600 Radian (84 - 92)	2100
Yamaha XJ600S (Diversion, Seca II) & XJ600N Fours (92 - 99)	2145
Yamaha YZF600R Thundercat & FZS600 Fazer (96 - 01)	3702
Yamaha YZF-R6 (98 - 02)	3900
Yamaha 650 Twins (70 - 83)	0341
Yamaha XJ650 & 750 Fours (80 - 84)	0738
Yamaha XS750 & 850 Triples (76 - 85)	0340
Yamaha TDM850, TRX850 & XTZ750 (89 - 99)	3540
Yamaha YZF750R & YZF1000R Thunderace (93 - 00)	3720
Yamaha FZR600, 750 & 1000 Fours (87 - 96)	2056
Yamaha XV (Virago) V-Twins (81 - 03)	0802
Yamaha XJ900F Fours (83 - 94)	3239
Yamaha XJ900S Diversion (94 - 01)	3739
Yamaha YZF-R1 (98 - 01)	3754
Yamaha FJ1100 & 1200 Fours (84 - 96)	2057
Yamaha XJR1200 & 1300 (95 - 03)	3981
Yamaha V-Max (85 - 03)	4072
ATVs	
Honda ATC70, 90, 110, 185 & 200 (71 - 85)	0565
Honda TRX300 Shaft Drive ATVs (88 - 00)	2125
Honda TRX300EX & TRX400EX ATVs (93 - 99)	2318
Honda Foreman 400 and 450 ATVs (95 - 02)	2465
Kawasaki Bayou 220/300 & Prairie 300 ATVs (86 - 01)	2351
Polaris ATVs (85 to 97)	2302
Yamaha YFS200 Blaster ATV (88 - 98)	2317
Yamaha YFB250 Timberwolf ATV (92 - 96)	2217
Yamaha YFM350 (ER and Big Bear) ATVs (87 - 99)	2126
Yamaha Warrior and Banshee ATVs (87 - 99)	2314
ATV Basics	10450
MOTORCYCLE TECHBOOKS	
Twist and Go (automatic transmission) Scooters	4082
Motorcycle Basics TechBook (2nd Edition)	3515
Motorcycle Electrical TechBook (3rd Edition)	3471
Motorcycle Fuel Systems TechBook	3514
Motorcycle Workshop Practice TechBook (2nd Edition)	3470

◇ = not available in the USA   **Bold type** = Superbike

The manuals on this page are available through good motorcycle dealers and accessory shops.
In case of difficulty, contact: **Haynes Publishing**
(UK) +44 1963 442030   (USA) +1 805 498 6703
(FR) +33 1 47 17 66 29   (SV) +46 18 124016
(Australia/New Zealand) +61 3 9763 8100

MCL15.10/03